1985

Reading to Learn

in Grades
5 to 12

Reading to Learn

in Grades 5 to 12

Margaret Early
Syracuse University

with the help of Diane J. Sawyer
Syracuse University

HBJ

Harcourt Brace Jovanovich, Publishers

San Diego   New York   Chicago   Washington, D.C.   Atlanta
London   Sydney   Toronto

ISBN: 0-15-575625-7

Library of Congress Catalog Card Number: 83-82513
Printed in the United States of America

Copyrights and Acknowledgments continue on page 465, which constitutes a continuation of the copyright page.

Preface

As its title implies, *Reading to Learn in Grades 5 to 12* emphasizes reading as an aspect of language and language as a tool of learning. Learning through reading, then, is the central focus throughout the book. The first part examines language and the learning process itself; the second part discusses learning in the context of the school and the teacher; and the third part specifically relates reading and writing to learning, both inside and outside the classroom. A special feature of the book is the unit "Learning About Ourselves as Learners" in Part Two; it underlines a theme that pervades the entire text, the importance of understanding one's own learning processes. This idea applies to teachers themselves, as well as to their students.

The book is intended for both preservice and inservice teachers; it may be used at either the graduate or the undergraduate level. It assumes that readers will have taken introductory courses in educational psychology and perhaps one or more methods courses in other fields; there is, however, no formal prerequisite.

Many teachers have contributed to this book for teachers. Among them are those who taught me how to read, those who by their example and counsel urged me to become a teacher, and those at Boston University with whom I studied the teaching of reading. I owe a special debt of gratitude to Olive Niles and Donald D. Durrell.

For their helpful reactions and suggestions to the prospectus or the manuscript, I would like to thank Robert A. Bennett, San Diego City Schools; Peter Hasselriis, University of Missouri; and Florence M. Taber, Nazareth College, Kalamazoo, Michigan.

Many other teachers and writers, most of them unknown to me personally, are quoted in the boxed materials that illustrate this text. To me it seems important that a text for teachers include the voices of other teachers speaking of their experiences in contemporary classrooms. This book also owes much to my colleagues at Syracuse University, especially to those with whom I have worked in the Reading and Language Arts Center.

Like all teachers, I learn from my students. Out of the hundreds I have taught at Syracuse University, I have been able to mention only a few by name in the

v

pages ahead, but many more are represented there, more often as my teachers than as my students. My special gratitude goes out to them and to the many teachers who have welcomed me into their classrooms to observe, to learn, and sometimes to teach their students.

Margaret Early

Contents

Reading to Learn

in Grades 5 to 12

Purpose and Plan

This book will make demands on you—as a reader, as a student, and as a teacher. The first demand—that you read this book self-consciously—may seem a little odd. You may never have read a book self-consciously. As a skilled adult reader, you have long ago forgotten how you learned to read. As a good student, you have developed techniques of selecting, remembering, organizing, and applying information that have become so habitual that you probably no longer think much about them.

If you are an avid reader, indeed a compulsive reader, you lose yourself in reading. Certainly, you take in plot and character, image and idea, story line and argument with little awareness of how you are doing it. You are no more conscious of the miracle of your brain than you are of the electronic miracle that transmits moving images into your home via television. With most books you should be as little concerned with how you read as you are with how you walk, eat, or sleep.

But in reading this book, we ask you to be self-conscious.

We ask you to examine your own reading process because introspection is one of the best ways you have of understanding how people read. But you probably won't be able to comprehend the message and *at the same time* think about how you are doing it. You'll have to pause in your reading occasionally and ask yourself: What's happening when my eyes transmit and my brain reacts?

To a large extent, your insight into how the process works in others will be based on your understanding of how it works in yourself. But other people's guesses (theories) and the research findings that support these theories will enhance your understanding.

As a teacher, what you believe about how and why people read will strongly affect how you teach. Your strategies as a reader and as a student—and how you apply them to the study of this textbook—will influence how your students approach their own texts.

The Purpose

You begin the study of this book with a purpose. You want to find out all you can about how adolescents read and study. How can we help you to help them grow as readers and as students?

First, we can help you to sort out what you already know about learning and teaching in today's secondary schools. We can help you to compare what you know from your experience with what psychologists and reading specialists have been learning in the past several decades. We can help you to learn new concepts and to use new vocabulary that will help you to think through the problems that only you can solve. No one can make decisions for you. But if you use this book well, you will be able to base your decisions on knowledge of the reading process and its relationships to other language and thought processes.

As teachers in grades 5 to 12, your primary concern is that students learn content. You recognize reading as one way of learning, an essential way in secondary schools, and an efficient one. If you make good decisions about teaching reading, your students should learn content more effectively. In this book, which we do not intend to be exhaustive (nor, we hope, exhausting), you will explore concepts that can help you to make basic decisions about teaching reading as a means of learning. These concepts involve process, the variability of learners, the settings in which you teach, the materials of instruction, and the out-of-school influences on students' reading skills and habits. Although we offer examples of what some teachers do in particular circumstances, this book is not a "how to do it" manual. Each of you must make your own plans to suit your style of teaching and your students' styles of learning.

Just as there is no one best way to teach reading, there is no one best way to organize school or classroom reading programs. So our purposes are to remind you of many methods, to help you set criteria for selecting instructional materials, and to suggest contributions you and others can make to a school-wide reading program.

The Plan

We begin by looking at the students and how they learn, especially how they learn through language, and that particular phase of language with which we are most concerned—reading. The students are in middle school or junior high school or high school. They have attended school for six, nine, even eleven years, learning to read, most of them, and learning how to use reading as an important means of understanding the world. Increasingly, their success in most school subjects has depended on their ability to read. They will be even more dependent on this ability in post-secondary schools and in the technological society they live in.

If you are teaching in any of the grades from 5 to 12, you are impressed with how different each student is from the next one, but you also know that they have many common characteristics. So, allowing for exceptions, in Part 1 we describe early and middle adolescents as learners, concentrating especially on how they acquire language tools.

In Chapter 1 we ask you to think about what psychologists, linguists, psycholinguists, and teachers have been discovering about normal language development as we present some speculations about what happens in the brain when people read. We try to present research findings without becoming overly technical and jargon-ridden, and we urge you to add your experiences to the researchers' findings and the theorists' hypotheses. We suggest you draw your own conclusions and consider how these shape your actions in the classroom.

The quick overview of reading in kindergarten through grade 4 in Chapter 2 will acquaint you with the instructional materials and teaching methods that help children to learn to read.

In Chapter 3, we continue the discussion of reading as a means of learning, focusing on comprehension as it is influenced by memory, intelligence, prior knowledge, motivation, the student's language, and the language and structure of the text.

Having explored how average students acquire oral language and subsequently develop the ability to read, write, and use language as a means of learning, we turn to the fact of life we have dodged to this point: Although there is a normal sequence in acquiring language, students arrive in secondary schools at various stages along this sequential route. In Chapter 4, we consider the range of readers in the grades between 5 and 12, describe characteristic learning strategies, habits, and attitudes among several types of students, and point out how these will be dealt with in succeeding chapters.

By raising issues, presenting theories, and describing students' reading development prior to the middle school and secondary years, Part I sets the stage for the practical problems discussed in the next two sections.

Part II begins with an examination of the school setting, because the curriculum determines most of the reading adolescents do. Until now, in secondary schools, learning content rather than learning to read has been the dominant factor, but changes in the student population and in the teaching force are reordering the goals of secondary education. We discuss these changes and define the roles of the whole school staff in serving students' development in reading and language generally. Here we deal with questions of accountability not for teachers alone but for every member of the school community—students, parents, faculty, administrators, and support staff.

Chapter 6 describes how administrators and teachers use standardized tests and informal measures to assess the reading achievement of large groups of students.

Between Chapters 6 and 7, a resource unit—"Learning About Ourselves as Learners"—illustrates how students can evaluate their status in reading, writing, speaking, and listening. This unit can be adapted for use in junior or senior high school in reading classes, English courses, or special electives. It illustrates our conviction that self-assessment motivates students and improves their understanding of the learning process. The results of this unit can make it easier for content teachers to know their students' language skills and so set directions for further learning.

Chapters 7 and 8 focus on poor readers in the secondary schools, adolescents who for various reasons are still in the beginning stages of learning to read.

These chapters describe diagnostic and remedial procedures that classroom teachers should know about even though they cannot be expected to undertake remedial tutoring. However, because they continue to have responsibility for nonreading adolescents in their classrooms, "regular" teachers must cooperate with remedial reading specialists.

Another type of nonreader is the subject of Chapter 9—the adolescent who has learned to read but chooses not to. Problems of motivation affect not only poor readers but good readers who are uncommitted students of academic subject matter.

Because the best way for you to examine issues related to teaching and learning is to study what teachers do and what materials they use, the chapters in Part III contain many concrete examples.

In Chapter 10, we describe how teachers can evaluate the usefulness of textbooks and judge their readability in order to use them appropriately in the whole process through which students assimilate ideas.

At least half our high school graduates will have little reason to use reading for further academic learning—but all students have reasons for reading outside the requirements of the curriculum. Chapter 11 is devoted to this out-of-school reading which yields information of a nonacademic nature and serves personal and social needs.

Chapter 12 deals with vocabulary development and its relationship to success in school and in every walk of life. It concludes with a discussion of students' needs in the areas of word identification and spelling.

Chapter 13, "Reading as Reasoning," elaborates on ideas introduced in Chapter 3. In it we focus on how students assimilate ideas through text, and suggest steps students can take (both independently and under teachers' guidance) to strengthen their powers of comprehension. Questioning and predicting to aid literal comprehension lead to higher-order skills such as recognizing the writer's intent and making judgments about the accuracy and worth of fact and opinion.

The title of Chapter 14—"Study Skills = Reading + Writing"—telegraphs our message: Writing is as important as reading when the aim is to learn through text. In secondary schools, the teaching of writing like the teaching of reading is a responsibility of all teachers.

Chapter 15 turns away from the study of informational writing to consider students' responses to imaginative writing. Although this final chapter deals with the study of literature, it is meant for reading and content teachers as well as English teachers. Many of the higher-order skills which students develop most effectively through responding to imaginative writing are also applicable to texts in history and science.

A Note on Our Language and Meaning

Because this book is for teachers, we try to convey in print as closely as possible what we would say if we were talking to you. We hold technical vocabulary to a minimum, use footnotes sparingly, and put into boxes some of the special features we'd show on an overhead projector if you were in the same room with us. Instead of appendixes and long bibliographies at the ends of chapters, we put into the body of the text references we think you'll find useful or intriguing.

This book is about how to teach reading in grades 5 to 12. We mean by this helping students to comprehend meanings through relating them to what they already know, to talk or write about these meanings, to use them to make decisions, and to judge them. In short, most of the job of teaching reading in grades 5 to 12 is teaching students how to study texts and learn from them.

Learners and the Learning Process I

1 *Language, Learning, and Reading*

Let's begin by putting reading in its place. Reading is just one way of using language to learn. It may be one of the handier tools for acquiring information or ideas, but it isn't the only one. In the past, whole societies have prospered without written language; and even in literate societies today, people can get along without reading. But without language, human society could not exist (see Box 1-1). So the place of reading, as a process to be learned, as a "subject" to be taught, lies within the larger context of language.

If you are to teach reading, or assist in its development, you must know something about the larger context of language. Just as you can't teach science or mathematics without using language, you can't teach reading without using all that you already know about language. You have responsibilities not just for reading as a tool of learning but for language itself. Don't be alarmed. You're a teacher, not a linguist; you need working knowledge, not scientific knowledge, of this basic human trait.

The purpose of this chapter, then, is to remind you of (1) how and why your students learn to speak; (2) what language is for; (3) how oral language development affects development in reading; and (4) how your attitudes toward your own language and your students' language help determine the kind of teacher you are.

What Language Is

Language is a system of symbols, or labels, that represent the world and our experiences in it. The primary language is oral, comprising symbols which are, first of all, arbitrary *sounds* that a group of people (a speech community) agree upon as representing the same object, event, idea, or experience. For English-speaking persons, the word for the liquid which chemists identify as H_2O is *water*; for the French, it is *eau*; for Spanish speakers, it is *agua*; and for each group, the string of vocal sounds is an arbitrary symbol standing for the thing (water). (For the child Helen Keller, without sight or hearing and still without language, there was only the experience of wetness itself.) That arbitrary symbol system

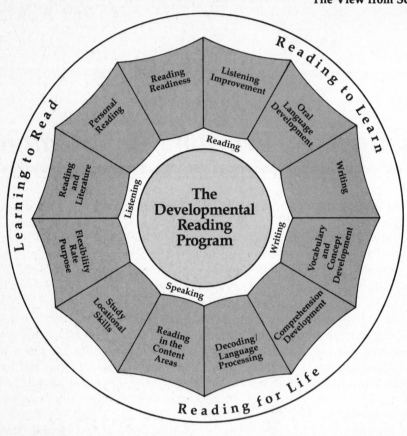

The developmental reading program is viewed as involving three levels: (1) learning to read; (2) reading to learn; and (3) reading for life. These levels should be viewed as continuous and interrelated.

SOURCE: From *Reading Framework for California Public Schools*, Kindergarten through Grade Twelve, California State Department of Education. Sacramento, 1980.

permits members of the same speech community not only to communicate in one another's presence—as some animals, notably bees and dolphins, seem to do—but to plan for the future and to recall the past. So far as we know, only human beings can use language for these purposes. Other animals communicate, of course, and some may have a kind of symbol system which can be seen or heard or felt. (For Helen Keller, without sight and hearing, there was only communication by touch until she discovered language.)

How does the mind work when it connects language with experience of the world? We can only guess at the nature of the mental activity that occurs. These guesses (theories) suggest that the mind organizes and builds associations out of experiences, pairing these experiences with labels and storing the labels in

BOX 1-1

A BIOLOGIST'S VIEW OF LANGUAGE

It begins to look, more and more disturbingly, as if the gift of language is the single human trait that marks us all genetically, setting us apart from all the rest of life. Language is, like nest-building or hive-making, the universal and biologically specific activity of human beings. We engage in it communally, compulsively, and automatically. We cannot be human without it; if we were to be separated from it our minds would die, as surely as bees lost from the hive.

We are born knowing how to use language. The capacity to recognize syntax, to organize and deploy words into intelligible sentences, is innate in the human mind. We are programmed to identify patterns and generate grammar. There are invariant and variable structures in speech that are common to all of us. As chicks are endowed with an innate capacity to read information in the shapes of overhanging shadows, telling hawk from other birds, we can identify the meaning of grammar in a string of words, and we are born this way. According to Chomsky, who has examined it as a biologist looks at live tissue, language "must simply be a biological property of the human mind." The universal attributes of language are genetically set; we do not learn them, or make them up as we go along.

We work at this all our lives, and collectively we give it life, but we do not exert the least control over language, not as individuals or committees or academies or governments. Language, once it comes alive, behaves like an active, motile organism. Parts of it are always being changed, by a ceaseless activity to which all of us are committed; new words are invented and inserted, old ones have their meaning altered or abandoned. New ways of stringing words and sentences together come into fashion and vanish again, but the underlying structure simply grows, enriches itself, expands. Individual languages age away and seem to die, but they leave progeny all over the place. Separate languages can exist side by side for centuries without touching each other, maintaining their integrity with the vigor of incompatible tissues. At other times, two languages may come together, fuse, replicate, and give rise to nests of new tongues. . . .

SOURCE: Lewis, Thomas, *The Lives of a Cell: Notes of a Biology Watcher.* New York: Viking Press, 1974

memory for reference through action or language. In normal language behavior, this activity is too instantaneous to be analyzed. For most people, language is like air; just as they breathe, they take in what linguists call "the referencing function of language." But Helen Keller, without sight or hearing, had to discover consciously the connection between language and experience. Do you remember from the film or the play *The Miracle Worker* that vivid scene in which the seven-year-old Helen rediscovers the gift of language that she had possessed at birth but had lost in infancy with the onset of blindness and deafness? In *The Story of My Life*, Miss Keller wrote:

Someone was drawing water and my teacher placed my hand under the spout. As the cool stream gushed over one hand she spelled into the other the word *water*, first slowly, then rapidly. I stood still, my whole attention fixed upon the motion of her fingers. Suddenly I felt a misty consciousness as of something forgotten—a thrill of returning thought; and somehow the mystery of language was revealed to me. I knew then that w/a/t/e/r meant the wonderful cool something that was flowing over my hand. That living word awakened my soul, gave it light, hope, joy, set it free!

Helen Keller's moment of discovery came after many months of practicing what for her was a meaningless exercise in which her teacher, Anne Sullivan, spelled words by tracing letters on her pupil's palm. Helen learned eventually to imitate this practice, but she had no idea that she was spelling a word, or indeed that words existed. She didn't know what language was for until that dramatic instant at the well when one of Miss Sullivan's repeated attempts to connect the experience of water with the patterns of touch that represented water succeeded in awakening the memory of verbal thought.

Early Language Development

Your students were born knowing how to use language. They were endowed at conception, as part of their genetic make-up, with the biological potential to perceive the world they were born into and to construct representations of this world in memory. These representations may be thought of as "structures" or networks of associations across brain cells. To communicate their representations of their world to others, your students have used (and continue to use) actions, images, and language.

With hearing and sight, your students had the sensory pathways along which language sounds and images usually travel to the brain. They also had the biological equipment to produce language. They were programmed genetically to acquire the sounds of the language (phonology) and the form (or syntax) of whatever language was used in the speech community they were born into.

The biological potential to acquire language must be accompanied by opportunities to explore the environment and to hear human speech. The extent to which these opportunities are present determines how quickly and how fully the potential can become reality as children acquire the sounds, words, and rules for ordering words in sentences. All healthy children who have these requisite opportunities to explore and to listen can learn a language that is sufficient to their needs. Whatever language they learn, they acquire it in the same order: sounds, words, syntax. They learn the vocabulary and the grammar of the language they hear, but they do more than imitate. They are able to make up sentences they have never heard anyone else express. Knowing instinctively how the language works—how to order words in sentences to express meaning—is the gift of language every child is born with. (The order in which children learn to use this gift of language is summarized for your quick review in Box 1-2.)

Becoming Aware of the Reference Function of Language

The first communication modes infants experience are the body language and vocal signals used by the adults who care for them. By five weeks infants can begin to distinguish some language sounds, and it has been shown that the amount and kind of talking that adults direct to infants from birth on probably affect the rate at which they develop language.

BOX 1-2

NORMAL LANGUAGE DEVELOPMENT

At end of	Vocalization and Language
12 weeks	When talked to, smiles, followed by "cooing," which is vowel-like in character and pitch-modulated; sustains cooing for 15–20 seconds.
16 weeks	Responds to human sounds; turns head, eyes seem to search for speaker; occasional chuckling sounds.
20 weeks	The vowel-like cooing sounds begin to be interspersed with consonant-like sounds; all vocalizations are very different from the sounds of the mature language of the environment.
6 months	Cooing changes into babbling resembling one-syllable utterances; most common utterances sound somewhat like ma, mu, da, or di.
8 months	Continuous repetitions become frequent; intonation patterns become distinct; utterances can signal emphasis and emotions.
10 months	Vocalizations are mixed with sound play such as gurgling or bubble blowing; appears to wish to imitate sounds, but the imitations are never quite successful; beginning to differentiate between words heard.
12 months	Words (mamma or dadda) are emerging; signs of understanding some words and simple commands.
18 months	Has repertoire of words—more than three, but less than 50; still much babbling but now of several syllables with intricate intonation pattern; no attempt at communicating information and no frustration at not being understood; understanding is progressing rapidly.
24 months	Vocabulary of more than 50 items; begins spontaneously to join vocabulary items into two-word phrases; all phrases appear to be own creations; definite increase in communicative behavior and interest in language.
30 months	Fastest increase in vocabulary with many new additions every day; no babbling at all; utterances consist of at least two words; many have three or even five words; sentences and phrases have characteristic child grammar, that is, they are rarely verbatim repetitions of an adult utterance; intelligibility is not very good yet, though there is great variation among children; seems to understand everything that is said to him.
3 years	Vocabulary of some 1,000 words; about 80 percent of utterances are intelligible even to strangers; grammatical complexity of utterances is roughly that of colloquial adult language, although mistakes still occur.
4 years	Language is well established; deviations from the adult norm tend to be more in style than in grammar.

SOURCE: Abbreviated from "Table 4.1 Developmental Milestones in Motor and Language Development" in *Biological Foundations of Language* by Eric H. Lenneberg, pp. 128–30. Copyright 1967 by John Wiley and Sons, Inc., New York.

When children achieve sufficient body control to reach for, look at, and crawl toward objects and people, they begin to explore their immediate world and to store in memory whatever they take note of. During the sensorimotor period (birth to two years), detailed in the writings of Piaget, infants "construct" their *impressions* of the world of space from their physical experiences of it. These impressions tend to be inaccurate or incomplete, because infants' observations are limited only to those direct experiences which they select as being important to note. Two factors limit what children can elect to notice—the environment which adults have provided for them and the level of mental development which they have achieved at any given age.

Feeling, touching, tasting, hearing, seeing, manipulating objects—these sensory experiences provide the raw material for constructing representations of the world in memory. The adult practice of giving children the names for things begins to impress upon their consciousness a symbolic reference system for the real world. Gradually, children come to use those labels for things they can point to and, later, for things which are out of reach and out of sight. We say they realize the reference function of language. Words are tools for retrieving the representations of reality which have been stored in memory. And though they first become aware of the reference function of language in infancy, children develop this awareness throughout their elementary school years.

Acquiring the Phonological System

The stage of life from birth to six or eight months is sometimes labeled the "precommunication period." Recordings of infant babbling show that during this period babies produce sounds common to all languages as well as sounds specific to the language of their home. Then, at about six months of age, the sounds not common to the home language begin to disappear, and the sounds of the home language become dominant. From these data, researchers infer that at birth children are capable of producing the sounds needed for communication in whatever speech community they are reared.

As the central nervous system matures, infants become increasingly able to identify speech sounds among other noises in the background. Further maturation of the auditory perceptual system permits children to compare the features, or distinguishing characteristics, of spoken words and to note the different sounds—between *mamma* and *kitty*, for example. Along with the ability to distinguish sounds grows the need to reproduce them, because babies also have an inborn need to communicate. As they practice sounds that are meaningful in their particular environment, they drop from their repertoire those which are not used by adults in their speech community. So children learn the "mother tongue" and whatever speech dialect of that language is common to their home and neighborhood. Mastery of all the sounds of the mother tongue occurs at different ages, but most children have achieved control by the time they are eight.

Disuse of sounds not in a child's first language makes the speaking of a second language—or dialect—increasingly difficult with age. After adolescence, learning to speak a foreign language like a native speaker requires intense desire, concentration, and practice—and perhaps some aptitude for mimicry.

Acquiring a Lexicon

Along with learning to perceive and reproduce the sounds of language, children learn to use words to label their experiences. Acquiring a lexicon—a stock of personal words—is always driven by intention, usually to communicate but also to plan, to play, to imagine. (We'll speak further about purposes in the next section.) On the way to achieving maturity in the use of words, children search and find the rules which govern their language. They differentiate only gradually, and in the process, they overgeneralize. Overgeneralization is at work when the four-year-old refers to Mrs. Jones as her husband's mommy. (All women are mothers.) "Are you a mother?" a little girl asked me. When I said no, she concluded I must be a teenager, showing that she'd begun to differentiate but still had a long way to go.

As children grow older and become more adept in communication, they are influenced by others in selecting what is important to note and store away in memory. Whatever they abstract from experience they add to their existing impressions. If the new information noted is consistent with information they already have, they simply add it onto the appropriate structure (which some psychologists call a *schema*). Take ten-year-old George. He already has a label for the smelly stuff women dab behind their ears—perfume. When his sister says they can't afford to buy Mom perfume for her birthday but can get her a bottle of cologne instead, George is able to add the new word to his lexicon. He understands that cologne has some of the same properties as perfume, and he appreciates at least one important difference—the cost.

Since learning a semantic system overlaps so much with cognitive development, we'll return to this discussion in the section below that deals with language and learning.

Developing Syntax

At the same time that children are acquiring their first words they are realizing that things (real objects and states of being) exist in relation to other things. (The toy is *beside* the chair. The plane landed *yesterday*. The sand is *hot*.) But children's first words—labels for things—are not sufficient to express relational contexts. To compensate for their limited lexicons, very young children use tone of voice, gestures, and facial and bodily expressions along with the essential noun. They make themselves understood usually because the whole context (gestures and setting as well as the few words) supplies meaning. Hearing a child say, "Daddy shoe," you can figure out from the context whether the meaning is "Daddy, I have a shoe," or "This is Daddy's shoe," or "Daddy, you forgot my shoe." Two-word sentences that contain a verb as well as a noun are easier to interpret—*Throw ball. Molly drink. Cookie gone*—though context is still revealing. Parents often expand on two-word utterances, saying, for instance, "Does Molly want a drink?" or "Molly drank all her milk." Some parents consciously expand their children's utterances and encourage the youngsters to do the same. Other parents unconsciously repeat, correct, and add to utterances. While it may seem that the conscious expansion would greatly assist children's language development, at least one study suggests that children learn syntactic control without this aid.

Words that signal relationships give children increasing power over syntax and hence over communication. Relational words help reduce their dependence on context to convey part of their message. They can place objects in space, events in time, people in relation to one another; they can say how they felt yesterday, what they plan to do tomorrow, what caused something to happen, and who owns what. Expressing relationships like these involves word order and inflectional endings on verbs and nouns, "irregular" past tenses, and tricky prepositions and connectives.

Programmed to understand the system of language, children quickly recognize the rules that constrain language usage. English-speaking children almost never generate sentences that fail to observe English word order. They don't say: "The kids ragged and dirty home walked tired." But just as they do in learning the semantic system, they overgeneralize the rules for forming past tenses, for example, or plurals or possessive pronouns. The mistakes young children make are clues to their rule-forming habits: *catched, gooses, goed, brang*. School-age children continue to work out the morphological rules (such as forming plurals and tenses) and the syntactic rules (such as eliminating double negatives and recognizing when to use "I" and "me"). Still, uncertainty resulting from overgeneralization persists into maturity. How many times have you heard someone say "between you and I" or "it was laying on the desk"? Learning the rules of syntax, particularly as they apply to certain verbs and pronouns, is often complicated by regional and social dialects, a subject to which we will return later in this chapter.

Learning What Language Is For

As children are learning the sounds, syntax, and semantics of language, they are also learning the functions of language. These activities are simultaneous— and we only separate them here so that we can talk about them. We began with understanding the reference function of language (page 12) because that awareness is basic, but so too is children's innate understanding that language is instrumental in satisfying their needs.

The functions of language which appear earliest in children's development have been classified by a linguist named Halliday into seven functions—a list that has become familiar to teachers of preschool and primary grades. We comment on Halliday's seven functions here because they underscore for teachers in the upper grades a fact of persisting significance: learning language is a purposeful activity. Young children learn to speak because they have real reasons for doing so. Older children—some of them—fail to learn the more mature functions of language (oral as well as written language) because they have not realized any compelling reasons for using reading or writing.

In their first years of life, children put language to work for them in the seven ways that Halliday specifies (see Figure 1-1). The first use he designates as *instrumental*, suggesting that language is an extension of the infant's use of hands and limbs to reach for objects. Four other functions on Halliday's list record small children's use of language to regulate other people's actions (*regulatory*), to express their emotions and their sense of self (*personal*), to find things out (*heuristic*), and to inform others (*representative*). A sixth function of language is to make connections with other people. Halliday calls this function *interactional*. It employs words that are not intrinsically meaningful, as when adolescents use such locutions as *you know*, or when adults use conventional chatter

FIGURE 1-1

HALLIDAY'S SEVEN FUNCTIONS

Let me—   *(instrumental)*

Be quiet!   *(regulatory)*

I miss you.   *(personal)*

How come?   *(heuristic)*

Jupiter is the largest planet
    in the solar system.   *(representative)*

You know.   *(interactional)*

Tyger! Tyger! burning bright   *(imaginative)*

such as *Howdy. Cold enough for ya? Have a good day.* Small children are often using language for the purpose of human bonding when they seem to be asking questions or making demands. Halliday's seventh function (*imaginative*), represented in the figure by the first line of Blake's poem, appears before children learn words and continues through adulthood as an essential human characteristic: delight in the sound of language, the poetic impulse.

As you might expect, children do not develop these uses of language as neatly or as uniformly as a sequential listing suggests.

Another student of children's uses of language, Joan Tough, has shown that children from educating homes use language at ages three, five, and seven for a wider variety of purposes than do children from less advantaged homes. Children from both groups find the language they need for their purposes, but the result of having a more restricted range of purposes is that the less advantaged children use more limited linguistic structures; they don't need them. The implication for teaching is evident: To develop children's vocabularies and their mastery of complex sentence structures, one must see that they have reason to use *all* the functions of language frequently. Among the uses of language that Tough found some children to be especially in need of experiencing in school are the following: (Paraphrased from Tough, page 169. See the Recommended Reading list in Box 1-3.)

❖ recalling past events in detail
❖ reasoning about present and past experiences

✛ anticipating future events

✛ predicting outcomes

✛ recognizing problems, offering solutions

✛ planning possible courses of action

✛ suggesting alternate plans

✛ projecting into other people's experiences and feelings

✛ using imagination in play

For teachers of older students, this list offers uses of oral language that translate to development of skills in reading, writing, and reasoning. Perhaps it is reasonable for teachers to question at first whether those students who have somehow missed out on sufficient early practice can develop these skills according to secondary school timetables and standards. Their next concern, however, is how to provide such students with opportunities for using oral language in these ways in anticipation of the demand for these skills in reading.

Clearly, the uses of language suggested in this section continue to develop throughout our lives so long as opportunities call them forth. The need to use language for varied purposes seems to promote the fullest development of our innate gift of language.

BOX 1-3

FOUR BOOKS ON EARLY LEARNING

Beard, Ruth M. *An Outline of Piaget's Developmental Psychology for Students and Teachers*. New York: Basic Books, 1969. (Reprinted as A Mentor Book by the New American Library (paperback) 1972.)

Boden, Margaret A. *Jean Piaget*. New York: The Viking Press, 1980. (Published in Penguin Books, 1980.)

Papert, Seymour. *Mindstorms: Children, Computers and Powerful Ideas*. New York: Basic Books, 1980.

Tough, Joan. *The Development of Meaning*. London: George Allen and Unwin Ltd., 1977.

Language Development in the Upper Grades

From the oral language base developed in the preschool years, children move on to the acquisition of reading and writing, learning to use these more abstract tools for the same purposes for which they learned to speak. (Consider how Halliday's seven functions can also be applied in reading and writing.) But with the acquisition of reading and writing, the uses of language become more versatile, sophisticated, and intricate.

Branching out from home to school, children learn to speak in more than one register, matching their usage to that of the person or group with whom they are associating. *Register* is a word linguists use for a variation of language; it may be applied to one kind of language (for instance, the oral register is different from the written register) as well as to variations of dialect. Additionally, the term *register* is applied to language which is used in one social situation and not another. Used in this sense, it may refer to several language variations within a dialect. Thus, a Texan, speaking in the same regional dialect, may use one register to address a political meeting, another to chat with neighbors, and still another to talk to a kindergarten class. Any one of these registers shares common features of lexicon, syntax, phonology, and body language with the others; but each has some features that make it different from the others. Most people speak in more than one register and readily shift from one to another. This practice is sometimes called code-switching.

Often, school language is the first new register that children learn. For many, the language of the classroom is not remarkably different from the language they use at home or in the playground. But for children coming from homes in which a foreign language is spoken, or a dialect that is markedly different from the mainstream dialect of the particular community, the switch from one register to another may be emotionally charged and linguistically demanding. Richard Rodriguez, born into a Spanish-speaking family in Sacramento, had to give up the private language of his home for the public language of the school (and all the other institutions of our society) in order to succeed in the mainstream culture. Moreover, Richard's teachers convinced his parents that they, too, must give up their mother tongue and adopt the public language (see Box 1-4). Today a heated controversy exists between those who would immerse children in the second language (as Richard's teachers did) and those who would keep the language of the school the same, or nearly the same, as the language of the home. Richard Rodriguez, while acknowledging the pain of breaking out of childhood and the language of the home, nevertheless opposes bilingual education.

Teaching reading and writing in English, it is important for you to know which language and what kind of dialect is spoken in your students' homes. You should learn as much as you can about the beginnings of language development in students who have been unsuccessful in switching to the language of the school for either writing or speaking. We shall have more to say in Chapter 7 about systematic ways of observing students' language production; at this point, however, we want you to think about the possible effects of language differences on learning.

What Effect Does Bilingualism Have on Learning to Read and Write in English?   Theoretically, becoming proficient in a second language would be no more difficult than learning one's mother tongue if similar conditions prevailed in both learning situations. But, of course, they don't. We can only approximate some of them, such as immersion in the second language in the home, community, and school; an intense need to learn; and strong positive attitudes toward the new language. Very often bilingual students consciously, more often unconsciously, reject English because it threatens to replace the mother tongue and the warm associations it holds for them. More than any other single factor, negative attitudes toward the language of the school and the establishment impede progress in the second tongue.

BOX 1-4

ON GIVING UP A PRIVATE LANGUAGE AND ADOPTING A PUBLIC LANGUAGE . . .

Because I wrongly imagined that English was intrinsically a public language and Spanish an intrinsically private one, I easily noted the difference between classroom language and the language of home. At school, words were directed to a general audience of listeners. ('Boys and girls.') Words were meaningfully ordered. And the point was not self-expression alone but to make oneself understood by many others. The teacher quizzed: 'Boys and girls, why do we use that word in this sentence? Could we think of a better word to use there? Would the sentence change its meaning if the words were differently arranged? And wasn't there a better way of saying much the same thing?' (I couldn't say. I wouldn't try to say.)

Three months. Five. Half a year passed. Unsmiling, ever watchful, my teachers noted my silence. . . .

Until one Saturday morning three nuns arrived at the house to talk to our parents. Stiffly, they sat on the blue living room sofa. From the doorway of another room, spying the visitors, I noted the incongruity—the clash of two worlds, the faces and voices of school intruding upon the familiar setting of home. I overheard one voice gently wondering, 'Do your children speak only Spanish at home, Mrs. Rodriguez?' . . . The moment after the visitors left, the change was observed. *'Ahora*, speak to us *en inglés,'* my father and mother united to tell us. . . .

My awkward childhood does not prove the necessity of bilingual education. My story discloses instead an essential myth of childhood—inevitable pain. If I rehearse here the changes in my private life after my Americanization, it is finally to emphasize the public gain. The loss implies the gain: The house I returned to each afternoon was quiet. Intimate sounds no longer rushed to the door to greet me. There were other noises inside. The telephone rang. Neighborhood kids ran past the door of the bedroom where I was reading my schoolbooks—covered with shopping-bag paper. Once I learned public language, it would never again be easy for me to hear intimate family voices. More and more of my day was spent hearing words. But that may only be a way of saying that the day I raised my hand in class and spoke loudly to an entire roomful of faces, my childhood started to end.

SOURCE: Richard Rodriguez, *Hunger of Memory, An Autobiography.* David R. Godine, Publisher, 1982.

Not only attitudes affect second language acquisition. We have already mentioned the difficulty many persons have in producing speech sounds that do not occur in their first language. There is also the component of memory in language learning. Children under five remember words and syntactic constraints easily perhaps because they are less distracted by other information: They do not suffer the information overload of older learners. For these reasons we believe children should be introduced to second language learning as early as possible. But until they achieve ease in speaking the second language (English in the context we are discussing), they probably should learn to read and write in their mother tongue—provided that teachers of the first language are available in primary grades (this may be more likely for Spanish than for a multitude of other tongues). When children begin reading and writing in their mother tongue, the transition to English for instruction should occur as soon as possible, certainly no later than the third year of literacy training. In schools where teachers speak only English, and children have to learn to read in English, nonnative speakers need intensive oral language practice for many months before beginning reading.

As you think about problems of bilingualism among your students, it may be well to remember your own experiences in learning a second language. After acquiring a high standard of literacy in English, it was not so hard for you to understand the abstractions of reading and writing in another language. Even so, you may never have learned to use a foreign language easily in relating to native speakers. In contrast, many persons living in polyglot communities acquire an oral language sufficient to their needs without being able to read and write at standards set by educated speakers.

When you think of yourself learning French in high school, for instance—struggling for proficiency in speaking, reading, and writing—you may realize that what bilingual students need most is abundant practice in a setting free from embarrassment. In second-language learning you do not have the same freedom to make mistakes and so to discover the rules of the language that you had in learning your first language. You don't have the luxurious time frame of those first five years of life. But you have the advantage of greater experience; you've already figured out one language system.

In sum, the bilingual students in early secondary years need strong reasons for reading and writing English, intense and abundant practice, freedom to make mistakes, and help in profiting from their mistakes—help which is sensitively timed to reduce embarrassment. (Remember that if you're too embarrassed to try your high school French in Paris, you'll avoid the occasions, thus reducing your practice and limiting your chances for proficiency. So will bilingual students.)

Do Social and Regional Dialects Interfere with Learning to Read and Write in Standard English?   Just as with bilingualism, attitudes toward the language of the school affect the proficiency with which students switch to that language from the language of the home. In the next chapter, on reading acquisition, we shall assert that the greater the difference between children's oral language and the language they are expected to read, the harder it will be for them to learn. But not impossible. Native speakers of English, if highly motivated, can learn to read and write French in high school and college without learning to speak like a Parisian. Londoners who speak a Cockney dialect that a St. Louis businessman strains to understand learn to read and write standard English. However, teachers who know that distances between registers make learning in the other register that much harder, do everything they can to familiarize children with the language of print before expecting them to read or to learn through reading.

The distance between teenagers' oral language and the standard English of textbooks is likely to be wide whether or not they have a marked regional dialect, such as Appalachian English, or a social dialect, like Black English. Adolescents' own register cuts across American dialects to produce a language meant to exclude nonadolescents. (Many groups besides adolescents also develop their own lexicons at least partly for the same reason: to exclude the uninitiated. Think, for example, of the language of musicians, gourmet cooks, and computer technologists.) But the questions teachers must ask about the teenagers they teach include these: Do students switch registers readily? If not, is the reason chiefly attitudinal or chiefly lack of familiarity with instructional language, especially the language of textbooks? How can teachers increase students' familiarity with the language of text? Since familiarity develops over time, how much time is a reasonable allowance—months? years? Which years are crucial in developing readiness (another word for *familiarity*) for textbook prose? We shall explore some answers to these questions in subsequent chapters (especially Chapters 10 and 13), but you should be thinking now of the issues involved.

How Do Language Skills Affect Each Other?   We have focused in this chapter on children's development of language in order to make the point that learning to read and write is an extension of learning to produce and comprehend oral language. In beginning reading, children's success in seeking meaning through print depends very much on their understanding of how the oral language system operates. Children who learn to read easily in the beginning stages are the ones who enter primary school speaking fluently for a variety of purposes, are familiar with the language of print from having listened to many stories read aloud, and are eager to figure out for themselves what the words say.

Is the relationship between *oral language* and *reading ability* as significant beyond the stage of beginning reading? Our comments on the effects of bilingualism, private and public languages, and social dialects including "teen talk" suggest that teachers must take into account the potential effects of students' oral languages on their proficiency in reading and writing standard English.[1] But we must be wary of assuming too quickly that students whose speech varies from standard English will have difficulty in comprehending text. Differences in dialect which are mostly a matter of pronunciation have little serious effect on ability to read and write. Even differences in syntax may not be very serious. Research supports the observations of teachers that students in grades 5 to 12 can understand many linguistic structures that they do not produce. Similarly, a student's speaking vocabulary is only a partial clue to his or her reading potential. People recognize the meanings of many more words in print than they use in conversation or even formal speech. On the other hand, to the extent that a person's use of certain labels suggests understanding of the concepts they represent, oral vocabulary is a clue to reading ability.

We believe secondary teachers waste time in trying to change students' oral usage when the primary goal is to improve reading and writing. You don't have

---

[1] By "standard English" we mean the language spoken, written, and edited by educated persons, heard in public forums, theaters, and television, and appearing in newspapers, magazines, and books from reputable publishers in these decades. We do not refer to "correct English" because in agreement with most linguists we avoid judging correctness. We recognize considerable variations in standard English as produced by educated Americans, though the differences are more likely to be items of pronunciation and word choices than of syntax.

to talk like a textbook (indeed, no one does) in order to understand text. Variations from standard English pronunciations and syntactic patterns need not prevent students from receiving or expressing ideas they genuinely understand. Teachers should help students say what they mean as precisely and clearly as they can, but the focus on meaning may well be shattered by teachers nagging about *you know's*, double negatives, and *it don't*.

An important relationship between oral language and reading is that improvement of the former often results from more of the latter. Many students are motivated to add to their repertoire of oral language as reading expands their world, giving them new ideas to talk about, new words to use, new reasons for using language. English teachers who save time for silent reading by cutting down on language drills probably do more for some students' speech habits than they give themselves credit for.

This relatively relaxed attitude toward students' oral language doesn't mean that reading teachers and content teachers can afford to ignore nonfluent, imprecise, repetitious, slangy, jargon-ridden speech. However, because direct attempts to reform speech habits are usually futile and damaging if they cut down communication, reading and content teachers have to compensate for impoverished speech by making sure that students have plentiful opportunities to hear standard English at roughly comparable levels to the texts they will be expected to read. That is not the whole story—we'll go into more detail in Chapter 9—but it is a point worth repeating. Be sure that students listen to standard English; read aloud to them.

As receptive skills, *listening and reading* have many parallels that teachers can take advantage of. Because comprehension of oral language calls for many of the same skills as comprehension of written messages, teachers can provide instruction and practice in listening, confident that there can be transfer to reading. Nonetheless, since reading and listening are not exactly the same skills, given the differences between the oral and written registers, you cannot expect automatic transfer. Good readers are often notoriously poor listeners. Secondary teachers can no more assume that students know how to listen than they can assume they know how to read. As with reading, the ability to learn through listening depends on the text, on the context, including purposes, and on the learner's attitudes. But listening to the reading of a text by someone who understands it gives students a leg up on comprehension because they are not distracted by figuring out unfamiliar words or putting words in meaningful phrases or recognizing which words deserve emphasis.

The fact that *writing and reading* are mutually reinforcing language acts is a pervasive theme of this book, and we won't belabor it here. One point, however, needs emphasis. In our society the most practical reason for writing is to learn, and in our schools we teach writing as a vehicle for thinking and learning. Making ideas clear to oneself is the chief reason for committing them to paper when you are a student. To deny students this exercise by permitting them instead only to respond to other people's ideas by circling choices on a workbook page or making checks on a ditto sheet stultifies their growth in thinking and, of course, in mature reading.

You would think that the relationships between reading and writing are so obvious that in our school curriculums the two would never be separated. But such is not the case. In many reading classes, pupils do workbook exercises instead of summarizing, paraphrasing, notetaking, and responding to the author's ideas by adding their own examples or raising arguments and additional questions. We are sympathetic to the many reasons teachers give for requiring only minimal amounts of writing (large classes and lack of confidence in their own abilities to judge and guide writing, for instance), but these reasons do not alter the principle that students must write to learn. The other side of the picture is that many writing teachers disregard the need to teach students how to read other people's writing analytically and responsively.

In summary, the lowest correlations between language skills occur when one of the skills has little to do with meaning. Mastery of the conventions of language correlates erratically with maturity in reading and writing; some good spellers exhibit limited comprehension and many good readers and writers spell badly. By contrast, the important relationships among language skills derive from the common element, meaning. That is, reading reinforces writing, listening reinforces reading, and more precise and complex oral language results when speakers have ideas to express which they have absorbed through reading and thinking. So when you are teaching reading effectively, you are also teaching all other aspects of language. Even so, demanding as that charge may seem, it still does not fully describe your responsibilities as a reading teacher or as a content teacher. Your principal concern is with the meanings that language both carries and gives shape to. Your task is to help students understand how they can discover and create meaning through the vehicle of language. Accordingly, both you and your students go beyond studying language to studying learning itself and the part language plays in learning. The next section, therefore, reminds you of what psychologists, especially Jean Piaget and his followers, have been telling us in this century about how children and adolescents learn.

Language and Learning

Preschool children not only learn oral language at a very rapid rate, acquiring a speaking vocabulary of several thousand words by the time they enter first grade, they also assimilate through experience a great deal of knowledge about whatever they can see, hear, smell, touch, and taste in the world around them. From these experiences they construct in their minds theories of how their world operates and how they operate in it, changing these theories continuously as they assimilate new data. This learning results from the interaction of many factors, of which three are especially significant: (1) genetic properties and physical maturation; (2) exposure to unfamiliar things, events, ideas; (3) intent to learn. We have already noted how these factors affect learning to talk (pages 12–18).

From observing the learning behavior of children at different ages from infancy through adolescence, Piaget developed a theory of how learning proceeds, of which factors dominate learning at different times or stages, and of how errors or mistakes can be interpreted as evidence of the kind of learning a child is capable of undertaking at any given time.

Experiences in the world provide the input out of which learning grows. In infancy these experiences are sensory and motoric (reaching, grasping, stretching, throwing, and so on). As the central nervous system matures, children construct in memory representations of integrated aspects of their experience and begin to use these representations or structures, (sometimes called *schemata*)[2] to think about the world, thus adding thought processes to perceptual and physical manipulation as tools of learning. Since children do this on their own, independently organizing aspects of their own experiences into these mental structures, they develop their own schemata, perhaps different from other people's, because they not only have had special sets of experiences to organize but they've made their own selections as to what to include. As they get older, however, social interaction—talking, playing, and working with others—influences their selection of what is important to note and take away from experience.

Whatever children abstract from experience they must add to their existing impressions of what is true about the world. If new information noted is consistent with existing information, then the new information is simply added to the appropriate schema. When new information is encountered which is inconsistent with previously organized information, the existing schema must be adjusted or revised to accommodate the new information and make it compatible with what is already known.

Suppose, for example, you read that the Great Pyrenees is the largest breed of dog in existence. No illustrations are provided, so you must imagine what this big dog looks like, using your concept of *bigness* as it applies to whatever dogs you've met. You go through a similar mental process when a friend describes a new recipe or a commercial building under construction in your town. You try to relate the information you are hearing to your schemata for beef casseroles or office buildings and make the new information fit. However, when you see a Great Pyrenees for the first time, or taste the dish made from your friend's recipe, or drive past the new downtown office building, you may find that you had not made sufficient adjustments in your schema to accommodate the new information received. So now, with experience as well as language to guide you, you make the necessary adjustments, or accommodations.

Piaget uses the word *equilibration* to describe a state in which the number and kinds of features that a child has noted are in balance with the kinds of features that his central nervous system allows him to notice at a particular stage of maturation. In a state of equilibration, children are unable to grasp that something they observe about the world is not consistent with what others understand to be true. That is, while the central nervous system is still maturing, children often find it impossible to recognize that some features of things, conditions, or events actually exist, or that certain facts are inconsistent with mental structures they have established for understanding the world. And they cannot revise a particular schema until they are capable of noticing new features of information and of recognizing that those features do not fit the established structure (see Box 1-5).

According to Piaget, changes in physical development are, in part, responsi-

---

[2]*Schema* is the singular, *schemata* the plural of this word borrowed from the Greek by modern psychologists. You may as well learn this term now because it is currently used in educational textbooks as a synonym for *structure* or *mental construct*.

BOX 1-5

PIAGET SPEAKS TO TEACHERS

1. Thought grows from actions, not from words.

2. Knowledge cannot be given to children. It must be discovered and constructed through the learner's activities.

3. By nature, children are continually active. They must find out about and make sense of their world. As they do so, they remake the mental structures that permit dealing with ever more complex information.

4. This remaking of mental structures makes possible genuine learning—learning that is stable and lasting. When necessary structures are not present, learning is superficial; it is not usable and it does not last.

SOURCE: C. M. Charles, *Teacher's Petit Piaget*, Belmont, CA: Fearon Publishing Co., 1974, p. 4.

ble for the different stages of mental development that we observe among school children. He defines three major stages of mental development and shows that at each successive stage children are capable of more sophisticated levels of reasoning.

During preschool and kindergarten (approximately ages four to six), children reason on the basis of impressions gained primarily from *perceptual* experiences. They may, for instance, choose a nickel over a dime because they equate size with value. In first grade, children may repeat "five pennies equal one nickel" but still not truly understand the relationship; it may be some time before they can learn the concept of equivalence. Similarly, preschool children, too young to learn the conservation concept, are likely to be more satisfied with a small glass full of juice than a larger glass which is only half full. "Full is more" at their stage of mental development, because they are not yet able to recognize the significance of the relative size of glasses in making judgments about which contains more juice.

Between ages seven and eleven, approximately, children recognize the relationship between the size of a container and the amount of liquid it holds. Seven-year-olds are rarely fooled by mothers filling the smaller glass to the rim. However, most children between seven and eleven think in *concrete* terms; that is, the relationships they can think about are predominantly those they can see as a result of manipulating objects and events in the real world. Sixth graders may assert that air has weight, recalling the information from a science text, but most of them probably won't believe it until they have conducted an experiment, such as comparing the weights of a balloon before and after it has been blown up. Once they become convinced through experience that air has weight, they may be able to form at least tenuous concepts of psi, barometric readings, and differences in air pressure at different altitudes. Without concrete references upon which to base new learning, students can memorize new information but cannot apply it in solving problems. They are storing facts but not creating schemata, since at this stage they cannot build relationships in the abstract.

When students enter the stage of development referred to by Piaget as the stage of *formal operations*, they begin to be capable of using abstract thought. They can impose a kind of reality on highly abstract considerations. Algebraic equations can be considered in the theoretical sense now, and previously memorized facts, such as "light travels through space over time," become concepts with both theoretical and concrete dimensions.

This theory of mental development is a means of explaining children's behavior which Piaget and his coworkers carefully observed, recorded, and analyzed. Because Piaget's theory serves to explain many of the learning problems we have observed among students, we consider it important for teachers to understand it and to learn to work with it. If Piaget's theory is indeed an accurate interpretation of how mental development proceeds, then any teaching approach that ignores the capabilities of the age group is destined to be only marginally effective. (This cursory description of Piaget's theory is meant to serve you as a review; if it is instead an introduction, you should read one or more of the references on Piaget cited in Boxes 1-3 and 1-5.)

Teachers' Attitudes Toward Language, Learning, and Reading

This is a book about teaching reading in the upper grades, yet it starts out way back in infancy with the beginnings of speech. Why? Because the way you teach reading in the upper grades will be shaped by your understanding of the way language begins, of how reading is related to the other language skills, and what you believe reading is for—which is both the same as and different from what listening, speaking, and writing are for. By way of summarizing this chapter, therefore, we restate below what we consider the most important implications for teaching reading in secondary schools. These implications will be enlarged upon in the chapters that follow.

1. While reading is an important means of learning, the end itself is more important than the means. Especially in secondary schools, students' opportunities to acquire information, ideas, and skills other than reading should not be disregarded. Of course, deficiencies in reading cannot be ignored; but if careful study of students' language capabilities and the school's facilities for providing remedial teaching suggest that their reading may never match their potential, they should be encouraged to use other means of learning content.

2. Learning to read is a natural extension of learning to speak. Secondary students who have been delayed in acquiring proficiency in oral English for any reason—physical impairment, mental retardation, non-English-speaking environment—are likely to show developmental delays in reading. With these students, secondary teachers should expect to spend much effort in helping them develop ease in listening and speaking before expecting marked growth in reading.

3. Older students go through the same developmental process in learning to read that normally developing students go through much earlier, except older children proceed at a different pace because they have lived longer and have developed socially, emotionally, physically, and cognitively. If they have already learned to speak and read in another language, they

may learn to read in English quite rapidly and competently. If English is their native language and they have failed to learn to read, their progress is likely to be slower and more laborious than it is for young beginning readers.

4. Anyone who teaches reading must also teach how to speak and listen and write. Content teachers who are also reading teachers contribute to whole language development; they cannot isolate reading as the only language skill that concerns them.

5. Secondary teachers should study the difference between the language students hear and use and the language of their textbooks. To do so, they need opportunities to listen to students in class and outside, and to study fairly extended samples of their writing. They need to determine how much distance between and among the various registers of language is tolerable, and to consider ways of helping students become sufficiently at ease with the language of textbooks that they can indeed learn through reading.

6. Teachers in middle schools must consider the extent to which learning at this stage is dependent upon concrete experience and ask what role reading can best serve. In senior high school, students acquire more capability for abstract reasoning but do so at uneven rates. High school teachers, therefore, may expect textbooks to serve a larger role in learning, especially for those students who are developing normally as readers and as thinkers.

We turn next to a review of how normally developing children learn to read. This subject occupies two chapters, one on reading acquisition and one on reading comprehension.

RECAPPING MAIN POINTS

Human beings are born with the biological equipment to produce and comprehend language, which is an arbitrary symbol system through which we represent our world and our experiences in it. Provided they can explore their environment and hear human speech, all children learn language, first acquiring sounds, then words, then syntax. They become aware of the reference function of language, and they use language to satisfy their needs.

All children use oral language purposefully, but some of them acquire more mature vocabulary and syntax earlier than others because their environment supplies greater opportunities to use language for a wide variety of purposes. Just as with oral language, children acquire reading and writing to satisfy purposes which they recognize as really theirs. Without such purposes, they may not learn to read and write well.

The greater the differences between the language children learn at home (their mother tongue) and the written language they must learn to read, the more difficulty they are likely to experience in school. It is easier to learn to read and write in one's first language than in a second language. But children who have learned to read and write in one language are better prepared to become literate in a second language.

The level of development that children attain in oral language, whether English or another language, is the best predictor of success in reading and writing. Richness of vocabulary and diversity of syntax are the crucial items. Dialect differences are of less importance. Nevertheless, one important reason why children should be read to is to familiarize them with written language, which may be quite different from their speech.

Since secondary teachers expect students to learn through reading and writing, they should understand not only how language develops but how learning proceeds through various stages of development. Piaget's theories suggest that children's mental development is closely related to physical maturation and therefore, in some degree, predictable. Emerging from the stage of perceptual learning at about the age they enter school, children move through a stage of thinking characterized by a need for concrete references. Most students remain in this stage through the early secondary years; they develop capabilities for abstract thought gradually and unevenly, approaching Piaget's stage of formal operations late in their high school career.

FOR DISCUSSION

1. Read the excerpt from Lewis Thomas's essay on language in Box 1-1, page 11. Why is language like nest-building? Explain Thomas's point that human beings have no control over language. In contemporary society, what groups or individuals might disagree?

2. From your own experience, or that of someone you know or have read about, give an example of a person realizing the "reference function of language," as Helen Keller did when she connected the word symbol with the reality of water.

3. From your experience, compare learning a second language (perhaps in high school) with learning your native language. How are your experiences similar to and different from the experience of a nonnative speaker of English enrolled in an American school? Why does age make a difference in language acquisition?

4. Bilingual education is a controversial issue in this country. After gathering facts and opinions from journal articles, books like Richard Rodriguez's *Hunger of Memory* (see Box 1-4, page 20), educators in your community, and bilingual acquaintances, present the pro's and con's of the debate either in a panel discussion or in an essay. Address questions like these: Should any communities in the United States have a dominant language other than English? Must all high school graduates be literate in English? When is a bilingual home an advantage in learning to read English and when is it a hindrance?

5. In a small group, think of other examples to illustrate Halliday's seven functions of oral language. (See Figure 1-1, page 17). Suggest a comparable list for reading. How does this list differ from Halliday's?

6. What implications should teachers in a junior high school draw from Piaget's research on the stages of mental development? How might their ideas about reading instruction be influenced by their understanding of Piaget? (To enrich this discussion, members of your group might consult the references in Box 1-3, page 18; and review chapters on cognitive development in their psychology texts.)

FURTHER READING

Brown, Roger, *Words and Things*. Glencoe, IL: The Free Press, 1958.
This is background reading of much interest to teachers who must be concerned in their classrooms with the psychology of language both as content and method. Especially readable chapters on language development, reading and writing, descriptive linguistics, and semantics.

Cazden, Courtney B., *Child Language and Education*. New York: Holt, Rinehart and Winston, 1972.

Cazden, Courtney B., Vera John, and Dell Hymes, eds. *Functions of Language in the Classroom*. New York: Teachers College Press, 1972.
A collection of essays. See especially those on the language of "different" children in primary classrooms.

Chomsky, Carol, "Stages in Language Development and Reading Exposure," *Harvard Educational Review*, 42 (1972): 1-33.

Dale, Philip S., *Language Development*, 2nd ed. New York: Holt, Rinehart, and Winston, 1976.
A comprehensive text on how language develops in normal children.

DeStefano, Johanna S. *Language, The Learner and the School*. New York: John Wiley and Sons, 1973.

Gibson, Eleanor J., and Harry Levin. *The Psychology of Reading*. Cambridge: The Massachusetts Institute of Technology Press, 1975.
Part I, Concepts Underlying the Study of Reading, develops in depth the discussion introduced in the chapter you have just read.

Halliday, M. A. K., "Learning How to Mean." In *Foundations of Language Development*. E. H. Lenneberg and E. Lenneberg, eds. New York: Academic Press, 1975.

Parker, Robert P., and Frances A. Davis, eds. *Developing Literacy: Young Children's Use of Language*. Newark, DE: International Reading Association, 1983.
An inviting collection of essays of special interest to experienced teachers and scholars. Authors include Joan Tough, Courtney Cazden, Yetta Goodman, Louise Rosenblatt. Topics include the social and cognitive bases for literacy, purposes of reading and writing, and the effects of schooling.

Temple, Charles A., Ruth G. Nathan, and Nancy A. Burris. *The Beginnings of Writing*. Boston: Allyn and Bacon, 1982.

2 Learning to Read

Generally, teachers in the upper grades are more concerned with how their students use reading to learn than how they learned to read in the first place. Yet an understanding of students as readers and as learners requires teachers to give thought to the beginnings of literacy. In Chapter 1 we traced those beginnings back to infancy as we reviewed how children learn to use oral language to satisfy their needs and orient themselves in the world. In this chapter we propose to show how language development in normal children extends beyond speaking and listening to include the more abstract forms, writing and reading. We will also consider how learning to read, as it occurs in school settings, affects the later development of learning processes which make use of literacy skills. Then in the next chapter we shall continue this discussion of the reading process, with additional attention to the development of comprehension.

"I suppose I learned to read in first grade with those Dick and Jane books, but it's all very hazy now," said Bob Costello to a group of teachers in the faculty lounge at Ames Central. They were considering with some apprehension the principal's announcement that staff development in the coming year would be centered on reading in the content fields. As a science teacher, Bob hasn't given much thought to reading instruction up to this point, and he's not alone in this respect. His colleagues are equally vague about "who teaches phonics these days" and "why reading scores look pretty good at the end of third grade and pretty bad at the end of sixth" and "whether all kids learn to read in basal readers." These teachers don't have time to take a course in teaching reading in the elementary grades, but they need to know what reading skills their students can be expected to bring to their content courses, and how they can help students refine these skills. As content teachers, they'd like to become familiar with some of the vocabulary that reading experts use. So Bob and his colleagues jotted down some of their questions:

+ If children perceive words accurately, have they "learned to read"?
+ How do you know whether they are doing this unless they read aloud?
+ Suppose the reader "says" the words accurately but doesn't understand the meaning of the message. Is that reading?

BOX 2-1

WHAT IS READING?

It may even be *necessary*, if the reader is to really tell what the page suggests, to tell it in words that are somewhat variant; for reading is always of the nature of translation and, to be truthful, must be free. . . . [Reading must] be dominated only by the purpose of getting and expressing meanings; and *until the insidious thought of reading as word pronouncing is well worked out of our heads, it is well to place the emphasis where it really belongs, on reading as thought-getting.* . . .

> —Edmund B. Huey. *The Psychology and Pedagogy of Reading*. First edition, 1908. Reprinted by M.I.T. Press, Cambridge, Mass. 1968. pg. 349-50)

Reading is not a simple mechanical skill, nor is it a narrow scholastic tool. Properly cultivated, it is essentially a thoughtful process. . . . It should be developed as a complex organization of patterns of higher mental processes.

> —Nelson B. Henry, ed. "Character and Purposes of the Yearbook," *Reading in the Elementary School*. NSSE 48th Yearbook, Part II. (Chicago: University of Chicago Press, 1949), p. 3.

You see, words have names and they have certain letters. You look at the letters and you put them together and you read a whole bunch of words together.—A fourth grader

Reading is when you read a word and it tells you something.—A sixth grader

> —Jerry L. Johns, "Reading: A View From the Child," *The Reading Teacher*, 28:7(1970).

✢ What if a reader miscalls one or more words when reading aloud but generally understands the passage? Is this O.K.?

✢ Do they teach phonics these days in elementary school?

✢ Why do so many kids seem to dislike reading?

✢ Are primary teachers as competent as they used to be? Or are the kids lazy and unmotivated?

We've shortened the list. Even so, we can only make a start on the answers to these questions in the pages that follow. In subsequent chapters, however, we will continue to address these questions.

What Is Reading?

Bob Costello and his colleagues didn't come right out and ask: What is reading? In a commonsense way they know what reading is and are willing to leave to academicians the niceties of definition. Their questions, however, betray their uncertainties about how they should judge reading. As we answer these questions in this and succeeding chapters, you'll get an idea of how we define reading. In the meantime, the definitions in Box 2-1 and the model of the reading

FIGURE 2-1

A SIMPLIFIED MODEL OF THE READING PROCESS

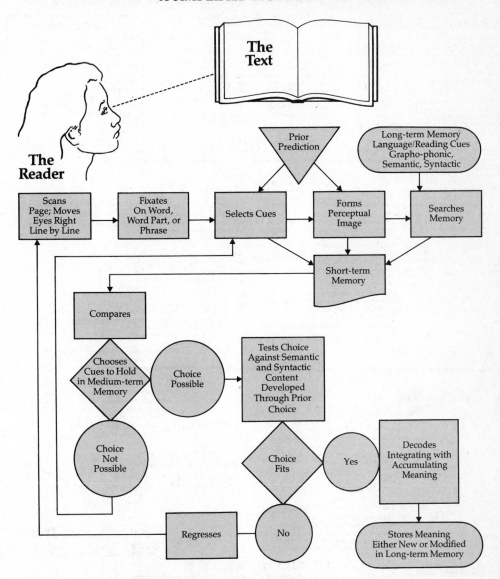

SOURCE: Goodman Model of Reading adapted from Kenneth S. Goodman and Olive S. Niles, eds., *Reading Process and Program*. Commission on the English Curriculum, Urbana, IL: National Council of Teachers of English, 1970.

process in Figure 2-1 suggest the way reading theorists visualize what probably happens in the mind during reading.

Another insight into reading instruction, can be obtained from diagrams and charts prepared by teachers and authors of instructional materials. Page 10 in

FIGURE 2-2

GOALS FOR READING INSTRUCTION IN THE CLEVELAND PUBLIC SCHOOLS

General Objectives

THE PUPIL WILL:

Develop an understanding of the interrelationship of listening, speaking, reading and writing

Apply knowledge of basic reading skills to reading tasks

Derive meaning from what is read

Apply reading skills to content area materials

Develop discrimination in selecting reading materials for personal needs and recreational interests

... To raise the reading ability of every child in the Cleveland Public School System to an acceptable level ...

The Education Committee's Report on Reading, Cleveland Board of Education—February 18, 1975

... That each pupil develop to his fullest capacity the competence in reading and in critical thinking skills that will enable him to meet the demands of school, job, and citizenship. Moreover, we want for each the personal enjoyment and enlightenment that come from wide, insightful, appreciative reading of the rich body of literature that has accumulated through the ages and that flows from the fertile minds of the great thinkers of our day.

The Cleveland Board of Education's Statement of Policy on Reading—August 10, 1972

Appreciation

THE PUPIL WILL:

Value reading as a resource to be used in evaluating everyday experiences and culture

Understand that reading influences attitudes and broadens the scope of home, community and world

Use reading as a continuing source of knowledge and pleasure through the independent use of libraries, media centers and other home and community resources

Develop an appreciation for words as essential and powerful tools of communication

SKILLS OBJECTIVES

PRE K	K	1	2	3	4	5	6	7	8	9	10	11	12

The Pupil Will:

Recognize that a word or a group of words represents ideas

Restate the meaning of simple words and phrases

Develop stories through pictures and words

Relate story content to pictures

Recognize that the ending of a story results logically from the preceding events

Distinguish between what is real and what is fanciful

Recognize the meaning of words in context

Predict word meaning using context clues

Utilize punctuation as a signal to meaning

Recognize the relationship between an illustration and its caption

Recognize directly stated details

Recognize a topic of a paragraph or selection

Identify the main ideas in a simple paragraph or story

Recognize simple relationships

Summarize the events in a story

Draw conclusions from given facts and statements

Recognize simple inference

Predict outcomes

Recognize that many words have been derived from other languages

Use structure and position as signals to meaning

Classify and generalize words based on their meanings

Interpret homonyms, synonyms and antonyms

Expand the vocabulary to include concept words from various content areas

Analyze words that contain shades of meaning

Differentiate between abstract and concrete words

Reorder and interpret facts

Perceive relationships between main ideas and supporting details

Arrange events chronologically and establish relationships

Determine cause-effect relationships

Distinguish and evaluate facts and opinions

Recognize inference in given reading selections

Differentiate various kinds of writing: e.g., prose and poetry

Differential various kinds of content: e.g., fiction and non-fiction

Understand and differentiate propaganda and editorial techniques

Demonstrate an understanding of language variations: e.g., cliches, puns and dialect

Interpret figurative language

Interpret analogy

Extend meanings of indefinite or incomplete statements and ideas

Evaluate attitudes of fictional characters

Recognize author's intent

Recognize and evaluate author's assumptions

Compare, test and evaluate author's conclusions

Recognize author's use of mood and tone to influence the reader

Recognize and compare authors' writing styles

Grasp general principles based on reading specific information

Respond to allusion in writing

Determine credibility of writing

COMPREHENSION
(ACT OR POWER OF UNDERSTANDING, INCLUDING VOCABULARY BUILDING)

The Pupil Will:

Recognize that spoken words are represented graphically by printed symbols

Identify sounds in oral words

Recognize sound-symbol relationships

Order sound elements in a prescribed sequence

Utilize configuration appropriately

Recognize prefixes, suffixes, syllables, endings, contractions, possessives and root words

WORD ATTACK
PHONICS AND STRUCTURE
(PRINCIPLES USED TO DETERMINE PRONUNCIATION OF WORDS)

The Pupil Will:

Follow appropriate directions

Use parts of informational books: e.g., index and table of contents

Locate information in simple reference materials: e.g., picture dictionary and basal text glossary

Use the dictionary for pronunciation and meanings

Expand word study using varied reference sources: e.g., glossaries, dictionaries and thesauruses

Use reference aids: e.g., atlases, encyclopedias and card catalogue

Develop skimming and scanning techniques

Read and interpret the significance of charts, graphs, tables and diagrams

Develop various notetaking and summary techniques for organized reading

Make judgements about the reliability and usefulness of various sources

Utilize SQ3R (survey-question-read-recite-review) system for reading content material

Adjust reading rate according to difficulty of materials

Understand use of footnotes

Use appropriate research tools and techniques: e.g., resource guides, periodical guides, special content indexes and biographical dictionaries

INDEPENDENT STUDY
(SKILLS THAT AID THE STUDENT IN USING READING AND REFERENCE MATERIALS)

The Pupil Will:

Develop perceptual awareness

Recognize sounds in the environment

Perceive likenesses and differences

Follow verbal and non-verbal signals

Utilize listening and speaking vocabulary to transmit and receive meaning

Comprehend oral and standard English

Use words, phrases and sentences based upon development level and experiential background: e.g., dialectal, bilingual and colloquial

Recognize symbols: e.g., trade names, signs, posters and pictures

Identify objects according to given characteristics

Focus attention on an assigned task

Listen to a story being read aloud

Recognize that a story has a beginning and an end

Interpret pictures according to experience

Use pictures to understand a story

Establish a left to right progression

Identify letters of the alphabet

PREPARATION
(PHYSICAL, MENTAL AND EMOTIONAL PREPAREDNESS FOR A GIVEN LEARNING ACTIVITY)

PRE K	K	1	2	3	4	5	6	7	8	9	10	11	12

STANDARDIZED ACHIEVEMENT TESTS

DIAGNOSTIC TESTING

Chapter 1 shows how a committee of California teachers visualized reading as one phase of language development. Figure 2-2, an adaptation of a chart produced by teachers in the Cleveland Public Schools, represents reading as composed of four major skills clusters—decoding, word meaning, comprehension, and studying—and suggests the grade spectrum in which these clusters are best emphasized. (The fine print identifying subskills in each cluster is worth the eyestrain!) Still another source that the teachers in Ames Central might investigate is the list of reading skills to which elementary teachers in their district refer. This might be a scope and sequence chart included in a basal reading series or a list that a reading committee has refined for a local curriculum guide.

Probably everyone who defines reading by way of a scope and sequence chart hastens to add: "But reading is more than the sum of its parts!" That well-worn caveat cannot entirely erase the possibility that the charts dictate a concept of reading which is in fact quite at odds with the true nature of the process. So we cannot make light of charges that skills charts impose a style of teaching that emphasizes bits-and-pieces drill to the detriment of meaning-seeking, which children should always associate with reading. Nevertheless, reading *is* a complex skill (knowing *how* rather than knowing *that*), we can manage it only in terms of subskills.[1]

To offset the dangers of atomistic teaching, we would cluster the subskills as the Cleveland teachers have done, select sparingly the ones for direct instruction, and follow such instruction with immediate and plentiful application of the subskill in the context of the whole reading process.

Although teachers, researchers, and theorists often define reading differently, the following characteristics of reading are generally accepted:

1. *Reading is a receptive language activity.* As a listener seeks to hear and understand the message being conveyed by a speaker, so a reader is concerned with recovering the message which was intended by a writer.

2. *Reading is a cognitive activity.* Reading requires thinking which is both conscious and unconscious, deliberate and automatic. For skilled readers, some of the mental activity—notably decoding—is automatic. For beginning readers, however, the decoding process requires some deliberation until recognizing most words becomes automatic. Among skilled readers, conscious and deliberate mental activity is usually required to consider the author's meaning in light of past experiences or previous knowledge.

   The cognitive processes believed to be required for reading are selective attention, imagery (the ability to create mental images), verbal encoding (the ability to use language to describe or discuss objects, events, and experiences), memory, and retrieval.[2]

---

[1]Running the risk of seeming to endorse mechanistic approaches, we cling to the old words *skill* and *subskills* in preference to *strategies*, which appears to be a fashionable new label for the same mental acts represented by the older terminology.

[2]Merlin C. Wittrock, "Education and the Brain." In *The Seventy-seventh Yearbook of the National Society for the Study of Education*. Ed. by Jeanne Chall and Allan F. Mirsky. (University of Chicago Press, 1978.)

Though no one can know exactly what activity goes on in the brain during reading, it is likely that it involves at least four kinds of processes—reception, sorting and organizing, relating, and storage.

3. *Reading is directed by the brain, not the eye.* While it looks as though a reader's eyes scan print and transmit information to the brain, research has shown that the neural structures of the brain actively influence the selection and interpretation of information; hence, these structures do more than passively receive and respond to sensory information.[3] The brain uses the eyes as we use windows in a house. People, not windows, look out onto the world. The one who is looking decides where to look, what to notice, and how to interpret what is seen. A window is a complete structure but it has no independent function. So it is with the eyes. The visual system is one of the means the brain uses to gather information which the brain has determined it wishes to receive.

This understanding of the relationship between brain and eye has changed our attitudes toward many aspects of reading instruction. For instance, we once believed that eye training is an aid to reading. We have learned, however, that exercises and equipment developed to increase eye span, prevent regressions, and move the eyes more rapidly across the page work with some children but fail with others. The children who become faster readers seemingly as a result of eye training are the ones whose brains have already worked out the "mechanics" for reading but have not achieved a smooth integration of the parts. Eye training is futile for poor readers because what the brain has not grasped it cannot be coerced into applying more efficiently.

4. *Reading is more than a decoding task.* During the 1960s, researchers in computer engineering tried to figure out how the brain performs the reading task in order to construct a computer that could simulate reading. They attempted to isolate each separate step the brain takes in processing information received from print. In working through the technical details, it became apparent to these researchers that the speed at which the brain is able to perform the reading task is very rapid—too rapid to permit the letter-by-letter processing that would be necessary if reading were chiefly dependent upon translating all print symbols to sound symbols. It became clear that the brain must attend to larger units of information for a significant proportion of the time.

Information available within the printed language is *phonemic* (related to the sounds within words) or *syntactic* (related to the sequencing of words in phrases and sentences) or *semantic* (related to the meaning conveyed through words and word parts). During the reading act the brain uses information from each of these sources in combination with prior knowledge, which tends to shape and limit what is gleaned from the printed message. Expectations based on the reading of a previous word, phrase, sentence, or paragraph also help determine what information the reader considers important or relevant in subsequent text.

---

[3]Wittrock, pp. 2–5.

SOME WORDS USED IN DISCUSSING BEGINNING READING—DEFINITIONS FROM A DICTIONARY OF RELATED TERMS*

decode (dē kōd') 1. v. to change communication signals into messages; especially, to get the intended meaning from an analysis of the spoken or graphic symbols of a familiar language, as decode a word in one's mother tongue. Note: to learn to read, one must learn the conventional code in which something is written in order to decode the written message. In reading practice, the term is used primarily to refer to word identification rather than higher units of meaning. We also speak of decoding Morse code signals, decoding body language. 2. v. to translate an unfamiliar code of symbols into a familiar one, as decode a secret message.

grapheme (graf'ēm) n. a written or printed orthographic representation of a phoneme, as b and oy for /b/ and /oi/ in boy. Note: In English, a grapheme may be a single alphabet letter or a group of letters as in boy above, and includes all of the ways in which it may be written or printed.

morpheme (môr'fēm) n. a meaningful linguistic unit which cannot be divided into smaller meaningful elements. Note: A morpheme may serve as a word, cat, or as a component of a word, as -s in cats.

phoneme (fō'nēm) n. a minimal linguistic unit in spoken language whose replacement can result in a meaning difference, as /p/, /b/ in pin, bin. Note: The application of this definition to a particular language is a linguistic problem, since phonemes must be determined by the nature and extent of their distribution in the language, their etymology, and their reality for speakers of the language.

phonetic (fə net'ik, fō-) 1. adj. referring to the nature, production, and transcription of speech sounds. 2. adj. corresponding to pronunciation. 3. adj. agreeing with pronunciation. 4. adj. referring to the description of nondistinctive elements of a language. Vowel length in English is phonetic but not phonemic.

phonics (fon'iks, fō niks) (with sing. v.) 1. n. an approach to the teaching of reading and spelling that stresses symbol-sound relationships, especially in beginning reading instruction. 2. n. instructional activities designed to teach reading and/or spelling through an emphasis upon the relationship of speech sounds to the letters and letter combinations that represent them. 3. adj. referring to such an approach or activities.

structural analysis a word identification technique for breaking a word into its pronunciation units. Note: Structural analysis elements commonly taught are the identification of roots, affixes, compounds, hyphenated forms, inflected and derived endings, contractions, and, in some systems, syllabication.

word recognition 1. the process of determining the pronunciation and some degree of meaning of any word in written or printed form. 2. the quick and easy identification of the form, pronunciation, and appropriate meaning of a word previously met in print or writing.

---

*Theodore L. Harris and Richard E. Hodges edited this dictionary with the help of a committee of reading specialists. It was published in 1981 by the International Reading Association, Newark, Delaware.

While evidence suggests that decoding visual information into acoustic signals significantly aids the efficiency of the storage and retrieval processes, the meaning of a word or phrase can be grasped without actually "saying" the words. So, too, the overall meaning of a passage may be grasped even though several word-calling errors are made while reading it. It is apparent, then, that getting meaning is not exclusively bound to the sound elements of language. Rather, meaning is achieved through an integration of the information already in the reader's mind with the information available from the semantic, syntactic, and phonemic components of printed language.

From Speaking to Reading

When Bob Costello remembered vaguely that he learned to read in first grade, he was overlooking his first five or six years when he not only learned to use oral language in the ways described in Chapter 1 but also, if he was a "paper and pencil kid," began to scribble–write, to print his name, to identify letters—like the M's on McDonald's—and to recognize words in the print surrounding him—words like *stop, corn flakes, on sale*.[4] Between birth and the time he entered school, Bob developed the skills of *attention* and *perception* as well as a *desire to achieve* and an *interest in stories*.

Attention refers to the ability to direct mental and physical activity to a given task. Infants learn to attend to speech sounds, selecting these from background noises, distinguishing between a parent's voice and the hum of the refrigerator. Later on they learn to attend selectively to certain objects or to pursue certain goals, whether to satisfy curiosity or to win a tangible reward. Some children select print for careful scrutiny earlier than others, sometimes by chance but perhaps more often because they are encouraged to do so. The ability to focus attention, screening out distractions, is obviously a valuable trait in figuring out print symbols.

Perception refers to the brain's ability to organize information coming into the nervous system through the various sensory modalities—vision, hearing, taste, touch, smell, and muscular awareness. It is in the brain that distinctive features in the visual world are sorted out. With respect to reading, such features include directionality (Is the circle on the right or the left of the stem in *d* and *b*?) and figure–ground distinctions (the way printed letters stand out from the space surrounding them). It is in the brain that discriminations between similar speech sounds are made. Perception is a process which integrates receptive acuity, ability to discriminate, and memory. Well-developed auditory and visual perception abilities help children organize (that is, make sense of) print and associate speech sounds with printed symbols.

Some children learn early in life to enjoy a sense of satisfaction when they accomplish something. Psychologists refer to this trait as *achievement motivation*. Other children learn to respond to promises or threats. The children who learn personal satisfaction are more fortunate, since much of the hard work involved

---

[4]Probably his kindergarten teacher gave him a "reading readiness" test, taping a supermarket's advertisement to the chalkboard and asking him to circle the words he recognized.

in learning anything requires persistence in the presence of few and usually distant rewards. Personal satisfaction lasts longer and motivates future efforts. Compare, for example, Jason's satisfaction with Jenny's. He announces: "Listen, Mommy, I can read this story we wrote in class today!"—and is spurred to further effort. Jenny says: "Hi, Mom, I got another happy face on my workbook page"—and that's that.

The extent to which early growth in language, and therefore in reading, depends on the preschool environment cannot be definitively assessed. Obviously, learning is the result of a multitude of interactions between nature and nurture, between heredity and environment. But the beneficial effects of an enriched environment have been demonstrated over and over again in recent decades by research, such as the long-term evaluations of Headstart, the preschool project for disadvantaged children, and by anecdotal evidence. A most dramatic example of the latter is the story of Cushla, a severely handicapped child who was introduced to books when she was only four months old. In her first years Cushla couldn't sit up, crawl, hold objects, or focus properly on what was happening around her. She could only be cuddled and read to. Yet at three and a half, this child who had been diagnosed by a succession of doctors as mentally retarded was demonstrating well-above-average language and intelligence. (see Box 2-2).

In short, children are well along their way to reading before they enter school. How far along the way varies greatly and in direct relationship to what each child found in his or her preschool world and was able physically and mentally to take advantage of. Cushla's story is an extreme demonstration of how far intelligent adults can extend whatever equipment a baby is born with. Conversely, Cushla's story warns that without the proper kinds and amounts of nurturance, most children cannot make full use of whatever nature has given them.

It is not a new idea—the impact of the home on school learning—but it is one that hit hard in the 1970s. One study after another related school achievement, particularly success in reading, to students' socioeconomic backgrounds. As long ago as 1945, Helen Robinson's study of *Why Pupils Fail in Reading* revealed

BOX 2-2

HOW BOOK LANGUAGE AFFECTS ORAL LANGUAGE

[At 3 years, 8 months,] Cushla's vocabulary certainly reflects . . . conversance with books. Words and phrases of increasing complexity and expressiveness are used correctly: 'doing nothing in particular', 'an amazing sight', 'terribly frightened', 'difficult', 'silent', 'strange', 'ridiculous'. At the time of writing, she gets in first while listening to *Make Way for Ducklings* by Robert McCloskey, with "a great responsibility", and "bursting with pride", phrases which are used to describe the duck parents' attitude to the new ducklings. Cushla's expression, a model of expansive satisfaction, leaves no doubt that these phrases, unheard several weeks ago, have acquired meaning and will be available for use before long in other contexts.

SOURCE: Dorothy Butler, *Cushla and Her Books* Boston: The Horn Book, Park Square Building, 31 St. James Ave., Boston, MA 02116.

that while causation is multiple, home background carries the heaviest weight of all factors. When that finding was echoed in later large-scale studies, new attention was directed to the home curriculum. The effects of these studies were both positive and negative. On the one hand, schools and professional organizations reached out to parents, offering advice on how to talk with children to further develop their uses of language, how to provide more experiences relating to school learning, and especially how to share books with children. On the negative side, research that correlated reading achievement with socioeconomic status gave some teachers an excuse to attribute poor achievement to home conditions beyond their control.

To be fair to themselves and to parents, teachers give enormous amounts of credit to the home for its influence on children's learning. At the same time, they remember how many children have achieved academic success even though their parents, for one reason or another, did not read to them or even spend much time talking with them, and had little sense of the values of education. These children, undoubtedly gifted with intelligence and the will to learn, still had to have someone or something to take over where their parents left off. The "someone" may have been a teacher or friend; the "something," a school, library, church, or community organization. Of necessity, home and school are mutually reinforcing in educating children, and these institutions are supplemented by the rest of the culture, including television. The important point for reading teachers is that just as children learn to speak through interacting with parents who teach, they learn to read by interacting with books and teachers as these are organized in the system we call school.

How the School Contributes to Learning to Read

In this section we attempt a bird's eye view of reading instruction from kindergarten to the beginning of middle school (grade 5 or 6 in most systems). We intend this section to provide you with sufficient markers or signposts so that you can investigate what is happening in the primary grades in the school system you are closest to. Since as teachers in middle, junior, and senior high schools, you continue a process begun many years earlier, you should know at least the outlines of what you are building upon.

Even primary teachers are continuing a process already well underway before children reach them. Using words loosely, people say children learn to read in first grade, but in fact they enter first grade as users of language and most of them have acquired at least the beginnings of reading. They continue to learn. Schools assist in the process by providing the appropriate atmosphere, opportunities, support, challenges, and rewards. It is in this sense, assisting the process, that we use the phrase "teaching reading" in the discussion that follows.

Instructional Goals in Beginning Reading

Kindergarten Through Grade 2   The major goals in the earliest years are three: (1) to keep children interested in learning to read and in enjoying the fruits of their labor; (2) to further develop the oral language and the cognitive and motor skills children bring to reading acquisition; and (3) to help children integrate several approaches to identifying (or decoding) printed words. Implicit in the first goal is that reading must satisfy children's quest for meaning. So attention to specific comprehension skills is present from the beginning and increases toward the end of this period.

That reading should be interesting and enjoyable is crucial—in the beginning and, of course, thereafter. Also, the more time beginners spend reading, the more fluent they become. Reading independently, they discover for themselves many routes to meaning that later will be "taught" as skills lessons in reading groups. Children who don't read for pleasure in primary grades, applying skills between lessons, may never become fluent readers. And if reading is never easy for them, they will fail as students—later if not sooner.

Among the basic skills to be developed in kindergarten and first grade to support reading acquisition are: (1) an understanding of the links between spoken and written language; (2) a familiarity with the conventions of print, such as left-to-right word order, capital and lower-case letters, punctuation, including designation of who is speaking, paragraphing, and the use of illustrations; (3) the ability to distinguish letter shapes and sounds; (4) coordination of hand–eye movements; (5) an understanding of how syntax for writing may be different from oral conventions (for example, inverted sentence structure).

Throughout this period, accompanying and dominating the language development suggested by these five components, students are acquiring new concepts and the words that label them. That's what all those trips to the fire station, the zoo, and the airport are about. That's the reason for all that cutting, pasting, labeling, coloring, and sorting of shapes, colors, and textures. And that's what's behind all that playing store and keeping house; all that singing and playing of instruments; and all that acting out of "Billy Goats Gruff" and "The Three Little Pigs." The kids are learning concepts and practicing skills which are vital to reading; they're not just fooling around.

Decoding is what most secondary teachers identify as the primary goal of the early grades. In our goal structure, it ranks below interest, enjoyment, and meaning. In sequence of instruction, decoding comes after the five readiness skills previously enumerated. But no one denies that learning to decode is essential business in primary grades. What causes the great debate is the question of how to assist children in this essential business. Within educational circles, the question in its starkest form is this: Do children learn to decode through reading, or do they learn to read by first learning to decode printed symbols into speech sounds? As with most dichotomies in education, this one will persist only if we fail to agree on definitions and look at generalizations instead of specifics. Does reading begin as soon as children attach an oral symbol (*Pac Man*, for instance) to the printed symbol? If we answer yes, then we should agree that children learn to decode by "reading," or by recognizing many symbols like *Pac Man* and using them to figure out letter–sound relationships. At the same time, they are enhancing their ability to recognize printed symbols by gradually learning all the letter–sound relationships.

In recent years, psychologists pursuing the question of how children learn to read have identified two contrasting theories as the "bottom–up" and "top–

down" views of reading acquisition. The former holds that learning to read depends on mastering the sound–symbol correspondences at the level of single letter sounds or on mastering clusters of sounds referred to as *phonograms* or *spelling patterns*. Mastery of these elements leads to accurate naming of words, which then triggers recognition of the meaning of the words as stored in auditory memory.

The top–down view holds that readers approach print expecting to get meaning. So from their past experiences, knowledge of language patterns, and selected information on the page, they construct the message. According to this view, the difference between what a child calls a word and the actual word on the page is not always significant. Only when the difference interferes with meaning is it deemed an error. For example, if Robbie says "airplane" when the print says "toy" in a story about choosing an airplane in a toy shop, the top–down view explains that he correctly perceived an intended relationship in the passage. Reading "airplane" instead of "toy" was a miscue, not an error, since Robbie's command of meaning overpowered the print features in his "reading out" the message as coded by the author. The top–down view thus asserts that print features guide but do not dominate the reading process.

Few practitioners adhere completely to one view over the other. However, these views do influence the degree to which educators emphasize decoding in the instructional materials they prepare for beginning reading. Moreover, primary teachers tend to shape their teaching strategies toward one side or the other of the "bottom–up," "top–down" controversy.

Regardless of which view is in favor in a particular school, most children by the end of second grade have learned to use meaningful context in combination with letter–sound relationships to help identify words. Average readers can recognize a thousand words automatically, on sight, without thinking consciously about "sounding them out." For words they must decode, they use structural analysis—employing word parts larger than phonemes—as well as phonic analysis backed by context. They use context clues, which encompass syntactic as well as semantic cues. To aid comprehension, they have had lessons on following the sequence of events, on seeing cause–effect relationships, on following directions, and on drawing inferences from text and pictures.

Grades 3 and 4   The major instructional goals in these grades are: (1) to establish independence in decoding; (2) to apply comprehension skills to increasingly complex materials, including content textbooks; and (3) to begin in earnest the development of study skills. By the end of grade 3, average readers have learned basically all the sound/symbol correspondences in English. New lessons in grade 4 give additional practice and emphasize supplementary strategies such as structural analysis and the use of glossaries. Grade 4 is the year of the dictionary, with much practice in alphabetizing, locating words, and using pronunciation keys, and perhaps not enough in interpreting and using definitions.

In fourth grade, too, children have their first serious encounters with the language and organization of content textbooks. Vocabulary study broadens to include specialized as well as general meanings.

During the third and fourth grades, virtually all comprehension skills are either extended or newly introduced. Although longer lists are available, the following includes the major skills:

word meaning

literal recall

sequencing events

recognizing the stated main idea

finding supporting details

inferring details

inferring the main idea

noting cause–effect relationships

distinguishing relevant from irrelevant information

classifying ideas

noting contradictions

distinguishing reality from fantasy, fact from fiction

recognizing author's purpose

using patterns of organization such as time order and comparision–contrast

understanding figurative language

predicting outcomes

drawing conclusions

Success in applying these skills, at rudimentary levels, distinguishes the "functionally literate" from the "illiterate" in society.

Instructional Materials and Teaching Strategies

As soon as the printing press made literacy a common ambition, primers for teaching reading began to appear, along with advice on how to use them. Today the production of instructional materials is a major industry in which books still figure prominently, though they compete with workbooks, kits, cards, ditto sheets, toys and games, puppets, kid-size alphabet figures, recordings, films and filmstrips, educational television programs, like *Sesame Street*, and computer software. Many commercial packages are advertised as programs designed to take care of *all* reading instruction—not only in primary grades but beyond.

We would like to say that reading programs are created by teachers and that instructional materials are no more than teachers' tools; but the truth is that you can get a pretty good idea of how reading is taught in most primary grades in this country by studying the commercial "programs." Nevertheless, since some primary teachers prefer to create their own instructional packages, and many others combine elements from several sources, we discuss in this section not only materials but approaches to teaching beginning reading.

Basal Reading Series   Probably a half-dozen basal reading series account for most of the instructional material in primary grades across the nation, though at least fifteen are presently on the market. (If you want to know more about this subject, see Robert Auckerman's book *The Basal Reader Approach to Reading*, John Wiley & Sons, 1981.) Although one series differs from another, they have enough common characteristics to constitute a type. A series begins with one or two prereading or readiness workbooks followed by three preprimers, a primer, and a first reader; there are two books each for grades 2 and 3, and one book for each subsequent grade through 8 in most cases. Beyond the preprimers, the pupil texts are hardcover anthologies of short stories, nonfiction articles, poetry, sometimes a play or two, and usually skills lessons. Especially at the primary level, contemporary basal readers are likely to contain a "whole book," one that is sold as such in trade bookstores.

Vocabulary control is the chief characteristic of the first nine texts (the first preprimer to the second book for grade 3); that is, words are introduced gradually and repeated frequently. As children move from book to book in the same series, they encounter those words which have been introduced in previous books or selections, with only a few new words introduced in each new selection. Since sentences gradually become longer from book to book, the readability of basal readers, at least as measured by word difficulty and sentence length, is graduated, or "leveled." Instead of designating the grades for which texts are intended, publishers are likely to refer to levels, with a grade 1–8 series having fifteen levels.

A set of graduated texts does not in itself define a basal series. What accomplishes that is the teacher's manual or guide which accompanies each text and contains explicit directions for how to teach each selection. In many cases, lessons in the guide are *scripted*; that is, the teacher is told exactly what to say in introducing a selection, teaching vocabulary, asking questions, and initiating skills practice. Often the expected responses from students are also included. The typical basal manual employs a method that has come to be known as the Directed Reading Lesson (DRL) or Directed Reading Activity (DRA). This consists of: (1) *preparation*, which covers motivating interest, preteaching new words, relating concepts to pupils' experience and prior knowledge, and setting purposes; (2) *guided silent reading*, which at the earliest levels often means reading page by page in response to the teacher's injunction, "Read to find out"; and (3) *discussion and follow-up*, which usually includes both skills practice and "enrichment activities" related to the content of the selection.

Pupil texts and teacher's editions are the core of the basal series. In addition, there are workbooks, ditto sheets, kits of skills exercises, and "libraries" of extra reading—to name the major supplements. The illustrations in Figure 2-3 give you an idea of what one basal series looks like.

Perhaps because they are so widely used, basal reading series are easy targets when criticism is leveled at primary reading programs. (By the same token, they should be widely praised when the evidence shows improvement in reading across the country.) Granted that the texts children read are only one of the variables that influence how they read, basal reading series nevertheless carry a heavy weight of responsibility for the quality of instruction in beginning reading. On the debit side, the series encourage standardization of instruction within a classroom, among classes in the same school, and from one school district to another. Along with standardization may come boredom. Although most primary teachers have three or more groups of children reading at different levels, groups are likely to be at different places in the same series. The sameness of the basal lesson format can become boring to teachers and pupils alike when it is repeated several times a day, day in and day out. Despite this, many teachers become wholly dependent on the series, following every suggestion mindlessly and asking for more supplementary materials. And because most series have extensive built-in testing programs to be administered at the end of each book—and often each unit—teachers work for "results" and let the basal reading program consume more of their curriculum than it ought to.

These same features we have noted as potential problems are often seen by supervisors and administrators as advantages, since the inherent standardization of instruction promises to be "teacher-proof." Moreover, if every teacher follows the same basal program, the administrators can persuade themselves that they're in control. Far from complaining about the basic similarities of the leading series, many school people complain of their differences. They say that shifting students from one series to another places too great a burden on beginning readers and their teachers.

But whatever one's view, basal reading series have become the most widely used vehicle of instruction in primary grades—for good reasons as well as for the less creditable ones just mentioned. While we would argue that no materials are "teacher-proof," the series can compensate, in part, for some teachers' temporary lapses—inertia, limited knowledge, lack of ingenuity, or skimpy preparation. The manuals are a daily reminder of principles learned, and perhaps forgotten, from courses and professional reading. The best of the manuals implement sound recent research while making proved old practices freshly appealing to today's children.

As for pupils' texts, no expense is spared to make them attractive and readable. Although easily parodied by sophisticated adults, preprimers can be exhilarating to children who are reading on their own for the first time. Critics often forget that the preprimers are only a small part of the first-grade program. Beyond the preprimers, most series contain collections of traditional tales, classics, and current literature by respected children's authors, much of it reproduced with little or no adaptation from the trade texts. On the credit side, too, is the careful and comprehensive skills development program which accompanies the readers. Many secondary teachers, when they understand the purposes and appreciate the comprehensiveness of basal reading series, wish that their subject-matter specialties were as well served with published materials. (Chapter 10 has more to say about textbooks.)

Still, a basal reading series is only one part of a well-balanced beginning reading program. Good primary teachers complement their series with one or more of the approaches described below.

The Language Experience Approach   As children move from oral language to the more abstract registers of reading and writing, they should, in the view of

FIGURE 2-3

3 Maintaining Skills

Comprehension Skills

Recognizing multiple meanings of words Display word cards *like*, *plant*, and *light*, and have them read. Discuss with pupils the various meanings of each word.

> *like:* to enjoy or be fond of; the same as
> *plant:* something that grows; to put a seed in earth to grow
> *light:* not dark; not heavy; something that gives off brightness

Then read the following sentences, and have pupils tell which word makes sense in the sentence. Read the completed sentence aloud.

> A feather is very _____. *(light)*
> My notebook is just _____ yours. *(like)*
> Let's _____ the flower seeds today. *(plant)*
> When the sun comes up, it gets _____. *(light)*
> Your _____ is beginning to grow. *(plant)*
> When it gets dark, the _____ will come on. *(light)*
> I _____ green peppers better than red ones. *(like)*

Have pupils use each word in a sentence to illustrate each meaning.

Direct pupils to page 106 of *Reading Skills 4*.

Reading Skills 4, Page 106

Recognizing cause and effect Direct pupils' attention to the pictures at the top of the page. Be sure pupils understand the cause-and-effect relationship depicted.

Have pupils read the first sentence on the left—the cause—and find a sentence on the right that tells the effect. Ask them to draw a line between the two sentences. Have pupils complete the page independently. When pupils are finished, have the cause-and-effect statements read aloud.

See "Providing for Individual Differences" for additional practice with this skill.

Recognizing time relationships Discuss with pupils the time it takes for most plants to grow. **Usually we plant tomato seeds in the spring and pick tomatoes in the late summer. How many months is it from early spring to late summer?** (about five months) Help pupils count the months from March to August.

Discuss the fact that sometimes growth and change can occur quickly, but other times they occur slowly. Have pupils compare the following activities and decide whether each requires a long or a short time. Also, you may wish to discuss why some things only *seem* to

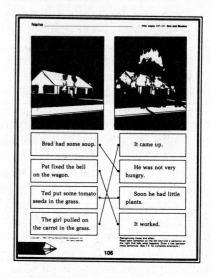

take a longer or shorter time than they really do.

> painting a picture
> making a cat mask
> making your bed
> the school year
> growing tomatoes
> making tomato soup
> riding to school
> growing up
> grocery shopping
> one birthday to another

Literature Appreciation

Comparing and contrasting selections Have pupils open their books to the table of contents. Review the theme of each section, and discuss the various selections in *Sun and Shadow*. You may wish to use the following questions:

> How many sections or groups of stories have we read in our book so far? (5)
>
> In which group were all the selections make-believe? ("On the Magic Hill")
>
> Which group told about life in the city? ("In the City")
>
> In which group did the selections take place at night? ("After Dark")

Sun and Shadow and Reading Skills 4 Teacher's Edition

many teachers, use their own language as the medium. Teachers who subscribe to this approach begin by writing down what children dictate and using these dictated stories as the reading text. Initially, teachers help a child recall the words dictated by reading along with her (or him) and pointing to the printed form that

FIGURE 2-4

A BASAL SERIES

encodes the spoken word. On subsequent days, the child is encouraged to recall the words (that is, read them) again and again. Gradually, the young reader begins to recognize many high-frequency words (*the, and, but, I, went, mother*) and high-interest words (*dinosaurs, snowmobile, computer*), as well as the names of friends, family members and pets. To enhance the children's personal experiences and interests, and thus to increase the variety of their dictated stories, teachers spend time reading aloud; showing posters, pictures, and films; taking them on field trips; planning special events; and helping them make things. These activities provide sources not only for stories but for other forms of writing, such as directions, letters, recipes, captions, charts, and records. To go with the texts which the children provide and share with one another, teachers devise lessons on decoding and on the basic comprehension skills.

The Language Experience Approach depends greatly on children's books—at first for listening and then, as the children gain skill in reading, for replacing the dictated texts. Often this approach leads to the independent reading of books, including basal series, which teachers using language experience treat no differently from trade or library books.

A common criticism of the Language Experience Approach is that it is too time-consuming and unstructured for reasonable management. Except in the hands of a highly competent teacher, it can easily allow some children to get lost. Teachers who forgo the guidance of a packaged program must have confidence in their ability to observe and assess growth, to sequence skills practice, and to move individual children along at just the right pace to maintain interest and challenge. Perhaps this approach works best when the teacher has aides and the children come from homes where reading is prized and encouraged.

The Whole Language Approach This is a variation of the Language Experience Approach. It makes much of the idea that reading is one of the language arts but not necessarily the most important one. From the first, children are immersed in experiences that require use of all the language arts—listening, speaking, writing, and reading, in that order. Writing to share thoughts with others is encouraged even at the scribble stage. Personal journals provide opportunities to record important experiences, ideas, and impressions in pictures and in words. Gradually, the journals contain more words than pictures. By third and fourth grade, as children's skills mature, they can write at length about topics important to them. In addition, their concerns for legibility, spelling, and clear development of relationships become heightened.

Using references to search out personally interesting information fosters positive attitudes toward reading and learning. Through listening to the reports of classmates, discussing findings, and defending interpretations, students are able to place reading and writing in realistic contexts from the outset. They come to view the language arts as personally useful, even powerful, tools necessary for understanding themselves and communicating with others.

Again, classroom management is more difficult with this approach than with a basal series. Monitoring individual progress requires more of the teacher's time and a greater awareness of the relatedness of reading skills.

Skills Management Systems Teachers vary in their ability to perform essential tasks, such as evaluating children's progress, guiding their skills development, and interpreting their behavior with a view to selecting texts and planning future lessons. Because teachers are different, skills management systems were developed in an attempt to ensure that beginning readers would be taught appropriate skills at appropriate levels. Essentially, skills management systems are an implementation of mastery learning theories. As each component of the grapheme/phoneme code is introduced to beginning readers, or as each skill of comprehension is about to be rehearsed, teachers administer a pretest to determine the nature and amount of drill the children should receive. At the conclusion of the lesson and/or practice, the students are given another test to see if mastery has been achieved. If the criterion for mastery is met, students move to the next skill; if not, they work through additional practice materials. Usually the criterion for mastery is set at 80 percent correct response; and children cannot try the next designated lesson or reading level until they obtain this score.

Adoption of a management system permits teachers to use a basal series or other instructional materials, but many systems provide their own materials. Management systems are intended as a check on teacher judgment as well as a means of identifying the reading status of any pupil at any time.

Management systems have spurred controversy among reading educators over the last decade or more because the systems run counter to the theory that reading is a unitary process in which many skills work in combination. Instead, management theory asserts that skills can be extracted from the whole process, tested individually, and taught sequentially and systematically, with the result that reading performance is improved.

In schools where management systems have been adopted, emphasis on isolated skill instruction tends to replace actual reading of text in the classroom. Thus, children who are least able to read spend most of their time practicing skills, and little if any time engaged in reading. However, many schools employing skills management systems show gains on reading tests. Critics claim that these gains are artificial indicators of reading performance, since the reading measures used—chiefly, standardized group tests—assess skills mastery, not functional reading performance. Clearly, views of what reading is and how it should be measured are at the heart of this controversy and others that debate which materials and instructional approaches best serve children who are learning to read. And until research studies ask the right questions and find conclusive answers, the controversies will persist.

Computer-Assisted Instruction

A new electronic aid for teaching reading is finding its way into the primary grades and beyond. At this stage, it is fair to describe the bulk of available *courseware* (as computer programs are called) as electronic workbooks. Most of the courseware for beginning readers provides practice in recognizing letters, identifying sound–symbol correspondences, and building words by letter substitutions. Some vocabulary or word meaning courseware and comprehension exercises are available for grades 1–6; however, most comprehension programs are designed for higher grades.

The major advantage of computer-assisted instruction appears to be the immediate feedback children receive on each task they complete. Coupled with built-in graphic motivators (the computer world's equivalent of the "happy face" sticker), the immediate feedback tends to keep students focused and lessens the likelihood they will practice errors. Because computers satisfy children's love of gadgetry and their need for motor involvement (pushing the joy stick), many teachers and administrators predict they will become as useful a tool in learning to read as more conventional conveyors of print.

However, the immediate prospects for widespread computer-assisted instruction are still not glowing because of the dearth of courseware and because the cost of personal computers for every classroom—and preferably for every student— is still a staggering sum for tax-supported schools, in spite of what the silicon chip has done for national computer sales. Whether miracles in electronic engineering can be matched by ingenious programming is anyone's guess. But as long as courseware for reading instruction is limited to skill/drill exercises, it seems doubtful that computers will play an integral role in developmental programs, even at the reading acquisition stage. Probably their major use will remain where it is today—in remedial programs—for as long as their novelty provides motivation.

Weaknesses in Beginning Reading Instruction

By the end of grade 3 or 4, most children have learned to read grade-level texts, if not flawlessly at least well enough to make sense to a listener when they read aloud and to grasp meanings when they read silently. But some youngsters arrive in middle school and even in high school unable or unwilling to read for their own pleasure and so not ready to learn to use reading as a tool.

To what extent are elementary schools responsible for the small minority who fail to acquire beginning skills even though they have had the opportunity to learn and have no major physical or mental handicaps? And to what degree are they to blame for the larger number of students who learn how to read but choose not to? These questions naturally occur to teachers in the upper grades when they encounter students who are still in the beginning reading stage. And they are not referring to new arrivals in American schools or to youngsters with clearly identified disabilities. Rather, their concern is for seemingly normal students who have passed through all the earlier grades—perhaps in their own school districts—without learning to read. When children fail, we rightly look for weaknesses in school practice.

As suggested in the previous section, the most common overall weakness of beginning reading instruction is too much emphasis on a single approach to the exclusion of others. When too much emphasis is given to phonics, for instance, children forget meaning, refuse to take chances, and sound out words letter by letter. Even in classes where phonics is introduced as one of several means of decoding, most children enter a sounding-out phase in the middle of first grade and emerge from it unscathed, and become fluent in identifying words using all the cues provided. But for those who continue to find reading a laborious decoding game, the desire to read disappears.

Too much drill on any of the skills—not just phonics—can confuse children as to what reading really is. Whether time-on-task means responding to flash cards, matching sentences and pictures in a workbook, or tracing a left-to-right track on the computer screen, children learn the immediate task rather than the ultimate purpose for it. A serious weakness of well-intentioned, task-oriented teachers is that they keep children busy without seriously questioning the worth of what is being learned. Too little time spent pursuing meanings in printed messages is characteristic of too many primary classrooms.

The way that children learn what books are for is by reading them. When they are too unskilled to read for themselves, they learn this all-important lesson from listening to teachers read whole books aloud to them. Teachers in the first three grades discharge this responsibility more faithfully than do those in later grades, but teach-and-test programs allow them too little time. And beyond grade 1 the need continues even though children can supplement listening with "real" reading. They also get a better idea of what reading is for when they are allowed to read to the end of a story without the interruption of teachers' questions, promptings, and corrections.

Other weaknesses which have been noted in beginning reading instruction include too much emphasis on oral reading and overcorrecting children's miscues. While teachers need to hear children read aloud as a check on their progress, this purpose can be achieved without having the daily routine of the reading circle extend all the way to middle school. This practice often results in word-by-word reading, washes out meaning, bores the children who are waiting their turn, and encourages the listeners to "pick on" the inexpert reader. It is also often blamed for inducing slow and inflexible habits of silent reading that persist into adulthood. Overcorrecting and prompting prevent self-monitoring and self-correcting, essential characteristics of independent, meaning-seeking readers.

Insufficient variety in the kinds of reading matter children encounter in primary grades accounts, in part, for difficulties in approaching content textbooks later on. If their diet is restricted wholly to basal readers, they may have a sampling of all genres but inadequate exposure to information presented in modes other than narrative. As basal series editors yield to reading supervisors' demands for more attention to skills, including comprehension lessons in the pupils' texts, the series skimp not only on informational selections in several modes but also on variety in literature, especially poetry. So if basal fare is not generously supplemented with books from the library, children miss the chance to become versatile readers.

All the weaknesses noted thus far are related to a single failure—the failure to recognize and respond to the many different ways children learn to read. The weakest programs are the ones that adopt a single method and fail to embellish it with borrowings from other methods. The strongest programs balance the careful monitoring of children's progress in reading with abundant opportunities to read all kinds of books, including basal series. Not just opportunities, of course, but reasons for reading must be clearly present in every classroom.

In a balanced beginning reading program, children should make progress in learning to read according to their own developmental timetables. They are most likely to do that when teachers figure out how each child is learning, the kinds and amounts of help each needs, and how to deliver it. It is an enormously complex job, this matter of responding to individual differences, and primary teachers seem to be better at it than many of the rest of us. School staffs made up of teachers who can identify and respond to different learning styles are most likely to avert the common weaknesses enumerated here.

Beginning Reading: A Growing Success Story

More children succeed in beginning reading today than ever before. Nationwide test results, such as the National Assessment of Educational Progress, record the strides we are making in primary grades, especially among disadvantaged populations in big cities and in rural areas where poverty, bilingualism and dialect differences, and limited instructional resources have had to be overcome. More important evidence can be found in parents' increasing satisfaction with early schooling, in the growth in children's book publishing (more titles, more sales, more children's bookstores, more lively libraries), and in the shift of public attention away from primary grades to the middle and upper grades.

Improved test scores at the end of grade 3 (and among nine-year-olds on the National Assessment) are the result in large measure, we believe, of improved instructional materials and better preparation of teachers. Much has been learned about the beginning reading process as a result of the efforts made throughout this century by educators and psychologists whose attention has been focused on early learning and language acquisition. Their research has been translated into materials and methods of instruction with good effect. While much remains to be learned about beginning reading and writing (especially the latter), we can now afford to give attention to later stages of development, both as researchers and as teachers.

The need to do so is imperative, for while beginning reading may be characterized as a "growing success," there is depressing evidence that many children do not grow appreciably beyond the levels they achieve by the end of grade 4. The reasons children slow down or cease to develop in reading beyond grade 4 are many, but surely a major one is a diminution of interest in reading as other concerns capture their attention. To counteract any lessening of interest and to develop learning through reading, teachers in junior and senior high schools need the same kind of support from researchers, publishers, and educational leaders that primary teachers have had for nearly a hundred years. Such support has indeed been increasing over the last several decades, but its effects are only now beginning to be felt.

Meanwhile, there is one thing teachers, parents, and other educators can do to help children preserve and capitalize on the beginning skills they have acquired. That is to keep them reading at levels they can read easily until they have overdeveloped, if you will, the habits and skills of easy intake. On this foundation, which for some may take several years to establish, students can develop, with your help, the skills of learning from text. Which is what the rest of this book is about.

RECAPPING MAIN POINTS

Beginning reading, sometimes referred to as reading acquisition, is an extension of oral language development. Psychologists define reading as information processing which employs selective attention (the brain directs the eye), sorting and organizing visual information (what is on the page), relating it to information which is stored in memory and retrieved for immediate purposes related to the current reading task, and storing the new or modified information thus absorbed.

Teachers and others who create instructional materials tend to define reading "operationally," that is, by what they observe readers doing. In scope and sequence charts and basal reading series, they describe reading in terms of skills and subskills.

In primary grades, basal readers are the most common materials teachers use to assist children in learning to read, but language experience approaches, "whole language" programs that stress independent reading of trade, or library, books, systems approaches that are strongly skills-oriented, and in some classrooms today, computer-assisted instruction complement the basal programs and, in some instances, have replaced them.

Beginning reading focuses strongly on learning to decode the meaning of written messages. So in primary grades comprehension is as important as decoding. By the intermediate grades, comprehension skills outweigh decoding skills in schemes for teaching reading.

Learning to read begins in primary grades and continues throughout a student's life. Most children today succeed in the beginning stages, that is, in reading acquisition. But some children who acquire beginning skills don't choose to read very much and so their skills are stunted. All students, even though they "learn to read" in elementary school, require continued support in learning to use reading as a tool of learning.

FOR DISCUSSION

1. Recall your experiences in the reading acquisition stage and discuss them with other adults of various ages. Include your earliest experiences with print. How does learning to read initially differ from the fluent reading you do now? Do you recall instruction in phonics? Do you ever consciously apply phonics now? Do you skip words that you don't know how to pronounce?

2. A clear and detailed presentation of the psycholinguistic view of reading is *Understanding Reading* by Frank Smith, which we frequently assign in classes for secondary teachers. We divide the text into sections of three or four chapters each, assign one section per week, and form study groups to summarize and react to Smith's thinking.

3. Interview a first-grade teacher, asking such questions as: How do children learn to read in your classroom? What are the strengths and weaknesses of a basal reading series? Had some children in your class this year begun to read before they entered first grade? What are the characteristics of first graders who make rapid progress? little progress? Add other questions that interest you. Prepare a report on reading in first grade that you can share with others. If four or five people take on this assignment, a panel report will be informative to other members of your class and will provoke discussion.

4. Interview elementary teachers at grades other than first. Include, if possible, a special reading teacher. Treat these interviews in ways similar to the above.

5. Why is it important for teachers in grades 5 to 12 to understand how children learn to read?

6. Prepare a group report on a basal reading series. Assign different levels or components to individuals in your group and prepare a guide sheet (or use

one provided by your instructor) that will structure your investigation and report.

7. If you have had a course recently in the psychology of learning, review your text and notes and prepare a report (oral or written) on how a particular psychologist (or psychologists) view the learning of language. We recommend Chapters 12 and 13 in *Human Information Processing* (see Further Reading), but you may wish to use a text with which you are already familiar.

FURTHER READING

Cronbach, Lee J. *Educational Psychology*, 3rd ed. New York: Harcourt Brace Jovanovich, Inc., 1977.
    See especially Chapters 11 and 12.

Durkin, Dolores. *Teaching Them to Read*, 3rd ed. Boston: Allyn and Bacon, 1980.

Goodman, Kenneth. "Behind the Eye: What Happens in Reading?" in *Theoretical Models and Processes of Reading*, 2nd ed., Harry Singer and Robert B. Ruddell, eds. Newark, DE: International Reading Association, 1976.

Holdaway, Don. *The Foundations of Literacy*. Gosford, New South Wales, Australia: Ashton Scholastic, 1979. Distributed by Heineman Educational Books, Inc., Exeter, NH.

Johnson, Dale D. and P. David Pearson. *Teaching Reading Vocabulary*. New York: Holt, Rinehart and Winston, 1978.

Lindsay, Peter H. and Donald A. Norman. *Human Information Processing: An Introduction to Psychology*, 2nd ed. New York: Academic Press, 1977.

Ollila, L. Q., ed. *The Kindergarten Child and Reading*. Newark, DE: International Reading Association, 1977.

Smith, Frank. *Understanding Reading*, 3rd ed. New York: Holt, Rinehart and Winston, 1982.

3 *Using Reading to Learn*

When Bette Mantaro bumped into Joe Wilder as they entered Room 206 in Parkview Middle School that September morning, they were both novices. He'd never taken a course in U. S. history before, and she was about to teach one for the first time. Although each was a newcomer, neither was unprepared for the months they would spend together. Each came equipped with considerable mental baggage, including attitudes toward reading, opinions and assumptions about each other, varying amounts and kinds of prior knowledge about American history, quite different views of life resulting from their quite different experiences, many common understandings (fortunately!) about the school and community they inhabited, a common language, and parallel, though of course not identical, development in using it.

How these two would get along in the months from September to June depended on how well they communicated with each other and with the others in the class and how well they understood the language of the texts they would use.

Ms. Mantaro was 23 and Joe was 13—a ten-year gap that was wider and deeper than it would ever be again. (At 53 and 43, Bette and Joe would both be middle aged; at 83 and 73 they would be contemporaries.) At 23, Ms. Mantaro had already forgotten how she had learned all that U. S. history which qualified her to teach what Joe was supposed to learn. She remembered an inspiring history teacher or two in high school, and was grateful to her college professors, but she had a notion that most of what she had learned about U. S. history she had acquired on her own, through reading textbooks and supplementary histories, making notes, reviewing, cramming with her college roommate, and writing papers. She had dim recollections of her own eighth grade history class, but it seemed that there, too, she had learned chiefly through reading the textbook. Her teacher hadn't been much help, but she hadn't needed much. She'd liked history ever since she'd read the *Little House* books in fourth grade and made a trip with her family the summer she was twelve and they'd stopped at places like Valley Forge and Gettysburg and Monticello and St. Augustine.

So far as she could tell, everyone who had been in eighth grade history class with her had been able to read the textbook, which was an earlier edition of the one she'd be teaching from this fall. But she knew from the reading course she'd taken as a master's student that she couldn't expect everyone in her classes to read as well as kids did ten years ago. She'd been told that in a typical eighth grade she could expect a range of reading abilities from third grade to eleventh. But this third period class was not typical. According to the reading achievement test scores she'd checked in the guidance office, all the students in Joe's class were reading at or above the 50th percentile on the Iowa Test of Basic Skills. So she didn't have to worry about whether these kids could learn from the history textbook. Or did she?

Joe Wilder was a "good" reader. He had scored above the 80th percentile on achievement tests given at the end of sixth grade. He had read with ease and understanding the novels included in the language arts curriculum, books like *Island of the Blue Dolphins* and *The Loner*, and the selections in the literature anthologies. He'd found the reading improvement classes something of a bore but had made his way doggedly through the exercises in the workbooks, ditto sheets, and skills boxes, earning A's and B's each marking period. Occasionally, he chose a novel like *My Brother Sam Is Dead* to read in the SSR sessions[1] that were held schoolwide every morning from 10:25 to 10:45, but usually he stuck to magazines and sports books. He read the sports pages in the daily newspaper delivered to his home, and he swapped comic books with the kids in his gang. Would he be able to learn basic concepts of American history from that five-pound textbook Ms. Mantaro was already passing out?

To put that question more precisely, but more abstractly: To what extent and in what ways does the use of language (reading and writing in particular) contribute to students' understanding of concepts or ideas? This is a question for which educational psychologists and reading specialists have as yet found no definitive answers. It is a question, however, to which teachers need immediate answers if they are to do their jobs. So they draw tentative answers from three sources: introspective analyses of their own language processes, observations of their students' uses of language, and the research and theory presently available. From like sources we draw the following speculations on the extent to which "good" eighth grade readers like Joe Wilder can use reading as an aid to learning concepts in history, science, math, and, indeed, whatever in the world they are curious about.

Learning Through Reading

Learning and comprehending are not quite the same, but they are closely related, and at this point in our discussion they are treated as one in order to invoke the wisdom of Henry David Thoreau, who put a fundamental psychological principle into plain English when he said that "we apprehend only what we already half know." Psychologists are making the same point when they say that

---

[1]Many schools set aside a period of time each day when everyone—teachers, students, secretaries, janitors, nurse, librarian—drops everything and reads. (See Chapter 9 for more details on SSR.)

comprehension depends upon prior knowledge and that learning can take place only when the learner is able to connect a "new" idea with what he or she already knows. I like Frank Smith's metaphor for prior knowledge—"the theory of the world in your head"—because much of what we "know" may be erroneous and is, in fact, subject to change as new ideas are assimilated.

What a reader already "knows" may clarify new ideas or distort them. Once when I was teaching American history my class read a short passage about the Know Nothing Party, which was formed in the mid-nineteenth century with the express purpose of keeping out of the United States Irish, German, and Scandinavian immigrants whom the party considered "undesirable." There was no question that the students were able to decode the words of the text accurately and rapidly, and they seemingly understood the meanings of individual words and the syntax of individual sentences. But when I asked them to identify statements about Americans' attitudes toward immigrants in the period we were studying—statements with which the text agreed—they responded, not according to the text they had just read, but with their ingrained beliefs that immigrants from Western Europe had always been welcomed to the United States.

Most teachers readily accept the idea that reading comprehension depends to a great extent on prior knowledge, but they are constantly surprised, as I was in the example just given, when students who bring different sets of experience and different "theories of the world" to their reading come away from it with different kinds and degrees of understanding. That we should not be surprised when students take away different meanings from a text does not imply that we should accept all interpretations as correct. Readers of expository text have an obligation to come as close as possible to the meanings set forth in that text by the writer. And teachers have a moral obligation to find out why students are wide of the mark so that they can help them achieve a more accurate understanding.

Nevertheless, we are likely to be surprised. Ms. Mantaro will be surprised when Joe Wilder fails to comprehend a passage in the textbook in the same way that she does. As a good reader of history herself, she expects others to see the world as she does. That's a failing that even experienced teachers have, for it is one thing to "learn" a psychological principle in the abstract and quite another to recognize it operating in the classroom.

Recently, despite having known for years that prior knowledge affects comprehension, I was still surprised by the results of experiments which demonstrated how powerful that effect is. The data that surprised me were reported in two doctoral studies conducted at Syracuse University, and are reproduced in Boxes 3-1 and 3-2. In the first study, 21 ninth grade boys read two short stories and two selections from science textbooks. They were encouraged to read carefully, to review if necessary, and to then tell a listener what they had read. Box 3-1 shows the scores obtained from analysis of their tape-recorded retellings.

You can see that the boys remembered more ideas from the short stories ("The Sniper" and "The Bet") than they did from the science passages (on the atom and on the concepts of volume, density, and mass). That is not surprising, for

BOX 3-1

HOW 21 NINTH GRADE BOYS SCORED IN RETELLING SHORT STORIES AND SCIENCE PASSAGES AFTER READING

Retelling Score	Sniper	Bet	Volume	Atom
More than 75%	—	—	—	—
51% to 75%	15	13	—	—
25% to 50%	6	5	6	6
Less than 25%	—	3	15	15

Average and above-average readers as measured by standardized reading test (Stanford).
SOURCE: Data adapted and reported with permission from Lorraine Dagostino, "An Exploratory Investigation of the Strategies Used by Ninth Grade Boys When Reading Short Story and Science Material." Ph.D. diss., Syracuse University, 1981.

the short stories, even though one is set in Ireland and the other in Russia, are about human emotions and actions that are recognizable to adolescents, whereas science concepts explained in abstract textbook prose are remote from their experience. However, the differences in the amount of recall are dramatic. None of the boys recalled more than 50 percent of the science content and most of them recalled less than 25 percent. In the next section we shall consider the relationships between recall and comprehension, but at this point let the data in Box 3-1 speak for themselves. If you were these boys' English teacher, you would have reason to worry about how well prepared they might be for a discussion of "The Sniper" or "The Bet" if you had done no more than assign the reading. If you were their science teacher, you would probably not have made an assignment simply to read the text (as the researcher did) because you would not expect much understanding of scientific concepts solely as a result of reading. But sometimes we forget the principle of prior knowledge and depend too heavily on textbooks as an aid to learning.

The second study relates directly to the issue of prior knowledge in the form of concept development. An Englishman, Michael Shayer, with colleagues, has standardized group tests[2] for measuring students' progress through the stages defined by Jean Piaget as "concrete operational" and "formal operational" thought. We found one of these tests, Task II, useful for assessing another group of ninth grade boys' understanding of the concepts of volume, density, and mass, which they would read about in a selection similar to one of those used in the first study. Box 3-2 shows that all the boys in the study were "good" readers, and that one group had mastered the concepts of volume, density, and mass which they would encounter in the reading passage while the other students had not quite arrived at this stage of cognitive development.

How well would both groups of students comprehend the selection? Analysis of the tapes made of each boy as he told another student what he recalled from

---

[2]M. Shayer, H. Wylam, P. Adey and D. Kuchemann, *CSMS Science Reasoning Tasks*, NFER Publishing Company, Darville House, 2 Oxford Road East, Windsor, Berks SL4 1DF.

BOX 3-2

36 NINTH GRADE BOYS' UNDERSTANDING OF ARCHIMEDES' PRINCIPLE BEFORE AND AFTER READING

Recall Scores

	N	Mean	Range
Concrete operational thought:	19	40%	11%-75%
Formal operational thought:	17	57%	35%-78%

Could Apply Principle

	N	Yes	No
Concrete operational thought:	19	32%	63%
Formal operational thought:	17	65%	34%

Before reading, two groups were identified as "concrete thinkers" and "formal thinkers" according to their scores on CSMS Science Reasoning Tasks. In both groups, all students achieved above the 60th percentile on reading achievement measures. After reading "The Discovery of Archimedes' Principle," each boy told a partner what he had read. Listeners had also been identified as concrete thinkers.

SOURCE: Data adapted and reported with permission from Marianna K. McVey, "The Role of Prior Knowledge in Ninth Grade Boys' Comprehension of a Concept in Science." Ed.D. diss., Syracuse University, 1981.

the selection reveal that, on the average, the boys who had mastered the concept before reading reported more fully than did the other boys. When both groups of students were asked to apply the principle in solving a new but very similar problem, the results were emphatic. Most of the boys who had not mastered the concepts, according to the Shayer test, came up with an incorrect solution while most of the boys who "knew" the concept before reading the selection were able to apply it.

Was reading the selection of any help to good readers who had not quite learned the concepts discussed in the selection? "Yes, probably." The post-test performance of "concrete thinkers," some of whom had read the selection and some of whom had not, showed that those who had read and talked about the selection improved their scores on the CSMS Science Reasoning Task II to a significantly higher degree than did those who had not read it.

Comprehension and Retention

We do not mean to imply by the foregoing discussion that students' retelling of what they have read is a completely reliable clue to their comprehension. For one thing, they may remember more than they care to report. And they may report ideas they do not fully comprehend. In the experiments just described, the students who seemed to know most about the concepts under discussion tended to ignore many specific details and get right to the point in explaining the science selection to another student. However, most of the students earned their recall scores by reporting specific details rather than generalizations.

Students filter the meanings that reside in text through their own experiences. Therefore, they tend to recall details they recognize and ideas they are already familiar with. Even when an author has stated generalizations plainly, readers may not recall these ideas unless, or even when, they are prompted. When we asked probing questions about generalizations expressed in the science selections, those students who had not volunteered these generalizations in their free recall of the material tended not to answer the questions accurately or fully.

This discussion may remind you of two facts about recall that you have observed both in yourself and others. First, it is easier to recognize an idea than to recall it. For example, which of these questions is easier for you to answer?

1. Which was the first state admitted to the Union after the Constitution was ratified by the original thirteen states?
2. The fourteenth state admitted to the Union was (a) Ohio, (b) Illinois, (c) Vermont, (d) Maine.

And, obviously, we can vary greatly the cueing values of recognition questions by controlling the wrong choices. For example, you would have had less trouble "remembering" that Vermont was the first state admitted (1791) after the Constitution was ratified if the other choices had been Missouri, Texas, and California.

You can test a second observation about recall by considering what this next question demands of you:

3. How did the issue of slavery affect the expansion of the U. S. after the defeat of Mexico in 1848?

This question requires you to recall events and issues, sort them according to a particular time frame, and then arrange them in an order that supports effectively the generalizations you make about the struggle between slaveholders and free-soilers in the decades preceding 1861. More *knowing* than *recalling* is involved in answering the third question.

Teachers, then, can control the quality of the comprehension they ask students to exhibit. If Ms. Mantaro asks Joe Wilder chiefly questions which require recognition of a right answer, she may make him look like a better reader of U.S. history than he actually is. As he becomes familiar with the kinds of questions Ms. Mantaro typically asks or that the workbook pages call for, Joe, who is eager to earn A's and B's, will store up facts that can be readily triggered by recognition items. Through this process, Joe and Ms. Mantaro, too, may delude themselves into believing that he comprehends the textbook and is learning about U.S. history.

Having students retell a story or explain ideas they have just read, as in the experiments just reported, is an inadequate measure of comprehension but a better one than having them answer multiple-choice items, which tap recognition rather than unaided recall. We understand why teachers prefer to score recognition-type exercises and short-answer questions rather than analyze "free recall" performances, whether oral or written. Nevertheless, we urge you to balance the two kinds of responses for several reasons, the less important one being that you want to measure both kinds of comprehension.

A more important reason for having students talk and write as a follow-up to reading is that these uses of language help them absorb what they have read. Even more important: Writing and talking compel readers to try to make sense of something they may have only partly understood.

Is it useful to remember much of what we read? Yes, of course, because that prior knowledge we referred to—that "theory of the world in your head"—is fed by what we retain from experiences, including the experiences and the thinking of others transmitted through the medium of print. A lot of the ease with which Joe Wilder will comprehend his eighth grade history textbook will depend on what he remembers from previous encounters with U.S. history, including those social studies texts in grades 4 and 5 as well as any historical fiction he may have read, and including, too, whatever conceptions and misconceptions he has picked up from films, television, travel, teachers, parents, and people generally.

Do remembered details influence the quality of comprehension? Of course they do, for the "theory of the world" is composed of details. For the students who read "The Bet" and remembered (from previous reading, probably) that a *kopek* is a Russian coin the setting of the story was instantly established. To be sure, recognizing the setting of the story is a minor matter compared with understanding the range of human emotions it expresses, but easy recognition of minor details often puts readers at ease so that they are able to grapple with the important issues. However, to say that facts are useful mental baggage implies no injunction to "teach" facts, supposing that we can do so by the questions we ask and the drills we set. Rather the implication is that we should encourage students to think about how they absorb details and to reflect upon the usefulness of such details to their developing theories of the world.

To be useful to Joe in comprehending text, the facts or ideas he has learned ("prior knowledge") must be easily accessible; that is, readily cued by meanings in the text. Furthermore, his brain must be ready to make connections between these meanings and what he knows already. What we are referring to as "what he knows" psychologists refer to as *cognitive structure*. This term, which is no more real for being high-sounding, implies some kind of systematic storing up of ideas that can be retrieved on demand and applied to a new situation. Cognitive structure is a metaphor, perhaps a helpful one, which leads us to think of the brain as if it were a hugely complex and computerized storage system. As teachers we have to be concerned rather less with what goes into that storage system and rather more with how to pull out what is needed.

We retrieve stored information—that is, we recall what we already know—when we make connections between one idea and another. A kind of chain reaction sets in. You've had the experience of attempting to recall a half-forgotten incident in your life, say, graduation from high school. You think you have forgotten the names of most of your classmates. Then someone reminds you that Jeff was going steady with Linda, and thinking of Linda puts you in mind of Susan, who was her best friend. Pretty soon, by a series of connections, you've recalled many of the actors and events of those last few months of high school. Because events in your life are associated with feelings, chances are you can retrieve them more easily than events in history, or scientific concepts, mathematical abstractions, and the beliefs of the world's religions, but the processes of recall are similar. So teachers invoke a discussion about a topic to be studied knowing that an idea contributed by one student may cause other students to recall a bit of information here or a half-understood concept there.

We shall have more to say in later chapters about the teacher's role in facilitating comprehension. Here let us simply reiterate the point that memory is one very important factor in comprehension, one which is intricately bound up with all other components of reading comprehension. Keep in mind the complexity of the comprehension process as we go on in the next sections to consider other factors, attempting to disentangle for the sake of clarity factors which are, of course, inextricable.

Comprehension and Language

When people who theorize about the reading process speak of "prior knowledge" they refer not only to ideas and facts, which they often label "content," but also to the reader's understanding of how a language works in various kinds of writing. Readers know, for example, what letter combinations to expect in written English, and they are familiar with the patterns of English sentences, expecting, for example, that an adjective will be followed by the noun it describes. These are examples of a very basic understanding of language codes. As readers meet more complex ideas expressed in writing, their knowledge of language codes expands. They learn, for example, that *or* sometimes introduces a synonym and sometimes an alternative idea. They realize that punctuation is a writer's device for presenting ideas more clearly, and they learn such conventions as: a colon directs the reader's attention to what is coming; a semicolon separates one complete thought from another; a comma joins ideas or words in lists. When readers consider chunks of language larger than words and sentences, they begin to merge language codes with structural codes (which are discussed in the next section).

What we want to emphasize here is that a large part of the prior knowledge that a student brings to reading a specific selection is familiarity with language structures or codes. Language codes differ slightly or greatly from one mode of discourse to another. For instance, the structures that a teenager uses in oral language are very different from the structures a newspaper columnist employs. Familiarity with the language codes of contemporary writers is insufficient preparation for easy understanding of the language codes of nineteenth-century novelists. Nevertheless, an adolescent reader who speaks English like a native and has read a good many books of any kind brings a great deal of familiarity with language to the reading of whatever subject you are teaching. Part of what the reader "half knows" is an expectation about what the written language does.

Sometimes it is more important to remember the language code than the content. Most of what elementary school children read in basal readers and in self-selected fiction illustrates this point. We expect them to gain familiarity with language codes; we don't expect them to remember the content. Another example is that of reading to follow directions. When we read directions for assembling a lawn sprinkler, for example, we expect to remember how to do it only long enough to complete the task. However, familiarity with the language code used in writing directions grows as we read more directions. We remember the code and forget the specific content.

Comprehension and Structural Codes

The metaphor *cognitive structure* suggests a grid or a network of connected meanings which are capable of being disconnected and reassembled in different patterns as new meanings are added and old ones revised. These patterns of meanings are undoubtedly shaped by the language structures in which the individual thinks, speaks, reads, and writes, as well as by the person's nonlanguage experiences and the mores of his society. The extent to which a network of meanings—a cognitive structure—is affected by reading depends on how thoroughly the reader internalizes the structural codes used by the writer. Thus, one reason that the ninth graders comprehended the short stories better than the science selections may have been their greater familiarity with the structural codes of narratives as compared with the structural codes of exposition.

From babyhood, children in our society learn how stories are structured simply from listening to "this is what happened to me" stories in the family, to say nothing of folk tales, nursery rhymes, anecdotes, jokes, fables, and the formal stories (including those in comic books) which are read to them at first and which later they read for themselves. Even children who have very little experience of stories, told or read, understand narrative structures which are basically the stuff of television dramas. Expanding on this point, Roger Brown (see Further Reading, page 30) once told an audience of the National Council of Teachers of English about sitting behind a pair of TV-wise eight-year-olds at a James Bond movie. When the scene shifted to a glass works in Venice and the camera lingered on a million-dollar vase, one boy said to the other, "They're gonna mess up that vase." And of course they did. The children knew as well as any adult the narrative methods of an adventure film. And this sophistication in viewing film carries over to reading stories. To be sure, adolescent readers still have to learn some conventions of story, such as flashbacks and point of view, but for the most part they have internalized narrative codes sufficiently to be able to hang new story content easily onto familiar forms.

Writers and teachers for thousands of years have sought to convey complex ideas through the medium of story, from the parables of the Old and New Testament to the illustrative examples used by contemporary textbook writers in explaining concepts in science, history, and even mathematics. As a matter of fact, the point we made earlier about thought patterns being dictated by the language and culture in which the individual lives may be reinforced if we repeat a story here. No doubt you have heard Shakespeare's *Hamlet* (a story still, even though it is told through dialogue and action) characterized as "universal." Seemingly, that overworked epithet means it is a story that can be understood at any time in history and at any place in the world. An American anthropologist staying with tribesmen in Tiv, in West Africa, decided to put it to a test. During a rainy spell, when boredom was sitting heavily upon the tribal elders and their visitors, she decided to tell them in their language the story of the prince who was ordered by his father's ghost to avenge his murder.

Did the tribesmen understand Hamlet's motivation, his actions, the outcome? Not at all. Their interpretations were completely at odds with what the visitor had expected. Not only were the tribesmen's structural codes for story mismatched with Shakespeare's, the cultural mores of the Elizabethans simply would not translate into the language and culture of the Tiv. If you ever teach *Hamlet*, or if you simply want to understand *comprehending* better, you may want to look up Laura Bohannan's delightful account of her retelling of *Hamlet*.[3]

The structural codes of expository prose may be as foreign to the adolescents you teach as Hamlet's story was to the Africans. While experience with stories has helped them internalize narrative codes (fortunately for Ms. Mantaro and Joe Wilder most of *history* is narrative), too little experience with the structural codes of other kinds of prose accounts for some failures in comprehending and remembering text. But inexperience with the structures of textbook prose may be too simple an explanation. It is quite possible that inexperienced readers apply codes learned from other media to the reading of textbooks.[4] For instance, adolescents who have watched 16,000 hours of television, on the average, may have learned a structural code that tells them that the most repeated piece of information is the most important. Applied to reading, this code leads them to generalizations derived not from perceiving logical relationships but from *lexical density*, that is, how often certain words and phrases are repeated. And often they arrive at correct understanding of the main idea through this method. The fact that most early adolescents and many late adolescents have not yet reached the stage of cognitive development in which formal logical thinking is operational lends credence to this speculation.

For many years, teachers have analyzed the structural codes of text, especially that found in secondary-school textbooks, and have identified common patterns of organization. In the 1930s, two teachers in the Reading Clinic at New York University, Gladys Persons and Stella Center, tabulated the frequency with which certain patterns of organization appeared in the textbooks of that decade. On the basis of this study and of other more theoretical analyses, teachers have been supplied with instructional materials which aim to acquaint students with such common structural coding patterns as:

+ main ideas and elaborating details
+ comparison and contrast
+ sequential ordering

---

[3]Laura Bohannan, "Shakespeare in the Bush," *National History Magazine*, (August–September 1966): 28–33.
[4]Dr. S. Penelope Wood raised this speculation as a result of studying adolescents' reading of paragraphs which were written in three kinds of organization from highly structured to unstructured. See her doctoral dissertation, "The Effects of Paragraph Structural Explicitness on Main Idea Comprehension of College Level Students with Varying Abilities," Syracuse University, 1979. Ann Arbor, Michigan: University Microfilms, 1980.

❖ order of increasing or decreasing importance

❖ cause and effect

We, too, shall advise teaching these patterns of organization (see Chapter 13) both for reading and writing exposition and for other types of nonnarrative prose. But we record here the following caveats:

1. Recognizing the author's organization (i.e., structural code) is only *one* factor in comprehension.

2. Internalizing such codes results less from exercises and lessons than from familiarity built up over a long period of time spent reading informational books. By a "long period of time" we mean ever since first grade.

3. For many adolescents who may already be using codes from nonprint media, traditional workbook exercises may be too little and too late. If used at all, such exercises must be constantly reinforced by teachers who call attention to how and where these "common patterns" are found in content textbooks.

4. Exercises based on analyses of the prose styles of early twentieth-century writers may match only very imperfectly the way writers currently organize their ideas for presentation in text. Moreover, *text*, referring chiefly to information-bearing prose or argument, is by no means limited to textbooks in our students' lives. (See Chapter 10 for a further discussion of textbooks, and Chapter 11 for other kinds of reading materials.)

5. While understanding contemporary styles of writing is essential for all students, some secondary-school students must also learn the structural codes of writers of the past.

To conclude this brief discussion of comprehension and structural codes, we remind you that learning through reading occurs when the reader can connect ideas (meanings) presented in the text with ideas in his or her head. We have referred to the reader's "known" meanings as a "cognitive structure" and have used the same word, *structure*, in a slightly different sense to refer to the patterns of organization writers use to transfer *their* "cognitive structures" (or parts thereof) to print. We have said that reading comprehension is facilitated if the reader is familiar with the structural codes of the writer.

Comprehension and Inference

From the early years of the twentieth century, models of the reading process have designated three (sometimes four) levels of comprehension: literal, interpretive, and evaluative or applied. Edgar Dale popularized the three-level model in this way: "We read the lines, we read between the lines, and we read beyond the lines." The persistence of this model over several generations of reading teachers testifies to its usefulness. It is useful as a guide to framing questions to test comprehension. And it reminds teachers to include instruction on all these levels:

1. Getting the plain sense of a text
2. Drawing inferences from what the author chooses to say or not to say
3. Making judgments about what the author has said
4. Applying in new situations what one has taken from the text

Readers of the same text may operate on different levels; some absorb the writer's literal meanings (what the words say); others find implicit meanings in the author's text and interpret them in the light of their related experiences; and still others, in addition to achieving the first two levels of comprehension, evaluate the worth of the author's argument and apply the author's meanings in their own lives.

While recognizing the usefulness of this model as an aid to understanding comprehension and therefore as an aid to teaching—one that we will use again and again—we must nevertheless caution you against accepting too readily the notion of levels of comprehension. The concept of levels implies a step-wise process in which one first comprehends literal meanings and then interprets those meanings. There is the further implication that readers develop through discrete stages, learning to read first at a literal level, then at an interpretive one. And then there is the implication that the third level is a part of *reading* comprehension when, in fact, *evaluating* and *applying* are ways of using the products of comprehension. Let's look more closely at these misinterpretations of the levels model of comprehension.

The comprehending reader is not merely translating printed words into their oral counterparts. That act, sometimes referred to as decoding or recoding from print to speech, is not reading at all. A machine can decode[5] but only the human brain that receives and reacts to the words can be said to be reading. So if reading is something more than oral transcription, or "hearing" the author's words in one's mind, that "something more" is making sense of meanings in the text by connecting them with meanings in the head. There is almost always an element of interpretation in taking in the sense of the text. When students recall what an author says, they rarely do so verbatim. (When they do, they probably are not understanding the message.) Instead, they report what meaning they found in the text, translating it into their own selection of words. They may select many of the same words that the author used (there may be no other words to use for a given subject), but they are using them now as their own. When they use synonyms and alternative phrases, they clearly are interpreting meanings.

It seems impossible to disentangle the first two "levels" of comprehension, but if they are to any degree separate, they occur simultaneously most of the time.

If this is true, then the first two levels of comprehension are in use from the very beginning of learning to read. Children in the primary grades connect the

---

[5]*The New York Times* (18 January 1976) reported that an experimental machine, demonstrated by Kurzweil Computer Products, Inc., of Cambridge, Mass., scanned a printed text and produced "generally understandable speech that sounded vaguely Swedish-accented."

meanings in the text with their understanding of the world, just as beginning readers in junior high school do if they are making sense of what they read and not merely mouthing the English text as they would a text in a language that is foreign to them.

But all reading materials demand varying kinds and degrees of interpretation. There's even a measure of interpretation in reacting to a stop sign; in England some signs say DEAD STOP, implying degrees of stopping. Literature permits more latitude of interpretation than does informational prose. If, as the semanticists tell us, all language is metaphorical, then some language, at least to the ordinary reader, will seem more richly metaphorical than others. And readers often make literal connections when they miss the cues that signal that the author is being fanciful.

In *Johnny Tremain*, Esther Forbes writes that the beautiful Lavinia had one blemish; it was as if the sculptor's chisel had slipped and cleft a vertical crack between her eyebrows. Florio, my ninth-grade student, at first took Forbes literally and figured that Lavinia was probably lucky to be alive, letting a sculptor fool around her with a chisel. On second thought, he connected his teacher's one-lined scowl with the description of Lavinia and suddenly recognized that the writer was "speaking figuratively"; he had found meaning in the metaphor.

Because language always falls short of reconstructing an entire experience— the whole meaning, or the total "cognitive structure" in the writer's head— authors depend on their readers having sufficiently comparable experiences (meanings) to make sensible connections. We could describe all reading—that is, comprehending—as the making of inferences. In any subject, good readers need fewer clues than do poor readers from which to extract data that will yield new relationships. The "ability to extract relationships from minimal data" is a definition that fits the drawing of inferences as well as it fits intelligence (to which psychologist R. F. Herrnstein applied it in an essay we shall refer to below). Does that mean that IQ and ability to comprehend through reading are closely related? Yes. (We shall discuss that relationship later.) Here, we will simply reiterate that drawing inferences is something that all comprehending readers do all the time, mostly below the level of awareness.

A particular kind of inference is the prediction, or the hypothesis about what is to come next in the text. The fluent reader makes predictions constantly and, again, usually below the level of awareness. Prediction is involved in decoding as the reader anticipates the next word or phrase before turning a page. (You are probably conscious of predicting at the turn of a page, but when reading fluently you are always predicting the rest of the word, as well as the rest of a phrase; as a fluent reader you *never* examine every letter of every word.) Beyond decoding—and you realize that it is artificial to separate "decoding" and "getting meaning"—a reader's predictions are related to the construction of sentences, paragraphs, and longer units of prose such as a story, a chapter, or sections in a textbook.

In comprehending the meanings conveyed in sentences and from sentence to sentence, students' command of the language tells them what to expect next—a verb following a subject, a noun following a preposition, an independent clause following an introductory adverbial clause. Preschool children can make predictions about oral language, and adolescents are thoroughly conversant with how oral language operates. They may, however, have more difficulty predicting the structure of long units of language. This, as we said earlier, may be the result of their unfamiliarity with the structures of prose writing. For example, the fluent reader, seeing a sentence like this one

> As a rule, buildings constructed before World War II are safer than modern build-ings because they were built brick by brick and floor by floor.

at the beginning of a paragraph, predicts that the rest of the paragraph will describe old and new buildings, expanding on the topic sentence. Or, seeing this sentence

> Steamboats soon traveled upstream at ten miles an hour or more, competing with land traffic on toll roads or turnpikes.

early in a section of the chapter, the good reader predicts that the rest of the section will describe aspects of frontier life at the time of the first steamboats.

A reader familiar with the style of the science textbook predicts that the introductory paragraphs about how a bucket brigade doused a fire in a house near a river will lead to a generalization of some kind, probably about the nature of energy.

After reading just the first paragraph of "Weep No More, My Lady," (see Box 3-3) a fluent reader makes hypotheses and raises questions like the following: The man and boy are probably out hunting. Or they may be fugitives running away from the law. They may be father and son. How old is the boy? Why is the man described as gaunt? Will the boy be punished for causing their presence to be discovered?

BOX 3-3

The moonlight symphony of swamp creatures hushed abruptly, and the dismal bog was as peaceful as unborn time and seemed to brood in its silence. The gaunt man glanced back at the boy and motioned for him to be quiet, but it was too late. Their presence was discovered. A jumbo frog rumbled a warning and the swamp squirmed into life as its denizens scuttled to safety.

SOURCE: James Street, "Weep No More, My Lady" (Reprinted by permission).

Predictions like these are hunches that readers almost never put consciously into words, as we have done in this illustration. These hunches will be thrown out or revised or confirmed as the reader gathers new information from con-tinued reading. If they were phrased at all, these predictions or hypotheses would probably come out as questions. When we read without asking questions or making predictions, however fleetingly or even subconsciously, we come to the end of a passage without knowing what we have read. We have simply been turning the pages.

Teachers can make students aware of the need to ask questions or make predictions, and they can show them how to do so (as we suggest in Chapter 13), but if students continue not to extract meanings which are implicit, teachers should examine the nature of the materials being read. To say, as many secondary teachers do, that their students "read okay at the literal level but haven't learned to draw inferences" is to make a loose diagnostic statement. Drawing inferences in reading is making sense of written language; it *is* reading. If the teacher means that in specific instances the students are not extracting all the meanings that she (or he) is, that is a different matter. Many kinds of literature have more than one layer of meaning, and English teachers often deliberately choose selections from which everyone in a group can take obvious meanings and a few can take subtle meanings.

Informational prose is less likely to have layers of meaning or to be subject to various interpretations, but it, too, demands inferential reading. Good readers make inferences more easily and accurately than poor readers; that's why they are called "good" readers. Asking what teachers can do about "failure to draw inferences" is almost the same question as: What can secondary teachers do about "poor readers"? (You will have some answers for that question by the time you finish this book.)

The third "level" of the comprehension model we are discussing has to do with evaluating what has been read or applying what has been learned. While evaluating and applying often follow from reading, they are not integral parts of the reading process itself. Thinking about and acting upon what one has read is no different from thinking about any learning experience.

Why is it important to recognize that evaluating and applying are *not* reading when we are going to insist upon including both in the goals of the secondary school curricula? It is important to understand the processes involved in learning so that you can know the kinds of instruction, and the timing and pacing suitable to each, and how to measure students' development. Making critical judgments about a text requires background in the subject and even more "prior knowledge" than does assimilating ideas from the text. Moreover, your evaluations of the judgments students make should take into consideration the likely limits of their experience of the subject at hand. Similarly, as you encourage students to apply knowledge gleaned from reading, your aim is to promote habits of careful thinking, and you must judge your success by students' willingness to try rather than by rigid criteria of right and wrong.

To refer once again to the question we raised in the experiments discussed on pages 57-59: How much can students learn through reading text? The fact that most of those students did not apply the concepts of volume, mass, and density which were explained in the text does not mean that they were poor readers. It indicates that they were not ready to learn the concepts and that their performance after reading is more of a comment on the inadequacies of our teaching than on their abilities to read. That is, in an investigation focused on students' learning, we intentionally failed to pre-teach key concepts in the assigned reading.

Moreover, what students do at this so-called third level of comprehension is governed by their abilities to produce language rather than to receive it. In any case, we ought to ask students to demonstrate what they think by writing or talking and occasionally by doing. When instead we measure evaluating and applying in a more passive way by having students react to others' reactions and applications, as tests and textbook exercises often do, we fail to stimulate their active thinking. Since this is our true purpose, exercises of this kind may lead up to, but they do not substitute for, having students express their own ideas.

One more point: We should distinguish between comprehending a writer's conclusions and forming one's own conclusions based on ideas from several sources. The first is more clearly "reading"; the second encompasses all of learning. Reading to understand an author's argument or conclusion can be guided in a particular text, and students may learn a strategy for "drawing conclusions" that can be carried over to the reading of other texts. Forming one's own conclusions is a matter of concept development for which strategies are acquired over years of living and learning.

Comprehension and Intelligence

We have been leading up to the question of how reading comprehension correlates with IQ. Correlations between reading test scores and IQ scores are low in primary grades (about .35) and high in secondary schools (about .80) because beginning reading is more a matter of translating print into speech and less a matter of comprehension. (Beginning readers understand what they decode; more advanced readers can decode words they don't comprehend.)

Some reading specialists used to suggest that high correlations between reading and IQ at the high school level showed only that group IQ tests require a great deal of reading. They do, of course, but nonverbal tests of intelligence also correlate highly with reading at advanced levels where the reading measure focuses more on comprehension than on word recognition. Most students who read poorly in secondary schools also have problems comprehending oral language, involving no reading. On the other hand, a small group of adolescents, some of whom may be dyslexics unable to decode accurately or rapidly from text to speech, can obtain high verbal IQ scores if the test does not require extensive reading. (See Chapter 6.)

In the past decade or two, intelligence testing has become very unpopular and the tests have been criticized as biased against minorities and the poor in our multicultural society because, so the argument goes, they reveal what the subjects had opportunities to learn rather than their capacity for learning. R. J. Herrnstein, the Harvard psychologist referred to on page 00, makes a persuasive argument that IQ tests are vital safeguards of minorities' rights to be "pushed up the occupational ladder, via higher education or otherwise."

Herrnstein says that only people who don't know much about the variety of IQ tests can believe that they are limited to specialized vocabulary or knowledge, to particular cognitive skills, or are explicitly slanted toward or against various subcultures. Having asked what links together such an assortment of skills and knowledge as are measured by the various tests, he concludes that:

> . . . the common trait involves extracting relationships from minimal data and applying the results to new data. The many different tests are different ways to tap the process. Vocabulary or word-usage tests sample the accumulated harvest of the

underlying ability, for we learn most of language from everyday contexts, not from the dictionary or by rote memorization. How well we extract subtle relationships from scant data has much to do with our command of language. Tests of inference or perceptual analysis confront directly the ability to extract and apply relationships.[6]

This definition of intelligence—extracting relationships from minimal data and applying the results to new data—underscores why reading comprehension and IQ scores are closely, though not perfectly, correlated. The fact that comprehension depends so heavily on intelligence should not frustrate teachers. The statistics, after all, only affirm what everyday experience tells us as soon as we begin to think about other people: They are different in every way but especially in their capacities to learn.

Since the paragraph we have quoted from Herrnstein's article makes the same point that we have made in this entire discussion—that reading comprehension is a facet of language development, which is a facet of intelligence—we must have had an additional reason for including it. We did. We meant you to realize—again—that one reason you read is to find affirmation of what you already know. Of course, you say, I always knew bright people can solve problems faster because they need fewer clues.

Knowing that intelligence is a large factor in learning through reading helps you to set reasonable expectations for yourself and your students. The low correlation between beginning reading and IQ suggests that almost everyone in school today *can* learn to read well enough to translate print into speech. The high correlation between IQ and advanced reading abilities suggests that all students should be able to comprehend written language as well as they can understand spoken language. (This is an oversimplification but a useful rule of thumb.)

The high correlation between IQ and reading comprehension in no way diminishes your responsibilities as a teacher. You still have to help students to make the most of what they've got. Fortunately for most of us, other factors influence how people use their intelligence in reading to learn.

Comprehension and Motivation

All things being equal (and they never are), people will learn what appears to be useful to them. "Useful" here is not to be equated with "utilitarian." A person might learn to read certain things (popular fiction, for example) because reading is an easy and inexpensive means of entertainment. Or someone who wanted to invest money wisely might put herself through a heavy course of reading in economics and finance. People also read carefully if they must; many citizens have worked assiduously to comprehend tax manuals, and many cooks have labored over instructions for operating a food processor. There is, of course, a limit to what motivation can do for the learner. Besides the desire to learn, the student must also have the requisite mental abilities, sufficient background skills

---

[6]R. J. Herrnstein, "In Defense of Intelligence Tests," *Commentary* (Feb 1980):44.

and knowledge to permit the next step, plus self-confidence, an idea of what there is to be learned, and a plan for proceeding. The most vital of these may be self-confidence, which withers or flourishes on the basis of past successes.

Apart from the overall will to succeed (characterized by some pedagogues as "achievement motivation"), the most telling influence on an individual's comprehension is a sense of purpose. If Joe Wilder turns to Chapter 3 in his textbook looking for nothing in particular, that's probably what he will find. Although there are times when aimless browsing is appropriate behavior, it becomes rewarding only when the mind focuses on a topic of interest and begins reading to satisfy an aroused curiosity.

Your best readers, of course, will be those with the most lively curiosity. They may not always be your best students, however, since creatures of "insatiable curiosity" may not have the self-discipline needed for the rigorous pursuit of learning in your particular field. Capable readers who couldn't care less about academic learning are familiar figures in contemporary classrooms. They may be easily outdistanced by less capable readers who love your subject, or you, or the approval of others, or the satisfaction of learning, or whatever tangible rewards for learning may be offered by parents or schools or society.

Interest may be a variation on the theme of purpose. It is possible, as no doubt you know from experience, to read with purpose on a subject in which you have but a modicum of interest. In that case, self-discipline takes over, bolstered by the promise of future rewards. (You need the course for certification; you are hedging your bets in view of a tight job market; you need the credits to satisfy the requirements for a "liberal" education.) Mature students can work for deferred rewards; it's harder for 13-year-olds to switch off television and spend thirty minutes on the economic grievances of the American colonists.

So in evaluating the reading behaviors and outcomes exhibited by your students, you must always reckon with motivation. Are they confident that they *can* learn through reading? Are they willing to try? Do they have a chance for success? Are they interested in the subject? Do they approach the text with a purpose and a plan?

How Text Affects Comprehension

Reasons for faulty comprehension reside in the text as well as the reader. We discuss the shortcomings of secondary-school textbooks in more detail in Chapter 10 and simply summarize for you here the responsibilities of writers and editors for successful communication. Students' search for meaning of text will be handicapped by vocabulary which is archaic, ornate, esoteric, technical, abstract, and idiosyncratic. It will be assisted if the writer uses technical vocabulary sparingly, defines words in context, chooses the simpler word whenever possible, and remembers that redundancy (repeating words and ideas) is an aid to readers whose vocabularies are still limited. Language that is idiomatic and contemporary is easier for today's adolescents than stilted and formal prose. Liberal uses of examples and figurative comparisons should help to explain new concepts. The language of fiction may be easier for adolescents to comprehend than the language of exposition because it is more likely to mimic oral dialect, it includes conversation, and it uses nouns and pronouns that refer to people. And, as we have said, adolescents are more used to the structure of fiction than the structure of textbook writing.

Sentence structure affects comprehension adversely when it is convoluted, positively when it is simple and direct. Short sentences are not necessarily easier than long ones. Students need to have relationships spelled out for them, and dependent clauses starting with words like *because, since, until* do just that.

Larger elements of organization are crucial, too. Especially for immature readers in secondary school, the structural framework should be clearly visible, made more so by the use of strong signal words *(in the first place; 1, 2, 3; as a result; next in order)* and typographical aids.

What makes informational texts especially hard to comprehend is fact-packing, which is the major sin of school textbooks. Summarizing and digesting ideas in order to get everything in increases the difficulty.

Since interest is a factor in comprehension, writers of text have an obligation to avoid the bland and the dull. Can texts be scintillating as well as simple? Can they be attractive to adolescents as well as true to their subject? Maybe not. But as you contemplate your students' efforts to comprehend, ask yourself how interesting and readable the author made the medium of the message.

How Teachers Affect Comprehension

Naturally, we believe teachers make a powerful difference in how well students use reading as a tool of learning; if we didn't there would be no reason for this book. But we have placed quality of instruction last among the factors affecting comprehension because, in a sense, teachers are outside agents in the transaction between reader and text. So far as reading is concerned, teachers can set up the transaction and strengthen it but they are not directly a part of it. Of course, important kinds of learning also take place in transactions between teachers and students directly, but our topic here is learning through reading.

Comprehension, we have said, is determined by prior knowledge and skills, command of language structures, prediction, memory, intelligence, and motivation, including purpose and interest. We have not said explicitly that practice is a factor, but we have repeatedly emphasized that previous experience in reading is a powerful source of prior knowledge and develops familiarity with language structures. So add *practice* to the list of factors. And let us consider that some of these factors can be heavily influenced by the quality of instruction and some can be only minimally affected by what the teacher does.

By *quality of instruction* we mean all the formal teaching that students experience from their first days in school. The long developmental process of which reading comprehension is a part is shaped by an accumulation of teaching practices. No one teacher can be totally responsible for students' growth in reading (though the best teachers act as though they are). So when we enumerate the teaching practices which retard growth in learning through reading, we are not casting blame on individual teachers.

Practices in the primary grades which retard reading for meaning are an overemphasis on decoding—too much time and attention given to phonics—

and, when meaning is attended to, an unnecessary emphasis on inconsequential details. Teachers guided by basal reading manuals often ask too many questions about reading texts that deserve to be enjoyed and forgotten. From primary grades, children should use reading not only for entertainment but for learning. Recent basal readers balance literature content with informational selections, but this step in the right direction needs to be followed up by many opportunities to read easy informational books. There is an unfortunate tendency for teachers (and others) to equate reading with literature, thus diminishing time available for reading to learn content of other kinds.

Instruction which best prepares students to use reading for learning begins in the primary grades with familiarizing children with the language of informational texts. At first, teachers read informational books to children and then they provide reasons for students to read trade books[7] as well as textbooks and references. They set up situations that capitalize on children's natural curiosity and send them to media centers or libraries for sources of information. (See Chapter 11.) In these ways teachers help individuals to expand their views of the world and to build up their store of "prior knowledge." But good teachers do more than encourage wide reading of informational texts. In addition, they continually help students to categorize and synthesize knowledge in any school subject by putting it to use. Students who use what they are learning this year in science, for example, will be more able to learn from future science texts.

From the beginning, but increasingly as students move through secondary schools, teachers can help them to develop the memory factor. Too often students left to their own devices engage in passive rereading of the text and develop other inefficient study skills and habits. They fail to realize that paying attention to organizational patterns strengthens recall as well as initial comprehension.

Motivation to learn school subjects, which is powerfully influenced by attitudes and customs of the home and community, is also shaped by the quality of instruction. Attitudes toward the self as a learner may have already been set by the time students reach the grades you teach. (Some research suggests that children have decided by the end of grade 3 whether or not they will be successful in school learning.) Nevertheless, we have the testimony of countless successful persons that teachers have altered their will to learn. We cite just one example in Box 3-4.

Their greater freedom to select materials that develop process rather than emphasize knowledge gives reading and English teachers a wider opportunity to appeal to the interests of adolescents than is usually afforded content teachers. For content teachers, the effort to link adolescents' natural interests to academic content often proves frustrating. These teachers might better focus on those elements of reading comprehension over which they have more control: choosing texts that are readable, carefully preparing students for reading a selection, seeing that they have a purpose and a plan for completing assignments, using immediate rewards or withholding privileges, and setting realistic short-term goals for the uninvolved.

---

[7]Trade books is the term used for all books which are not textbooks.

BOX 3-4

HE SAVED MY LIFE

Newspapers of November 2, 1979, carried a syndicated column in which Richard Reeves described a reunion of graduates of Abraham Lincoln High School in Brooklyn. The columnist wrote about retired principal and former English teacher, Abe Lass, who was flying from New York to Los Angeles to attend the reunion, which was held in California because, said Lass, "that's where a lot of Brooklyn is now." Reeves wrote in part:

"... I knew about Abe Lass before he sat down next to me on that plane. A friend of mine, who was a hood thrown out of Abraham Lincoln, had told me about Lass many times. 'I was on the streets and that's where I'd still be,' said Ken Auletta. 'Mr. Lass sought me out at home and got me back into school and then into college. He saved my life.'

Auletta, a writer for the *New Yorker* and a columnist for the *New York Daily News*, couldn't make it to California because he was finishing up the manuscript of his second book. . . .

"'We were hostile kids,' Auletta said, 'and he was a tough guy, compassionate but tough. God, I owe him.'

"We all owe him."

The least alterable variable affecting learning through reading is IQ. Perhaps the most that teachers can do is to understand intelligence in the abstract and how it is measured, to accept it as a factor in comprehension, and to continue to think of students as individuals, not as members of a group in an IQ range, such as below 90 or over 135 or between 90 and 115. And be prepared to be surprised.

A Final Word

To reiterate a theme of this book: Good teachers understand the process of learning through reading, and excellent teachers help students to become aware of that process. In learning the process yourself, in teaching others about that process, you begin to feel the full impact of a word we use freely in educational circles: *developmental*. It means *becoming*. Both students and teachers remain "unfinished" so long as each continues to learn and to teach. In the successful relationship that began when Bette Mantaro and Joe Wilder bumped into each other in Room 109, they exchange roles often; both of them are learners and each, on occasion, teaches the other.

RECAPPING MAIN POINTS

The effectiveness of reading as a means of learning the content of school subjects depends on factors residing in the reader, the text, and the teacher. Within the reader, the most potent factor is prior knowledge: what is already known about the subject at hand and what is known about language, particularly the conventions of written language.

Two other powerful factors affecting comprehension or learning through reading are the student's intelligence and motivation.

Linked to prior knowledge and so also affecting comprehension is memory. Students comprehend ideas with which they have some familiarity. Conversely, it is easier for them to recall ideas they comprehend. So good teaching helps students to remember useful ideas and to retrieve from memory whatever is relevant to the subject they are going to read about.

Perceiving the organization of a text aids comprehension and retention.

The conventional idea of "levels of reading" may be misleading. Teachers should be sensitive to the fact that the simplest act of getting meaning requires readers to make inferences. Evaluating or applying what is comprehended reinforces learning, but it is not really a "level of reading" so much as it is a type of thinking.

Making predictions, like drawing inferences, is applied in identifying words (decoding) as well as in comprehending.

Within the text, factors that affect comprehension are the writer's style (choice and arrangement of words), the way the text is organized, and the density of ideas (fact-packing).

Teachers influence how effectively students learn through text. They can improve students' chances by (1) familiarizing them with the language and content of informational text from first grade onward; (2) preparing them for the key concepts of a particular reading assignment; (3) teaching them how to recognize and remember important ideas; (4) setting goals that students can reach and holding them to these expectations.

FOR DISCUSSION

1. "Cultural Literacy," an essay by E. D. Hirsch, Jr., in *The American Scholar*, Spring, 1983, should provoke lively discussion. The essay illuminates points made in this chapter about the nature of comprehension and argues that high school students should learn a common body of knowledge.

2. Choose a short story, an essay or editorial, or a poem. Divide the selection into four or more parts. Present each part in sequence to an audience (perhaps a group of colleagues). At the end of each segment, have them predict what will happen next (in a story), or what argument the writer will present next (in an editorial), or what expectations are aroused in each part of the poem. From this activity, discuss the role of prediction in comprehension.

3. How does a student's motivation affect learning through reading? List as many aspects of motivation as you can and consider the weight each might have in influencing the quality of a reader's comprehension of a particular text. Also consider factors that affect the student's motivation.

4. If interest in reading a text is sufficiently strong, is a student sure to understand it? Discuss the issues involved.

5. What can teachers do to improve the likelihood that students will read a particular text with understanding? Which variables affecting comprehension do teachers have most control over? Are any factors beyond a teacher's influence?

6. Think of a book which you found hard to read. What made this text difficult for you? What symptoms of your difficulties might have been apparent to an observer? If you succeeded in making sense of the subject, what helped you? How might a teacher have helped you? What did you do to help yourself?

FURTHER READING

Bloom, Benjamin S. *Human Characteristics and School Learning*. New York: McGraw Hill, 1976.

Hirsch, Jr., E. D. *The Philosophy of Composition*. University of Chicago Press, 1977. Especially Chapters 4 and 5 on readability.

Olson, David R. "From Utterance to Text: The Bias of Language in Speech and Writing," in *Harvard Educational Review* 7(8), (1977).

Pearson, P. David and Dale D. Johnson. *Teaching Reading Comprehension*. New York: Holt, Rinehart and Winston, 1978.

Smith, Frank. *Comprehension and Learning: A Conceptual Framework for Teachers*. New York: Holt, Rinehart and Winston, 1975.

4 Many Kinds of Readers and Learners

"Tell me," said a Russian journalist to his American counterpart, "what is so special about democracy in the United States? Tell me in one word what makes it work."

"That's easy," said the American. "The word is *access*."

Access to education for all school-age youth is a mission very nearly accomplished in these last decades of the twentieth century. Today between 75 and 80 percent of youths aged 15 to 19 are full-time students. In 1954, only 55 percent of youngsters who had been in fifth grade seven years earlier graduated from high school. By 1977 the figure for high school graduation had risen to 75 percent. Today almost everyone in the United States reaches the early secondary grades, more than three-quarters of them stay through twelfth grade, and half the graduates go on to college or another form of post-secondary education.

These statistics suggest why dramatic changes have taken place in secondary schools in recent decades. Selection is no longer a characteristic of public high schools. With the exception of large urban schools specializing in science or in creative and performing arts or in vocational education, most schools must admit everyone of the appropriate age who lives in the designated district. And, in the comprehensive high schools, only admittance to advanced courses is on the basis of achievement.

How Schools Differ

Ethnic diversity is typical of many high schools today. While some urban schools are still segregated racially, and some rural schools serve the same ethnic groups that established them a hundred years ago, in the majority of large suburban and small city schools the student body is a melange of ethnic, racial, and socioeconomic differences. Even though we have used terms like *multicultural* and *bilingual* freely in educational circles for a decade or two, we are astonished to realize that 12 million immigrants settled in the United States in the 1970s, giving that decade the greatest wave of immigration of any in our history.

It is no wonder that high schools still confront problems of diversity. With every decade the student population becomes more ethnically, racially, and socially mixed, while the original purpose of the old secondary academy—to prepare students for college—is appropriate to an increasing proportion of its graduates. Trying to serve as a preparatory school and at the same time to serve youth who will not go to college, high schools continue to experiment with accommodations to individual differences. Two major administrative measures have been (1) tracking students according to their measured achievement and intelligence and (2) creating different programs for students who choose to pursue academic, commercial, vocational, or general (unspecified) goals. Since neither of these measures has proved wholly satisfactory, variations are numerous. Tracking, which was widely condemned in the 1960s as undemocratic, unworkable, and unnecessary, is limited in most schools today to making special provisions for the gifted and setting minimal standards for the least able. Differentiated programs in many high schools have been reduced to two: college preparatory and noncollege preparatory. In the 1960s, following the lead of colleges, high schools of sufficient size made most of their offerings elective and described them in college catalog style. More recently, still following the lead of colleges, high schools have retreated from their commitment to elective curricula and have increased the number of required courses.

Schools that are too small to offer many sections of required courses or much variety in electives, as well as schools that reject the philosophy of student options, leave to teachers the whole task of adjusting to individual differences. Whether motivated by the constraints of their budget and staffing problems or by their educational philosophy, many administrators permit classes to form on no other basis than the students' years in school. The ultimate responsibility for adjusting to individual differences, they believe, rests with teachers. With minimal help from state and local curriculum guides, teachers must decide how to define goals, organize their curricula, select materials, and teach individuals, small groups, and whole classes.

Debate about the feasibility and wisdom of scheduling students so that the range of differences within classes is narrowed intensifies as secondary-school populations become more diverse. To the extent they are unsuccessful in making within-class adjustments, teachers work for alternative schemes. For example, rapid growth of electives in high school English programs in the late 1960s reflected, it seems, teachers' frustrations in putting into effective use the recommendation that students of differing abilities should read different texts and work on different assignments. But elective systems didn't work perfectly either, and they were cited as one of the reasons for declining scores on aptitude and achievement tests across the nation. So now they have been put aside (temporarily, we predict) while the pendulum swings toward more commonality of course offerings for everyone.

Today, questions of curricular or administrative adjustments to individual differences are much the same in middle and junior high schools as they are at the senior high level. The range of differences in achievement has always been widest at the grade levels just below that in which dropouts begin—tenth grade these days. Additionally, however, the influx of immigrants and the mainstreaming of handicapped youngsters have made early secondary populations even more diverse than they were two decades ago. These changes in early secondary grades seem not to have flagged the attention of school-watchers to the same degree they do in high school grades, perhaps because the public's concern for the mid-span of schooling is more easily neglected than is its concern for either beginners or graduates, or perhaps because longer experience with diversity is helping middle-school staffs adjust more smoothly. In any case, in the early secondary grades as in the senior high school, schemes for adjusting to individual differences fluctuate between leaving everything to the teachers or depending on administrative planning to achieve more homogeneous classes. Middle and junior high schools have become increasingly departmentalized; relatively few schools today retain single classes at each grade from first through eight. Still, there is less specialization in early secondary schools since most students are assumed to have common purposes in learning and have not yet defined their career goals.

These shades of difference between early secondary and senior high schools do not alter very much the main point we wish to make: Great diversity is characteristic of this nation's schools. Teachers whose first task is the improvement of literacy will teach whoever comes through the school door; so they will encounter (though not necessarily simultaneously) students who run the full gamut from illiteracy to maturity in communication skills.

But individual schools are different, too. They can be categorized— as students can—but, like students, each school has unique traits and therefore in some measure defies categorization. Someone has said that schools fifty miles apart may differ as much from one another as schools fifty years apart. In the same day, a reading consultant may work in a high school that sends 80 percent of its graduates to college and in another where only 20 percent are college bound. So, what we have said about the range of differences among school-age youth nationally has to be modified considerably to fit particular schools.

Schools differ from town to town and within the same city. Obviously, geography is a factor that affects the homogeneity of a school population; a prairie school serves a different ethnic, racial, and social mix than does a ghetto school in Chicago, and both are different from one in a bedroom community in the Washington–New York megalopolis.

But more potent factors than geography account for school differences; one of these is money. In the same county, one school system has a better tax base because of the industries in its district than a neighboring system that is dependent mostly on residential taxes; yet the first community is considered less affluent than the second. Support for schools changes as communities attract young families that are concerned but poor, and changes again when upwardly mobile parents seek better neighborhoods, or when housing patterns shift to accommodate childless adults.

Even more influential than geography or economics on the range of achievement within a school is the kind of leadership it receives from its principal and how much he or she is backed by the superintendent, school board, parents, and concerned citizens. Principals are key figures especially with respect to reading achievement, but even here their effectiveness is tempered by the faculty mix. The right mix requires enough teachers with the same convictions who can work together on the improvement of reading and study skills to outweigh the few who remain unconvinced. School populations change and some faculties keep pace; others do not. Some faculties overcome impediments to learning that stem from community conditions; others do not.

Nevertheless, schools with generally low-achieving populations also enroll high achievers; and elite schools, public and private, have nonreaders—fewer of them, it is true, than poor schools, but such youngsters are often least recognized where general achievement is high.

Because schools differ along such dimensions as community support, administrative leadership, faculty strengths and weaknesses, and the student body's ethnic, racial, social, and economic characteristics, reading teachers have to expect different ranges of achievement in different schools. For example, in a ghetto junior high, almost every student may fall below the national average in reading achievement. In a suburban high school, nearly all the juniors and seniors may score above the national norm.

Within a single class, it is unlikely that you will have the typical range of achievement that reading authorities like to quote: that is, a span equivalent to the number of years in the grade, or a ten-year span in tenth grade stretching perhaps from grade 4 to college freshman. (Unlikely but not impossible.) Similarly, you would be surprised to find in a single class at seventh grade level the range that might be expected of the whole grade, that is, from primary level to senior high. In short, you may never have in any one class all the different kinds of readers and learners we describe below, beginning with the great majority called average.

Nevertheless, having reminded you that schools are almost as different as the individual youngsters they serve, that classes within the same school and grade may differ from one another, and that each student remains an individual in any group, we shall go on to generalize about some of the types of readers and learners you are likely to encounter in grades 5 to 8 or in grades 9 to 12. We warn you against assuming that students in any class you teach will match the profiles we present here; and in Chapters 6 and 7 we discuss ways for you to assess differences in achievement among your particular readers and learners. However, because we believe teachers have a right to expect equal years of schooling to produce similarities among learners even though differences also prevail, we proceed in the next two sections to describe "typical" learners, first in grades 5 to 8 and then in grades 9 to 12.

Readers and Learners in Middle School

Average Readers

What—besides variety—can you expect of "average" readers in middle school? (For the sake of this discussion, accept as "average" students those who have been so defined by former teachers and whose scores on reading achievement tests were close to grade placement at the time the tests were administered.) You can expect these students to read aloud fairly accurately and fluently from grade-level textbooks. Their oral reading performance verifies that they have mastered decoding to the degree that printed words are generally familiar, unmysterious, pronounceable. To be sure, average readers may mispronounce some words, even common ones, but their pronunciations will not be bizarre, even when they are working out the pronunciation of technical terms they have never seen before. Occasionally, they may misread words (saying *valuable* for *voluble*) or omit words (sometimes crucial ones like *not*) or insert words that distort the meaning. But such errors result from carelessness, haste, misapprehension of meaning, and not from serious deficiencies in decoding skills.

Average readers in middle school have pretty much mastered phonics; they know generally how sounds are represented by letters in the English language though they may not be able to remember a rule on demand. They recognize compounds, can divide words into syllables, and can identify common prefixes, suffixes, and roots. They may hesitate to apply this knowledge when confronted with a new and formidable polysyllabic word, but what they lack is confidence, not basic knowledge. They know how to locate words in a desk dictionary, especially a school dictionary edited for early secondary grades, and they can use a pronunciation guide, though they may not make a habit of doing so.

Average readers in middle school no longer need workbook exercises on decoding skills. They may continue to learn more about how the English language functions orthographically and syntactically, but such learning aids them as writers more than as readers. Average readers represent a wide range of spelling ability, and for weak spellers a review of phonetic principles, syllabication, and the ways in which derivatives are formed may be in order, as we shall note in Chapter 12.

So far we have said nothing about average readers' comprehension; only that they can read aloud accurately in grade-level texts. For reasons noted in our discussion of comprehension in Chapter 3, it is much more difficult to generalize about how average readers apprehend meanings than how they decode. Bob, who is reading at sixth grade level according to standardized tests and his teachers' judgments, is quite a different reader from Susie, who is similarly ranked. He is interested in science and nature study, retains knowledge from previous science lessons, recalls information from books and magazine articles related to these interests, notes details, can follow written directions, interprets tables, graphs, and maps, and carefully observes cause–effect relationships that lead him to solve problems he is interested in. He reads slowly and carefully and earns points on standardized tests chiefly on passages that present information in a straightforward manner. Susie, on the other hand, reads rapidly, covering more items on a standardized test than Bob, losing points on some questions that require her to note details in factual passages but making up her score on inferential items on passages high in human interest.

Bob's and Susie's different reading styles reflect their different interests, learning patterns, personalities, and perhaps physical make-up. These characteristics are, of course, shaped by other factors that are bound to make for differences: home environment, influence of siblings and childhood friends, their interaction with former teachers, their parents' interests and levels of education. We point out these differences between Bob and Susie to emphasize that the generalizations that follow, while useful data for teachers, contain a multitude of exceptions.

Average readers have for the most part acquired basic comprehension skills. That is, they can recall short passages written at appropriate readability levels on subjects with which they are familiar. They can answer questions about matters that the text states rather explicitly and they can connect details that are rather obviously related. They understand generally how sentences convey meaning so long as these sentences are not overly complex or elliptical. They tend to be literal minded and may, therefore, be confused by metaphors and symbols, and to miss historical and literary allusions because they haven't read widely. They can think critically about text which refers to concrete experiences; they have trouble dealing with abstractions.

The chief characteristic of average readers in the middle years is that they don't read very much. They have lived just long enough to acquire the basic skills but not long enough to refine them. They have missed out on literature that would have helped them develop their imagination and inferential skills, and supplied them with ideas that are frequently alluded to. They lack background because they were not read to very much, and their developing skills in earlier grades while "on schedule" were insufficient to make reading on their own truly enjoyable. So what they need in middle grades more than anything else are good reasons for reading widely and the time to do so. Most of the time will probably have to be found in school because out-of-school interests multiply rapidly in early adolescence.

Some average readers may be performing as well as they are able; many are not. For example, students of average intelligence who need more time to learn are often the least motivated to spend time outside of school on homework. They need encouragement from parents and teachers to reduce excessive amounts of television and other distractions and to increase the amount of time spent at home not only on school assignments but in reading books and magazines of their own choice. How much "encouragement" average readers receive from home varies as widely as every other dimension of individual differences; so teachers can expect varying degrees of success in enforcing out-of-class reading requirements. Still, the chief responsibility rests with teachers: They must make known their expectations and present their students with attractive reasons—as well as means—for meeting them. Nothing is more important to the development of reading power than that students read widely in their middle years. (See Chapter 9 for specific suggestions on how to motivate wide reading.)

It may be well to interrupt our consideration of average readers' skills in middle grades to pursue briefly our concern for home influences, since research repeatedly shows them to be associated with learning. This comes as no surprise to experienced teachers, but occasionally we need to remind ourselves of obvious truths. In the middle grades, when preteens and early adolescents have great need for parental support, such support is quite likely to diminish; perhaps because the parents are having crises in their personal lives—such as divorce, remarriage, or new relationships—or going through changes in their working lives—such as promotions, transfers, or loss of jobs—or perhaps because of increasing economic pressures brought on by a maturing family with new and expensive tastes. Caught up in their own problems, parents sometimes pay less attention to children in these crucial years because they assume the children are more independent than they actually are. Thus, whereas parents may have the time and inclination to stay close to the learning process of beginning readers, they often have less of both for the learning activities of older children.

Teachers may be more aware than parents of the volatility of middle school students, observing how quickly they change from eagerness to boredom, from delight in learning today to active resistance tomorrow. Both teachers and parents are sensitive to the physical changes of early adolescence, though they may not always relate growing pains to learning plateaus. But teachers may not be as sensitive to the impact of family situations on learning behaviors. Even though there is nothing they can do about disruptions in a student's home life, teachers can modify their expectations for performance during a difficult period so that the student can experience success and gain satisfaction in school if not at home. That is, knowing that Jenny is struggling to accept her mother's new husband and his children, Jenny's teachers may make special efforts both to direct her attention to school work and at the same time to understand her distractibility.

Teachers have to keep in mind not only that changes are taking place in their students' personal lives and in their bodies but also in their school lives and in their learning styles. An obvious change is the transition from the self-contained classroom to the departmentalized curriculum, but teachers sometimes forget the impact this change can have on average students. Whereas in fifth grade, Joe had to get used to the demands and idiosyncrasies of just one teacher, now in sixth grade he must respond to the differing styles and assignments of a science/math teacher, a reading/language arts/social studies teacher, and assorted other teachers for art, music, and beginning French. (In eighth grade instead of two teachers for five subjects, he'll have five teachers.) Unless those teachers work as a team, they may give Joe more assignments in content textbooks than his average skills can cope with.

The chief service that reading teachers can render average students in these difficult middle years is help with consolidating the skills they have brought with them from the elementary grades. Through careful observation of the kind described in Chapter 7, and through developing self-assessment units like the one described on pages 166–83, reading teachers can help "kids in the middle" to sort out their strengths and weaknesses and to set reasonable goals for themselves. Content teachers are, of course, very much a part of this process of helping students to define themselves as readers and learners. Their assignments and expectations are the yardsticks students measure themselves by. And the accuracy of those measuring instruments depends largely on how well teachers understand what is "normal" for the middle years.

What is normal as far as study skills are concerned? From primary grades onward, normally developing readers will have had lessons in study skills: how to find main ideas, how to recognize patterns of organization, how to follow a writer's argument, how to decide which ideas they should remember. They will have had practice in outlining, mapping, and other ways of making the organization of ideas graphic. They will probably have written summaries and taken notes. Much of this practice, however, will have been assigned through workbook exercises and lessons in their basal readers unrelated to content assignments. Although they may have had research topics to pursue in encyclopedias and other reference books, the strong likelihood is that these lessons have not "taken." So if Randy and Steve are bewildered when you ask them to outline a section of their social studies text, don't be surprised and don't charge their former teachers with negligence. Your only recourse is to evaluate your assignment. If you decide it is reasonable to ask for an outline, you will first have to show Randy and Steve how to outline (after you've convinced *them* that the assignment is reasonable!).

Most students entering middle school have little or no grasp of study skills. With good teaching, much practice, and real reasons for studying content textbooks, references, and other subject-centered materials, they may leave middle or junior high school with fair abilities in outlining, summarizing, paraphrasing, and discussing ideas that are presented in texts at their levels of understanding. But for average readers in these years, sophisticated study skills are not a first priority. They are not much use to kids who are still not using reading to learn. So study skills follow in emphasis (that is, time allotted, energy expended) the major goal of expanding these students' interests in reading first for pleasure, then for learning.

Shouldn't average readers in grades 5 to 8 be expected to learn from text? As we shall say repeatedly in this book, the answer is no. But all yes/no answers on this topic must be qualified. Initial learning from text—especially content textbooks—is not a reasonable expectation for average readers in middle or junior high school. These students can, however, use grade-level textbooks to confirm and expand upon learning they have already achieved through other media: discussions, first-hand experiences, your reading aloud to them from various sources, demonstrations and explanations, simulations and games, films, filmstrips, still pictures, and diagrams. Text is useful for average readers just emerging from the beginning stages of learning to read, but its best use—so far as content textbooks are concerned—is for consolidating learning. At the same time, average readers pursuing their own interests in reading trade books and magazines are learning they *can* learn from text. If they have sufficient experience of this kind of learning from text, they will move into grades 9 to 12 ready to apply serious study skills to their content textbooks. We should add, of course, that students' interests *can* be related to the curriculum, and good teachers steer them in that direction.

Meanwhile, teachers continue to direct students' attention to simple study skills. They ask students to give the main idea of a passage in their own words as often as they resort to the recognition-type exercises found in workbooks. From time to time, they model how to outline a section of the social studies text, showing how such an outline aids comprehension and retention. (For more ideas on teaching study skills, see Chapter 14.)

Problem Readers

Although the wide span of "average" covers readers with problems of many varieties, we also recognize the presence in many middle school classrooms of students whose reading skills are so far below average we can scarcely call them "readers." These boys and girls—of the same age as their classmates—are still struggling to acquire beginning reading skills. For example, still in the reading acquisition stage, Bill and Marie have very similar reading profiles. They use phonics as their only approach to word identification. They read word by word, identify very few words at sight, and are insensitive to context as an aid to guessing words. They appear to view reading as a difficult decoding game having very little to do with meaning. Although depending solely on phonics, neither Bill nor Marie has a very good ear for the separate or blended sounds in spoken words. Except in reading performance, however, Bill and Marie are very dissimilar. On an individually administered intelligence test, Bill achieved an IQ of 116, whereas Marie achieved a score of 82.

Some preadolescents and teenagers who are still in the beginning reading stage are there simply because they haven't had sufficient time to acquire the skills. Chief among these are nonnative speakers of English, many of them having recently arrived in schools requiring English for learning. If they have good instruction paced to their varying learning rates, they should acquire literacy skills just a little behind their acquisition of the oral language. Other

BOX 4-1

ALL CHILDREN BRIGHT AND BEAUTIFUL . . .

I faced my classes of bright-eyed and energetic seventh graders with great optimism. In this agricultural southwest area, my classes were filled with predominantly Mexican-American children. These children, I discovered, spoke English well. They reacted to what I said to them intelligently. Their dark eyes would light up with understanding when I engaged them in conversation. I expected these children to be top students. Imagine my surprise when I discovered that almost three-fourths of these Mexican-American children were seriously retarded in reading; i.e., they read two or more years below their grade level in school. They had not learned to read well in spite of six long years already spent in the American classroom.

I used every trick in my bag to recapture the dying embers of their interest, seizing as the major objective of my reading program the simple goal to *keep them reading.* . . .

BUT WHY CAN'T THEY READ?

There was not *one* single reason why these children could not read well but a multiplicity of reasons, combining in different strengths and patterns in different individuals . . . (Linguistic deprivation . . . feeling different and so inferior . . . the clash of cultures . . . attitudes toward academic success . . . poverty . . . poor teaching.)

SOURCE: Marilyn L. Peterson, "All Children Bright and Beautiful: But Why Can't They Read?" *Contemporary Education*, (Fall 1981).

delayed readers may have physical disabilities, such as hearing losses or visual defects that caused them to be slower than their age-mates in developing literacy skills. Some visual and hearing impairments go unnoticed and are compounded by poor teaching in the early grades. Learning disabilities that are related to minimal brain dysfunction are often undetected in the crucial early years. In other cases, severe physical disabilities in childhood have shortened the time for learning, and these children are just catching up in middle grades.

Some children arrive in middle school as nonreaders or as barely beginning readers even though they have spent the requisite time in American elementary schools. They may, however, have moved from one school to another in different parts of the country or even from abroad (from American dependents' schools, for instance). Others who have done no moving themselves still may have experienced disruptive learning because their primary teachers moved frequently. For whatever reason, they may have had poor teaching in primary grades, but when poor readers have seemingly had the opportunities to learn and have not, the causes are likely to be related to severe emotional or social disturbance.

Obviously, both kinds of problem readers, those who have not had sufficient time and those who have, need more time. They also must have expert teaching during this period. In Chapter 8, we shall have more to say about remedial readers—those readers who will profit from more time and expert teaching—but the point to be made here is that problem readers, with or without remedial teaching on the side, will appear in middle school classrooms along with all the average readers. They won't be isolated from the mainstream. In content classes they must be reckoned in the accounting of individual differences that this chapter addresses.

It is perhaps unnecessary to add that as a group the problem readers don't look very different from the average readers. The range of IQ scores in both groups may be very similar; though most of the below-average readers probably have limited verbal intelligence, some have normal to superior intelligence. Among the average readers are also students with physical disabilities, disruptive home situations, bad experiences in school, emotional disturbances, and other handicapping conditions. They have learned to read "on schedule" anyway. Problem readers are only superficially similar to each other in their lack of skills; they differ widely in the reasons for their disability.

Superior Readers

The superior readers in middle school also defy generalizations. True, they are fewer in number—in most schools—than average readers, but it is quite possible to have classes containing only superior readers since "skimming off the cream" is a common practice. But within classes for the gifted, the mixture is as various as we have noted for the average, except, of course, that the range of IQ is certain to be narrower.

What characterizes the reading performance of superior readers in grades 5 to 8? Let Penny and Chris represent two somewhat contrasting types. The only child of university professors, Penny began to read before she was three. Her precocity was deliberately fostered by both parents, who read aloud to her daily from infancy and read with her all through school, sharing her current enthusiasms and guiding her into classics and the best of contemporary children's literature. By seventh grade, Penny was reading serious adult fiction, which she alternated with the latest best-sellers of so-called junior novelists like Madeline L'Engle, Susan Cooper, and Ellen Raskin. While she had a special liking for fantasy, her tastes in fiction encompassed almost all categories. Waiting for her mother in the college bookstore, she would skim the paperback novels: mysteries, westerns, romances, gothics, classics, war stories, social problem novels— the lot—and make additions to her "to-be-read list." She also kept up with the self-help books and the current nonfiction, at least to the extent of skimming the book jackets. Her vocabulary reflected her wide reading; she kept word cards faithfully; and she held her own when the family played charades or Scrabble or imitated TV quiz shows. Keenly competitive, she aimed for an A in every course and succeeded even if she didn't really understand all the concepts in science and the equations in math. She read rapidly whether the text was self-chosen or assigned. Her competence in writing kept pace with her reading. She could paraphrase and summarize and outline. She knew the value of taking notes and giving teachers back exactly what they wanted. Sometimes school assignments bored her, but her academic home had instilled habits of self-discipline early on; she didn't stint homework for the sake of pleasure reading.

Equally bright, equally competent in reading by all the standard measures, Chris had developed very different habits from his classmate Penny. In the early years, his parents had had very little time for reading to him, though they had showed him how pleased they were with his good reports. Now that his parents were divorced, Chris and his younger brother pretty much ran their mother's house. Only the nine-year-old had time for TV; when Chris was at home, he studied. He read all assignments thoughtfully, tempering his rate of reading to the demands of the text. He wanted to be sure he understood even if he didn't always have time to show the fullness of his understanding in the written work the teacher required. Outside of school he had to be as selective about his reading as he was with his other leisure activities. So he hurried through the sports section every night when he got home from hockey practice, and if there was time after homework, he turned to the library book he'd chosen for that week. It was usually a historical novel if he had a book report due, although recently he'd begun to look for books on energy resources because his science teacher said that was an expanding field. Chris knew the value of a good vocabulary, and he picked up new words easily, trying them out when he could on his brother and his mother. His imagination was more limited than Penny's, so he didn't earn as many A's for creative writing, but he was good at explaining a process, giving clear directions, and presenting an argument, whether orally or in writing. He didn't read as much as Penny, but he got a lot of mileage out of his reading time.

Is there any need to teach reading to seventh graders like Penny and Chris? Not if you define reading instruction in terms of workbook exercises and lessons divorced from content. But superior readers in middle school are still developing their powers, still refining their learning tools and techniques; they still need their teachers' help in applying their skills. The fact that Penny has acquired a good deal of background (on some subjects) doesn't mean that she is always ready to use it. And while she reads a great deal, she is ony 12 and is constantly venturing into unknown territories. So like any other 12-year-old, she often finds learning from text a challenge. Her advantage over average readers is that she has had more successes to give her confidence in approaching the unknown.

What Chris needs now and will need increasingly as he moves into high school and college is the ability to read faster. Since he will have limited time for academics, what with his part-time jobs, sports, and home responsibilities, he will have to study efficiently and budget his time to allow for scanning more than the newspaper. More than Penny, he needs teachers who can widen his view of the world's possibilities. And, so that he can develop higher order skills later, he needs time for relaxed reading now, time to educate his imagination.

Superior readers don't need special reading classes. They may be excused from many of the skills practice sessions that English teachers in middle school regularly incorporate into their curriculum. But they can profit from many of the electives listed on page 118 (Chapter 5).

Readers and Learners in Grades 9 to 12

Average, superior, and problem readers are found in roughly the same proportions and varieties in the high school as in the middle school. As individuals, they may change dramatically in the four years between grades 5 and 8, but to describe their group characteristics will require us to repeat much of what has already been said. To minimize repetition we'll characterize each group briefly as readers and then generalize about teenagers as students.

Average Readers

Emerging from the junior high school, average readers who have continued to develop normally through grades 5 to 8 should be able to derive more than they used to from their content textbooks, provided these are at appropriate readability levels. Average readers will continue to need the same kinds of help in approaching grade-level textbooks, however, because vocabulary and sentence structure have become increasingly complex as concepts have become more sophisticated. Whether the subject is a new one like biology or a continuing one like American history, teachers will have to probe students' prior knowledge and, of course, expect it to be present in varying amounts among any group of average readers and learners.

For all students, but especially for the average, entrance into the senior high school signals new routines, new expectations, additional conflicts between academic demands and personal desires that can shake, if not shatter, their learning styles. We said that average readers at the beginning of middle school had fragile reading skills. Now we can say that, if they have been well taught, they enter high school with their general reading skills strengthened but with study skills that are frail. All of them who are college bound will need serious and consistent work on textbook study techniques, reference skills, and writing-from-reading in such forms as note-taking, precis writing, reports based on multiple sources, and critical evaluations.

In ninth or tenth grade many average students need more help with study skills than they can get from their content teachers, and a semester in a special reading class may be in order. But, on the whole, average students in high school benefit most from reading/study skills instruction that is part and parcel of their content courses.

The broad span of average doesn't narrow in high school even though some of this big middle group may drop out as soon as they reach the legal school-leaving age. Some drop-outs will be intellectually able youth, even good read-ers, who resist the confines of an academic or a vocational curriculum, or whose personal lives are in disarray. Some will be the least able readers whose skills, far from developing normally in middle school, remain at fifth or sixth grade level, presenting a formidable handicap for ninth or tenth graders expected to learn from grade-level textbooks. Discouraged, they quit at 16. To be sure, many others on the low end of average will reach twelfth grade and a diploma, having squeaked by proficiency tests and course requirements.

Problem Readers

Some who were almost illiterate in middle school will arrive in high school having made rapid progress during the four middle grades. These are most likely to be bright youngsters whose deficiencies stemmed from lack of experi-ence with the English language. Less capable nonnative speakers will continue to lag behind their normally developing age-mates. And, of course, newly ar-rived immigrants may be placed in high school classes even though they are not

---

BOX 4-2

DEFINING DYSLEXIA

dyslexia *(dis lek'sē ə)*

The concept of dyslexia, like that of learning disability, has a long history of differing interpretations. The medical profession tends to regard it as a disease for which there is a causative factor; the psychological profession, a serious problem of unspecified origin. The education profession has wavered between these positions.

1. *n.* a medical term for incomplete alexia; partial, but severe, inability to read; historically (but less common in current use), word blindness. *Note:* Dyslexia in this sense applies to persons who ordinarily have adequate vision, hearing, intelligence, and general language functioning. *Dyslexia is a rare but definable and diagnosable form of primary reading retardation with some form of central nervous system dysfunction. It is not attributable to environmental causes or other handicapping conditions—J. Abrams (1980).* 2. *n.* a severe reading disability of unspecified origin. 3. *n.* a popular term for any difficulty in reading of any intensity and from any cause(s).

SOURCE: *A Dictionary of Reading and Related Terms*, Theodore L. Harris and Richard E. Hodges, eds., 95. International Reading Association, 1981.

yet literate in English. (In fortunate circumstances, such youths may continue to study content subjects in their native tongue while taking ESL classes.)

Some who were beginning readers in middle school may continue to struggle with reading acquisition skills in high school even though they have had excellent remedial teaching. Those who become discouraged drop out. Those who have learned to compensate for dyslexia (if that is the problem) continue as successful learners in high school, using oral/aural methods. Also in this group are physically disabled students who may be developing normally as readers but because of their slow start are not yet at expected high school levels.

All the problem readers who remain in high school need continuing support not only from content teachers but from remedial teachers. The remedial help may be intermittent, depending on the student's progress, others' needs, and the availability of experts; but every high school should have a resource for disabled readers however many, or however few, are enrolled.

Superior Readers

Just as the rich get richer, superior readers in middle school continue, with rare exceptions, to make big gains throughout their years in high school. If they hit the ceilings of standardized tests, their gains may not be demonstrated by those instruments, but their increasing maturity should be manifest in the books they choose, the essays they write, the colleges they apply to, the scholarships and prizes they win, and the enterprise they show in extracurricular projects as well as in academic subjects.

We are not suggesting that all superior readers are superior students, or that all gifted students attain the highest levels of literacy. Exceptions stand out, however, because they *are* exceptions: the excellent reader who spurns academic success; the facile reader who chooses not to read; the doers to whom reading appears too passive an activity. On the more significant side, students with high grade-point averages are almost without exception superior readers. They have learned not only to read widely and selectively, but they make use of ideas learned from text in their own thinking, writing, and discussing. They are on friendly terms with dictionaries, knowing when to seek confirmation of a word's

BOX 4-3

WRITES HIS OWN TEXTBOOK

David Price was only 14 when he published his first article on computers in *Byte*, a computer-science journal. Now a sophomore at the College of William and Mary, he has written a textbook, *PASCAL: A Considerate Approach* (Prentice Hall), because he thought the one he had to use in his freshman computer course was "really bad." Altogether, Price figures he had about twelve articles and book reviews on computers published while he was in high school, even though he took his first formal course in computer science at William and Mary last year.

—As reported in *Chronicle of Higher Education*, (16 March 1981)

meaning and when to trust their guesses. They use words precisely and effectively. They have learned to use a library's resources fully when needed. They help themselves comprehend complex ideas by seeking out related texts and additional information. They read with pencil in hand, to underscore, to annotate, to diagram complex ideas. Their interests explode in language—they write for themselves and for publication. (Of course, such students exist! See Box 4-3).

Do superior high school readers need reading instruction? If a course promises to improve their speed, increase their efficiency, improve their writing, they'll be the first to sign up. Will they challenge the teacher? Will they make gains? Yes, if the teacher responds to the challenge and acts on the assumption that a group of superior readers has even less homogeneity than most other groups.

Bard College, an elite liberal arts college in upstate New York that sends most of its graduates in pursuit of advanced degrees, has answered in its own way the question we raised about superior readers needing further instruction in reading and writing. All freshmen entering Bard in 1981 and thereafter, no matter how superior their grades, SAT scores, and reading achievement records, were required to arrive on campus three weeks before the college opened for an immersion program in logical thinking, close reading, and articulate expression.

Teachers' Concerns About Adolescents as Students

Near the end of a discussion of individual differences in RED 627, a course on secondary school reading, Ruby Thomas said she'd rather teach problem readers. "Because," she explained, "they'd be less of a problem. At least, you'd know what they didn't know. You could see the goal and aim for it."

Some members of the class sympathized with Ruby's need to unravel the tangles of individual differences and to identify a corner of the fabric they could work on. But others said no, that working with problem readers was too uncertain in its rewards. "Listen, Ruby," said one of her classmates, "there's no real future in remedial reading. If it's really successful, it will self-destruct. So you get all the kids through the acquisition stage, and then they're average readers. They're somebody else's problem then. Or you figure out how the kids who don't learn to read can learn in other ways. Pretty soon you're out of a job."

"You should be," Doug said. "There's no way high schools can afford remedial teaching—not for long, anyway. Sooner or later we've got to teach all those kids—all different—in regular classes."

"So, sure, there are individual differences," said Janet, who'd been teaching at North High for several years, "but there are lots of ways that adolescents are alike. As a matter of fact, they don't want to be different, most of them, anyway. Oh, they want to be an identifiable group, different from adults, different from little kids, but not different from each other. Shouldn't we think about some of the things that are affecting most kids in the 1980s and that should probably affect the way we teach reading and study skills?"

So in the sessions that followed we faced Janet's question and raised others, and did not settle any of them. But since they are questions you also may raise, we'll summarize the discussions here.

What is there besides high school in an adolescent's life?

In many ways high school is the dominating force in adolescents' lives, isolating them from the rest of society. However, it is not necessarily the curriculum that dominates, but the extracurriculum: being with friends in the corridors and cafeterias, the locker rooms and the libraries, participating in sports and dramatics, working on school publications, science fairs, history projects, raising money for school trips and dances, cheerleading, playing in the band or orchestra. Adolescents associate with few adults except teachers (whom they don't really count as *people*); even outside of school, theirs is an inbred society restricted to teenagers. The result is a narrowing of interests against which teachers have constantly to contend. The reason for education, for learning to learn, is to broaden one's world, but that is a concept that teachers have a hard time establishing as long as society seals teenagers off in their own narrow world.

High schools as institutions reinforce the trend, since together the curriculum and the extracurriculum conspire to consume as much of teenagers' waking time as possible. The best teachers push their subjects hard, hoping to fire students with their enthusiasm. "You'd think anthropology was the only subject we took," complained Sylvia, leaving Mr. Walters' room with his exhortations to read that book on the Tasaday and that article in *National Geographic* still ringing in her ears. Each of Sylvia's other teachers assigned homework and extra reading as if the others didn't exist. Though a conscientious student, Sylvia did the least possible to complete each assignment; that year she had the starring role in the spring musical.

Should teachers show less enthusiasm for their subjects? Surely not. But somehow they must resolve the tensions they provoke between learning for learning's sake and working only for a grade. Indeed, for many students, that's not the real tension; the conflict is between meeting teachers' requirements and yielding to out-of-class demands. How much and what kinds of homework to assign is a central issue in secondary school reading programs. It can be resolved only by faculty groups who share the same values about secondary education. Not all teachers, or parents or students, share the view presented in this text that learning how to learn—becoming eager to learn something new—is a goal for high schools that must take precedence over particular content, though, of course, it cannot displace content.

As well as considering the role of homework and motivating students to learn, high school faculties should weigh ideas for moving students out of the teenage ghetto whenever possible and mingling them with other age groups. Community projects are frequently recommended for this purpose; a more recent scheme is the "adoption" of a school by a local industry, which brings technologists and business executives into classrooms and students into the workplace.

Teenage culture, more than the high school itself, dominates students' lives, and sets up competing demands on their time. The high cost of adolescent living makes part-time jobs a first priority for most kids, and the lack of a job a desperate and humiliating circumstance for poor youth. It's not just part-time work that steals attention from studies; so do financial worries and the pastimes from cars to electronic games that consume "pocket money." Nor is all teenage earning for frivolous pastimes; since few parents can afford the whole cost of college education, many high school students work as much as they can to supplement college scholarships and financial aid. Between cramming for the high grade-point average and adding to the savings account, one more tension is added. So serious is the need to work that many high school students have become in fact half-time scholars, present in class but too tired to engage in learning. (See Box 4-4.)

Not surprisingly, stress among teenagers has become a media topic, its high incidence verified by statistics on suicide,[1] use of alcohol and drugs, and driving accidents. Even discounting for media hype, however, teachers are left with a problem of sufficient magnitude to justify its inclusion in any discussion of reading and study skills in secondary schools. It may be that management of stress is a 1980s label for a long-standing topic in the study skills course: how to budget your time. But the topic needs revitalizing; all content teachers must consider it as they try to agree on reasonable expectations for high school students.

Are changing family patterns affecting high school students' learning?

Because many of the teachers and prospective teachers in RED 627 were themselves single parents or in two-paycheck households, they were especially sensitive to this question. Noting that 45 percent of all children born in 1977 will spend part of their childhood in a one-parent family and knowing that correlational studies associate socioeconomic status with success in reading, they were especially interested in figures from the U.S. Bureau of the Census that showed the average income in 1976 of families of divorced mothers was $9,608 compared with $13,206 for married-couple families, and that 28 percent of all families headed by a divorced woman were below the poverty level, compared with 6 percent of married-couple families. Some of the disparity, they guessed, was related to two other factors: the growing number of two-paycheck married couples and the fact that women typically earn less than men (more than 40 percent less according to at least one report).

Do working mothers adversely affect the learning skills of their children? Accumulating evidence says no. Apparently, the most potent factor for future learning is the quality of interaction between mother and child in the first year of life, a conclusion related also to findings that first-born children and those from smaller families tend to achieve at higher levels.

---

[1]Suicide is the third ranking cause of death among children under 18. (In 1978, approximately 5000 children aged 10 to 18 committed suicide in the U.S. In the past decade, the rate of childhood suicide has risen more than 100 percent. In 1983 a Boston University sociologist, Lee Ann Hoff, reported that in the past five years the rate of adolescent suicide has risen 250 percent in urban and rural communities. Hoff is the author of *People in Crisis* (Addison-Wesley, 2nd edition, 1984).

BOX 4-4

IS WORKING PART TIME GOOD FOR STUDENTS?

"Today, proportionately more American teenagers are working while still in school than at any other time in the past quarter century. Between 1940 and 1979, the proportion of 16-year-old males attending high school and working part time increased from 4 percent to 27 percent. . . . Not only are more adolescents working part time now, they are also working longer hours. In 1960, only 44 percent of the 16-year-old male workers who were still attending school worked more than 14 hours a week; in 1970, the figure was 56 percent. For 16-year-old females, the increase was from 34 percent to 46 percent." (Sheila Cole, *Working Kids on Working*, Lothrop, Lee and Shepard, 1980)

Questioning the value of working part time, its effect on "a student's grades, educational plans, friendships and family relations," Cole cites findings such as these from the research of social psychologists:

✤ Youngsters get very little valuable on-the-job training which will be useful later in life.

✤ They usually don't feel close to the adults they work with.

✤ Students who work use more alcohol and marijuana than those who don't—probably because they have more money for such things.

✤ Students who have the most trouble learning in school learn the most from their jobs.

✤ Students who worked "felt less involved in school than did their nonworking classmates, were absent more, and did not enjoy school as much. . . .

✤ Workers got lower grades than nonworkers.

✤ Tenth graders who worked more than 14 hours experienced lower marks, as did 11th graders who worked more than 20 hours.

SOURCE: Reported in "Where We Stand," by Albert Shanker, the New York *Times* (28 June 1981). Shanker's column is an advertisement of the United Federation of Teachers.

That working parents spend less time with their children may be offset by the expanding role of the father, the spur to ambition that working mothers set for their daughters, and the developing self-reliance of children who have household chores to perform. One researcher reported that daughters of working mothers set higher goals for themselves and are "more self-reliant, dominant, independent, autonomous, and active" than girls whose mothers remain at home.

In spite of some positive findings like these, high school teachers and administrators are sensitive to predictions that in the 1980s high schools will have many more students who have been born to unwed teenage mothers or who have been "latch-key" kids or who have grown up without male role models. For some the disadvantages inherent in such early home conditions will have been minimized by effective day care and excellent primary schooling, but for others the effects of a bad start (so far as school success is concerned) will persist into high school and accentuate the need for wide-range secondary reading programs.

What do kids expect from high school?

If half of them answer "a job" and the other half "admission to college," we should not assume that either answer betrays a cynical disregard for learning for its own sake. On the other hand, we cannot be sure that desire for a diploma is equivalent to desire for an education. Previous schooling, parental attitudes and the community's drive for accountability have taught most students to work for grades and test scores. This compulsion does not prevent them from questioning: "Why do we have to learn this stuff?" But it is discouraging to find them satisfied with answers like: "Because it's on the test" or "The curriculum requires it." This acceptance of authority, grudging though it may be, is characteristic of more of today's students than it was in many of their teachers' high school years. As the pendulum swings away from progressive ideals toward conservative values, students, too, develop conformist attitudes, buckling down to the kind of drill which seems to benefit basic skills and produce respectable test scores but does little for higher-order skills like reasoning and critical thinking. Since it's really the latter we want youngsters on the threshold of college to display, we must present them with sounder reasons for whatever we require than our assurance that "It's good for you," even though they settle for that.

Passivity toward learning seems to be characteristic of many teenagers. Did they learn this from schooling? From the spectator role many have assumed since infancy, when they were first exposed to TV? They are so used to being

BOX 4-5

WHAT DO YOU LIKE ABOUT THE WAYS TEACHERS HELP YOU TO LEARN?

1. *Clear, complete explanations and concrete examples.* The teacher spends enough time (but not too much) explaining what students do not understand . . . gives examples whenever possible . . . gives students time to think . . . reviews materials and concepts.

2. *Positive, relaxed learning environment.* The teacher has rules but allows students freedom to talk and to learn with others . . . expects that all the students will learn.

3. *Individualized instruction.* The teacher knows that students are different and have different abilities . . . sometimes divides students into groups . . . informs students of their progress . . . works with students and assigns a variety of tasks and projects.

4. *Adequate academic learning time.* The teacher gives students time to work in class . . . helps students to keep working so that they will learn.

5. *Motivation and interest.* The teacher makes students want to learn . . .

These five factors, listed in descending order, were the ones most often mentioned by 566 student in grades 7 through 12 in Little Rock, Arkansas, in answer to the question headlined. Reported by Mary H. Mosely and Paul J. Smith in *Phi Delta Kappan*, December 1982.

---

acted upon that they see motivation as the teacher's responsibility, not theirs. (See Box 4-5.)

To a degree they are right. If the system has taught them not to question, or to be satisfied with irrelevant answers, then the burden for motivating passive students rests with their teachers. As far as reading and learning from text are concerned, motivating students—getting them to see the reason for doing it—is nine-tenths of teaching, but not solely the responsibility of teachers, since adolescents' attitudes toward learning are derived also from home, peers, the media, and the whole social climate.

So what kids expect from high school is germane indeed to the reading teacher. Of course, instead of generalizing about their expectations, you should ask them. If the answers are no better than the ones we've hypothesized here, you and your colleagues must set about changing them.

Where are these kids headed?

Although we were told throughout the 1970s that the United States was entering a post-industrial economy, high school teachers may still not fully realize the implications of this transformation for their curriculum. Two statistics first: Today more than 65 percent of U.S. workers provide information or services; fewer than 20 percent manufacture products. The ten most rapidly growing jobs in this decade are shown in Box 4-6. Nine job skills predicted to be most in demand in the 1990s are listed in Box 4-7.

These figures make clear that the new technologies, far from diminishing the need for literacy, demand steadily higher levels of literate performance. They demonstrate why educators in this latter half of the twentieth century have insisted that learning *how* is even more important than learning *what*, especially in the pre-college years. Since one cannot learn how to learn without also

BOX 4-6

TEN MOST RAPIDLY GROWING JOBS, 1978-90

Jobs	Growth Rate
	%
Data-processing machine mechanics	147
Paralegal personnel	132
Computer systems analysts	107
Computer operators	88
Office machine services	80
Computer programmers	74
Aero-astronautical engineers	70
Food preparation personnel (fast foods)	69
Employment interviewers	67
Tax preparers	65

SOURCE: Max Carey, "Occupational Employment Growth Through 1990," *Monthly Labor Review* (August 1981):48.

BOX 4-7

JOB SKILLS FOR 1990

1. Evaluation and analysis
2. Critical thinking
3. Problem solving (including math)
4. Organization and reference
5. Synthesis
6. Application to new areas
7. Creativity
8. Decision making with incomplete information
9. Communication skills in many modes

SOURCE: *Information Society* (Denver: 1982).

acquiring knowledge, no dichotomy is implied. Rather, the statement is simply another way of saying that content teachers should demonstrate how to study their subjects and why these subjects are of interest and importance.

The growing variability of jobs in the future, merely hinted at in Box 4-7, is still another facet of the individual differences which have been the theme of this chapter. Not that high school teachers should strive to prepare students directly for jobs as diverse as handling fast foods, servicing data processing machines, and managing employment offices. But by keeping in mind the kinds of careers that high school graduates in the 1980s and 1990s will seek, teachers will be better able to decide whether, for instance, it is more important to have students explain in their own words why an effect resulted or to have them mark T or F beside a text editor's explanation. Awareness of the world their students will enter permeates the decisions that high school faculties make, decisions that range from the kinds of tests a teacher gives to the selection of content for the required curriculum.

Parenthetically, we cannot resist observing that education itself is a major information service enterprise. Many of the students we teach in grades 5 to 8 and 9 to 12 are being prepared quite directly by their current experiences for how they will teach whether they enter traditional roles as teachers and parents or such new teaching roles as communicators through the mass media, writers of texts, instructional technologists, and creators of computer software.

So what can teachers do about individual differences?

This question came up in almost every session of RED 627 and seemed to invite more detail than the students could encompass in finite answers. Pressed to generalize, however, they offered these three precepts:

(1) Identify the differences within any group you teach. But focus, too, on the similarities so that you can form groups in which students learn from one another as well as from you. (Techniques will be described in subsequent chapters.)

(2) Don't settle for a single method of organizing classes, of teaching concepts, or of eliciting responses. Experiment with many methods. Beware of formulas; beware of ruts. Try out the ideas in books like this one; adapt them to your personal style; vary them to suit your moods, and your students'; decide why some ideas work and others don't; keep looking for better ways to meet your goals, but be clear as to goals.

(3) So far as you are able, respect the person behind the cumulative records, the diagnostic reading profile, the unfinished workbook exercise, and the mangled syntax of yesterday's homework assignment.

RECAPPING MAIN POINTS

Individual students differ as readers, as learners, and as human beings. Schools are also different, as are individual classes within the same school. Categorizing schools as urban, rural, or suburban may tell little about the ethnic, social, economic, and cultural variety of their student bodies. Within each category, the range of students' abilities may be very wide or relatively narrow. Similarly, within a school, some classes may be more homogeneous than others.

Nevertheless, teachers in grades 5 to 8 and 9 to 12 can expect to have students who are barely literate and students who read easily and well on any topic with which they have had prior experience. Most of their students will exhibit reading abilities between these two extremes.

Average readers in middle school represent a wide range of intelligence. Their reading scores on standardized tests are close to grade placement—the reason for characterizing them as "average"—but the details of their reading performance may vary widely. Average readers in middle school are most in need of expanding the amount and range of their reading.

Average readers in senior high school need emphasis on study skills; they should respond to their reading in various written forms. They also need to sustain habits of wide reading developed earlier, since these will support the development of higher-order skills. Increasing their rate of comprehension is also of concern to average and superior readers.

How adolescents read and learn is very much affected by the social and cultural world of adolescence. Teachers need to understand changing social patterns in order to counteract potentially negative effects on adolescent learning.

FOR DISCUSSION

1. Why is it important to increase the amount and range of reading of average students in grades 5 to 8? What is the relationship between wide reading and higher-order comprehension skills such as reasoning about what is read?

2. Discuss the types of differences you are likely to find in a so-called average class in a junior high school in a middle class suburb.

3. If adolescents differ so widely in reading abilities, attitudes, habits, and learning styles, is there any point in generalizing about methods of teaching reading and studying? Why is it important to think of the ways in which adolescents are similar as well as different?

4. Think of a class in which you are, or were, a student. Perhaps you can remember a pre-college class. What differences in learning ability and literacy levels among your classmates were you aware of? If you were not aware of differences, how do you account for this? In your experience, what have teachers done to accommodate to individual differences?

5. Describe the characteristics of superior readers in secondary schools. What kinds of instruction in reading and writing do these students need? Why is it not sufficient to make sure they have opportunities to read and write?

6. In what ways may students' time be wasted in high school? Discuss possible ways to prevent this waste.

FURTHER READING

Artley, A. Sterl. "Individual Differences and Reading Instruction," *Elementary School Journal* 83 (Nov. 1981):143–51.

Fenstermacher, Gary D. and John I. Goodlad, eds. *Individual Differences and the Common Curriculum*. Eighty-second Yearbook of the National Society for the Study of Education, Part I, 1983 (distributed by University of Chicago Press).
  A collection of essays. See especially "Individual Differences in the Classroom: A Psychological Perspective" by Thomas Good and Deborah J. Stipek.

Glanz, Ellen. *What Are You Doing Here? or School Days for the Teacher*. Council for Basic Education, 725 Fifteenth Street, NW, Washington, DC 20005, Occasional Paper No. 26, 1979.
  A social studies teacher in Lincoln-Sudbury High School (Massachusetts), Ms. Glanz became a student for a semester, going to classes, the cafeteria, the girls' room with other students; taking the same tests, doing the same assignments, making the same kinds of excuses.

Naisbitt, John. *Megatrends: Ten New Directions Transforming Our Lives*. New York: Warner Books, 1982).
  This compact analysis of current trends aids in understanding today's students and the world they are growing into.

Owen, David. *High School*. New York: Viking Press, 1981.
  A view of "nonacademic" high school youth as seen by a recent Harvard graduate who goes undercover in an upstate New York high school.

Learners and Teachers II

5 *The School Setting*

"Talk all you want to about the importance of the individual," Smothergill was saying, "but the fact remains: We teach kids in groups—big groups. We've got three thousand kids in this high school."

"And I have thirty-two essay exams to finish before fourth period," said Elaine Verbrugge in a tone to stifle further conversation. It was the day after the professional development seminar on providing for individual differences.

"Smothergill's right, though," said Virgie Wilson. "That guy from the university talked as if there'd be no one around but you and the kid who can't read."

"As if teaching took place in your living room instead of in this zoo," said Mike Ferrari.

And let's tune out right there because the teachers have made the essential point: Teaching and learning take place in complex educational systems peopled by actors and onlookers. Education is a public enterprise. Indeed, teachers often complain that they live in a goldfish bowl, but while that figure of speech suggests the public scrutiny, it fails to invoke the complex relationships within the system. Although we don't much like metaphors which imply schools are factories (*school plant, educational products, cost effectiveness*), the factory image suggesting churning activity, meshing gears, chain effects, and assembly lines seems much more evocative of the schools than does the placidity of a goldfish bowl.

One small indication of the complexity of the system is how hard it is to define secondary schools. In 1980, the National Center for Educational Statistics named five categories of secondary schools: (1) middle schools; (2) junior high schools; (3) four-year high schools; (4) combined junior–senior high schools; and (5) vocational/technical high schools. Some middle schools were counted as the end of elementary schools and others as the beginning of secondary. Two other patterns, common to rural schools, are the K–8 unit and the central school which houses all 13 grades. In this book, because we are concerned with the teaching of reading in departmentalized curricula, we cover grades 5 to 8 in departmentalized middle and junior high schools, referring to them as "early secondary." We refer to grades 9 to 12 as "senior high school."

It is absurd to generalize about an organization as vast as the schools, but we must risk the absurd in order to avoid talking about reading instruction in the abstract. In the last chapter we dared to generalize about the biggest segment of the school population, the approximately 25 million public school students in grades 5 to 12. Now we risk similar sweeping generalizations about the other occupants of public schools—the instructional staff—which in 1981 numbered about two and a half million, of whom one million were classroom teachers in four-year high schools.[1] Given these numbers, the following generalizations could be matched by staggering numbers of exceptions. Nevertheless, because people, not machines or textbooks, teach reading, we plunge ahead.

Teachers are themselves the products of the system they serve. In no other profession do the practitioners become a part of the system at the age of five and continue therein for 16 to 18 years until they reach the other side of the desk. Lawyers don't begin as children to observe the practice of law, nor do physicians experience hospital life daily for fifteen years before they begin to study medicine. The closest counterpart to teaching in this respect is parenting, which is also, of course, part of the educational process. The chief effect of the cyclical nature of the educational system is that teachers tend to teach as they have been taught. From kindergarten on, every teacher contributes to future teachers' concepts of teaching. Given this condition, it is understandable that reading instruction has crept so slowly up the grades from primary to senior high school; teachers have had very little experience themselves of being taught how to learn through reading.

Because reading instruction in secondary schools has been very limited over the past forty years, today's secondary teachers have few experiences of their own to call upon. The younger members of a faculty may recall having had reading classes in grades 7 and 8, but not beyond. Most high school programs have been targeted on remedial reading, and few would-be teachers need these services. A more common experience is the speed reading courses taken in high school or college. In any case, few teachers remember their content teachers teaching them how to read and study. Among the attitudes and impressions that far too many future teachers carry away from their secondary years is the conviction that teachers assign and correct, ask questions and evaluate answers, but seldom teach how to read and study.

To correct such misapprehensions, to help future teachers think about learning, is the reason for Education courses. Few teachers in secondary schools in the 1980s have escaped such courses. Why, then, do many of them still shy away from teaching reading?

A young English teacher said, "Oh, but I don't know how to teach reading. I just had one methods course in college and I wouldn't know what to do."

"How many courses did you take in how to teach English?" we asked.

"One," she said, and hesitated at the incongruity. "But," she said, "English was my subject!"

---

[1]Statistics in this paragraph are estimated from figures reported in *Digest of Education Statistics*, 1982, National Center for Educational Statistics, U.S. Government Printing Office.

This young woman had some confidence in teaching ninth grade English because she had studied world literature, Shakespeare, the contemporary novel, and other literature and language courses to a total of 36 college credits. To teach reading, she thought she would have to pick up comparable numbers of credits and become a "reading specialist" who would "diagnose and remediate."

Today several states require at least one course in reading for certification to teach any subject in grades 7 to 12. "Necessary but insufficient" is our reaction to this requirement, as we observe practices and talk to teachers who have had a reading methods course. What is needed, however, is not a piling up of preservice requirements but changed attitudes in the school environment which the novice teacher enters.

Attitudes *are* changing, almost imperceptibly in some places, with more dramatic effect in others. Some of these changes are due to the changing student population, others to the social climate. Today's teachers are the products not only of the schools of the 1950s, 1960s, and 1970s but of the drastic social upheavals of those decades. They have learned that everyone in our society must become literate though many may read very little.

TV babies themselves, young teachers read less than "academic types" once did, or were supposed to. They have less time to devote to class preparations because they have families to raise and educate, houses to renovate, degrees to earn, political issues to debate, bodies to keep fit, personal lives to disentangle, divorces to finalize, relationships to fulfill, retirements to plan for, inflation to fight, volunteer work to do, professional status to defend, union meetings to attend, social wrongs to right, pleasures to partake of, the local and world news to keep up with, decisions to make. Ah, those decisions! We blithely say that teaching is decision-making, failing to notice the surfeit of choices that teachers must make *outside* their working lives as well as in their classrooms. One person who noticed is Ed Farrell. (See Box 5-1.)

It is no wonder that teachers burn out. But this is not necessarily a tragedy

BOX 5-1

WHY TEACHERS BURN OUT

All decisions take their human toll. . . . Teaching, particularly if it is student-centered, requires constant and accumulatively wearying decisions from teachers. When I left the high school to become a university instructor, I found my workweek equally long but my fatigue not nearly so great: I was no longer in the classroom five hours a day, where I often had to call on one of thirty hands waving in simultaneous frenzy; I no longer had clusters of bodies at my desk asking what we are going to do today, asking what we did yesterday, asking to be excused to go to the gym, asking why I gave Sue an *A* and my inquisitor only a *B*—and all this under the incessant tick of the classroom clock and the inexorable clang of a class bell. We burn out good teachers because of the untoward number of decisions we compel them to make, decisions correlated directly to the number of students they face.

SOURCE: Edmund Farrell, "Wading for Significance in Torrents of Trivia," *English Journal* (September, 1978), 29.

unless they remain on the job in their burned-out condition. Calculating the stress factor in teaching, young people entering the profession might predetermine how long they will remain in the classroom before moving into different roles within the profession or making a new career outside it. Very few teachers should permit themselves to teach the same subjects or grade levels for 25 or 30 years. And a major responsibility of the caring administrator, as we shall note below, is to shield the staff from burnout, so far as possible, and to help teachers plan changes in their roles and careers.

How Secondary Schools Organize Instruction

Relatively speaking, schools are oases of order in the confusion of contemporary society. To describe schools as orderly is redundant, of course, since schools are *systems*, which is another word for order. The system that schools have become has been dictated by necessities, some logical, some psychological in nature. Necessities of both kinds have dictated the departmental organization, which facilitates the teaching of subject matter and complicates the teaching of reading/study skills.

This feature, which divides the curriculum into subjects and assigns subjects to specialists, must have seemed an absolute necessity to teachers and principals in the early days of secondary education, when the chief purpose of the high school was to prepare students for Ivy League colleges. Later, as the comprehensive high school emerged as the best way to accommodate all students, including those who would go on to jobs instead of college, programs designed as college preparatory, commercial, technical–vocational, and general made the case for departmentalizing even stronger.

As is so often the case in education, departmentalization drifted downward. In the junior high school, which was developed as a preparation for high school, specialization also began to seem a logical necessity. Then, as the curriculum seemed to become increasingly sophisticated even in the elementary school, and as the middle school became an organizational unit for grades 5 or 6 to 8, it seemed efficient to make teachers subject-matter specialists in these grades as well.

The chief advantage of specialization is that it permits teachers to master what is to be learned in a field such as earth science, Afro/Asian studies, or computer technology. Moreover, specialization makes it possible to plan similar lessons for more than one class. With so many detailed decisions to make, teachers, and therefore students, stand to benefit from whatever devices reduce planning time and increase a teacher's mastery of his or her field. The disadvantages of specialization are, however, serious. First is the practical matter of increased pupil load. Surely, the need to react to 125 instead of 25 different personalities during a day raises the stress factor. Perhaps reacting to the same 25 students all day long is equally stressful, but in one respect this arrangement is more effective: The teacher of 25 can observe and assist transfer learning much more easily than can the teacher of five groups of 25, each seen once a day for 40 minutes.

A second and more serious disadvantage of a departmentalized curriculum is that multiple classes and short periods deflect teachers' and students' attention from learning how to learn. Subject matter seems *all* important; furthermore, in the student's view, each kind should be kept separate from another. "Don't try to teach me how to read in math class," says Joe, "that's Ms. Keppler's bag." It's not just the students' view. Secondary teachers have been known to submit grievances to their unions that they were hired to teach science, not reading. In one high school, the principal walked out on his observation of an untenured teacher who was demonstrating reading strategies needed for the next chapter, leaving a note that he would be back when she was teaching history. The attitudes expressed in these examples are natural outgrowths of a curricular plan whose purpose is to facilitate teaching subject matter.

For students, multiple classes mean multiple assignments, each done without regard to the other. This compartmentalizing of learning obviously diminishes the possibilities of transferring skills or relating ideas from one subject to another. From a practical point of view, multiple classes can overload the students as well as the teachers. For example, in one school where every teacher became convinced of the values of teaching vocabulary as a result of an in-service course in reading methods, the students were held responsible for roughly ten words a week in four or five areas; as a result, what started as a worthwhile effort proved self-defeating.

Another danger of departmentalization is that specialist–teachers begin to think that their subject is the only one students have to pursue. The effects of such thinking include not only increased and unrelated tasks for students but the repetition of ideas and information from class to class, accelerating boredom and cutting down on students' opportunities to learn what is of value to them. A different and perhaps worse effect of departmentalizing is that teachers may neglect important learning because they assume someone else will do it.

In spite of these disadvantages, departmentalization remains the most common way to organize teachers, students, and curricula in secondary schools. For teachers as they are presently trained and for those students for whom subject-matter preparation is of considerable importance, the division into subject specialties is practical. The problems of the segmented curriculum are not insurmountable so long as they are recognized and dealt with. We believe that excellent reading instruction can be achieved even in a departmentalized school if teachers and administrators are convinced that

+ students have an increased need for instruction in how to learn through reading when they enter a departmentalized curriculum, whether that is at grade 5, 7, or 9.
+ teaching reading/study skills requires team teaching or at least team planning.
+ reading teachers and content teachers can understand their respective roles and work together.
+ helping students use language to learn ideas is at the heart of every subject in the secondary school curriculum.

Improving Reading Programs at Secondary Levels

If by "program" we mean what shows up on the scheduling computer in the main office, then the ideal school would have no "reading program" at all: The reading/study needs of every student would be served through the teaching and learning of content. In an ideal school, the "program" might be no more than a clear statement of (1) the role of reading and writing in the total learning repertory of students at various stages of development, and (2) reading strategies clearly described as they are used in every content area. This program would be the product of all the faculty and administrators in that school; at least they would all subscribe to it and make it happen.

It may be because *program* is such an ambiguous label that surveys of secondary schools yield such depressing results—for example, those shown in Boxes 5-2 and 5-3. At least four decades after reading instruction in secondary schools was recognized as a subject for professional books and articles, research, and methods courses, the schools in these surveys are reporting that every teacher is *not* a teacher of reading, that the needs of poor readers in secondary schools are being served in few places, and that if developmental reading is recognized as being taught anywhere it's being done in English classes.

Sixty years after William S. Gray[2] recommended that in secondary schools "remedial" emphasis should give way to developmental reading taught by teachers in all content areas, we still have arguments in staff rooms and in professional journals as to whether schools should set up special classes for reading or by-pass them in favor of an all-out effort to "infuse" reading in all content areas.

This old argument preserves one more useless dichotomy in Education. Convinced that there is merit in both approaches and even more merit in combining them, we remind you again that there is no one best plan for introducing or extending reading/study skills in secondary schools. Schools are almost as various as the people who attend them, and each school works within its limitations of budget and personnel. Box 5-6 provides a checklist of criteria you might use to decide whether a particular school "has" or is approaching a "total" reading program.

A total reading program, in our view, provides instruction for all students. Most students could be well served through their content courses, provided that their teachers were concerned and competent enough to teach them how to learn through reading their text materials. Students whose reading skills are still at the beginning level need expert help beyond their content courses, however. We would place these students in remedial services.

In that large number of schools where content teachers are not yet concerned and competent with respect to reading instruction, students need support outside their content classes. The majority of students need this support, especially in the early secondary years, and they are best provided with it through reading

---

[2]*Report of the National Committee on Reading*, W. S. Gray, ed., Part I of the Twenty-fourth Yearbook of the National Society for the Study of Education (University of Chicago Press, 1925).

BOX 5-2

READING "ACTIVITIES" REPORTED BY 172 SECONDARY SCHOOLS

Population: 172 schools (7–12) in 8 counties
School size: under 250 to over 3,500

100% of junior high schools reported "some organized activity"
 62% of senior high schools reported "some organized activity"

Type of "organized reading activity"

Corrective classes	78%
Remedial	74
Developmental	68
Content-oriented	41
Disadvantaged	35

Major emphasis

Developmental	33%
Corrective	32
Remedial	20
Disadvantaged	9
Content-oriented	6

Developmental

Required reading courses	35%
Individualized "lab"	18
English units	17
English/reading combination	14
Elective skills improvement	14

Content-oriented

Limited to certain curricular areas:

English	86%
Social studies	10
Miscellaneous	4

25% increase since 1970 but less than for developmental, corrective, and remedial.

Professional duties of reading personnel

Corrective–remedial teaching	86%
Helping content teachers	61
In-service education	27

In 31% of schools, reading teachers also taught a content subject.

SOURCE: Adapted from data reported by Walter Hill in "Secondary Reading Activity in Western New York," *Journal of Reading*, 19:1 (October 1975):13–19.

BOX 5-3

SECONDARY READING PRACTICES IN NEW ENGLAND

From 290 Massachusetts schools surveyed, 187 responses were received, and of these 81 percent reported having planned reading programs in secondary schools and 19 percent reported no programs.

	Schools	
Types of Reading Programs Provided	**Number**	**%**
Elective course in reading	106	70
Individualized laboratory or instruction	94	62
Required reading course	45	30
Federally-funded programs for the disadvantaged	26	17
Methods For Selecting Students		
Teacher referral	127	84
Individual diagnostic testing by the reading teacher	107	71
Standardized tests	104	69
By grade level	50	33
Elective—student's choice	32	21
Competency testing	19	12
Types of Students Served		
Students revealing some difficulty	127	84
Students with severe problems	121	80
College bound students	80	53
Students preparing for SAT, PSAT, or CEB exams	62	41
All students	31	21
Students failing minimum competency exams	11	7

NOTE: Data reported for Massachusetts only are generalizable to all six New England states, according to survey conducted by New England Reading Association in 1978.
SOURCE: Carol Sager, *Secondary Reading Practices in New England* (NERA, 1980). Information regarding this publication should be addressed to Mr. Charles Flaherty, 21 Silver Lake Ave., Wakefield, RI 02879.

classes which we refer to as *developmental*. Schools that cannot afford these extra classes, or that are staffed with teachers who can successfully integrate reading skills with content instruction, may leave direct instruction in reading to the English faculty.

Whether reading instruction for most students is provided solely through English classes and content classes or through "extra" developmental classes, arrangements must be made for students at beginning levels and for the very able readers at the other end of the range. Box 5-4 illustrates one way of sorting out and providing for these various needs. We suggest that you turn to this chart now and study it with reference to the needs of students in the school that you know best.

We have contrasted direct instruction with application in content fields and said that the secondary programs we favor provide a balance between these two emphases. The spirals in Figure 5-1 (page 116) demonstrate such a balance from

BOX 5-4

PROVIDING FOR DIFFERENCES IN READING ACHIEVEMENT

Diagnosis shows:	Focus on:	Through:	Content Class Adjustments:
Nonreaders (can't read)	Functional literacy	Tutorial (Load: 35 weekly)	Oral/Aural
Nonreaders (won't read)	Pleasurable literacy	Speak/Read Service to others Out-of-school projects	Nonprint to print
Deficit: Compre- hension	Meaning Sentences Paragraphs	Reading Classes (Class size: 15–20)	DRL* in content fields
Deficits: Mixed	Long-range self-diagnosis	Learning to learn	Motivation through content
Deficit: Study reading	Comprehen- sion/retention	Efficient study and research tools	Application to content
Advanced, Able	Responsibility Ability to respond	Speed reading Understanding doublespeak Junior Great Books Nonfiction: The World of Issues	Much independent research Responsibility to group Strong content em- phasis

*See Chapter 13, page 378.

first grade through twelfth. The table at the bottom specifies skills or strategies to be emphasized in "direct" and "applied" instruction. This scheme shows that from grades 5 through 8 almost equal time and resources should be devoted to "direct instruction" and "content application." It also shows that beyond grade 8 greater emphasis should be given to applying strategies in content courses than to direct instruction either in English classes or in "extra" reading classes. However, the spirals show that although direct instruction absorbs less time and fewer resources in the senior high school it does not disappear from the curriculum.

BOX 5-5

THREE KINDS OF PROGRAMS*

	Remedial†	Corrective†	Developmental†
Who is served?	Students who have not yet acquired basic skills—but are capable of doing so.	Students who read 1 to 2 years below grade level, but have mastered most basic skills and are capable of improving.	All students
Main purpose?	To provide basic skills instruction in reading and writing.	To help students correct specific skill weaknesses.	Ongoing program to help students refine and extend skills which they already possess.
Setting?	Special reading class. Intensive 1–1 or small-group instruction.	Reading class or English class.	Instruction given in all content area classes, in addition to reading and English classes.
Teacher?	Clinically trained teacher or tutor.	Reading and/or English teacher.	All teachers

*The main reading program for learning disabled and other special education students is usually in a separate setting with a special education teacher.
†These three labels are variously applied, depending on such factors as funding, available staff, scheduling, physical plant, and so on. Other labels are also used, such as: reading lab, Chapter I reading, remedial English, basic communication skills, or Reading Improvement I and II.

Problems in the Early Secondary Grades

Reading programs are more commonly found in middle schools and junior high schools than in grades 9 to 12. In grades 5 and 6, reading classes for all students—that is, "developmental" classes—are usually continuations of the basal reading programs found in the lower grades. Frequently, basal programs are continued into grade 7 as "extra" classes (in addition to English or language arts), but by grade 8, it is common to find only underdeveloped readers assigned to "extra" instruction in reading; all other students now get what they will from English teachers and, in some cases, from content teachers.

The effectiveness of reading instruction in the early secondary years is not well documented; our impression is that direct instruction programs need to be

BOX 5-6

TEN CRITERIA FOR A GOOD SECONDARY SCHOOL READING PROGRAM

1. Reflects administrators' and teachers' convictions that reading is a tool of *learning* and that *learning how to learn* is the essential goal of secondary education.
2. Provides *direct instruction* in how to read and study for every student at every grade level as needed through:
   Special reading classes
   English classes
   Corrective instruction
   Remedial services
3. Provides *instruction* and *practice* in learning from text in the content fields.
4. Involves all teachers in *cooperative planning* so that reading and study skills are neither overlooked nor overstressed.
5. Provides *multi-level text materials* in every subject so that slow, average, and superior readers can learn from text at levels appropriate to their development.
6. Emphasizes *personal reading* out of school as well as in school as a source of information, an aid to personal and social development, and as a pleasure.
7. Promotes *alternatives to reading* as ways of learning when students can learn more effectively from:
   Listening (to live and taped presentations)
   Viewing (including films and television)
   Participating (in discussions, experiments, improvisations)
8. Assesses individuals' *growth in reading* through:
   Informal testing and observations
   Standardized tests
   Choices of reading
   Responses to reading
   Achievement in all school subjects
9. *Evaluates program* regularly through analyzing students' achievement and attitudes; teachers' opinions and work loads; cost effectiveness.
10. Continues and varies *staff development* so that administrators and faculty are always aware of an all-school *language policy* and are improving their abilities to implement it.

SOURCE: Adapted from Margaret Early, "What Does Research in Reading Reveal About Successful Reading Programs?" in *What We Know about High School Reading*, M. Agnella Gunn, ed., National Conference on Research in English, 1969. Reprinted in *English Journal* (April, 1969).

improved as much as content application programs need to be started in the first place. The chief fault of direct instruction programs is that reading teachers are likely to be inexperienced and poorly prepared; many are drafted from subject specialties and assigned to teach reading in extra classes which have been mandated by local boards or state legislatures. Inexperienced teachers are likely to rely heavily on instructional materials, sometimes inappropriate materials purchased before students' reading skills have been carefully assessed.

FIGURE 5-1

A TOTAL READING PROGRAM

GRADE

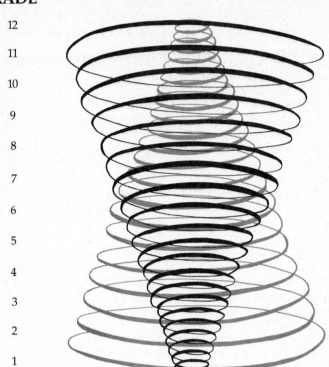

12
11
10
9
8
7
6
5
4
3
2
1

The direct-instruction program, strong in primary grades, narrows as it spirals through grade 12. The second spiral represents content applications. Beginning in first grade, it grows wider and stronger as it spirals outward through grade 12. Strategies developed through direct instruction are applied in the content fields.

Direct Instruction	**Content Applications**
Word Recognition Techniques Structure Content Dictionary	Special Vocabulary of Subject Applying All Techniques of Word Study *and* Direct Teaching
General Comprehension Skills Study Habits Retention	How to Study Particular Texts Understanding Structure of Writing in Special Fields
Rate of Reading Locational Skills	Adjusting Rate to Purpose and Subject Research

Extra classes in reading for everyone may be more expensive than a middle school or junior high school can afford. For instance, an extra class for everyone in grades 7 and 8, offered five times a week, requires as many reading teachers as English teachers. An unfortunate solution for the school which can hire only one reading teacher is to schedule reading two or three times weekly for every student; this results in overloading the reading teacher. For example, instead of five classes of 25 students each five times a week (load = 125), the reading teacher is assigned eight classes of 25 three times a week (load = 200). Faced with a load of 200 students, only extraordinary teachers can cope with normal ranges of abilities and learning styles. Even with fewer than a hundred students at this crucial stage of development, teachers may do little except follow the basal manual (or worse still, ignore the manual and simply assign the pupil texts) or depend too heavily on skills kits and "reading lab" equipment or settle for periods of "sustained silent reading," which have their place (see Chapter 11), but do very little to foster the study skills that some of that total population of seventh graders need.

The chief shortcoming of many developmental reading classes is that they provide inadequately if at all for individual differences. We believe that a first step toward providing individuals with the instruction they need is to remove the least developed readers and the most capable from these classes. The least developed readers should be assigned to remedial services if they are available and appropriate; if not, these children would be better off without "developmental" reading. At the other end of the range, the most capable students may develop reading and study skills on their own or with the help of content teachers. The "average" readers left for the developmental reading classes will still present a broad range of differences, but this range will be manageable for teachers who have learned to assess reading achievement and to match instruction and practice with what diagnostic profiles show. We emphasize *manageable*. A teacher's skill in arranging for students to learn to read as well as they are able develops over years of thought-about experience; it does not come from a single text like this one or a single course in teaching reading, even though both the text and the course offer knowledge as well as encouragement.

The rest of this chapter will reiterate that support for the reading teacher must come first from the administration, then from the rest of the staff in a particular school. When support is given, the effectiveness of developmental classes should show in students' performances in content courses, in their personal reading habits, and in their scores on formal and informal reading tests. If careful evaluation shows that reading classes are low in effectiveness, then administrators and teachers must decide whether or not direct reading instruction is worth the expense of extra classes.

Reading Instruction in Senior High Schools

As the spirals of Figure 5-1 suggest, direct instruction in grades 9 to 12 should be limited to a few groups at each level. Such instruction is remedial and corrective, aimed at selected students, not all of them. For those few adolescents who can profit from remedial instruction and are lucky enough to be in systems

BOX 5-7

SUGGESTED READING ELECTIVES OR UNITS*

1. *Learning About Ourselves as Learners.* Features diagnostic testing, self-evaluation, and goal setting. A nine-week offering might be wholly diagnostic, centering on students' understanding of themselves as learners and helping them to analyze learning processes, including reading, listening, and problem-solving. A unit under this title appears between Chapters 6 and 7.
2. *Personal Reading* should be minimally guided, permitting students to read popular paperbacks from junior novels to contemporary fiction. One focus might be selection of new books for the library. This elective offers opportunities for diagnosing and strengthening general vocabulary/comprehension.
3. *Choosing Literature for Children* might develop into a service to day care centers, preschools, and primary grades as students learn to select books and read them aloud. Slower learners and soon-to-be parents might be prime candidates for this elective. A variant offering might aim at a critical approach to children's literature.
4. *Oral Interpretation.* Just as the title implies, this elective or unit is based on a series of carefully designed sequential exercises in oral reading. One class began with choral speaking, went on to simple plays, teacher-written scripts, professional TV scripts, and readings of prose and poetry.
5. *Reading: The World of Ideas.* A semester or year's course devoted to the reading of nonfiction. Content is developed from students' interests, but skills of perceiving organization, recognizing author's purpose, drawing conclusions, and other critical reading strategies are emphasized.
6. *Reading Newspapers.* Several different courses might evolve under this general title. One for low achievers utilizes television news programs to prepare students for reading local newspapers. For average and more able readers, emphasis is on reading newsmagazines critically.
7. *Understanding Doublespeak.* A course in critical reading aimed at analyzing the language of advertising, government, diplomacy, industry, the military, journalism, education, and so on.
8. *Reading for College Success.* For eleventh and twelfth graders, a chance to reform study skills.
9. *Speed Reading.* Just that—for the motivated and competent reader.
10. *Words, Words, Words.* Ordinarily, we don't study vocabulary out of the context of ideas, but short electives featuring vocabulary development can be justified. The class might feature word games, etymologies, and neologisms.

*Adaptable as 9-week or 18-week electives or as units of study within English courses.

that can provide them, the kinds of remedial services described in Chapters 7 and 8 should be available.

Especially at the upper levels, a total program emphasizes content applications, and the reading personnel needed to bring that about will work more with teachers than with students. However, as Box 5-7 specifies, short-term intensive courses (electives or units within English classes) give added strength to reading instruction centered in content classes. Ten elective courses or units are briefly described in the box and more detailed plans for developing one of these, "Learning About Ourselves as Learners," appears between Chapters 6 and 7. Especially valuable to students continuing beyond high school are courses that brush up their study skills and rate of reading.

Effects of Competency Movements on Secondary Programs

Beginning in the 1970s and continuing into the 1980s, state-mandated competency testing swept the nation. In part a reaction to the anything-goes attitudes of the 1960s, in part a concern for minority youths' right to read, in part a further manifestation of the demand for accountability, the competency movement has been viewed with alarm by many educators, but endorsed by legislators, school boards and administrators, many parents, and especially by news columnists. On the whole, we believe that competency-testing mandates are proving a positive force for secondary school reading programs of the starter type. Ironically, the movement seems to have had largely negative effects on elementary schools, which have always given too much time to direct reading instruction and are now giving still more time to the "basics" at the expense of content, which furnishes the real reasons for learning to read in the first place.

However, among secondary school faculties that have been slow to admit any responsibility for teaching reading, the public pressure for minimal competency has led to worthwhile beginnings. Perhaps the experience of a small city in upstate New York is typical. When the school board ruled that graduation from high school should require a minimal level of reading achievement, set at eighth grade, they supported the expansion of reading programs in both the junior and senior high schools. What had been a remedial program restricted to the services of two teachers who "covered" five junior high schools was expanded to include a full-time reading teacher in each junior and senior high school. Each reading teacher was provided with a well-equipped center and aides to assist in organizing materials, monitoring students' individualized practice sessions, and keeping records. At first only students scoring two years below grade level on standardized tests were referred for additional testing and possible assignment to the centers. Over a period of five years, however, the remedial character of the program changed significantly. In each school the reading teachers were supported by a committee drawn from the content teachers, counselors, media specialists, and the administrators. Gradually, most teachers developed realistic notions of what students could achieve through the expanded reading services and, more important, they became aware of their responsibilities in working with underdeveloped readers. As students and parents became convinced that the school board was not simply setting standards but was willing to spend money on teachers, aides, and equipment, they borrowed confidence from the board's commitment. Emphasis on reading proficiency acted as both a carrot and a stick. Five years after the school board's mandate, graduating seniors were satisfying the minimal requirement in reading, the dropout rate had not increased, and few students were reaching twelfth grade still below the eighth grade standard. Of course, we cannot assume that every student who managed at least an eighth grade level on the standardized reading tests could actually read the local newspaper or a high school textbook. But the push for minimal competency in this instance is creating positive outcomes which are not limited to the reading program but are affecting the whole curriculum.

Staffing Secondary Reading Programs

The character of reading programs in early secondary years and in senior high schools can be seen in the job descriptions of personnel responsible for, or related to, particular programs. For this reason, in the following paragraphs, instead of describing various programs, we briefly describe what various staff members contribute to secondary programs, and refer you to a selective list of articles on page 190, Chapter 7, which describe in detail programs which we find commendable. Study also Boxes 5-8 and 5-9 that show how one middle school program expanded over an eight-year period.

To initiate or to expand a reading program beyond the elementary grades usually requires additional staffing, a condition that makes budget-minded school boards examine carefully the need for any kind of program. So secondary faculty and administrators who decide to move toward an all-school reading program should make very sure that additional personnel are necessary, thinking first of ways to maximize the effectiveness of present resources within present budgets. The following descriptions of personnel may guide such thinking.

Reading Consultant/Coordinator[3]   Large and middle-sized school systems usually have at least one reading coordinator who has responsibility for the K–12 program. Many split the job between two coordinators, K–6 and 7–12. Some have an elementary language arts coordinator and a secondary English supervisor in addition to, and sometimes instead of, the reading consultants. In situations where the coordinators' functions are largely supervisory, their chief responsibility is for staff development—visiting teachers' classrooms; responding to calls for help; evaluating, selecting, and distributing materials; arranging for schoolwide testing and sometimes for diagnoses of individual pupils; arranging for and often teaching in-service courses; applying for state and federal funds for research or special programs. Spread so thin, coordinators in large school districts spend more time in their offices or on the road between schools than they do in classrooms. They seldom have time to offer teachers the continuous help they need, and they almost never teach students themselves.

Reading consultants who get bogged down in administrivia are a luxury that few school systems can afford. In the long run, it is economical to design a position that focuses exclusively on one unit of the school at a time, so that the consultant can work with teachers closely and continuously. A secondary consultant is essential when the goal is to combine reading instruction with content and when teachers need to learn how to do it. A full-time on-site consultant is

---

[3]We use *coordinator* for the same position that many school districts designate as *consultant*. We use *consultant* also to refer to persons brought into a school system on a temporary basis to advise on programs and to conduct staff development.

BOX 5-8

A MIDDLE SCHOOL READING PROGRAM

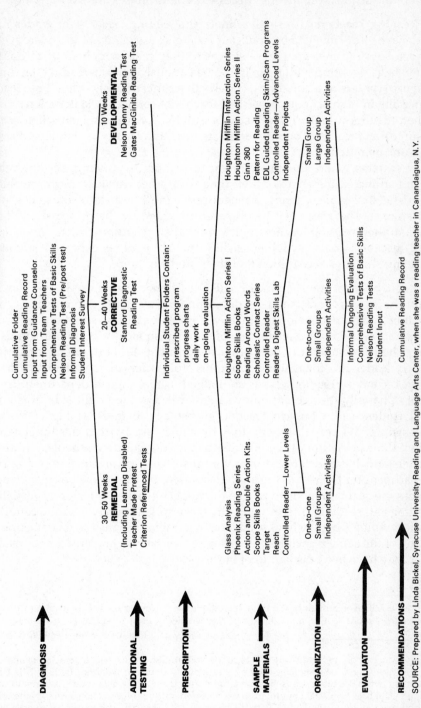

DIAGNOSIS

Cumulative Folder
Cumulative Reading Record
Input from Guidance Counselor
Input from Team Teachers
Comprehensive Tests of Basic Skills
Nelson Reading Test (Pre/post test)
Informal Diagnosis
Student Interest Survey

30–50 Weeks
REMEDIAL
(Including Learning Disabled)

20–40 Weeks
CORRECTIVE

10 Weeks
DEVELOPMENTAL

ADDITIONAL TESTING

Teacher Made Pretest
Criterion Referenced Tests

Stanford Diagnostic
Reading Test

Nelson Denny Reading Test
Gates MacGinitie Reading Test

PRESCRIPTION

Individual Student Folders Contain:
prescribed program
progress charts
daily work
on-going evaluation

SAMPLE MATERIALS

Glass Analysis
Phoenix Reading Series
Action and Double Action Kits
Scope Skills Books
Target
Reach
Controlled Reader—Lower Levels

Houghton Mifflin Action Series I
Scope Skills Books
Reading Around Words
Scholastic Contact Series
Controlled Reader
Reader's Digest Skills Lab

Houghton Mifflin Interaction Series
Houghton Mifflin Action Series II
Ginn 360
Pattern for Reading
EDL Guided Reading Skim/Scan Programs
Controlled Reader—Advanced Levels
Independent Projects

ORGANIZATION

One-to-one
Small Groups
Independent Activities

One-to-one
Small Groups
Independent Activities

Small Group
Large Group
Independent Activities

EVALUATION

Informal Ongoing Evaluation
Comprehensive Tests of Basic Skills
Nelson Reading Tests
Student Input

RECOMMENDATIONS

Cumulative Reading Record

SOURCE: Prepared by Linda Bickel, Syracuse University Reading and Language Arts Center, when she was a reading teacher in Canandaigua, N.Y.

better than a part-time person hired from a university or borrowed from another unit of the school system—but necessary compromises are worth trying.[4]

Reading Teachers   In small schools, the reading teachers for grades 7 and 8 and maybe 9 are likely to be "pull-out teachers" assigned to the underdeveloped readers. As the inelegant label suggests, they take students out of classes or study halls, working with them in rooms variously labeled: reading, learning, or resource centers or laboratories, (rarely clinics these days). Often these teachers, especially in high schools, are Title I teachers,[5] funded by state/federal monies. When they represent all that a school is doing for reading instruction, you can assume that the school board, administration, and faculty are largely uninvolved and uncommitted.

In systems where the commitment to reading is growing, reading teachers spend an increasing share of their time with other teachers. Inconceivable as it seems at first glance, many teachers resist the presence of outsiders in their classrooms. The way must be prepared for them by the principal and/or consultant; then reading teachers must prove their usefulness by recognizing content teachers' goals, avoiding clichés and a "reading expert's" jargon, and winning students' recognition that they can be of help.

English Department   Since English teachers are supposed to be concerned with the processes of language development, we cannot conceive of a sound reading program developing in any departmentalized situation without the cooperation and indeed leadership of the English faculty. (Good programs must have the cooperation of every other department, too, but we have no right to expect leadership for reading programs from science, say, or math teachers.) Most secondary reading efforts *are* lodged in the English department (see Box 5-2); unhappily they seldom move beyond it. On the bright side, it is good to find evidence that English teachers' resistance to the teaching of reading is weakening. Where it persists, that resistance arises from misunderstandings about the true nature of reading instruction in secondary schools, and from an understandable reluctance of many English teachers to function as the service department for the rest of the academic program. The whole point of "language across the curriculum" is to relieve the English teacher of *total* responsibility for writing and reading. Interestingly, the recent public outcry over the condition of literacy among high school graduates has rallied English teachers' support of many of the same principles (for example, "every teacher a teacher of reading") that they have been disdainful of in the past.

---

[4]For an excellent treatment of the consultant's role, see "Key Issues Facing Reading Consultants: Practical Solutions to Common Dilemmas" by Mikulecky et al in *Inchworm, Inchworm: Persistent Problems in Reading Education*, Constance McCullough, Editor, International Reading Association, Newark, Delaware, 1980.

[5]Title I was part of the Elementary and Secondary Education Act of 1965, federal legislation enacted to meet the special educational needs of educationally deprived children. In 1981 Title I became Chapter I of the Education Consolidation and Improvement Act, which stated its intent to continue financial aid based on Title I but to do so with less federal supervision and control. In the transition period, both labels—Title I and Chapter I—were used. Financial assistance goes to schools "with high concentrations of children with low-income families," as determined by state and local educational agencies. Teachers designated Title I were paid by federal funds; Chapter I, by state funds.

BOX 5-9

EVOLUTION OF A MIDDLE SCHOOL READING PROGRAM

Year	Schoolwide program		Title I* program	Summary of important changes
1	Remedial reading teacher	Separate reading classes 75 students		
2			Title I teacher — Students drawn from English classes 40 students	Title I added
3	2 reading teachers	Developmental and corrective Drawn from English 2 separate classrooms 140 students	Separate reading class 50 students	Reading teacher added Title I scheduled separately
4		Developmental, Corrective and Remedial Separately scheduled 2 separate classrooms Common planning time 350 students	45 students	Reading classes scheduled separately Schoolwide program expanded
5	3 reading teachers	Developmental, Corrective and Remedial 2 teachers share room 3 teachers coordinate program 580 students	Title I teacher and aide — 60 students	Another reading teacher and aide added 2 teachers share room Program expanded More coordination
6		Shared Title I students 640 students ←	→ 45 students	Sharing Title I students increased coordination of two programs
7	4 reading teachers	Share a lab room Common planning time 3 classrooms on same floor Consolidated materials and files All students (640)	45 students	4 teachers share lab Common planning Consolidation of materials
8	4 reading teachers (one—Title I) Aide, volunteers	2 large, adjoining classrooms with lab room Department coordination All students (640)		Volunteers added Common reading center Title I no longer separate

*See footnote 5, page 122.
SOURCE: Prepared by Linda Bickel, Syracuse University Reading and Language Arts Center, when she was a reading teacher in Canandaigua, N.Y.

Far from having to be wooed by the reading specialists, English teachers should be in the vanguard. And, of course, many of them are. They still make up the majority of secondary teachers in graduate reading courses and at reading conferences. The trouble is that many English teachers who become born-again reading experts leave their field behind them, never to return to positions of influence within the English department.

Since developmental reading has been lodged in the English department in most secondary schools that admit to having any program at all, and since most schools will not, and probably should not, hire reading teachers as "extras," we must improve English teachers' competence to teach reading and writing; but we should not expect them to hold reading certification of the same kind as that required of reading clinicians, coordinators, and resource teachers.

Remedial Teachers   Sometimes called reading resource teachers or specialists, these are highly qualified personnel capable of diagnosing and serving those adolescents who cannot read above a third grade level. Very few of the 23,000 secondary schools in the United States can afford these high-powered personnel, and there are not presently enough to go around in any case. Small schools look to cooperative arrangements with other schools (through regional organizations like the Bureaus of Cooperative Educational Services in New York State and intermediate district offices in Pennsylvania and other states) or to university and community centers for remedial services. As a rule, schools that employ remedial teachers should give them time to consult with classroom teachers. However, the more time remedial teachers spend in regular classrooms, the less remedial their services become. Gradually, many remedial teachers take on broader consultative roles and help schools move from a narrow remedial program to the ultimate goal of an all-school commitment to reading. In most secondary schools, however, the need for remedial services of some kind will persist no matter how proficient the preventive program in elementary grades becomes. See Chapters 7 and 8 for a more detailed description of these teachers' roles.

Media Specialists   Once known as librarians, the media specialists, whose domain includes all kinds of nonprint resources as well as books, are often in an excellent position to spark a whole-school reading program. Certainly, they know better than anyone else who chooses to read what—and why. In middle schools more often than in senior high schools, the media center sometimes includes teaching-to-read functions that go beyond the traditional roles served by librarians, even those who teach study skills. Our preference is to minimize this teaching-to-read function and to maximize the media specialist's unique opportunities to motivate students' learning. In either role, however, the media specialist is vital in the support network.

Guidance Counselors   Fifty years ago, when secondary reading was in its infancy, many programs began as an extension of counseling services. In postsecondary institutions, reading and study skills services are still likely to emanate from guidance and counseling services. The links between learning and counseling are vital, and no program can succeed without the support of the guidance staff.

Reading Committee   Whether the object is to initiate, improve, extend, or evaluate reading/study programs in small or large units, we recommend an active Reading Committee. (Better still, call it a Learning or Literacy Committee.)

It should be composed of representatives of all subject areas, all the personnel previously listed, and the administrators whose role we discuss below. We make this recommendation fully aware of the limitations of committees, their proliferating demands on our time and patience, their cold-molasses rate of progress, and the rank amateurism of most faculties with respect to group dynamics. Nevertheless, language/reading won't move across the curriculum without a committee to guide or push it. And, of course, someone has to keep pushing the committee.

The Key: Administrative Leadership

Like every other aspect of a good school, the reading program stands or falls on the quality of leadership. Administrative style affects all of the curriculum, but particularly influences learning-how-to-learn, which, as we have said, is not a "program" at all but a set of values shared by the whole staff. In a school where the administration is not committed to those values, you may find isolated instances of excellent teaching; but this is rarely so because good teachers desert poor schools—or lose their powers.

We speak here not solely out of personal conviction and experience. From various investigations into what makes a good school, the answer has come back again and again: the quality of leadership. One study characterized a good school as one in which the principal (1) promotes a learning climate that is orderly but not repressive; (2) places strong emphasis on acquiring, developing, and assessing literacy skills; and (3) encourages teachers to hold high expectations for their students. By contrast, in low-achieving schools the staff attributes students' learning problems to nonschool factors they believe are beyond their control, such as low IQ, nonstandard English, poor home background, and lack of motivation.

Since this book concerns the teaching of reading, we cannot elaborate on how the administrator achieves these three hallmarks of a good school. Obviously, some administrators possess the techniques for doing so and others do not, though probably every secondary school principal dreams of administering a school where students come willingly to learn. Apparently much can be achieved by principals who care enough to work at acquiring those techniques. "A caring principal," says Gerry Grant[6] in a line that speaks volumes, "is one who doesn't have his or her eye on the next rung of the ladder."

The administrators we refer to are at the building level, but their powers are constrained by the level above, that is, by the superintendent who chooses them and who controls the school board and budget. That person need not know the difference between building codes and structural codes, but he or she should know enough to listen to an advisory committee on students' learning needs (the Reading Committee), to evaluate the effectiveness of learning programs, and to persuade the public when programs need reform or reinforcement.

---

[6]Gerald Grant reporting on "What Makes a Good School," in Street Lecture at Syracuse University, November 1979.

Having hired the best possible potential teachers and principals, he or she should recognize the school system's responsibility for continuing their education.

As for building principals, they must know in far greater detail than the superintendent what constitutes a schoolwide language-in-learning policy and what it takes to create and sustain such a policy. To continue learning themselves, principals must be in and out of classrooms, talking with individual students about learning (not just about disciplinary matters) and frequently teaching groups and individuals. Given the constraints of time and energy, they will have to delegate some of their administrative duties to others in order to be free some of the time for teaching and learning. Administrators and teachers should always remember that in a learning climate, the staff as well as the students continue to learn.

Staff Development

Staff development has replaced *inservice education* as the catch-all term for describing ways in which teachers continue to learn. We use it here to refer chiefly to experiences in the school setting rather than to after-school workshops or courses or meetings of professional organizations such as the International Reading Association and the National Council of Teachers of English. Changes in teaching style and curricular content evolve gradually and are influenced much more by the school setting (one's students and colleagues, the physical resources available, and the community in which one works) than by ideas imported from afar and thrust upon a faculty that is not ready for them. Staff development can take many forms; we do not rule out inservice courses, professional days sprinkled over the school calendar, the occasional lecture or demonstration by the visiting expert, or visits to exemplary programs. These activities can catalyze ideas that are just forming in teachers' minds, or they can boost teachers' morale by affirming their long-time intuitions and practices. But they are limited to the extent that they are intermittent rather than continuous.

From what we have said earlier about teachers' growth on the job, you know how much we value staff development. But let us reiterate the point here. Because we believe that the success of secondary reading programs depends on what content teachers learn about the teaching of reading/study skills, we consider ideas for staff development to be of crucial importance to every person in the field of reading.

General Principles

No matter what form staff development takes, it should observe general principles such as these:

+ Values we teach by should be examined from time to time; because life styles change, students do, too.

+ The preservice preparation of secondary teachers rightfully emphasizes what is to be taught, and can only hint at how it should be done, through brief periods of student teaching and a handful of education courses.

✤ Since preservice preparation emphasizes content, most teachers have to learn on the job the processes involved in reading and writing.

✤ The best way to learn about a process is to take part in it. Teachers should examine their own study processes and do a lot of writing and reading in staff development sessions.

✤ Inservice study of learning *processes* should result in *products* teachers can use, such as planning guides, lessons geared to their students' needs, adaptation of text materials, and so on.

✤ Staff development should take place within the teachers' working day. Professionals, of course, continue studying and learning their craft even after hours; this cannot be assigned or enforced, however.

✤ Learning how to teach occurs most effectively in the teachers' own classrooms, with their students present, with their materials, and within their time constraints.

✤ Teachers learn from each other. This cannot be prevented. What is learned can be positive rather than negative, given the right school climate; but beyond incidental learning from each other, only careful planning will ensure that *good* teachers teach other teachers.

✤ Teachers are as individual as the students they teach; their learning styles will be as varied as their students'. How well do we respect individual differences in teachers' learning?

✤ Teachers who cannot or will not learn should not teach. Nor should they become administrators or consultants!

✤ A learning climate for the staff requires flexible scheduling, with opportunities for team teaching, planning and study sessions, and considerable extra help. For example, clerical help and/or teacher aides may be essential to teachers' growth on the job.

✤ Some time during a teacher's year should be reserved for thinking about teaching in situations free from actual teaching responsibilities. This implies summer workshops or weekend retreats as *part* of continuous staff development, not as the whole of it.

✤ Studying how to teach while you are doing it means understanding the rigors of disciplined inquiry. Teachers have much to tell researchers, but they also need the services of statisticians and other kinds of researchers to aid their inquiries.

✤ Budget plays a major role. Teachers should contribute to budgetary decisions, considering, for example, whether an expensive reading laboratory is as much needed as, say, clerical assistance or the advice of an experienced team of teachers from the next county.

✤ Personal learning of many kinds can give teachers insights into students' learning processes. Learning to act, speak French, play a musical instrument, design a dress, excavate an archeological site, research the history of a local industry, supervise a field trip to Scandinavia or Samoa—any such learning experience that teachers choose may contribute to the reading program if someone makes the connections.

✤ Staff development, which is continuous and incidental, must also be structured and scheduled. We suggest planning ahead in five-year spans—an early task for the Reading Committee. Plans are subject to change, of course, but somewhere in the principal's office should be a map of what lies ahead.

✤ Staff development plans should be long-range but flexible. Before reacting in panic to the latest local editorial on the decline and fall of literacy, a school staff should examine all the pieces of the plan for staff development and determine which piece should be brought forward this year for public scrutiny.

✤ Wherever possible, staff development projects should involve students and parents.

Goals for Staff Development in Reading

Most of the preceding principles apply to staff development in many areas besides reading. Specifically, staff development focused on improving the teaching of reading should aim at having the whole school staff—

1. understand how language affects learning;
2. agree on goals to be expected of various types of students;
3. accept that the whole staff contribute in different ways to students' abilities in reading, writing, and studying;
4. determine fair and practicable measures of students' progress in using language as a way of learning.

Stating principles, of course, is a snap compared to implementing them. Implementation requires energy, skill in human relations, common sense, determination, drive, knowledge of resources, humor, enthusiasm, a sense of timing, intelligence, self-confidence—and friends! Fortunately, some people muster all these resources and do, in fact, create secondary schools where teachers continue to learn, grow, and transmit to students their own enthusiasm for learning. In the following discussion, we summarize a few of the various schemes for staff development aimed at reading/study programs.

Team Planning

A large middle school in a suburban district is divided into three houses, each containing about 125 students per grade level. The principal has devised a schedule in which teachers at each grade level teach five classes and attend one planning period daily. In these planning periods, the teachers of reading, English, math, science, and social studies meet regularly, sometimes joined by staff members from art, physical education, guidance, and the media center. During informal sessions, the teachers share diagnostic information, tell each other what they are assigning, plan units which correlate English and social studies, for instance, or math and science. The reading teacher is a constant resource, and the content teachers, through studying the diagnostic profiles of students whom they all know, have learned much about processes of reading, writing, and studying.

Team Teaching

A senior high school staff approached the problem of teaching reading in the content fields first through their social studies teachers. Prodded by the principal and the reading consultant, five social studies teachers volunteered to take a university course, "Reading and Study in the Secondary School," during a six-week summer session. When classes were scheduled for the next year, the five teachers were assigned four classes each instead of the usual five. In place of the fifth class, each was assigned to team teach with a colleague who had not had the benefit of the methods course, thereby extending the benefits of the course to five additional social studies teachers during the first year. Team teaching in just one class reduced the hazards of trying out a new relationship. At the same time, this each-one-teach-one arrangement gave both members of the team a chance to learn from each other, adapting materials from the summer course to fit a real situation. Not all five partnerships were uniformly successful, but the experiment stimulated sufficient interest among the rest of the faculty that it was repeated the following year with a new set of teachers, this time from the science department. With a competent consultant in the district to give advice when called upon, this secondary school staff seems well on the way to an all-school program that incorporates both direct instruction and application in the content fields.

Reading Teachers in Regular Classrooms

A small 9–12 high school had only one reading teacher, and he was funded by Title I. He found the rest of the faculty indifferent to his efforts and not at all ready to think of themselves as teachers of reading as well as content. Along with the principal, the faculty assumed that if anything could be done with below-level readers, the reading teacher, backed by state and federal funds, was the one to do it. The Title I teacher knew the importance of reaching the content teachers but was frustrated in his attempts to lure them into his reading center or to engage them in professional discussion in the faculty room. He concentrated first on the principal, whom he convinced that he should have a couple of free periods in his schedule, provided he kept the same number of students. He used these "free" periods to follow selected students into their other classes, explaining to each teacher that he was there to observe the student's use of language skills. Gradually, he drew the visited teacher into discussing the student's progress and the teacher's goals. Occasionally, he could provide materials that the content teacher could use with other students. From this modest beginning, the reading teacher's role changed until he became a resource for many teachers. His aim is to do more team teaching with content teachers, thereby enlarging his knowledge as well as theirs and expanding his services to a much larger segment of the student body.

Introducing Reading to Content Teachers

A university reading team introduced all the teachers in the ninth grade of a city high school to the idea of integrating reading instruction with content. During the first half of the school year, the team visited with administrators and teachers, carefully laying groundwork for the effort to be launched in January. At midyear they were ready to open a Learning Center for all ninth graders. In one large classroom they had installed study carrels, reading texts and workbooks, a library of paperbacks and magazines, and a modest collection of filmstrip projectors, rate controllers, tape cassettes, and headsets. As an opening gambit, they invited all ninth graders and their parents to a party in the Learning Center and explained how it would serve them. Under the supervision of one reading teacher, the center would be open all day to students who could use it for study purposes as well as for improving their reading skills. Graduate students from the university aided the reading teacher in diagnosis and corrective practice, working with individuals and small groups. Although the center functioned legitimately as a service to students, its real purpose was to free content teachers for intensive study of reading theory and practice. For three weeks, the social studies teachers became students in a full-day workshop taught by university instructors. Their students went to the Learning Center during their social studies period. At the end of three weeks, English teachers replaced the social studies teachers in the workshop, and in fifteen weeks five sets of teachers had each spent three weeks learning how to integrate reading instruction with their content. During these classes, the teachers devised study guides and other materials related to their content, which effectively stressed strategies for learning from text. When they needed to try out these materials with their students, they could find them in the Learning Center.

This plan forced all content teachers in the ninth grade to meet head on the question of whether they should (and could) teach students how to study the materials of their course. Not all teachers entered the program enthusiastically, but after three weeks most of them left the workshop understanding what is meant by an "all-school reading program," equipped with techniques and materials which they had prepared themselves, and convinced that any effort they gave to teaching students how to read their textbooks would result in increased learning of content.[7]

Using the Outside Consultant

The foregoing plan illustrates one way in which schools can use consultants from a university reading center. There are many other ways, of course. At some schools consultants initiate staff development by surveying the achievement of the students, the attitudes of the teachers, and the resources at hand. Often the consultant gets a reading committee started and helps it to interpret the results

---

[7]The program described was set up in East Syracuse–Minoa School District with the guidance of Harold L. Herber and doctoral students from the Reading and Language Arts Center, Syracuse University.

of a survey, draw up recommendations, and begin to implement them. Some schools bring in consultants to work closely with individual students and to discuss the resulting case studies as a means of initiating staff development. Instead of attempting to involve whole faculties immediately, some consultants prefer to engage only the administrative personnel in continuing discussions of issues and solutions. In one school system, a university consultant was invited to meet once a week for lunch with changing groups of teachers to discuss in a very informal manner their questions and concerns. Whatever the plan, most consultants would agree that their services are most valuable when administrators and faculty have figured out how these services can be delivered during the school day, not after hours, and over a period of time that allows for both preparation and follow up.

Teachers as Students of Process

Teachers can learn a great deal about the processes of reading and writing by becoming students themselves. Instead of a methods course in how to teach reading and study skills, teachers may enroll in a course to improve their own reading or writing. It may be a speed reading course offered as part of the adult education program. It may be a course in writing reports or in writing for young readers. One language arts consultant persuaded a professional writer to give a course for the administrators in her district. They were anxious to improve their own skills in communicating with the public, and through learning about their own writing processes they enlarged their understanding of instructional programs in writing and reading, too.

Faculty Study Groups

A form of staff development that we strongly recommend is self-directed study groups, but we recognize that in teachers' busy lives these are unlikely to spring up spontaneously. They need direction and rewards. A skillful administrator can supply both, and eventually study groups should be their own reward. One principal initiated study groups by scheduling them during "free" periods, supplying books and articles to be read, and finding a discussion leader within each group. (At first the principal herself served in this role.) In another situation a television course on teaching reading in secondary schools became the focal point. Arrangements were made to rent kinescopes from the PBS (Public Broadcasting Service) channel which had sponsored the course through a university reading department. These were shown on a repeated schedule during the school day, and small group discussions were coordinated with the showings. When faculty requested them, the consultants who had developed the TV course were called in.

Reading Coordinators' Workshops

The reading coordinator in a midwestern high school persuaded his administration that the best way to reach content teachers was to run small workshops for them during the school day. By manipulating the schedule, the principal secured thirty minutes' "free time" for every content teacher. The reading coordinator then scheduled groups of teachers by subject and grade level, meeting four of these groups daily over a period of eight weeks. In a year's time he was thus able to work closely and continuously with more than a hundred faculty members. Working with small groups that shared common goals, he concentrated on developing study guides and other materials and practices which would provide for the range of differences in the teachers' classes. Because these workshops required two hours of his time every day, he could teach only one reading class for students and still have time available to follow up his workshop sessions in the teachers' classes.

Teacher Centers

Reading personnel in secondary schools and in teacher education have taken advantage of teacher centers, which are vehicles for staff development. Increasingly popular in the last decade, teacher centers have taken a variety of forms. In one model, a School of Education and a school district jointly sponsor a center which is managed by a director who reports to a board composed of faculty and administrators from the university and the school district. Among the purposes of this center is to provide field experiences for students in Education; the result has been a merging of preservice and inservice education, which is especially useful in furthering the growth of secondary reading programs in this school district. Students from the university assist the school's reading teachers in diagnosing individuals and setting up appropriate plans for improving their skills; they also work with content teachers in interpreting and implementing these plans. Instructors from the university reading and language arts staff present series of lectures and demonstrations at the request of faculty; and they assist the district's reading and language consultants as they select materials, order equipment, and set up schoolwide assessments. What makes teacher centers vital instruments of staff development is that they are run by teachers and respond to teachers' needs—although they reach beyond the school setting whenever necessary to bring in expert help.

Teacher-Centered Research

Teachers' participation in research or "disciplined inquiry" can yield at least two benefits: one for the field of secondary reading and one for the teachers themselves. Researchers have studied beginning reading and the reading of adults more diligently than they have studied reading in the secondary school. We need to know far more than we now do about the process of reading beyond the beginning stage and prior to fluent or mature reading. We know very little of how adolescents learn from text and how they use what they learn in speaking, writing, and further learning. We don't know very much about how teachers affect the learning process, and we have very little hard data to support recommendations relating to programs and personnel.

Secondary teachers can contribute richly to this needed research. They can identify important questions that research might answer. They can share with psychologists, sociologists, and psycholinguists what they have already observed of students' habits, attitudes, and strategies of learning. However, although teachers often know what works and what doesn't work in classrooms, they may not know why and may not trouble to find out. It is easy to suggest reasons why most teachers have not been actively involved in research. There are the constraints of time and budget, fear of statistics and other research tools, disappointment with the few studies we share with them, and distrust of findings which seem to contradict teachers' experiences. Most of all there is the lack of communication between teachers and researchers. "What does research tell the teacher?" is a popular topic in journals and at professional meetings. But a more appropriate question might be: "What does the teacher ask of research?"

Involving teachers in research requires a leader—perhaps the reading consultant or an administrator—who can convince them that the study is immediately practical, that it seeks answers to important questions, that it needs their advice from the beginning, and that it can be accomplished without undue hardship for them or their students. To satisfy the last condition, the administrator may need to provide released time, clerical help, statisticians, computers, and expert advice. Brainstorming with a group of content teachers, reading teachers, and consultants would yield dozens of questions suitable for research in a particular setting. The next step would be to set up a practicable study, calling in expert advice on research design. By working with the data and interpreting the results, teachers would grow measurably in their understanding of process and programs in reading. Staff development must go beyond listening, reading, and discussing. At some point and to some degree, teachers must be actively involved in finding out why—engaged, that is, in "disciplined inquiry."

Your Role in the Reading Program

You are not alone. Especially, when you teach reading in a secondary school, you function as part of a team. If you are a reading teacher, your chances of success with any student are affected by the five or six other teachers with whom that student spends the rest of the day. If you are a content teacher, your goal is to assist students to learn from text. You will be more likely to achieve that goal with those hundred or more individuals you're responsible for if you can turn to reading/learning specialists for guidance. In turn, you must contribute to the concept of secondary reading instruction by

+ sharing your observations of how students learn.
+ expressing your ideas of how teachers affect learning.
+ trying new materials and approaches to improve students' reading and study strategies.

As a first step, we hope you'll continue to learn from this text, observing as you do so *how* you learn from text.

RECAPPING MAIN POINTS

The individual differences of teachers as well as of students must be considered in planning reading instruction. This is especially true for secondary schools, where content teachers must teach reading to students representing extreme differences in abilities, achievement, interests, and backgrounds. In organization as well as population, schools that serve grades 5 through 12 are diverse institutions.

However, one common characteristic of school organization is the division of the curriculum into separate content areas, each taught by different teachers. In many school systems, departmentalization begins as early as grade 5. Departmentalizing increases the number of students each teacher must respond to individually, erects barriers between subjects in the curriculum, makes transfer of learning more difficult to achieve, and can result in both duplication and neglect of particular skills and knowledge. To counteract these disadvantages of departmentalizing, teachers must recognize language learning as basic to all subjects, work in teams wherever possible, and coordinate instruction across subjects as well as between grade levels.

From fifth grade to twelfth, teaching reading as a separate "subject" must give way to teaching reading in content classes. At the present time, however, most middle and junior high schools assign all students in grades 5, 6, 7 and sometimes 8 to separate classes for reading; many senior high schools have remedial or corrective classes. As the requirement of at least minimal levels of literacy for graduation has become widespread, so have "competency classes" in junior and senior high school.

Schools that employ no reading teachers probably depend on English teachers for direct instruction in reading. Whether or not special reading classes exist or the English curriculum includes instruction in how to read and study, content teachers are responsible for teaching reading along with their subjects. It cannot be assumed, however, that most content teachers either accept the responsibility or know how to apply it effectively.

There is no one best way to organize a reading program in secondary schools. Programs must be shaped according to a particular school's budget, student population, faculty, and support staff. The building principal is the key to the success of a reading program, but he or she must have moral and financial support from the superintendent and school board. Staffing a secondary reading program varies according to the school's size and budget. In addition to the regular faculty, most programs require the services of a full-time or part-time reading coordinator, possibly a visiting consultant, reading teachers, one or more clinicians, teachers' aides and volunteers, media specialists, guidance counselors, and a reading committee.

No secondary reading program is likely to succeed over time without continuous staff development. Among many kinds of staff development, team planning and team teaching are highly recommended. Other possibilities are (1) faculty study groups, (2) pairing reading and content teachers, (3) having teachers and administrators take courses to improve their own reading and writing, (4) engaging in classroom research, (5) organizing workshops and inservice courses, (6) observing programs in other schools, (7) calling in consultants from other schools, universities, publishers, and from district, county or state educational services.

FOR DISCUSSION

1. Visit a middle school or a junior or senior high school to collect information about the reading program, which you can share with your discussion group. Interview the principal, media specialist, guidance counselor, and chair of the English department in addition to reading teachers and aides. Ask about philosophy, goals, scheduling, materials, and the attitudes of faculty and students toward reading instruction. Try to arrange future visits in which you can observe classes.

2. Why is continuous staff development essential to maintaining sound reading programs in secondary schools? Of the several kinds of staff development discussed in this chapter, which appeal most strongly to you? Why? Add other ideas for staff development to the suggestions in this chapter.

3. What views of secondary education are held by opinion leaders in your community? Are they concerned about literacy and the teaching of reading? Consider these sources: files of local newspapers; calls to school board members and the superintendent of schools; interviews with officers of local or state teachers' organizations, including International Reading Association councils; the journals of state teachers' associations.

4. Read one or more of the journal articles listed on page 190 of Chapter 7 and report orally or in writing on the reading program(s) described therein. Review issues of the *Education Index* published since the most recent date of the articles listed on page 190 and add to this bibliography newer articles describing secondary reading programs. Be selective. Not all articles offer new information or give enough details to be helpful.

5. Why have secondary school reading programs developed so slowly over the last four or five decades? Consider these factors: changing school populations, teachers' attitudes, public expectations, school budgets, and others. Why do you think the pace of development will (or will not) accelerate in the immediate future?

FURTHER READING

Berger, Allen, and H. Alan Robinson, eds. *Secondary School Reading*. Urbana, IL: National Council of Teachers of English, 1982.

In this collection of essays two are relevant to the present chapter: "Organization and Management of Programs" by Joan Nelson and Harold Herber and "Specialized Services" by Virginia Palmer and Virginia M. Brannock.

Herber, Harold L. *Teaching Reading in Content Areas*, 2nd ed. Englewood Cliffs, NJ: Prentice-Hall, 1978.
   See especially Chapter 2, "Significant Problems/Promising Solutions."

Mikulecky, Larry J., Patricia Anders, Linda Ramig, and Norma Rogers. "Key Issues Facing Reading Consultants: Practical Solutions to Common Dilemmas" in *Inchworm, Inchworm: Persistent Problems in Reading Education*, Constance McCullough, ed. Newark, DE: International Reading Association, 1980.

Singer, Harry, and Dan Donlan. *Reading and Learning from Text*. Boston: Little, Brown, 1980.
   Chapters 1 and 2 treat issues raised in the chapter you have just read.

Thomas, Ellen Lamar, and H. Alan Robinson. *Improving Reading in Every Class*, 3rd ed. Boston: Allyn and Bacon, 1982.
   First author was the reading consultant for the University of Chicago Laboratory School. This is a practical text for reading specialists working with teachers in all content fields; especially practical suggestions on role of "non-academic" teachers.

6 Assessment and Evaluation in the Whole-School Program[1]

Joe Grabowski stood in the faculty room of Riverdale Junior High School drinking coffee, staring at the cars in the parking lot but not thinking about them. He was nearing the end of his third year of teaching. A biology major, with a minor in Education, he'd taken this job teaching general science to seventh and eighth graders because the year he graduated there were no openings in this system at the senior high level. As it turned out, Joe liked the school; he liked the kids and he enjoyed teaching. But today he was glum. Turning to Sam Kincaid, he vented his concern.

"That faculty meeting yesterday—about how our kids aren't scoring high enough on the reading tests. I know the kids in 7–C would do better in class if they could read the text, but I don't know the first thing about teaching reading. And I really don't know why I should have to learn. I was hired to teach science. Why should I spend next year in a staff development project on how to teach reading? If the kids can't read, they need more reading teachers. So—I know—the budget's strained as it is. Then why don't the elementary teachers do a better job? What do you think about this staff development business, Sam?"

"I used to feel pretty much the way you do, but that was before I took a week's seminar on improving math teaching. It was offered by the school district a couple of summers ago, before you got here, Joe. One of the five days was on how we could be more effective with low achievers just by taking a little extra time to help them use their textbooks. I began to do some of the things they talked about. Just little things, like showing the kids how to use the glossary during the first week of school and then using it in class regularly to look up words I'd be using in developing concepts. Another little thing that really pays off is checking to make sure all the kids know how to read a table before turning them loose with an assignment that requires them to use it. I used to assume that all the kids had learned these things before coming to junior high. Now I know a

---

[1] We use *assessment* to refer to measuring students' abilities before instruction; we apply *evaluation* to programs as well as to students' growth after instruction.

lot of them don't have good learning habits, and most of them forget to use what they *have* learned. I tell you, Joe, that one day with the district reading staff helped me to be a better math teacher. So I don't know about next year. I think maybe we'll learn something from the experience, but I worry, too. We don't want the math and science curriculum to suffer from this big to-do about reading."

There are lots of Joes around, not so many Sams. Nevertheless, this exchange between Joe and Sam represents the way many secondary teachers react to the idea that they should teach reading. Many are confused and angry, some are cautiously optimistic, and others remain passively resistant, thinking: "This too will pass, if we wait long enough." That's why "every teacher a teacher of reading" is a slogan to be avoided. Like most slogans, it oversimplifies. Not every teacher in the secondary school needs to teach reading, certainly not beginning reading; yet all teachers are concerned with how their students learn. Because reading and writing, as well as listening and speaking, are tools for learning, these language skills must figure prominently in teachers' efforts to improve learning. All teachers, we believe, define their roles as helping students to learn whatever subject they teach, and all good teachers want to become better at the "midwifery of ideas," as one writer, tongue in cheek, translated *maieutic* (bringing out ideas latent in the mind) and applied it to the teacher's profession.

Accountability and the Increase in Testing

Today, as never before, teachers are being held accountable for how well their students learn. After all, it is teachers who are directly responsible for planning and delivering instruction as well as for evaluating learning. "To read, to communicate, to compute, to make judgments, and to take actions resulting from them: these are legitimate expectations for our high school graduates in America in the late twentieth century," writes Patricia Graham, former head of the National Institute for Education (NIE), in the first sentence of an essay in which she argues that literacy, thus broadly defined, is the primary obligation of high schools today. Because high schools serve almost all our population, educators have been unwilling to commit them to a single overriding aim such as literacy for all. Graham recognizes that asking high schools to adopt this goal is asking them to try something that they have never undertaken before. We don't know, therefore, whether they can succeed. (See Box 6-1.) But in almost every state, schools are being required to show evidence of their students' literacy.

So far, and with considerable variation from state to state, competency tests have required students to demonstrate minimum levels of literacy—for example, to comprehend consumer "literature" such as recipes, directions, advertisements; to write letters expressing opinions, interests, and concerns; to recognize basic concepts of mathematics and perform basic computations. In short, the tests seek confirmation that schooling ensures that every student will achieve the levels of literacy necessary to participate in today's society. With this kind of pressure from state legislatures, it is not surprising that school administrators, who are also pressed by tightening budgets, are urging teachers in every

BOX 6-1

THE GOAL OF LITERACY

Many Americans today complain bitterly about the inadequacies of high schools and about the unsatisfactory preparation of high-school graduates. Such criticism of schools or concern about the young is not new; it is most common at times when substantial "new populations," such as immigrant, minority, or poor youngsters, are completing school. . . . For high schools to accept literacy as a primary aim for their graduates, to develop community support for such a goal, and then to demonstrate that they fulfill it would be vital steps in assuring young people that they are not being cheated educationally; it would also assure the communities they serve that the schools were assuming one, if not all, of their responsibilities.

SOURCE: Patricia Albjerg Graham, "Literacy: A Goal for Secondary Schools" in *Daedalus* (Summer 1981).

subject to provide instruction that extends students' competence in reading and writing as well as in knowledge of subject matter. Even in school systems that can afford them, administrators and school boards are recognizing that reading teachers alone cannot guarantee the universal literacy that Graham and others contend should be the primary goal of secondary schools.

Nor is public concern for education limited to the achievement of minimal skills. To be sure, the competency movement began with an emphasis on "survival skills," an emphasis that has met widespread criticism. New York State's first competency test in 1975 was branded "incompetent" by its critics; consequently, the difficulty of the math, reading, and writing sections has been increased over the years until it has become what many consider the stiffest minimum competency test in the nation. Of course, making the tests harder is a move toward placating only one set of critics—those who charge the competency movement with debasing standards for all students. Meanwhile, those who oppose inflexible standards for all are merely hardened in their opposition by the trend toward rising minimal requirements. Since our purpose here is not to debate the pro's and con's of competency testing but to acknowledge its current influence on secondary schools, we refer you to Box 6-2, which reproduces the position taken by the International Reading Association. Suffice it to say that the competency movement, whether or not it is here to stay, has already nudged many secondary teachers toward assuming responsibility for literacy skills.

Similarly, public alarm at declining scores on college entrance examinations has provided further impetus for reform in secondary schools. Like the tests of basic competencies, the Scholastic Aptitude Tests are not designed to measure students' recall of information from content courses. Instead, they measure ability to recognize a wide range of information (for example, through vocabulary and analogy items), to use background knowledge to comprehend reading passages, to employ logical thought processes, and to solve problems. Thus the scores on these tests reflect general attainment in vocabulary, reasoning, and reading comprehension. And all teachers, elementary through secondary, share

BOX 6-2

ON TESTING MINIMUM COMPETENCIES

No single measure or method of assessment of minimum competencies should ever be the sole criterion for graduation or promotion of a student. Multiple indices assessed through a variety of means, including teacher observations, student work samples, past academic performance, and student self-reports, should be employed to assess competence.

Furthermore, every effort should be made through every possible means to remediate weaknesses diagnosed through tests. Retention in grade or non-promotion of a student should be considered as only an alternate means of remediation and one that should be considered only when all other available methods have failed.

For these reasons, the Board of Directors of the International Reading Association is firmly opposed to the efforts of any school, state, provincial or national agency which attempts to determine a student's graduation or promotion on the basis of any single assessment.

SOURCE: The Board of Directors of the International Reading Association, "A Position on Minimum Competencies in Reading," *Journal of Reading*, 23:1 (October 1979):51.

in the credit or blame that accompanies any trends in national averages. It should be noted that the decline in SAT scores that began in 1963 was halted in 1980, but at this writing an upward trend has not yet begun.

Another testing program, the National Assessment of Educational Progress (NAEP), continues to keep the public as well as the schools alert to the achievement of 9-, 13-, and 17-year-olds, not only in reading, writing, and mathematics, but in all school subjects. NAEP reports in recent years have not been encouraging so far as the critical reading, reasoning abilities, and writing skills of 13- and 17-year-olds are concerned.

A Typical (Limited) Reading Program

Against this background, the principal and district administrators in our hypothetical situation have been setting plans for staff development next year—which will engage all the faculty in the improvement of reading and related language skills. Riverdale, a 7–9 junior high school, already has the beginnings of a whole-school reading program. Its trained reading teachers provide developmental classes for all students in grades 7 and 8; English teachers in grade 9 schedule a three-week unit in reading and study skills in September and again in January.

Because all seventh and eighth graders in this suburban junior high are scheduled for reading classes, no class is designated "remedial" or "corrective," but the poorest readers in each grade are assigned to the smallest classes with a teacher trained in a university reading clinic. The suite of classrooms and offices called the Reading Center is well furnished for small-group instruction and is well supplied with instructional materials including basal series and high interest/low vocabulary texts, reference resources, and files of Learning Activity

Packages (LAPs) developed by the reading teachers. Some LAPs give practice in skills used in reading math, science, and social studies textbooks; others feature more general learning skills in packets like "How to Study for a Test" or "Taking Notes and Making Outlines."

The Reading Center also provides for out-of-school reading interests with racks of popular paperbacks, a wide assortment of magazines including national news magazines geared to the reading interests and abilities of 12-to-15-year-olds, and, of course, local newspapers.

Report card grades in reading are based on students' accomplishment of specific objectives established by agreement between themselves and their reading teachers. These individual objectives are decided upon after studying a student's performance on both standardized and informal tests. Progress is assessed both by performance on daily work and by assessment packets that include some teacher-made tests as well as tests culled from workbooks and provided with basal series.

Briefly, that's the setting of the "direct instruction" program at Riverdale; it is not a whole-school program because it is only very tenuously related to the rest of the curriculum. The staff development planned for the coming year has four purposes: (1) evaluating the quality of the direct-instruction program and relating its objectives to the rest of the faculty; (2) studying how learning in the content fields can be improved if the content teachers make use of some of the strategies developed by the reading teachers; (3) deciding whether all or part of the direct-instruction program should be confined to the Reading Center; (4) laying plans for the next several years that will put Riverdale on a direct course toward a whole-school reading program.

The rest of this book is devoted to many of the issues with which the Riverdale staff will have to wrestle as they work toward improving their services to all students. This chapter takes up the first of these issues: assessing students' needs and making decisions based on the results of such assessments.

The Place to Begin: Assessing Needs

The first thing reading teachers want to know is how well their students use language skills in learning. The first thing content teachers want to know is how much their students have already learned about their subject, but they also want to know how capable students are of learning new content. Adolescents want to know who they are, what they can do, and where they are going. In the best of situations, these three groups (reading teachers, content teachers, and adolescents) would have their questions answered by working together on assessment and sharing their findings. Assessment of needs—sometimes called diagnosis or, more simply, analysis—is so important that we treat it in three places: in this chapter, where we address the content teachers' concerns; in Chapter 7, where the emphasis is on remedial readers; and in the between-chapters unit, Learning About Ourselves as Learners, where we describe how students can assess their own language performances. Because all three foci employ some of the same instruments and techniques, we shall cross-reference to avoid duplication.

This chapter considers published instruments which can be administered to whole groups. The next chapter discusses diagnostic instruments, most of which must be individually administered. Teacher-made tests are recommended in the unit on learning and are also illustrated in Chapters 12 to 15.

Standardized Tests

Every school system today uses standardized achievement tests to document students' current levels of achievement and growth over time. Because standardized tests, especially reading tests, are so widely used and so often misused, we urge you to understand their limitations as well as their legitimate uses. First we ask you to consult the test results in students' records (sometimes kept in the guidance office and not shared with teachers unless they insist). Then we warn you that individual test scores are not very reliable and can mislead you in estimating a student's ability. And you react: What good are they? Why should I waste my time studying students' scores if I can't trust them?

Standardized tests of reading achievement are among the best measurements we have in education, the result of many decades of experiment and refinement of testing procedures. The best of them are reliable measures for comparing the performance of one group against norms provided by other students' performances. The average score of all tenth graders in School A is a reliable score which can be compared with the average score of all the tenth graders in the norming population. The norms which offer the most meaningful interpretation to the teachers and administrators in School A are those derived from students most like the population of School A. That is, local norms developed over the years by a single school district or a group of districts with similar characteristics are better yardsticks than "national" norms, which are sometimes skewed ethnographically.

If standardized tests are intended to measure changes in groups, not individuals, why do we use them in making decisions about individuals? Because they offer *additional* information, of a very general nature, which may support (or contradict) observations of a student's abilities based on informal measures and teachers' reports. When planning for a new class, a teacher studies the range of reading scores and makes some guesses about the range of readable text materials that will be appropriate. We shall have more to say about interpreting test scores in the next section, but first we remind you of the limitations of reading tests.

Someone has called standardized tests "elastic yardsticks," capturing well the notion that measuring skills and knowledge is not an exact science. At best, reading tests take a sampling of students' knowledge of vocabulary, for instance, and their ability to recognize "right" answers after reading a passage which may or may not treat a subject that is familiar to them. Because tests must be administered in class periods of less than fifty minutes, reading passages are short, much shorter than typical reading assignments in secondary schools. Powers of concentration are not pushed as hard by tests as by homework. Multiple-choice items, the common pattern for objective testing, reflect the item-writer's understanding of the passage, not necessarily the test-taker's interpretation; especially with tests requiring inferential thinking, good scores go

BOX 6-3

SOME STANDARDIZED READING TESTS (GROUP SURVEY TESTS)

Note: Some widely used reading tests are a part of achievement batteries; others are published as single measures. Both types are included in the following selections.

California Achievement Tests. (Monterey, CA: California Test Bureau/McGraw-Hill, 1978).

Levels 4–19 (grades K–12.9) measure achievement of students in reading, language arts, math and reference skills. Overlapping levels permit individual students to be tested at an appropriate difficulty level. In addition to norm-referenced scores, anticipated achievement scores for individual students may be obtained by relating CAT scores to performance on Short Form Test of Academic Aptitude. The reading portion of the battery consists of two subtests: vocabulary (same, opposite and multiple meanings) and comprehension (literal, interpretive and critical reading).

Degrees of Reading Power Tests. College Entrance Examination Board, 1982. Distributed by DRP Services, The College Board, 888 Seventh Avenue, New York, NY 10106.

A new kind of test for students in grades 4–12, the Degrees of Reading Power program purports to match students' reading ability with the readability levels of school texts. Each DRP test is made up of a number of prose nonfiction selections each about 325 words long, each at a different level of difficulty, presented from easy to challenging. Seven sentences in each passage contain a blank to be filled by selecting from five single-word responses the one word which fits the meaning of the passage. All choices are common words and each fits the syntax of the sentence. The correct response, therefore, depends on the reader's understanding of the passage, not on vocabulary. The total number of correct items is converted to a DRP score which can be matched to DRP Readability scores. A Readability Report is published annually and gives a DRP readability covering more than 2,000 texts (1982–1983). Used together, the tests and the Readability Report should enable teachers to determine the texts which are at students' mastery, instructional, and frustration levels.

Gates–MacGinitie Reading Tests. Arthur Gates and Walter MacGinitie. (Boston: Houghton Mifflin, 1978).

Comprised of four primary levels and Survey D (grades 4–6), Survey E (7–9) and Survey F (10–12). Surveys D and E have three forms and Survey F has two forms. Speed and accuracy, vocabulary and comprehension are assessed in Surveys D–F. Comprehension is measured by a *cloze*-type test in which 2 or 3 words are deleted in each paragraph. Students select the correct answer from the five choices given. Vocabulary is tested in isolation. This test and its previous editions have been widely used for several decades.

Iowa Test of Basic Skills. A. N. Hieronymus, E. F. Lindquist, and H. D. Hoover. (Boston: Houghton Mifflin, 1978).

Levels 9–14 (grades 3–9) each contain a total of 11 subtests in the areas of vocabulary and reading, language, work-study, and math. Two forms are available at these levels. In the reading subtest, students read passages and answer questions in three categories (facts, inferences and generalizations). Vocabulary is tested in limited context. Total test time for these two tests is 57 minutes.

Iowa Tests of Educational Development. (Chicago: Science Research Associates, 1974).

Comprehensive battery intended to measure the achievement of students in grades 9–12. The abbreviated battery (the 3R core) consists of reading (vocabulary and com-

Continued

BOX 6-3 (continued)

SOME STANDARDIZED READING TESTS
(GROUP SURVEY TESTS)

prehension), language arts (spelling and usage), and math tests. Additional tests in the areas of social studies, science and use of sources are available. Science and social studies tests include items to test background knowledge and ability to read passages in these subjects.

Metropolitan Achievement Test. G. Prescott, I. Balow, T. Hogan, R. Farr. (New York: The Psychological Corp.: Harcourt Brace Jovanovich, 1978).

Consists of two components: the Survey battery (8 levels, grades K–12.9) with tests in reading, math, language arts (and science and social studies from grades 1.5) and the Instructional battery with a variety of subtests in reading, math and language (6 levels, grades K.5–9.9). Two forms are available at each level of both components. Eleven subtests are included in the reading instructional component. At the intermediate level (5.0–6.9) tests cover consonants and vowels, vocabulary in context, word part clues, rate of comprehension, skimming and scanning, and comprehension. The advanced level includes vocabulary in context, rate, skimming and scanning, and comprehension.

Sequential Tests of Educational Progress, Series II. Educational Testing Service, Princeton, NJ. (Also Addison-Wesley, 1972).

Four levels (grades 4–14) measure achievement in English expression, math concepts, reading, science and social studies. In addition, mechanics of writing and math computations are included in the first 3 levels (grades 4–12). Two forms are provided at each level. Subtest times range from 40 to 60 minutes.

Stanford Achievement Test. R. Madden, E. F. Gardner, H. C. Rudman, B. Karlsen, J. C. Merwin. (New York: Harcourt Brace Jovanovich, 1979).

Tests at the intermediate level are in the areas of reading, math, language arts, social science, science and listening comprehension. The advanced level contains the same tests with the exception of listening comprehension. Reading subtests assess vocabulary, comprehension and word study skill (structural and phonetic analysis) at the intermediate level, and vocabulary and comprehension at the advanced level. In grades 9–13, the Stanford Test of Academic Skills includes tests in reading, English and math. Performance on the dictated vocabulary assessment and the listening comprehension test at the intermediate level may provide diagnostic information when compared to word study and silent reading comprehension scores.

Stanford Diagnostic Reading Test. B. Karlsen, R. Madden, and E. F. Gardner. (New York: Harcourt Brace Jovanovich, 1976).

Four levels, two forms at each level, provide evaluations of reading skills in grades 1–12 and community college. The tests are designed to identify specific strengths and weaknesses in reading for both individuals and groups. The Brown Level (grades 5–8 and low-achieving high school students) has subtests in the following areas: auditory vocabulary, literal and inferential comprehension, phonetic and structural analysis, and rate. The Blue Level (9–12 and community college) includes comprehension, phonetic and structural analysis and rate, word meaning, and scanning and skimming.

to students whose thinking conforms to the norm, and divergent thinkers are penalized. Moreover, machine-scorable tests cannot measure ability to remember and restate ideas and information, the skills most needed in secondary schools.

The accuracy of even well-made tests may be vitiated by conditions over which the test-maker has no control, such as administering the test in a cafeteria with limited proctoring, crowded seating, poor ventilation or lighting. To these chance factors of administration, add the effects of students' attitudes, test-taking skills, personal crises, state of health, then consider the limitations of the tests themselves, and you can see why an individual's score may be far from the truth.

You can estimate your students' language abilities without standardized test scores. But with a hundred or more students to get to know quickly, it is foolish to ignore the general clues test scores provide. They are places to begin the diagnostic process, which will continue for as long as you teach these students. Although diagnosis, or assessment, is continuous, taking accurate measurements early is as important to the teacher starting instruction as it is to a tailor cutting cloth. The initial assessment must not be prolonged, however; neither teacher nor students should equate testing with teaching. Studying the most recent reading scores of the classes you are about to teach can help you to decide what further testing is needed and what can be eliminated.

Studying a Class Profile

Raw scores (the number right) are converted to grade equivalents, percentiles, percentile bands, or stanines in order to show how students perform in comparison with the norming population. Before you judge any students' scores, consult the test manual to determine which kind of score is reported on class profiles, how the converted score relates to the raw score, and how the test was normed. Ideally, you should study the test itself as well as the manual; the best way is to answer all items yourself.

Figure 6-1 represents a class profile that Joe Grabowski received from the guidance counselor in the one-day workshop that preceded school opening the year that staff development in reading was launched at Riverdale Junior High School. Remember Joe? He was the science teacher with whom we began this chapter. Actually, the class profile shows only half of Joe's 7–C section.

This class profile reports scores from the *Stanford Achievement Test Battery*, a series of tests given over several days. The reading section, as you can see, is comprised of vocabulary and reading comprehension. Most reading tests report these two subscores, and some give a combined score derived from two, three, or more subtests. The greater the number of subtests the less faith we have in the combined score; the shorter the subtests the less we trust the part scores.

Looking at the scores of Riverdale 7–C, note first that these are grade equivalent scores. Then notice that all the shaded scores indicate average performance. Knowing that one raw score point can make a difference of a full month in the grade score (and knowing that a lucky guess or a lost place on the answer sheet are accidents that make a difference), we consider converted scores as *estimates* of ability levels. Accordingly, we interpret as "average achievement" all scores that fall within six months (either way) of grade placement. Because this test was administered in May of sixth grade (6.8), scores as low as 6.2 and as high as 7.7 indicate average achievement.

The immediate impression Joe Grabowski has of this group is that they are average students, performing consistently like the students in the norming

FIGURE 6-1

RJHS SECTION 7-C, GRADE EQUIVALENT SCORES*
Stanford Achievement Test; Intermediate Level II Battery

Students	Vocab.	Reading Comp.	Word Study	Spelling	Language	Social Studies	Science	Listening Comp.
Andrea	6.5	4.1	4.2	5.1	4.5	4.0	3.7	6.2
Betsy	7.5	7.2	6.9	6.8	6.9	6.7	6.5	6.5
Chad	6.1	6.0	6.2	6.0	5.9	5.0	4.0	5.5
Dori	6.9	6.7	6.5	6.6	6.5	6.5	6.3	6.7
Eddie	6.1	3.9	3.7	4.6	3.9	4.2	3.7	5.7
Frank	6.9	6.8	6.9	7.0	6.9	6.8	6.6	7.1
Gary	7.2	7.0	6.9	6.9	7.0	6.9	6.8	7.2
Hal	6.7	3.9	4.1	4.9	4.2	3.6	3.0	5.9
Isobel	6.0	6.1	6.5	6.2	6.3	5.0	4.9	5.5
Jenny	7.0	6.8	6.6	6.6	6.7	6.6	6.4	7.2
Kevin	8.2	8.5	7.8	7.9	8.0	8.1	8.0	8.7
Lara	6.6	6.7	6.8	6.5	6.5	6.6	6.3	6.8
Melanie	8.5	9.0	8.8	8.5	8.7	8.5	8.5	9.4
Nancy	6.7	6.5	5.4	5.6	6.3	6.4	6.2	6.9
Omar	6.8	7.1	6.8	6.7	6.9	6.9	6.7	7.0

■ Average performance
◯ Seriously below average; should be followed up
*Battery administered in May of sixth grade.

population at their grade level. But there are a few exceptions. Andrea, for example, is below average on every test except vocabulary and listening comprehension. Checking the manual, Joe finds that the vocabulary test is administered orally, measuring understanding of word meanings without requiring students to decode, and similar in that respect to the listening comprehension test on which Andrea also scores in the average range. Andrea, Chad, Eddie, Hal and Isobel are below average in science. Their teacher wonders how much these low scores are affected by poor reading ability, how much by lack of interest in and knowledge of science concepts. Kevin and Melanie are well above average, not only in science, but across all areas.

It looks as though Andrea, Eddie, and Hal, whose listening comprehension exceeds their reading, language, and science scores, should be referred for further clinical diagnosis (see Chapter 7). Because they will continue in 7–C science, however, Mr. Grabowski observes carefully how they respond to science concepts which are demonstrated and discussed, and for the time being he requires little from them in reading and writing. From the Stanford Battery results, Chad and Isobel look like somewhat different problems, weak in science but only slightly below average in reading comprehension, with listening comprehension scores below reading. Differences of a few months are not sufficient evidence of better or poorer real achievement, but they are cause for speculation and follow-up testing and observation. Are Chad and Isobel poor listeners? Does their attention wander? Were the tasks on the listening comprehension test more difficult than those on the reading test? Do the low scores in social studies and science support the hunch made from the listening scores that Chad and Isobel are intellectually dull and unmotivated? It is unfair to interpret individual test scores too closely, but Joe Grabowski is right in responding to signals. At least, he guesses that Chad and Isobel—unlike Andrea, Eddie, and Hal—are no better listeners than they are readers and will need a still different approach to learning science. He decides to consult the reading teacher about these students, too.

Classroom Analysis of Language Performance

When recent standardized test data are not available in September, teachers must devise other means of estimating the range and general levels of reading abilities in their classes. Even with standardized test data of the kind we have been discussing, teachers must seek additional information before they can plan instruction. Of course, they continue to adjust their strategies throughout the year as they gather evidence of strengths and weaknesses from students' daily performances, but the initial assessment is most important. What you learn in September may save both you and your students the time and grief associated with relearning and reteaching. Following are a few ideas for the first quick assessment.

Written Recall   When testing time is limited (and it should be), a test of written recall will yield the most information. It is easy to devise. Select a passage of five hundred to a thousand words (depending on the maturity of your students) which is typical of the reading materials in your course. Content teachers usually search their textbooks for a clear, well-organized, short section. Reading teachers may find a suitable expository (not narrative) selection in a workbook, magazine, reference book, text or trade book. Judge the readability of the selection, perhaps using a formula (see Chapter 10) but, more important, be sure that three or four main ideas are clearly presented and supported by elaborating details. Avoid selections that are densely packed with new concepts insufficiently elaborated or explained. If textbooks are used, there will be no need to duplicate the selection. Make clear to students before they begin to read the passage that they should read with the intent of recalling it as fully as possible. They may reread if they wish but they cannot take notes, and they must record their study time. (You can keep the time check on the chalkboard, or students can return a duplicated selection to you before beginning to write, and you can note the time taken. Records need not be exact; you simply want to know who took a little or a lot of time when you evaluate the recall.) The whole exercise should take fifteen or twenty minutes.

You will already have explained the diagnostic nature of the test, impressing students with its serious purpose but assuring them that their efforts will not be counted as part of their end-of-term grades. To evaluate the papers, you may consult a checklist like the one in Box 6-4. Or you may grade holistically, sorting

BOX 6-4

WRITTEN RECALL CHECKLIST

Main Ideas

____ Taste is essentially a chemical sense.

____ Taste system is very complex and involves all the senses.

____ Many animals' taste sense is superior to ours and more important to survival.

Details

____ chemicals react with taste buds
____ signal then produced
____ and sent to brain
____ which classifies it
____ (salty, sweet, bitter, sour)
____ system so efficient
____ we can distinguish between tastes
____ and odors
____ of thousands of different substances

____ "tastes good" refers largely to *odor*
____ test by holding your nose
____ and trying to tell difference between raw mashed apple and raw mashed potato
____ *temperature* another factor
____ unmistakable difference in taste between hot and cold milk (beer or soup)
____ *texture* also important
____ lumps in pudding (or a gritty ice cream) affect taste reaction

____ wild rats sample foods by tasting them
____ only when food has been taste-tested will the rat eat enough to sustain life

SOURCE: Checklist based on "Accounting for Taste" by Fred Warshofsky. *Reader's Digest New Advanced Reading Skill Builder* (Pleasantville, NY: Reader's Digest Services, Inc., 1973):98–99. (This article might be used to test student's written or oral recall. Teacher checks off items recalled as student tells what he remembers. Or teacher checks items from written report.)

the papers into "good," "fair," or "poor" categories as you decide: "How well did this student recall the passage?" In any case, analysis of these papers should tell you which students

✤ remembered how many main ideas or major generalizations
✤ noted how many details and which ones
✤ recalled in the order used by the writer
✤ demonstrated fluent recall

✤ recalled ideas and details accurately

✤ paraphrased ideas showing understanding of the concepts

✤ used many or few terms from the passage

✤ showed mastery of sentence structure

✤ observed conventions (spelling, punctuation, usage)

Joe Grabowski should give a test of written recall based on his textbook to all students scoring average and above on the Stanford. (He does not simply assume that average-to-superior readers, according to that test, can read and recall the grade-level science text.) For those students whose scores suggest they may be reading well below average, he substitutes a much easier science-related passage for this test.

Some of the average readers may produce very limited written recall. Can we assume they have not comprehended the passage? No, because factors other than comprehension may inhibit their writing. If at all possible, Joe should individually retest students in the "poor" category, giving them a new passage of comparable difficulty and asking them to tell what they remember.

The test of written recall measures the appropriateness of the textbook for a particular group. (As in all testing, we are *sampling* the textbook as we are sampling the students' reading/writing abilities.) *Cloze* tests are also tests of the textbook.

CLOZE **Testing**   Many teachers use *cloze* exercises instead of, or in addition to, the test of written recall. Again, *cloze* tests are easy to construct. From the textbook in use, choose one or more passages, each at least 250 words in length. Leave the introductory sentence or paragraph intact, and thereafter delete every fifth word, leaving a blank of standard size for every deletion. The test consists of restoring the missing words, not answering questions about the passage. After taking the test, students can turn to the textbook passages and score their own or each other's paper, giving points only for exact restoration of the author's words. This scoring practice eliminates the subjectivity of judging synonyms and permits the application of criteria derived from research studies; that is, 60 percent restoration suggests the material is at the reader's "mastery level"; 40 percent and lower indicates material too difficult for the reader to learn from. It is important to assure students before taking a *cloze* exercise that exact restoration is virtually impossible; nevertheless, they should fill every blank. (See Box 6-5.)

Cloze exercises of this kind should be interpreted very cautiously. To say that a textbook is unreadable for all who fail to restore 40 percent or more of the author's words may be erroneous. Probably four or five *cloze* tests from the same source should be given and their results averaged before you hazard any guesses about the readability of a textbook for a particular group. Similar caution should be exercised in estimating the reading ability of students taking the *cloze* tests. Nevertheless, *cloze* testing can provide content teachers with insights into both readability and reading abilities and is probably worth their consideration. As a teaching rather than a testing device, we see many advantages to it: It focuses

BOX 6-5

CLOZE EXERCISE—GRADE 7 SCIENCE
Respiration

Animals are active. They need energy to _____ and function. Animals get
_____ from the food they _____. How does this happen? _____ obtain
energy from food, _____ need oxygen. The process _____ taking in and
using _____ is called respiration. In _____ cell of an animal's _____,
oxygen and digested food _____ in a chemical change. _____ the change,
energy is _____. Water and carbon dioxide _____ formed. Carbon dioxide
is _____ waste that is excreted _____ animals. The excretion of _____
dioxide is part of _____.

Different kinds of respiratory _____ are present in animals. _____
example, oxygen from the _____ moves into the blood _____ an earth-
worm through its _____ skin. Carbon dioxide moves _____ of the earth-
worm's body _____ the opposite direction.

Insects _____ tiny openings in their _____ called spiracles. Spiracles
lead _____ a complex network of _____. At the end of _____ tubes are
air sacs. _____ is pumped in and _____ of the air sacs _____ the movements of the _____ body. Oxygen from the _____ enters the insect's cells
_____ the air sacs. Carbon _____ leaves the cells through _____ air sacs.

Most animals _____ live in water have _____ they use for respiration.
_____ are organs that remove _____ oxygen from water. The _____ of a
fish are _____ inside slit-shaped openings behind _____ head. As a fish
_____, water flows over the _____ and an exchange of _____ is made.
Dissolved oxygen _____ removed from the water _____ diffuses into the
fish's _____. Another function of the gills is to remove carbon dioxide from
the fish's blood. The carbon dioxide diffuses into the water that passes over
the gills.

SOURCE: Charles H. Heimler and J. David Lockard, *Focus on Life Science* (Columbus, Ohio: Charles E.
Merrill Publishing Co., 1981):98–99.

Note: In this exercise, every fifth word has been deleted for a total of 50. In most cases, more than one
short sentence should be left intact before deletions begin. (If you restored 30 words correctly, you can
read this text without difficulty; if you restore about 20 you probably need help with this textbook; if
fewer than 20, you should have an easier text.)

Key:
(1) move, (2) energy, (3) eat, (4) To, (5) animals, (6) of, (7) oxygen, (8) each, (9)
body, (10) combine, (11) In, (12) released, (13) are, (14) a, (15) by, (16) carbon,
(17) respiration, (18) systems, (19) For, (20) air, (21) of, (22) moist, (23) out, (24)
in, (25) have, (26) exoskeletons, (27) to, (28) tubes, (29) these, (30) Air, (31) out,
(32) by, (33) insect's, (34) air, (35) through, (36) dioxide, (37) the, (38) that, (39)
gills, (40) Gills, (41) dissolved, (42) gills, (43) located, (44) its, (45) swims, (46)
gills, (47) gases, (48) is, (49) and, (50) blood

the reader's attention on the relationships among words, underscores the search for meaning, exercises the habit of predicting or anticipating meanings, and demonstrates the usefulness of guessing from context.

Oral Reading   A time-honored method for assessing levels of silent reading ability is to have students read aloud passages of increasing difficulty. Trained reading teachers can guess from a reader's miscues[2] the kinds of difficulties he or she may encounter in reading silently. For example, some readers ignore meaning in their zeal for decoding. Miscues that distort meaning are much more serious than those that ignore graphemic cues. Reading *pond* for *lake* is not serious in most contexts; reading *battle* for *bottle* probably betrays a total disregard for meaning. Repeated miscues on key words—*magician* for *musician*, for instance—are very serious indeed.

Should content teachers concern themselves with analyzing students' oral reading errors? Generally, no. They should know that most students who score below the sixth-grade level on a standardized reading test should be given an oral reading test by a trained examiner. If that kind of referral is impossible or inconvenient, however, the content teacher may want to know more about poor readers' decoding habits. A good way to find out quickly is to select ten multisyllabic words from a content textbook and ask individuals to read them aloud, noting the kinds of difficulties encountered. (Refusing to try? Skipping syllables? Guessing from first letters only?) We shall have more to say about testing poor readers in the next chapter. However, examples of informal ways to test decoding skills are found in Chapter 12.

Estimating Levels of Reading Ability

If no standardized test scores are available, or if reading or content teachers want to check further on low scorers, graded word lists can be used for quick estimates. We describe three sets of commercial materials that are commonly used and easily available. Total testing time required per student is about five minutes.

San Diego Quick Assessment[3]   This instrument was created to provide a quick means by which to gauge a student's reading ability. It consists of thirteen graded lists of ten words each, and each list is identified according to the level of reading difficulty it represents, from pre-primer through grade eleven. The teacher starts the student reading the list of words that is three years below his or her grade placement and records the words miscalled on a copy of the list. If any words are missed on the first list, the teacher drops back to easier lists until no errors are made. Then the student reads increasingly more difficult lists until at least three errors are made. The highest list on which no more than one error

---

[2]*Miscue* is a term contributed by Kenneth Goodman, who with Yetta Goodman has written widely on the analysis of miscues and the significance of guessing (or predicting) in learning to read.

[3]*San Diego Quick Assessment*, Margaret LaPray and Ramon Ross. Reproduced in "The graded word list: Quick gauge of reading ability." *Journal of Reading* 12:4 (1969):305–307.

is made represents the student's independent level, where he or she may be able to read without teacher assistance. That is, the level of the list at which nine of ten words are correctly identified suggests the readability level at which students are likely to have the greatest success.

Slosson Oral Reading Test (SORT)[4]   This test is made up of ten lists of words each drawn from grade level textbooks. The teacher selects a list below the student's grade placement and sets the base as the list on which all 20 words are correctly pronounced. From this base list, the student continues with successively more difficult lists until *none* of the 20 words can be read correctly. The total number of words read correctly (counting 20 for each list below the base list) is converted to a grade equivalent reading level using a table provided.

Zip Scale[5]   Intended as a survey of secondary school students' abilities to understand words, the *Zip Scale* consists of twelve lists of 20 words each. Students select the antonym from four choices for each of 20 target words, responding to all words on all twelve lists. The highest list on which 16 words are read correctly represents the student's independent reading level. Listening comprehension can be assessed by reading aloud the lists that follow the one defined as the independent reading level. The student responds orally. Testing continues until the student achieves less than 80 percent accuracy on three consecutive lists. The difference in performance between the two administrations suggests the gap between reading achievement and potential. Students who read poorly may be able to comprehend textbooks at the "listening level" if they are read aloud.

Listening Comprehension

Content teachers' study of their poor readers should include investigating students' ability to learn through listening. They can administer a whole-class test by selecting an appropriate short section of their textbook for reading aloud. Questions based on the text should also be read aloud and require true–false or multiple-choice responses. Because reliable objective tests are hard to write, teachers may look for publishers' tests or workbook exercises related to the class text. This measure of the appropriateness of the textbook may reveal: (1) who can profit from taped lessons based on the text; (2) who needs still simpler oral/aural approaches; (3) who comprehends better through silent reading than through listening.

Other Informal Tests

Reading consultants have been urging content teachers to construct informal tests of reading based on their textbooks and related course materials at least since the 1940s when the first edition of Strang, McCullough, and Traxler's *The*

---

[4]*Slosson Oral Reading Test*. Richard L. Slosson, Slosson Educational Publications, Inc., P.O. Box 280, East Aurora, NY 14052.
[5]*Zip Scale for Determining Reading Level for Junior and Senior High Students*. Ward Cramer and Suzanne Dorsey. J. Weston Walch, Publisher, Portland, ME 04104.

Improvement of Reading[6] appeared with excellent sample tests. Over the years, in reaction perhaps to some teachers' lack of enthusiasm, reading consultants and department heads have constructed "all-purpose" textbook tests or suggested formulas for "quickie surveys." The results have come to look more and more like the standardized tests to which informal testing is supposedly superior. That is, an "all-purpose content area reading test" contains subtests that are too short to be reliable; it also fails to provide sufficient analysis of the sustained reading of a particular content textbook.

With the advent of management systems, criterion-referenced tests matched to course objectives were urged upon us. These look rather like the informal tests described by Strang and others and can be made to serve purposes of prelearning assessment as well as end-of-unit evaluation. There are problems with such tests, however. Pre- and post-tests in each subject are more likely to display what students have learned of the subject than to measure their learning skills.

So, yes, whoever promotes "reading and writing in the content fields" is asking content teachers to give additional tests and to use them for new purposes. And content teachers resist—with good reason.

Ideally, the reading staff should assume the burden of testing learning abilities and interpreting the results for content teachers. But in many junior and senior high schools no such staff exists. An overworked "remedial reading teacher" cannot serve content teachers in this or any other way. Are there alternatives? The idea of pooling test results is worth pursuing since it saves students from being overtested and keeps teachers from duplicating their efforts. One possible alternative is to involve students in self-evaluation through a unit in reading or English classes such as we describe in "Learning About Ourselves as Learners" (pages 166–86). However, until that option is taken up by an English department or a reading staff, content teachers may have to fend for themselves. If you find yourself in such a situation, consider using a learning unit through which you can assess skills such as using textbook features, locating references, interpreting picture/text amalgams, reading maps, charts, and graphs. Box 6-6 classifies skills according to areas of the curriculum. From this chart select skills for informal testing.

Informal tests of learning skills, no matter who creates and administers them, should be brief and focused. Students should understand their diagnostic purposes; when these are established in students' minds, pretesting can motivate and improve subsequent learning. And having said so much about diagnostic testing and having still more to say about testing as evaluation at the end of this chapter, we still warn: *Don't overdo testing*.

Observation as Diagnosis

In many ways teachers' observations of language uses are the best indicators of students' learning skills, acquired and potential. But observations take time,

---

[6]Ruth Strang, Constance M. McCullough, and Arthur E. Traxler. *The Improvement of Reading*, 4th ed. (New York: McGraw-Hill, Inc., 1967).

BOX 6-6

A SAMPLING OF SKILLS USED IN THE CONTENT FIELDS

Sample Skills	Sample Applications in Content Fields
NOTING SPECIFIC DETAILS Following directions Recalling facts Observing punctuation	*Science:* Following directions in performing an experiment *Mathematics:* Understanding verbal problems *Homemaking:* Reading recipes, dress patterns, knitting instructions, etc. *Industrial Arts:* Reading manuals, how-to articles, warranties and instructions on use of equipment *Driver's Training:* Mastering driver's manual *All Courses:* Reading directions on exams
PERCEIVING STRUCTURE Identifying main ideas Following sequence Recognizing patterns of organization Outlining	*English:* Précis writing, summarizing articles and essays *Science:* Seeing cause–effect relationships *Social Studies:* Following time sequence *Homemaking:* Compiling information from text and magazine sources on child care, grooming, home and family *All Courses:* Using chapter headings, previews, summaries, etc., in textbook study
INFERENTIAL READING Drawing conclusions Distinguishing between fact and opinion Interpreting figurative language Recognizing mood and purpose Judging character Making comparisons	*English:* Studying writer's craft in poetry, drama, novel, etc. *Social Studies:* Interpreting point of view, analyzing propaganda, comparing emotive and report language *Science:* Anticipating results, determining validity of scientific writing *Business:* Interpreting statistics *Mathematics:* Seeing relationships and solving problems

Continued

teachers need to know in a hurry, and they may have a hundred to a hundred and fifty students to observe. Is it any wonder that observations can be chancy, unrecorded, and unanalyzed? Oral language, which may be very revealing of learning styles and attitudes, is the most difficult to capture. Samples of writing

BOX 6-6 (continued)

A SAMPLING OF SKILLS USED IN THE CONTENT FIELDS

Sample Skills	**Sample Applications in Content Fields**
GETTING INFORMATION IN GRAPHIC AND TABULAR FORMS	*Social Studies:* Reading pictures, political cartoons, maps, charts, graphs, etc.
Charts and graphs	*Business:* Reading timetables, lists, accounts, forms; graphs (line, bar, circle)
Maps	
Diagrams	*Science:* Relating text and diagrams, understanding scales, comparing specimens with verbal and graphic representations, reading cross-sectional and longitudinal models, etc.
Tables	
Pictures	
	Industrial Arts: Reading maintenance and lubrication charts, scale models, etc.
LOCATING INFORMATION	*All Courses:* Making reports
Dictionary and glossary	*Media Center:* Direct teaching of retrieval skills by media specialists, reading or English teacher—reinforced by all content teachers
Table of contents	
Index—cross references	
Card catalog	
Encyclopedias, almanacs, etc.	
Reader's Guide to Periodical Literature	

are easier to collect and analyze, but these, too, require a teacher's systematic attention. It was out of these conditions that schemes for systematic informal testing arose in the first place, but time has proved that tests are no substitute for teachers' daily observation of students in learning situations. This is easier said than done. In the typical 40–50 minute period, teachers are often so busy telling, showing, chatting, directing, questioning that very little time is left for students to demonstrate observable learning. Providing teachers with opportunities to observe is one of the most powerful arguments for small-group instruction.

Even so, admitting the difficulties doesn't dispense with the necessity for observing if we are to diagnose and evaluate. It simply underscores the need for arranging more opportunities for observing, for taking systematic notes, and for pooling the results. Teaching reading in secondary schools is, willy-nilly, a team effort. If observing is half of teaching, sharing is more than half of team teaching.

Using the Results of Assessment

The purpose of assessing students' language proficiencies is to make teaching and learning more productive and more interesting. But content teachers who assess their students' language needs still begin their instructional planning with content objectives. To identify them they turn to state and local curriculum guides, department meetings, textbooks, and their own knowledge of their subject matter.

Ordering Objectives

We suggest that when you have identified all the objectives for a unit, a marking period, or a year's course, you group them and rank them by priority. At least two groups will emerge: (a) knowledge and skills everyone needs for living in our society; (b) concepts and principles students must have to master the particular discipline. For example, math teachers identify "using contemporary units of measure" in the first category, "the history of measurement" in the second. A priority ranking of objectives helps you to differentiate goals to match students' needs. From this base you can maintain an appropriate balance in the amount of time devoted to each objective, and you can adjust teaching and evaluation to different levels of ability. You plan for all students to accomplish the basic objectives by whatever route is appropriate to them, but you hold only the above-average students responsible for accomplishing the extended objectives. You encourage average students who have the interest and independent work habits to go beyond the objectives set for them, but you don't penalize them for failure to achieve the extended objectives.

Next, as you specify how each objective can be achieved, you consider various resources and think about particular students who could effectively use each one. Working in this way in a particular unit, the math teacher, Sam Kincaid, might assign three or four of his poorest students to interview workers at a lumber yard or construction site and then report to the rest of the class what they had learned about measuring devices and computation processes used in the field. In Kincaid's class, students particularly interested in building might be given an architectural plan for a mountain cabin and asked to determine how many board feet of lumber would be necessary to construct it and how many trees should be harvested to supply the lumber. Others might try to determine how many bread boards, of certain dimensions, might be made from a tree near their school. Obviously, the purpose of these activities is to supply concrete experiences for those who have difficulty grasping concepts through print. In sharing their separate experiences with their classmates, these students develop readiness—their own and their classmates'—for learning from the math textbook.

Not every lesson can, or should, take students out of the classroom for hands-on learning. Only concepts of major importance would warrant the expense of planning time and energy. But Sam Kincaid, who is as interested as the next person in conserving time and energy, has learned a basic truth: Reading is the least expensive mode of learning—but only for students who have the requisite skills. One of those skills is the ability to think logically and deal with abstractions; few students in early secondary years can operate in many areas without concrete manipulations. As we shall reiterate in subsequent chapters, content textbooks are secondary sources of information; they are most useful in affirming and extending what students already know.

Selecting Resources for Instruction

When planning for instruction, teachers move back and forth between and among three elements: their curriculum objectives, their students' abilities, and the instructional resources at hand. With some clarity about the first two elements, you can decide how to use available materials and how to add to them. Beginning teachers often have little more than a class text, one that they did not select themselves. More experienced content teachers—probably the majority—decide to keep a textbook at the center of their instruction, adapting it to below- and above-average learners. With experience, teachers have more voice in selecting new textbooks, but because they choose for next year's classes on the basis of former students' needs, they always have to make adjustments. These kinds of adjustments are necessary: (1) differentiating assignments in the basic textbook; (b) adding print and nonprint resources to enrich the basic text; (3) moving to multi-text approaches.

Adapting a Single Textbook   If you have only one textbook and it is too difficult for some students, what can you do? The following are six suggestions. More detail on each of them can be found in the places noted in parentheses.

1. Assign the same reading to everyone, but provide study guides that make different demands on different groups of students. (See Chapter 13.)
2. Vary the reading assignments as well as the tasks according to students' abilities. For example, slow readers may be assigned only parts of a chapter. Some may be asked to survey a chapter, paying attention to pictures and captions, headings, previews and summaries. (See Chapter 13.)
3. Rewrite parts of the text at lower readability levels. Some teachers do this, but it is not a practical procedure unless many contribute to the effort. (See Chapter 10.)
4. Put parts of the textbook on tape for poor readers who can nevertheless comprehend at this level. This suggestion works best when teachers have assistance. (See Chapter 9.)
5. Provide glossaries for help with key vocabulary. (See Chapter 12.)
6. Provide advance organizers, simplified summaries, outlines or "maps" of the chapter content. (See Chapter 13.)

In many situations in secondary schools, we approve issuing the same text to all students in a content course, even though some of them cannot be expected to learn from it. While adolescents like to have choices, they also like to conform. Especially among their peers they hate to be singled out as "different."

Enriching a Core Text   While making do with a single text, using all the preceding suggestions—and others—teachers also enrich the core text with related trade books (especially paperbacks), magazines, newspapers, films, recordings, filmstrips, community resources including people, and "realia"—all those objects that relate to the concepts being studied. This is one of the points at which the media specialist is essential to the team-teaching effort. To be really effective, the media specialist must be invited by content teachers to search out available resources. When gaps in the media center collection are identified in this search, the specialist begins to shape the collection through future orders to better meet real, rather than presumed, faculty needs.

Multi-text Approaches   Teachers who adapt a single text or enrich the core text sooner or later replace the single textbook with several textbooks at different readability levels and a wealth of supplementary resources. A few teachers abandon textbooks altogether in favor of assembling and organizing their own print and nonprint instructional materials and learning experiences.

Teaching styles, like learning styles, vary widely, and effective learning takes place in many different kinds of classrooms. The best teaching embraces many styles and shifts from one approach to another, sometimes employing a single text, sometimes many, sometimes replacing text with oral and visual media. The worst teaching clings to a single method for everyone.

Grouping for Instruction

Organizing students and materials in ways that facilitate a good match between the reading abilities of the former and the readability of the latter is a continuing challenge to the professional teacher. We hesitate to advise any single organizational pattern and can only repeat with respect to grouping students what we have just said about using textbooks. No one method works all the time. Vary grouping patterns according to purposes. Sometimes the most effective learning takes place in whole groups, with everyone listening to the same lecture or viewing the same film or hearing the same story or contributing to a summation of the unit. Most secondary teachers use small groups effectively when the purpose is to discuss a common reading or to pursue a clearly defined purpose. Individual assignments can be guided by LAPs (Learning Activities Packets).

Groups may be made up of students whose levels of language abilities are similar or they may be deliberately constructed to include a range of language competencies. Poor readers who are highly verbal students with good reasoning abilities can be grouped with superior or average readers, as long as acting on information gained is a primary objective of the group. The better readers may do most of the reading, but the tasks of organizing information, discussing relationships, raising questions, and reporting to the class can be shared by everyone in the group.

Grouping students according to low reading ability alone should be done cautiously. Students with both high and low intellectual abilities may be equally poor readers. Grouping these students to synthesize the main points of a selection read by all of them could be useful. So, too, could their development of a joint report based on viewing films or listening to tapes or interviewing a local expert. But experiences like these could also prove frustrating to bright handicapped readers if they always are grouped with others who cannot stimulate and extend their thinking.

Teachers who use multiple texts and nonprint resources often find the best way to organize instruction is through units centered on a theme, a concept, or a problem. This is the most practical way to adjust to individual differences in departmentalized settings. However, the unit method is not always successful. When it breaks down, the causes may be traced to lack of resources, failure on the part of teachers and/or students to understand the goals of the unit, or, most frequently, students' inability to work independently because they have not developed necessary study skills (like locating references) and are being frustrated by reading and writing assignments that are ill-matched to their level of development. Teachers who can write excellent units can also be out of touch with their students' skills and prior knowledge. Like the single-textbook teacher, they can assume too much.

Adjusting Evaluation Procedures

Adjusting instruction to individual needs must extend to evaluating progress by different methods for different students. Able and average students should be required to write reports, essays, and thoughtful answers to test questions. They should not be limited to objective tests. But students with minimal proficiency in reading and writing need avenues for expressing what they have learned about the subject under study. Accordingly, teachers give oral tests to small groups and individuals, using tape cassettes, other students, teacher aides, and media center personnel to assist. Students respond by checking answers on the objective test form; additionally, they prepare taped and "live" oral reports.

Should content teachers subtract points for below-standard written English? Yes, frequently, but not always. One characteristic of a whole-school program is that students expect to be held to the same language standards in biology as in American history as in English. The faculty from every curricular area should agree on these standards (a necessary if not easy task). Some faculties agree to double-grading practices; others prefer single grades evaluating both substance and form. Practices vary according to the maturity and purposes of the students, but all grading policies should implement the faculty's beliefs about how language reflects and assists learning.

The significant issue for teachers is how to use grading to assist their main purpose: to elicit the best performance from learners. Conscientious and hardworking teachers often defer grades until students produce better work. But they reduce the likelihood of sloppy first attempts by preteaching that stimulates ideas, frames careful questions, reviews necessary skills, and offers models so that students thoroughly understand the dimensions of the task and the bases on which it will be evaluated. To protect themselves against the irritations of misspellings and other usage errors, teachers have students proofread each other's papers. They encourage poor spellers to refer to personal and class lists of important words for each unit while writing exams as well as out-of-class assignments.

No stickier problem than grading exists in all of teaching, and we would be presumptuous to offer advice to fit all situations. But you cannot dodge the issue: Evaluating learning is what teachers are for. As soon as possible, beginning teachers should ask department heads and other colleagues for grading policies (these may be written statements) and for examples of graded papers. In well-run departments, grading practices are reviewed frequently; at such times teachers can raise questions about practices that do not conform with their philosophy. Of course, staff development which seeks to move language across the curriculum must grapple with the fact that grading is the most visible interpretation of school policy.

Evaluating Students and Programs

We have used the words *assess* and *diagnose* to refer to testing which precedes instruction and helps teachers to make decisions about individuals' instructional needs. We use the word *evaluate* to refer to measuring growth after instruction. Evaluation of growth in literacy and in knowledge of content serves decision-making by administrators, teachers, and students. The chief reason for testing is to use the results to decide what steps to take next. If test results are not used for decision-making, testing is a waste of time.

Administrators' Use of Test Results

As noted earlier, standardized tests measure the performance of groups more or less reliably. Therefore, they are a valuable tool to adminstrators who must make decisions about students as groups and about programs and teachers. But even for administrative decision-making, standardized test results should be used in conjunction with other measures, especially teachers' judgments. (See Box 6-2.) Moreover, reading test scores should be compared with the group's scores on other achievement tests and on aptitude or intelligence tests. The scattergram shown in Figure 6-2 is a good way to make visual the relationship between a particular group's reading and intelligence. Administrators, too, should become familiar with test manuals and understand what the test measures, on whom it was normed, the effect of the standard error of measurement, the significance of the range of scores as well as the deviation of individual scores from the mean.

Standardized test scores contribute to administrative decisions on scheduling classes, assigning teachers, allocating dollars, planning staff development, and hiring personnel. If an entire grade level in a school shows significantly low reading and writing performance (compared with previous classes in this school or with a truly comparable population elsewhere), administrators have several decisions to make. They may consider lowering the teacher–pupil ratio in English classes during the coming year, adding a half-time reading teacher, or assisting the present reading staff with teacher aides. Additionally, the principal may request help with staff development from the district consultants or bring in an expert from outside. Because these possible actions require more dollars, more space, and special considerations for scheduling, decisions may have to be deferred or altered, but they should be kept on the agenda. If not, the question to be decided becomes: Is this testing necessary?

Administrators must report test results to funding sources, sometimes in connection with research studies, more often when a school receives aid for

FIGURE 6-2

SCATTERGRAM SHOWING READING ACHIEVEMENT AND IQ SCORES OF 169 TENTH GRADERS

Intelligence Test Scores†

Reading Score Percentiles*	Below 90	90–100	101–110	111–120	121–130	131–above	Total
90–100		*	*****	***	*** *****	**	19
80–89		**	* *****	***** *****	*		19
70–79	*		*** *****	****	*		14
60–69		**	* *****	*****			13
50–59		****	*****	*****	*		15
40–49		** *****	* ***** *****	***	*		22
30–39		***** *****	*** ***** *****	**	*		26
20–29	**	* *****	***				11
10–19	***	*** *****	****				15
0–9	***	** *****	****		*		15
Total	9	47	65	32	14	2	169

*Reading scores in percentiles from CTBS, *Comprehensive Tests of Basic Skills, Reading Comprehension, Test 2,* (CTB/McGraw-Hill).
†IQ scores are from *Lorge Thorndike Intelligence Tests* (Houghton Mifflin).

reading improvement and special services to handicapped children. Test data figure, too, in school accreditation. They are examined by school boards and parent organizations that want to know whether or not tax dollars are well spent. Although the taxpaying public surely has a right to hold schools accountable, the use of standardized tests as a single measure of accountability has led to serious abuses, such as teaching for the test, grading teachers on their students' achievement without due regard for factors beyond teachers' control, and comparing schools from dissimilar communities. Teachers' organizations have been in the vanguard in protesting such abuses, and they have been joined by some parents' groups that charge mismeasurement of their children's abilities. Even so, heated debate in print and in public forums has done little to correct the abuses and may instead have weakened evaluation procedures which, when well balanced between astute teacher judgment and objective measures of achievement, provide administrators with vital data for running a good school.

Teachers' Needs

While we disapprove of administrators' using standardized test results to judge teachers' performances (even when the results are reliable and are interpreted accurately), teachers themselves need objective test data to confirm and extend their necessarily subjective evaluations of their students *and* themselves. Evidence suggesting that a class has made better-than-expected overall growth motivates teachers to analyze what was right about the year's work. That analysis—as much as the boost to their self-confidence—will make them better teachers next year. By the same token, teachers' confidence may slump when group averages are lower than expected; however, good teachers rally, search for the causes of disappointing scores, and modify whatever of their methods may have contributed to them.

Another indicator of the success of the program is the range and median of report card grades for each marking period and the year as a whole. In computing final grades, teachers should weight daily work more heavily than unit tests. Evidence of interest in school, in assignments, in relating school work to experiences and problems in daily life should all be counted into an evaluation of competence. Teachers, not standardized tests, collect this evidence. Competence in this broad sense is what society means to assess when it asks how successful our schools are.

Even friendly observers of schools sometimes fail to appreciate teachers' astuteness in estimating the growth of individuals as well as whole classes. Of course, teachers make mistakes; sometimes they use grades to motivate rather than to measure, grading performances both above and below their real worth. Sometimes they grade to make themselves look good; they are not always fair and wise. But, on the whole, grades earned in high school are still the best predictors of success in college, more accurate indicators of future performance than achievement and aptitude tests. As teachers continue to refine their evaluative procedures, administrators and the public should add teachers' judgments to the objective data collected to describe a program's worth.

Students' Use of Scores and Grades

Students and their families use achievement scores, grades on papers, and report card grades to make decisions about future education and careers. It is crucial that these consumers understand the meaning of scores and grades. Very often grades received in school indicate to students only the extent to which their performance did or did not meet teachers' expectations. When grades go up or down over time, most students don't know precisely why. They guess "This was easier," "I studied harder," or "I liked the topic." But they may not understand what knowledge, skills, interests, and habits make one assignment easier or harder than another.

Teachers can help students make more effective use of evaluation data by making their evaluative criteria explicit and going over details of the test with individuals and groups. Pointing out that a third of the class missed the map question, for example, highlights the need for a special lesson on map-reading skills, not for everyone but for those who missed the question.

Students as well as teachers should have a sense of accomplishment at the end of a unit or at the end of a year—or, if that is not deserved, understand what they must do to improve. Far from being bitter medicine or a dreary exercise, evaluation procedures including test-taking can be motivating and enlightening. For this to happen, however, more class time must be spent before tests are administered, clarifying purposes and reviewing test-taking skills, and, after an evaluation has been made, in weighing and interpreting the results. Allotting sufficient time to the whole process means giving less time to test-taking itself in the year's schedule, so that standardized testing is ordered parsimoniously and care is taken that informal tests yield vital information.

The important goal of the unit that follows is to develop students' skills in taking their own measure.

RECAPPING MAIN POINTS

Public concern with the literacy of high school graduates has turned the attention of many school administrators to reading programs in the junior and senior high schools. In a typical situation in which emphasis has been restricted to reading classes, the administration now seeks to involve all content teachers in the reading program. They begin by evaluating present reading services and assessing students' abilities to use reading in learning content.

Standardized reading tests are a starting point. They are best used to compare the performance of one group with another, the norming population. Individual scores are subject to wide margins of error. Teachers use standardized test results to estimate the range of abilities in a class and to identify students who need closer study.

Informal tests based on the content teacher's textbooks and assignments provide more relevant and more complete data than standardized tests. When testing time is limited, teachers ask students to read and study a typical passage from a content textbook or equivalent materials and then write all they can remember from the reading. *Cloze* tests offer teachers clues as to the readability of texts in relation to their students' reading abilities.

Wherever necessary and possible, teachers supplement group tests requiring written responses with individually administered tests to which students respond orally. Another necessary supplement to formal and informal testing is observation of how students use language and approach learning tasks. Assessing students' listening comprehension is important for two reasons: (1) Most learning, especially in early secondary years, depends on listening, observing, and performing rather than on reading; and (2) the quality of listening comprehension is an indication of the reading potential of poor readers.

Preteaching assessments presume that teachers can adjust content and delivery of information to their students' abilities. Considering curriculum objectives, instructional resources, and the range of abilities in a class, they can (1) differentiate assignments related to a single text, (2) enrich a basic text, (3) replace a single text with many texts of varying readability. Good teaching employs many ways of organizing the class and setting up opportunities for learning.

Adapting instruction to individual needs must extend to varying the means of evaluating students' knowledge—for example, replacing reading/writing tests with oral tests.

Administrators, teachers, students, and parents should hold common beliefs as to the limitations and the uses of test results. The reason for assessing students' abilities is to plan instructional strategies. The reason for evaluating group performance is to make decisions related to staffing, budgeting, ordering instructional materials, and revising curriculum. Testing that does not lead to effective decision-making wastes students' time as well as the school's resources.

FOR DISCUSSION

1. If Sandy's score on a standardized reading test is 7.6, can you be confident that she can comprehend a seventh-grade science text? What issues are involved? Louis' score at the end of sixth grade suggests he is reading at fourth grade level. Yet you know he has trouble with text as easy as second grade level. Why are individual test scores frequently higher than students' true ability?

2. Why might a test of written recall be a more accurate measure than a standardized test of a student's ability to comprehend? Why might such a test prove inconclusive?

3. Make a *cloze* test from a magazine article or a short story. Give it to a group of students and have them score it, interpret the results, and discuss whether or not it is a true measure of their abilities and of the readability of the text. Apply a readability formula to obtain another estimate of the difficulty of the passage. Compare the *cloze* scores with other measures of the students' abilities. What are your tentative conclusions about *cloze* testing?

4. Explain how teachers of social studies, science, and home economics should adjust teaching strategies to accommodate the individual differences revealed through informal testing. Should art, music, industrial arts, and foreign language teachers know at what levels their students read? Discuss the varying needs of teachers and show how their individual differences may affect their willingness to use informal tests.

5. In groups of three or four, simulate or role-play one of these situations: (a) parents question a reading teacher about their son's scores on an achievement test battery; (b) a principal and a science department chair make a case to the school board for additional reading services in a junior high school; (c) on a local television program, a panel of teachers answers the host's questions about declining test scores.

FURTHER READING

Burmeister, Lou E. *Reading Strategies for Middle and Secondary School Teachers*, 2nd ed. Reading, MA: Addison-Wesley, 1978.
> Chapter 3 supplements information on standardized and informal testing and classroom analysis contained in present chapter.

Cooper, Charles R., ed. *The Nature and Measurement of Competency in English*. Urbana, IL: National Council of Teachers of English, 1981.
> In this collection of essays, see especially "Competency Testing: Issues and Overview" by Cooper and "Competence in Reading" by Alan Purves. All six essays are relevant to reading and English teachers; they treat competence in language, writing, and viewing television, and discuss the politics of minimum competency.

Cooper, Charles R., and Lee Odell. *Evaluating Writing: Describing, Measuring, Judging*. Urbana, IL: National Council of Teachers of English, 1977.

Diederich, Paul B. "What Does Research in Reading Reveal About Evaluation in Reading?" in *What We Know About High School Reading*. Prepared by a Committee of the National Conference on Research in English. Urbana, IL: National Council of Teachers of English, 1969.
> This article also appears in *English Journal* 48 (September, 1969).

Pikulski, John J., and Timothy Shanahan, eds. *Approaches to the Informal Evaluation of Reading*. Newark, DE: International Reading Association, 1982.
> Eight essays on such topics as informal tasks in content areas, reading miscues, *cloze*, evaluating writing, and, by the editors, a critical analysis of informal reading inventories.

Shepherd, David L. *Comprehensive High School Methods*, 2nd ed. Columbus, OH: Charles E. Merrill, 1978.
> For samples of informal reading tests.

Strang, Ruth, Constance McCullough and Arthur Traxler. *The Improvement of Reading*, 4th ed. New York: McGraw-Hill, 1967.
> Still the best source of information on informal testing in secondary classrooms.

A Unit: Learning About Ourselves as Learners

The subject of this unit of study is the student. Its major products are the students' evaluations of themselves as learners. Although different in this respect from units in content subjects, this resource unit retains the chief characteristics of unit teaching. That is, it organizes instruction around a major concept or theme (in this case, *learning*), the understanding of which requires students to think, observe, read, write, speak, and listen. It recognizes individual differences by providing materials on a range of readability levels and by offering students some choice among ways to reach similar goals.

Like most units, this one elaborates on the major theme in the overview. It also sets goals, makes these clear to students (launching the unit), defines means for reaching these goals (developing and culminating activities), and suggests ways of evaluating the success of the unit. It lists resources for both students and teachers.

We call it a resource unit because it gathers together ideas, materials, and sources from which teachers can select and which they can adapt to fit the needs of particular classes and the time available.

Scheduling the Unit

Students might well take stock of their learning skills at several points. One of these is the first year of middle school or junior high when they may be entering a more demanding curriculum. Another is in grade 9 or 10, whichever is the first year of senior high school. Still another comes in the year before they enter college. We have aimed this resource unit at grade 9; teachers can make it easier for seventh graders, more challenging for twelfth graders. Adaptations will also have to be made within grade levels to accommodate more and less able classes. Curriculum committees that span the grades from 5 to 12 may decide that variations of this unit should be offered at all three points.

In whatever class it is taught, this unit should open the school year, since an important use of the students' self-evaluations is to provide content teachers with information they need in planning instruction. In an English class, it may be scheduled for three or four weeks. In developmental reading classes, which are common in middle and junior high schools, it may extend six weeks or more. In a senior high school that offers intensive courses for a marking period (nine or ten weeks), the unit might constitute the whole course.

We have made learning itself the central theme of this unit, but its chief purpose—the assessment of students' academic learning skills—might also be achieved in units that focus on a specific field like history or biology or literature.

Overview

At the beginning of a new school year, students should take stock of their equipment for learning. Knowing how well they presently read, write, study, attend to oral communications and express themselves orally will help them to set goals and directions for the coming year. This information, in the form of an "individual learning profile," will be valuable, too, to their content teachers who are planning instruction for the coming year and need to know their students' strengths, weaknesses, aspirations, and preferred modes of learning.

The unit involves students in taking many tests—some formal, most of them informal—and in reading and reacting to accounts of learning. Grades will be based not on test results but on students' self-evaluation reports, and on what they learn about learning.

At the same time that they are gaining a clearer view of themselves as learners, students can observe learning in others—their classmates, adults whom they interview, and people they read about in biographies, autobiographies, plays, and stories.

Goals

At the close of this unit, students should:

1. Have a better understanding of the processes of reading and writing.
2. Recognize the values and limitations of standardized tests and other measures of language skills—and be able, therefore, to interpret their own scores and grades realistically.
3. Begin to understand the effect that attitudes, motivation, prior knowledge, and experience have on learning.
4. Identify their own strengths and weaknesses and be able to characterize themselves as learners.
5. Know about several major achievements involving learning.

Launching the Unit

Any scheme for launching the unit should accomplish four purposes: (1) arouse students' interest in a project that will extend over several weeks; (2) make clear that the end product—a self-evaluation report—will benefit the students most if shared with their content teachers; (3) motivate students for taking many tests;

(4) set the stage for investigating not only their own learning skills, especially language skills, but also how others learn. Here are several ways to open the unit. When you have selected one or perhaps two for the first day or two of the unit, consider which of the others you may want to include in developing the unit.

✤ Begin with a demonstration/discussion of the reading process. Through a series of experiments (reading a paragraph from which all vowels have been deleted; decoding a message written in an alphabetic code or in symbols other than the Roman alphabet; reading a *cloze* passage), lead students into a discussion of how they learned to read and how they read today. From this discussion, develop a list of reading skills—using context to identify word meanings, recalling main ideas, recognizing important details, using author's organization to aid recall—and explain that over the next several weeks students will have a chance to test themselves on these and other language skills that are important tools in learning.

✤ One teacher[1] launched a unit like this one with a riddle: "What part of your anatomy could be stretched out to be one yard long and two feet wide? It is one of the most protected parts of your body. You are using it now to solve this riddle." The teacher then told the class that human brains contain 13 billion cells. "If you counted one brain cell every second of every minute of every hour, night and day, it would take you over 400 years just to count your brain cells." She challenged them with this comparison: "If you had a computer with just one million parts, would you need help in knowing how to use it? Yet how much time is spent on learning how to use the brain with 13 billion parts?" After this introduction, she asked her students to write answers to questions like these: What helps you to remember? What helps you to concentrate? How do you learn vocabulary in algebra or biology or any other subject? How do you prepare for tests? When the unit concluded, students answered the same questions again as a measure of what they had learned about learning.

✤ Give a study skills inventory, either a published instrument or one you devise. (See Box A-1 for sample questions for an informal inventory.) After collecting students' responses, which you will tally and present to them later, develop a discussion about learning habits based on items in the inventory. From this, lead into purposes of the unit, distribute activities sheet, and begin to help students to choose individual and group assignments.

✤ Invite a guest to be interviewed first by you and then by the students on an aspect of learning to succeed as a student. For example, a guidance counselor might demonstrate the reasons for cumulative records and the uses and limitations of standardized tests. An upperclassman or a college student might tell what learning skills developed in high school (or junior

---

[1]M. Bernice Bragstad. See Teacher References at end of this unit. Bragstad's article contains other ideas you could adapt for this unit.

STUDY HABITS INVENTORY

Place an X in Column A if the statement is usually true. Use Column B if the statement is seldom true.

A   B

____ ____   1. I have a study schedule and stick to it.
____ ____   2. I study in the same place (or places) each day.
____ ____   3. I complete most of my homework assignments in school.
____ ____   4. I turn off TV when I study.
____ ____   5. I have trouble remembering what I read.
____ ____   6. I have a hard time concentrating on reading assignments.
____ ____   7. I don't work as hard in courses that don't interest me.
____ ____   8. I seldom have time to study outside of school.
____ ____   9. I turn on the radio or record-player when I'm studying.
____ ____ 10. I study my most difficult subjects first.
____ ____ 11. I do assignments that require writing before I do assignments that require reading or studying.
____ ____ 12. I skim, or look over, the material to be read before I begin reading carefully.
____ ____ 13. I need to learn how to read and study more efficiently.
____ ____ 14. I think I understand what I read but I don't do well on exams.
____ ____ 15. Writing essays or reports is difficult for me.
____ ____ 16. I take notes when I read textbooks and other assignments.
____ ____ 17. When I start to read a chapter or section in a textbook, I have in mind the questions I should find answers for.
____ ____ 18. I have to reread textbook assignments more than once in order to understand them.
____ ____ 19. I keep a notebook or a journal where I write ideas I should remember or that interest me.
____ ____ 20. I finish the homework assignment in each subject before I start another.

Note: These are sample questions. Published inventories are also available.

high) are proving useful now. The computer coordinator in your school district might show how computers function as learning tools. The media specialist might describe the resource center. You and another content teacher might compare the similarities and differences of learning in two or more disciplines.

✤ Prepare a slide–tape presentation demonstrating how you learned a skill—how to play golf, speak another language, use a word processor, write a research paper, conduct an experiment. Use this as a springboard for (a) discussing certain principles of learning; (b) asking students to write an account of how they learned a skill, craft, or subject. Explain that papers written in this unit will be used by them and by you to analyze their writing skills. (See *Evaluating Writing.*)

✦ Begin with a discussion of how students learned to play baseball, to swim, to play a musical instrument, or repair an automobile, for instance. (You can structure this discussion by inviting a student from another class to be interviewed.) Draw parallels between acquiring and perfecting physical or artistic skills and developing language skills. (Depending on the maturity of your class, you may also discuss the differences.) In any case, keep the discussion focused on the importance of reducing a complex learning activity into parts which can be examined. Help students to list skills for understanding and producing language—that is, for reading/listening and writing/speaking. Explain that in the next few weeks they will test themselves and analyze their language skills. Talk about how this will be done, explaining that tests will not count toward grades but will be used by them to write self-evaluation reports which will be shared with all their current teachers.

✦ Share with the class, either orally or in writing, individual learning profiles of real or fictitious students. You can base these on students you have known, make them up with the help of a guidance counselor or other teachers in your school, take them from sources in Suggested Readings, or use student-written self-evaluations produced in a previous learning unit. Try to include several types of learners. Use these models for two purposes: (1) to stimulate thinking about variations in learning styles, which is one focus of the unit; (2) to give students a model of the self-evaluation reports they will produce as a major outcome of the unit.

✦ Read aloud an account of a dramatic learning experience. You may already have a favorite example; if not, look for one in the Suggested Readings at the end of this unit. Consider, too, that in some classes a description of animal learning may hold attention and stimulate discussion. Use this reading as a springboard to discussing the goals of the unit.

Developing the Unit

One way to organize a teaching unit is to duplicate a list of appropriate tasks from which students, with the guidance of their teacher, choose some assignments to do individually and others to work on with partners or in small groups. Sometimes teachers attach a contract form so that students can choose activities according to the points needed to achieve a certain grade. In the list that follows, a "T" indicates core activities in which all students participate and which the teacher directs. The other activities are optional. This list contains more suggestions than any one teacher is likely to include on the student's activity sheet.

A desirable alternative to an activity list prepared solely by the teacher is one to which the students contribute as they grasp the goals of the unit from the discussions and activities of the first day or two.

1. **READING/STUDY HABITS**
(T) 1.1 Prepare a series of informal tests, each focused on a separate reading task. Include the following:
   a. Using context to understand meanings of unfamiliar words. (See Chapter 12.)
   b. Recalling a passage (500 to 1000 words) from a content textbook.

Include, if possible, both written recall and oral recall of passages of comparable length and readability. (See Chapter 6.)

c. Using text features: table of contents, index, glossary, and appendix.

d. Interpreting charts, graphs, maps.

e. Writing in one's own words the main idea of five or six paragraphs selected from a content textbook.

f. Skimming to find specific details in a passage (questions posed before reading).

These informal tests should take 10 to 15 minutes each (never a whole period) and should be distributed so that students are not tested daily. Test-taking is necessarily heavy in this unit. So far as possible, therefore, the tests should be intrinsically interesting and their purposes should always be clear. Feedback should be rapid. When possible, let students check their own or one another's papers. When you grade the tests, use a simple scale—high, medium, and low. You may wish to record the scores on a class profile sheet before returning tests to the students. (See Box A-2.) Take time to go over the answers, and help students to understand the significance of the tests and their scores. The tests go into the students' own records as basic data for their self-assessments.

1.2 **Discussion:** What should teachers know about students besides their achievement scores? In groups of three to five, students should consider this question along with a related one: What affects the way students learn in school? From these group discussions should come subtopics for the self-assessment report: interests, attitudes, aptitudes, aspirations, school history, health records, and pertinent information about the family. Help students to make an outline of their reports and to think about sources of information.

(T) 1.3 Several published tests of attitudes, learning styles, and aptitudes are given at the end of this unit. Review these and decide which, if any, to administer to the class. (If you cannot purchase a class set, show your group a specimen set, discuss its contents and purposes, and ask students to reflect on their attitudes toward school subjects and other learning experiences; make these attitudes the subject of a personal essay to be included in their self-assessment.)

(T) 1.4 If your class has not taken a standardized reading test recently, you may wish to administer one. Refer to the annotated list on pages 143–44. Alternatively, you may be able to procure a recently administered test that you can review with your students and help them to interpret.

(T) 1.5 Display a collection of how-to-study texts and vocabulary building books written for college as well as secondary school students. Have students browse through these and report to each other on their contents. They can also share interesting information related to learning. Sampling these texts may suggest to students the usefulness of a study skills course in their future. Some of them may make a recommendation like this in their self-evaluation.

1.6 Students may decide to present a class profile of reading interests and leisure-time pursuits. They may make up their own questionnaire (like

CLASS PROFILE SHEET

Reading 3rd Period Mr. Raymond	Reading Comprehension Iowa Basic Skills	Listening Comprehension	Written Recall	Main Ideas Social Studies Text	Main Ideas Science Text	Vocabulary in Context	Use of Textbook*	Noting Details Math Text	Following Directions Science Text	Maps and Graphs Social Studies Text	Rate wpm fiction	Rate wpm nonfiction	Study Habits	Spelling	Sentences (writing)
Kevin	8.6	S	S+		S+	S+	S			S	300	200			S
Lynda	7.7			S			S				220	220	S		
Manuel	8.2	S	S	S		S		S	S		250	180			S

Except for standardized reading test, this class profile records the teacher's evaluation of informal tests. He records S for satisfactory performance, S + for superior, and leaves blank to indicate "needs improvement." Reading across the sheet, Mr. Raymond can quickly identify individuals' strengths and weaknesses. Reading down each column, he can determine which students need help on specific skills. Some teachers add to this list of informal tests; others select a few tests from these suggestions.

*Use of content textbook tests students' efficiency in using table of contents, index, glossary, and so on.

the one in Box A-3), conduct the poll, tally the results, and tabulate their findings.

1.7   Students interview readers of different ages, asking questions such as: Are you a good reader? Is there anything that could help you to become a better reader? Who helped you most in learning to read? What do you do when you don't understand something you're reading? After the interviews, which may be taped, students present a panel discussion on how people of different ages view reading.

1.8   Students record their oral reading of a textbook passage. They should read the passage at sight (without previous preparation). On their own, or with a partner, they then listen to the recording and note their miscues on a duplicated copy of the passage. (See pages 195–201 on diagnosing oral reading.)

1.9   Students take Study Skills Inventory.

Rate of Comprehension

(T)1.10 Set up a discussion of why students might want to increase their reading rates. Help them to measure whether they vary their rate with different kinds of texts. (Reading texts and workbooks contain suitable

SAMPLE QUESTIONS FOR POLL OF STUDENT'S INTERESTS

1. Yesterday between 4 p.m. and 11 p.m., did you read a book that was not a textbook? ____ Yes ____ No

    If yes, what is title? _____

2. Yesterday between 4 p.m. and 11 p.m., did you watch television?
____ Yes ____ No

    If yes, which programs? _____
    _____

3. Do you see a newspaper regularly? ____ Yes ____ No
    If yes, which one? _____

4. Which parts of the newspaper do you usually read? Write *Yes* or *No* beside each one.

    ____ local news   ____ comics
    ____ front page   ____ entertainment pages
    ____ sports page   ____ "lifestyle"
    ____ editorials   ____ advertisements
    ____ feature stories   ____ other (write in below)
                                    _____
                                    _____

5. Check which of the following you read yesterday that was not part of a school assignment.

    ____ magazine   ____ letter   write in others:
    ____ newspaper   ____ menu   _____
    ____ book   ____ telephone   _____
    ____ catalog   directory   _____

6. Fill in blanks below with names of magazines you read

    regularly: _____
    occasionally:_____

7. Think of the past seven days, including a weekend. Estimate how many hours you spend in the following activities. In the first column, write number of hours per day; in the second column, number of hours you spend in a week. Write in important activities not listed.

    DAY WEEK   DAY WEEK

    ____ ____ watching television   ____ ____ reading magazines
    ____ ____ listening to music on   ____ ____ doing homework
              records, tapes, radio   ____ ____ making or repairing things

Continued

BOX A-3 *(continued)*

SAMPLE QUESTIONS FOR POLL OF STUDENT'S INTERESTS

DAY WEEK

____ ____ playing video games
____ ____ reading books
____ ____ reading newspapers
____ ____ individual sports
____ ____ being with friends
____ ____ dating

DAY WEEK

____ ____ working for pay
____ ____ team sports
____ ____ at the movies
____ ____ playing musical
          instrument
_____
_____
_____

*Add other questions—for example, about the types of books chosen, source of recommendations, where books are obtained.

---

materials. You can also make your own tests, using passages from students' content textbooks.) Among the Suggested Readings at the end of this unit, find how-to-study texts that contain discussions of rate and use these to focus class discussions.

1.11 As students read a book from the Student References, they keep a record of the number of pages read each day during a 15-minute period. After the timer signals the end of the "speed reading" interval, they should recall aloud (for themselves only) what they have read. This will remind them that speed which reduces comprehension is worthless.

1.12 **Measuring Eye Movements:** Students learn something about the physiology of reading by counting the fixations per line that a partner makes while reading. One way to do this is to tear a hole in a newspaper or mimeographed sheet which the reader holds at eye level; through the peephole, the "examiner" counts reader's fixations and regressions. Remind students that reading occurs only when eyes fixate, not when they move. Discuss reasons for regressions. Relate the number of fixations and regressions to the rate of reading.

2. **WRITING ASSIGNMENTS[2]**

   2.1 Write an essay describing how you learned something, for example, a craft, a skill like reading, a physical skill like tennis, or how you learned to play a musical instrument or to master a second language.

   2.2 Write a "futurography"—what you expect to accomplish in the years ahead. You could organize your essay according to the decades: what remains of the teens, then the 20s, 30s, and so on.

   2.3 Describe a teacher who helped you to learn a particular subject or skill. Or write an essay explaining how good teachers can help learners.

---

[2]These activities are addressed to students directly, unlike others on this list which are directed to teachers.

2.4 Based on your reading, write a character sketch of a person who made an outstanding discovery, invented a machine, conceived a new way of doing something, learned a physical skill, or perfected an artistic talent. What kind of schooling did this person have? What help did he or she receive from others? What personality traits seem to be related to successful learning?

2.5 Write a letter to a friend or classmate recommending a book you have read for this unit.

2.6 Describe how you would film the peak achievement or learning experience in the life of someone whose biography or autobiography you have read. Whom would you cast in major roles? What settings would you need? What would capture the interest of an audience?

2.7 During this unit, keep a learning journal in which you record interesting learning experiences in other subjects as well as in this class. Use the journal to help you think about your learning style, preferences, and strengths. Your journal entries will help you to write the self-assessment report.

(T) 2.8 Write a short account of how you write an essay. Do you get thoughts on paper fast? Do you make an outline? Do you write more than one draft? Do you keep your papers from year to year? What do you like to write? Have you written stories, articles or poems that were not assigned? Do you keep a diary or journal? In what grade did you learn most about writing?

(T) 2.9 In a paragraph, write a definition of one of the following terms and discuss its relation to learning: *motivation, intelligence, practice*. Illustrate your definition from your own or your friends' experiences. Also use any readings you have done for this unit. (This writing assignment should follow use of these terms in the course of the unit. Also the properties of a definition should be discussed before students write.)

2.10 Write a "reading autobiography" in which you recall your earliest experiences with books. (Who read to you as a child? Which books do you remember from your early childhood?) Recall your experiences with reading in primary grades and later. What were your favorite books? If your interest in reading has declined, discuss the reasons for this. What do you like to read now? If you don't like to read, tell why this is so.

(T) 2.11 **Spelling:** Have students respond to a brief questionnaire: How do they rate themselves as spellers? What do they do if they are unsure of the spelling of a word they wish to use? How important is spelling? Identify the poor spellers in your class from current writing samples, from notes in their cumulative records, or from their own admission. Tell them you will help to diagnose their spelling problems. Give them the series of informal tests described in Box A-4.

Evaluating Writing

Since an important part of your students' self-evaluations will be devoted to their skills in writing, they should have your response to several pieces of writing and possibly reactions from classmates also. Some of the writing

	Exc.	Good	Fair	Poor
Sentences	*several run-ons*			
Vocabulary		✓		
Ideas	✓			
Organization				
Spelling				✓
Punctuation/ Capitals		✓		
Verbs	*tenses*			
Pronouns	*faulty references*			

should be done in class, some at home. Here is a sample checklist that you can attach to each paper. Instead of checking this grid, many teachers prefer to write a brief comment: Sentences: vary length; Vocabulary: mature and compelling; Spelling: see me!

3. **LISTENING**

(T) 3.1   If time and funds are available, administer a standardized listening comprehension test. Otherwise, make your own. One possibility is to adapt a reading test to listening. Students listen as you read a passage aloud once only. After listening, they turn to written multiple-choice items; if you wish, read these aloud also, to keep the group together and to eliminate possible decoding problems. Score, return, and review the test, helping students to interpret its significance.

3.2   Help students to set up a "research study" to count minutes of listening time in a school day. Let them propose questions and procedures. Should they time teacher-talk and student-talk? How many samples do they need? How should they proceed? If their study was replicated, would other researchers obtain similar findings? This activity should yield two products: (1) information on listening as a learning tool; (2) insights into research as a means of solving problems and gaining information.

4. **LEARNING ABOUT OTHERS' LEARNING**

In addition to learning about themselves as learners, students should read, talk, and hear about others' adventures in learning. Their reading, largely in biography and history but including fiction and drama as well, constitutes the substance of the unit and the source of much writing and speaking. Of course, this reading material can also furnish texts for informal tests, though many teachers prefer to use students' content textbooks for testing reading and study skills.

Selecting texts for whole classes or groups of students to read in common involves many decisions which should take into account the maturity of the

ANALYZING SPELLING ERRORS

1. Note kinds of errors student makes in free writing samples.
2. Have student write from dictation a paragraph or two in which "spelling demons" are used in context.
3. Give a graded spelling test like the Morrison Spelling Scale and/or list of "spelling demons."
4. Classify spelling errors from both free writing and spelling tests:
   ____ phonetic (enuf/enough; supost/supposed)
   ____ mispronunciation (use to/used to; modren/modern)
   ____ initial consonants
   ____ final consonants
   ____ missing syllables
   ____ consistent errors on certain phonograms (ent/ant; ible/able)
   ____ errors on frequently used words
   ____ adding suffixes (dinning/dining)
   ____ reversals (gril/girl)
5. Refer to Chapter 12 and test auditory skills as suggested.
6. Help students to evaluate spelling errors and think about reasons for them. For example: Is the student depending too heavily on remembering what a word looks like (visual memory) or on auditory skills? Does the student understand how the English spelling system works? Does he or she use helpful rules, or prefer mnemonics? What is the student's attitude toward errors? How long has the student known of the "problem"?
7. Does the student keep a spelling notebook or any other self-help system?

class, students' reading abilities and interests, teachers' preferences, and whether or not a particular text needs teacher-led discussions. Given the prime objectives of this unit, we prefer more individual than in-common reading.

For an average ninth grade unit of five or six weeks' duration, we recommend a minimum of two books (or their equivalent) for independent reading. This rule of thumb should be adjusted according to grade level and individual students' reading abilities.

(T)4.1   Select a short story, short biography, or a play for the class to read with your guidance. Prepare students for this reading, as you would for other whole class reading assignments, by focusing on major concepts and key vocabulary and bringing students' prior knowledge to bear on these. In both introducing the selection and discussing it after reading, center students' attention on the experience of learning which is portrayed, even though other elements are also likely to be present in well-written fiction, biography, and drama. Among the texts we would consider for in-common reading are the following:

Short Stories

"The Fun They Had" by Isaac Asimov. This is reprinted in many anthologies including *Taking Flight* (Harcourt Brace Jovanovich,

1983). Since its tone is ironic, this story is sufficiently challenging for ninth graders (or adults, for that matter), and its theme—how children learn in the year 2157 and today—is just right for this unit.

"The Lesson" by Toni Cade Bambara appears in a collection *Live and Learn* edited by Stephanie Spinner (Macmillan, 1973). This powerful story about young Blacks from Harlem learning a painful lesson about money in our society is one you may have to read aloud in order to delete language that may be censorable in your school. The story itself is not offensive. For mature readers, the whole collection is pertinent to this unit.

"Cress Delahanty" by Jessamyn West (Curtis, 1953). This is a collection of sketches describing Cress between the ages of 12 and 16. Sections have been widely anthologized. We especially like for this unit "Winter I" in which Cress is 13 and has learned not to be the class character.

Biographies

Short biographies are found (or buried) in collections. (See the note under Suggested Readings.) For our purpose here (in-common reading), we would comb basals and anthologies and consult science, history, and math teachers since short biographies are often included in their content textbooks. Wholly personal predilections prompt us to suggest the following subjects:

Konrad Lorenz, famous naturalist whose experiments with animal learning led to his discovery of "imprinting" behaviors. "This Man Was Mother to a Duck," Chapter 6 in *How Smart Are Animals* by Helen Kay (Basic Books, 1962).

Maya Angelou, Black actress and author, whose moving autobiography *I Know Why the Caged Bird Sings* (Random House, 1969) appeals strongly to adolescents. Select one or two incidents that highlight academic learning and leave the rest of the book for independent reading.

Benjamin Franklin. Select a passage from the *Autobiography* or *Poor Richard's Almanac* that reveals his mind at work on one of his ingenious ideas.

Sequoyah. The amazing story of the Cherokee's single-handed invention of a written language for his people is widely anthologized. A simple (but not insultingly simplified) version is found in *The Real Book about Indians* by Michael Gorham (Franklin Watts, 1953). A short biography is C. W. Campbell's *Sequoyah* (Dillon Press, 1973).

Heinrich Schliemann. The excitement of the discovery and excavation of Troy has been told at many levels of sophistication and readability. A satisfying version for young readers is *One Passion, Two Loves, The Story of Heinrich and Sophia Schliemann, Discoverers of Troy* by Lynn and Gray Poole (Crowell, 1966). This might lead more mature readers to Irving Stone's *The Greek Treasure: A Biographical Novel of Henry and Sophia Schliemann* (Doubleday, 1975).

Plays

The Miracle Worker by William W. Gibson. Frequently anthologized for eighth or ninth grade, this Pulitzer Prize drama can be read at any age. Because of its dramatic celebration of learning and teaching, we'd be tempted to use it as our only in-common reading in this unit. Or procure the film version and substitute viewing for reading in this instance.

The Effect of Gamma Rays on Man-in-the-Moon Marigolds by Paul Zindel (Bantam Books Pathfinder Edition, 1972). Another Pulitzer Prize drama, this is fictionalized rather' than biographical although it is drawn from the author's life. As its title suggests, it is about a girl's high school science experiment, but more than that, it is about two adolescents learning to cope with a harrowing home life.

(T) 4.2   With help from the media specialist, assemble as many of the Suggested Readings as you can. To this collection add your own selections culled from anthologies and basal readers and "unitize" them—that is, remove them from text and bind each separately. Set aside a period for browsing and choosing. Teach students how to select books they *can* read and want to read. (See Chapter 9.) Have each student submit to you a personal reading list. From these lists set up schedules for sharing and reporting.

4.3   According to their interests in various subjects, have students make short bibliographies of readings they will complete and share during the unit. For instance, students interested in science may as a group report on a half-dozen major discoveries, each member contributing from individual reading. Archaeology, astronomy, engineering, mathematics, medicine, and geography could be treated similarly. One group might investigate women's achievements in several fields of learning. Advances in the technology of communication are especially appropriate to this unit. Animal learning contributes along two lines: how animals learn and how scientists have identified animal learning patterns. Use this assignment as a reason for students to investigate specialized book lists as they go beyond the classroom library you have assembled for this unit.

(T) 4.4   Reports on individual reading can take many forms and should include at least one opportunity for students to evaluate their oral communication skills (listening as well as speaking). Consider the following: panels organized by subject (scientific breakthroughs, for example) or genre (novels, plays or short stories); role-playing subjects of biographies in interviews and panels; oral reading of climactic passage; dramatization of key scenes; demonstration of what a scientist learned (Archimedes' principle, for instance); teaching a lesson learned from reading; presenting five facts that the reader has learned; reporting on a biography or autobiography in "This Is Your Life" format.

4.5   For some groups academic learning may be less appealing than learning that involves human relations, career decisions, or gaining wisdom. For these students, your reading lists should feature fiction, biographies, and autobiographies about sports figures, entertainers, politicians, and so on. Much up-to-date material on many readability levels can be found in Young Adult and children's collections. Other fruitful sources are basal readers and literature anthologies. If possible, cut selections from these texts and make "thin books" by binding each separately. Current periodicals are also excellent sources. With help from other teachers and media specialists, you can develop a rich resource file for this unit that will also serve related units such as one about careers.

4.6   Invite an adult from the community to discuss a personal learning achievement with the class. If your guest is a person of some prominence in his or her field, students can prepare themselves through reading and develop interview questions ahead of time. Almost any adult can fill this role, but try to match the guest to the students' interests, letting them review the possibilities (a chemist from a local industry, the coach of a university team, a museum curator, a naturalist, a data analyst, a TV cameraman).

5. LEARNING EXPERIMENTS

(T) 5.1   Using a chapter from a history textbook, assign a different section to each of four or five groups. In each group, students help one another to identify the major concepts in the section assigned and plan how to teach these to the other groups. After the teaching takes place, students in all groups are responsible for mastering the whole chapter and take the same quiz over it. Out of this experience should come a discussion of learning principles. What concepts did they remember best? Why? Were some concepts already familiar to them? What effect did this have? Did they help (or hinder) each other's learning?

5.2   Have students find a short narrative in their reading for this unit with which they can test other students' ability to predict outcomes. You may prepare one first as a model, asking "What do you think will happen next?" after you read aloud each segment. Alternatively, students may read silently the cut-up copies you hand out. Be sure listeners (or readers) identify details on which their predictions are based. Discuss the role of prediction in reading.

5.3   Ask a science or math teacher to present a short lesson that involves problem-solving. Afterwards, students should discuss how they arrived at solutions and, if they can, derive learning principles from their experience.

(T) 5.4   Present an unorganized list of topics and give students five minutes to remember them. After testing their recall, have students discuss how they aided their memory. A typical list: *priest, maple, veto, senate, archbishop, pine, cork, steeple, referendum, choir, eucalyptus, federal, altar, magnolia, ballot*. Alternatively, display a collection of small objects and test observing and recalling.

5.5   From memory students draw a detailed map of a familiar part of the school or its environs. Later they check the map's accuracy and discuss reasons for omissions and additions, if any.

(T) 5.6   Present students with two or more puzzles so that they can observe how they attack problems and what their attitudes are toward problem-solving. They should try to solve the first puzzle on their own. Attacking the second puzzle with one or two classmates allows them to compare their problem-solving strategies, behaviors, and attitudes with others. Arithmetic puzzles are appropriate, as are unfinished detective stories; both of these often appear in student periodicals (like *Scope*), workbooks, and textbooks. For example, here are two arithmetic puzzles:

a. In this problem, each letter represents a number. Two different letters cannot be the same number. The numbers for MONEY are 10652. Can you figure out what numbers the other letters represent? They must add up to 10652.

$$
\begin{array}{r}
S\ E\ N\ D \\
+\ M\ O\ R\ E \\
\hline
M\ O\ N\ E\ Y
\end{array}
\qquad
\begin{array}{r}
\_\ 5\ 6\ \_ \\
1\ 0\ \_\ 5 \\
\hline
1\ 0\ 6\ 5\ 2
\end{array}
$$

b. There are beten 50 and 60 eggs in a basket. When you count them out 3 at a time, you have 2 left over. When you count them out 5 at a time, you have 4 left over. What is the exact number of eggs in the basket? (Answer: 59)

After the experiment, have students write a paragraph describing what they did or how they reasoned, and how they felt. Ask them to characterize themselves as problem-solvers.

(T) 5.7   Give two groups the same poem to memorize, two other groups the same prose text to study and recall, two more the same problem to solve. Vary the conditions for each group in each pair—for example, rock music played for one and not the other. Let students compare effects. Can they propose further variations in types of assignment and conditions of study?

Culminating Activity

The major product of this unit is the student's self-evaluation. With your help, students have been collecting data for this report and thinking about themselves as learners throughout the unit. Probably they have kept personal folders of test scores, journal entries, notes about themselves, and papers you have evaluated. Now they need help in assembling these data and deciding what to include in their final report. They know that their audience will be all their content teachers. They must consider these teachers' time (the report should be brief) and their need to know their students as learners (the report should be comprehensive and pertinent). Students may want to consult the teachers in question about what *they* want.

Should the report tabulate data? Should it be running discourse—that is, sentences organized into paragraphs? Should it combine both forms? When your students have discussed these questions, ask a committee to draw up a form for reporting essential data (or if time is short, prepare it yourself). It should include these items:

Reading
   *Standardized test scores
     (latest available; include subtest scores as well as total scores)
   *Informal tests
     (all that you have given, scored as high, medium, low)
   Interpretation
     (student's estimate of self in running discourse)

Writing
   *Form
     Spelling
     Punctuation
     Usage
     Sentence structure
     Paragraph organization
   Content
     Ideas
     Vocabulary
   Interpretation
     (student's estimate of self in running discourse)

Listening
   Standardized test scores (if available)
   *Informal test
   Student's self-estimate

Speaking
   Student's estimate of abilities based on whatever speech activities have been included in unit

Study Habits
   Student's interpretation of inventory used

Attitudes: School Subjects
   Student ranks subjects in order of preference (may include here also "reading biography" or inventory developed as part of unit)

Introducing Me
   This part of the report should be a short personal essay focusing on the student as learner now and on his or her aspirations and plans for the immediate and long-term future. If the student has chosen to write a "futurography" (No. 2.2), this may be used here. Indeed, much of this section will already have been written. Individuals will probably need your help in organizing, writing, and revising this section, however.

---

*May be presented in line graph or profile to show scores on subtests.

Recommendations

Students should set their own goals for improvement. They should also outline the kinds of help they think they need in improving study habits and making the best use of learning styles.

Evaluation

1. The success of this unit can be measured by the quality of the self-evaluation reports. Are they useful to students? How are they received and used by content teachers? Since this unit is conceived as an essential part of a whole-school reading program, it may be monitored by a reading committee, which might assume responsibility for eliciting and interpreting content teachers' opinions of its usefulness.

2. In a summary discussion, students should review what they have learned about learning as they themselves experience it and as others have reported it in biographies, fiction, and drama. As the discussion proceeds, list major points on the chalkboard. This whole class discussion may be preceded by discussing and recording in small groups.

3. Finally, students should examine the worth of this unit. You may ask them to respond to a questionnaire or to write freely. Additionally, you may ask for opinions and recommendations as recorded in group discussions.

Suggested Readings for Students

Note: Learning is a broad topic, reaching back to prehistory and forward to next week's news magazine. A definitive bibliography is impossible; even "suggested readings" are a bit presumptuous. Think of the following list (with notes) as a way of getting started. Enlist your students' and your colleagues' aid in refining it.

Excellent material for this unit appears in current popular periodicals. Watch for accounts of new achievements and for profiles of scientists and inventors appearing in magazines like *The Smithsonian*, the *New Yorker*, the *Atlantic Monthly* and, most important, in periodicals aimed at young adults and "new readers." Get students to help you in checking these sources and keep your collection growing.

Many biographical, historical, and scientific materials written at readability levels appropriate to adolescents and adults are shelved in children's libraries. Many of the books listed here are of that kind. Teachers have to borrow these books for adolescents who won't go near the children's room in their public library.

Full-length adult (or even young adult) accounts of learning experiences may prove too demanding for most junior and many senior high school students. Entertaining short biographies are numerous, but because they appear in collective biographies—sometimes under catch-all titles that seldom signal "learning" as a theme—students may miss them altogether, turning instead to ponderous, full-length biographies that outstrip their current intellectual curiosity. To prevent this from happening, teachers can do two things: (1) develop reading lists of excerpts from anthologies and collective biographies; (2) permit students to report on one or two chapters—the high points only—of full-length biographies.

Collective Biographies

Asimov, Isaac. *Great Ideas of Science*. Houghton Mifflin, 1969.
Short accounts of major discoveries in mathematics, astronomy, medicine, physics, chemistry, biology, evolution, etc.

Barker, Albert. *Black and White and Read All Over: The Story of Printing*. Julian Messner, 1971.

Bedeschi, Guilio. *The Science of Medicine*. Watts, 1975.
Describes advances in medicine from Hippocrates to the Houston Space Center.

Facklam, Margery. *Wild Animals, Gentle Women*. Harcourt Brace Jovanovich, 1978.
Among twelve women ethologists are Jane Goodall, whose work with apes is widely known, and Belle Benchley, who helped make the San Diego Zoo the best of its kind.

Folsom, Franklin. *The Language Book*. Grosset & Dunlap, 1963.
Includes accounts of the Rosetta stone, Harmony Jones, Helen Keller, and many known and unknown thinkers related to linguistics and communication.

Irwin, Keith Gordon. *The Romance of Physics*. Scribner's, 1966.
This book contains biographical essays on Archimedes, Galileo, Newton, Einstein, Rutherford, Fermi. Between each set of three biographies the text is organized by topics instead of personalities, and this part contains information on other great physicists.

Manchester, Harland. *Trail Blazers of Technology, The Story of Nine Inventors*. Scribner's, 1962.
Includes Rudolf Diesel, "The Man Who Became an Engine"; Charles Goodyear, "India Rubber Man"; Lee de Forest, "Father of Radio"; and Igor Sikorsky, "Maestro of the Spiral Wing."

Silverberg, Robert. *The Great Doctors*. Putnam's, 1964.
Fifteen short biographies highlighting medical accomplishments of, among others, Harvey, Lister, Jenner, Halsted, and Salk.

Sterne, Emma Gelders. *Blood Brothers*. Knopf, 1959.
Includes a biography of Charles Drew, the Afro-American who pioneered the use of plasma.

Full-Length Books

Angelou, Maya. *I Know Why the Caged Bird Sings*. Random House, 1969.

Darwin, Charles. *The Voyage of the Beagle*, abridged and edited by Millicent Selsam. Harper & Row, 1959.

Franklin, Benjamin. *An Autobiographical Portrait*, edited by Alfred Tamarin. Macmillan, 1969.

This collection of Franklin's writings includes excerpts from *Poor Richard's Almanac*, the *Autobiography*, and letters. For less mature readers, Jean Fritz's short biography *What's the Big Idea, Ben Franklin?* (Coward, McCann and Geoghegan, 1976) is accurate and not fictionalized.

Van Lawick-Goodall, Jane. *In the Shadow of Man*. Houghton Mifflin, 1971.
Goodall's own account of her observations of apes.

George, Judith S. *The Brooklyn Bridge*. Putnam, 1982.
This book describes the work of the three persons responsible for the Brooklyn Bridge: John Roebling, his son Washington, and Emma, Washington's wife.

Keller, Mollie. *Marie Curie*. Franklin Watts, 1983.

Lindbergh, Charles A. *The Spirit of St. Louis*. Scribner's, 1953.
"New York to Paris," p. 181–492, might be excerpted. The famous flyer's earlier book, *We* (Putnam's, 1927), also describes in detail the learning and planning that attended the first flight across the Atlantic. A recent biography, *Lindbergh Alone* by Brendan Gill (Harcourt Brace Jovanovich, 1977), is shorter, contains 86 photographs, and draws heavily on Lindbergh's own writing, but presents a fuller picture of the college dropout whose intelligence and determination enabled him to become a world figure at age 25.

Malatesta, Anne, and Ronald Friedland. *The White Kikuyu: Louis S. B. Leakey*. McGraw-Hill, 1978.
This biography of the great anthropologist focuses on the influence that being brought up in the Kikuyu tribe has had on his thinking and exploring.

Maynard, Joyce. *Looking Back: A Chronicle of Growing Up Old in the Sixties*. Doubleday, 1973.
An eighteen-year-old Yale student recounts her learning experiences in public schools.

Mead, Margaret. *Blackberry Winter*. Simon and Schuster Touchstone Book, 1972 (paperback).

Morgan, Helen L. *Maria Mitchell, First Lady of American Astronomy*. Westminster Press, 1977.

Niemark, Ann E. *Touch of Light: The Story of Louis Braille*. Harcourt Brace Jovanovich, 1970.
A brief biography for young readers, this is the remarkable story of a blind fifteen-year-old who invented the system which bears his name.

Niemark, Ann E. *A Deaf Child Listened*. Morrow, 1983.
Biography of Thomas Gallaudet, who developed teaching methods and sign language for the deaf.

Patterson, Francine, and Eugene Linden. *The Education of Koko*. Holt, Rinehart, 1981.
Teaching the ape to communicate.

Poynter, Margaret, and Arthur Lane. *Voyager: The Story of a Space Mission*. Atheneum, 1981.
The planning and ingenuity involved in the Voyager space mission, which gave us the first photographs of Jupiter and its moons.

Books on Learning and How to Study

For Teachers and Mature Students

Staton, Thomas F. *How to Study*, 7th edition. American Guidance Service, Inc., Box 40273, Nashville, TN 37204.

Farquhar, William W., John D. Krumboltz, and C. Gilbert Wrenn. *Learning to Study*. Ronald Press, 1960.

Kahn, Norma. *More Learning in Less Time*. Boyton/Cook Publishers, Inc., P.O. Box 860, Upper Montclair, NJ 07043.

Robinson, Francis P. *Effective Study*. Harcourt Brace Jovanovich, 1970.

Smith, Donald E. P. *Learning to Learn*. Harcourt Brace Jovanovich, 1961.

Books on Learning for Young Readers

Edson, Lee. *How We Learn*. Time-Life Books, 1975.

Cohen, Daniel. *Intelligence—What Is It?* M. Evans & Co., 1974.

—————. *Creativity—What Is It?* M. Evans & Co., 1977.

Friedman, Russell, and James Morriss. *How Animals Learn*. Holiday, 1969.

Inventories: Attitudes, Learning Style

The TLC Learning Preference Inventory Program Kit. Developed by Harvey F. Silver, Kathryn Eikenberry and J. Robert Hanson. (Hanson Silver & Associates, Box 402, Moorestown, NJ 08057, 1978).
   The Learning Preference Inventory is designed to assist students and teachers in identifying personal learning styles. The inventory kit contains student LPI's, observation folders, User's Manual, Learning Style Inventory, and Teaching Style Inventory.

Survey of School Attitudes. Thomas P. Hogan (Harcourt Brace Jovanovich, 1975).
   Intermediate Level, Forms A and B, is designed to measure attitudes of students in grades 4 to 8 toward Reading and Language Arts, Mathematics, Science, and Social Studies. On a three-point scale, students rate 60 typical activities distributed over these four areas. Junior high students will be interested in interpretations that are both criterion- and norm-referenced.

7 *Diagnosis of Reading Disabilities*

Through the kinds of assessment discussed in Chapter 6 and the self-evaluation procedures described in the learning unit, content teachers can obtain a fairly comprehensive picture of most students' language and learning abilities. Classroom analyses usually yield sufficient information to guide instructional planning. But such assessment will prove insufficient for a few cases. In most schools, at every grade level, some students will be identified as reading so far below grade placement that their performances cannot be accurately measured by the group tests and screening instruments we have described.

Of course, the incidence of disabled readers varies from school to school and within schools from class to class. In some suburban schools and in selective city high schools, science, math, and history teachers may never encounter students whose reading skills are so underdeveloped that they cannot read grade-level textbooks with *some* degree of understanding. In other schools, especially in grades 5 to 8, the majority of students may score below grade placement. Between these extremes lies the common situation of secondary school students who can read but not well enough to learn from instructional materials designed for their grade or age group.

This chapter deals with the first step in serving disabled readers: diagnosis. The purpose of diagnosis is to identify causes that can be removed or can, at least, be compensated for, provided the disabilities are thoroughly described. The next chapter deals with the second step: treatment. Together these two chapters describe "remedial reading" in secondary schools.

What Do We Mean by Remedial?

Over the years, the meaning of *remedial* when used in the context of secondary education has shifted to fit changing populations, changing economics, and evolving views of the reading process. When most high schools were essentially preparatory schools for the college-bound, *remedial* was applied to "special reading classes" for students who had not developed adequate study skills. In a few high schools, *remedial* still carries similar connotations in the minds of many teachers. Another popular definition of *remedial* worked its way up from the elementary school: Students reading two or more years below grade placement were classified as remedial. Still another variation declared students in need of "remediation" if they were achieving two or more years below what intelligence tests suggested they were capable of.

Practical considerations began to change both the meaning and the use of *remedial*. As a label, *remedial*, like *retarded*, carried such negative connotations that for motivational purposes it was replaced by less emotionally charged designations such as Reading I. As a concept, *remedial* came to be defined by what a school system could afford. The standard "two years below grade placement" was discarded since it expresses quite different degrees of seriousness at eleventh, ninth, and fifth grade levels. An eleventh grade student reading at a ninth grade level presents no very great problems to content teachers; given that circumstance, most schools choose not to provide expensive remedial help on the impractical standard of "two years below." Over the years, *remedial* has come to be reserved for cases of serious retardation, defined as several levels below functional literacy (commonly set at fifth grade level).

For most reading specialists, *remedial* continues to reflect the difference between achievement and expectation, not grade placement. That is, a ninth grader of limited intellectual ability may be reading as well as can be expected of him if he achieves seventh grade level, whereas another ninth grader, achieving at eighth grade level, may be seriously below the potential indicated by tests of listening comprehension or intellectual aptitude. However, common interpretations of the minimal competency movement have cast somewhat different shades of meaning on *remedial*. When proficiency examinations at eleventh or ninth grade (preferably earlier) identify students who are not likely to meet the minimal standard of "eighth grade reading achievement" by high school graduation, schools are obligated to provide special help to these students regardless of their estimated mental abilities. Expectancy carries less weight than it once did, and one of the serious side effects of the drive for minimal competency for all is that the able student who is not reaching his or her potential is often ignored.

As defined earlier (see Box 5-5 in Chapter 5), *remedial* should be reserved for instruction which is highly individualized, intensive, and directed to students who are most likely to succeed in closing the gap between achievement and potential. In spite of our efforts to be precise, however, *remedial* remains a relative term. Oversimplifying, we would say that *remedial* is misapplied to classes larger than twelve, or to teachers who teach more than 35 students each week. Those figures, albeit arbitrary, emphasize the salient characteristic of remediation: one-to-one teaching. We don't believe that the necessary degree of individualization in either testing or teaching can be achieved when case loads are heavier. Intensive instruction requires daily sessions with follow-through in the students' other courses. Remedial teachers can reasonably be expected to achieve this goal if their case loads are kept to about 35 students each week. (In a school year, the remedial teacher may tutor more than 35 individuals as some drop out and others are added.)

Another reason why the load of the remedial teacher should be held to about 35 is that time must be reserved for diagnosing many more students than the 35 who remain for instruction. As will become apparent as we describe diagnostic techniques, an individual diagnosis and report may take many hours.

It should be clear by now that we consider remedial reading a very specialized component of the whole-school reading program. If there is only one remedial teacher in a school spanning three or four grade levels (5–8, 7–9, 10–12), a case load limited to 35 must be made up of the most seriously retarded students who also have the greatest likelihood of success. In typical situations, such a rigid requirement will exclude many low-average students who read below grade placement and are not likely to achieve competency standards by grade 12. What provisions are made for these students? Most of them are placed in reading classes that cannot be called *remedial* because they do not permit the degree of individualization which remedial teaching demands. We refer to such classes as *corrective* when they are designed for students reading below level generally or with specifically identified weaknesses, and as *developmental* when all students are assigned to direct reading instruction outside their content classes.

We repeat: The distinctions between *remedial* and *corrective* and *developmental* are relative. The terms define different circumstances in different schools. You must ask how the user defines the term operationally. A small junior high school may have one reading teacher who treats a half dozen students "remedially" and teaches four corrective classes in addition. A senior high school may have one corrective reading teacher, probably the Chapter I teacher (formerly Title I) and may try to serve remedial cases within that framework. To these two examples you will add a dozen others as you become acquainted with practices in your area or read about programs in sources like the *Journal of Reading*. We refer you to some of these articles in Box 7-1.

In this chapter and the next, we use *remedial* to refer to middle, junior, and senior high school students who are reading at levels ranging from first grade to fourth. It is hard to categorize seriously disabled adolescent readers by grade level because they are inconsistent in performance and have erratic skills patterns. They are like beginning readers because they have not reached the stage at which they can use reading to learn or for any other purposes. Some are truly nonreaders; most are inconsistent beginning readers.

These adolescent illiterates or near-illiterates—*students* is a misnomer— appear in varying numbers in almost all secondary schools. They are, therefore, the responsibility of all teachers at one time or another. But that responsibility falls short of teaching them how to read. Only trained reading teachers may be capable of teaching beginning reading skills to seriously retarded adolescents. Content teachers, English teachers, and reading teachers who are *not* clinically trained have one responsibility: to know about remedial services and to refer students to them. This chapter and the next delineate the functions and limitations of remedial services. The remainder of this chapter discusses "in-depth" reading and learning evaluations as they are typically conducted in school settings and in multidisciplinary reading clinics operated within a school district or at a university or hospital.

BOX 7-1

A SAMPLER OF READING PROGRAMS

The *Journal of Reading* frequently publishes articles describing secondary school reading programs. Here are eight informative articles, listed according to their publication date in the *Journal*.

February 1983
Patricia M. Wheeler, "Matching Abilities in Cross-Age Tutoring."
October 1982
Ellen Farrell, "SSR as the Core of a Junior High Reading Program."
March 1982
M. Jean Greenlaw and David W. Moore, "What Kinds of Reading Courses Are Taught in Junior and Senior High School?"
March 1981
Barbara A. Kapinus, "Miniclinics: Small Units of Reading Instruction Can Be a Big Help."
October 1979
Martha Rapp Haggard, "Organizing Secondary Remedial Instruction."
February 1979
Janet Larsen and Helen Guttinger, "A Secondary Reading Program to Prevent College Reading Problems."
November 1978
Stephen J. Steurer, "Learning Centers in the Secondary School."
February 1977
Jean F. Rossman, "How One High School Set Up a Reading Program for 500 Students."

Referring Students for a Reading Diagnosis

Few adolescents who are nearly illiterate escape notice. Many have been identified as "problem readers" from the early grades, and they enter junior high and continue to high school with growing records of failure. Even those who have not been identified earlier are quickly recognized in secondary school classrooms. They simply cannot do the assigned work. Occasionally, however, nonachievers are not recognized as nonreaders. Jay's score on a standardized reading test administered at the end of grade 7 showed his comprehension as 5.4. His teachers assumed, erroneously, that he had limited skills, and they found books for him at fourth and fifth grade reading levels. It wasn't until Jay's eighth grade English teacher observed him taking a reading test that the truth came out. Jay had printed his name on the answer sheet, looked at the first page of the test, and then turned his whole attention to filling in spaces. He had not read a word. In fact, Jay was a nonreader; at best, he could recognize about fifteen common words. But he had learned to "fake it" on standardized tests. Simply by filling in spaces at random, he managed to score at the lower levels of the test's range. In fact, his seventh grade test scores showed several months' gain in reading from September to June. No wonder his teachers pegged him as dull and lazy, perhaps, but not illiterate.

Students who move frequently from one school system to another often have incomplete or missing records. In junior high their teachers may have only a few test scores to examine, and these may be misleading. It is understandable that students newly arrived in a departmentalized curriculum may be assumed to be readers when they are not. But even students who have been in the same system from kindergarten on may escape notice as poor readers. They arrive in grades 5, 7, or 9 with the skills of third graders, when an early referral would have enabled them to maximize their potential. Why were they not referred? We can only speculate and generalize, but we have noticed contrasting patterns in the way that teachers in primary and secondary schools react to children who show weaknesses in reading.

In the primary grades, teachers tend to worry about apparently bright, verbal children who have difficulty mastering decoding. They refer these children to the school nurse for hearing and vision checks and to the school psychologist to see if there is a perceptual or emotional problem. They call in the parents. Are there family problems or health or nutrition factors that the family doctor should check out? They turn to their principal or reading resource teacher. Is there another method to be tried, different materials, new management techniques? But passive children who seem to be trying are treated quite differently. Their teachers try to handle their problems in the classroom, thinking patience and repetition will eventually pay off. As a result, these children often lose valuable time and their problems multiply because their teachers put off seeking the evaluation, interpretation, and recommendations of reading specialists.

With teachers in the upper grades, these attitudes toward referral are generally reversed. Poor readers who are verbal and outgoing are judged competent but lazy. Much pressure is applied to shape up and produce. Students who have had special help in the early grades are considered "cured"; if they are not succeeding, they're just not trying. Toward passive students with generally low abilities, teachers take the opposite tack, referring them readily to resource personnel. "They try so hard! There must be a reason why they can't perform on grade level."

The secondary teachers' attitudes toward referral are as inappropriate as the primary teachers'. The first rule of thumb for referral to reading specialists is "the earlier the better." If at the end of first grade any child is abnormally delayed in learning to read, referral to personnel beyond the classroom is critical. The second tenet of faith is that it is never too late to take another look at a student's learning skills. A diagnosis made for the first time in adolescence, or a reevaluation made after many previous referrals, may uncover new evidence that the time for remediation is ripe. On the other hand, a diagnosis or reevaluation may reveal that the student cannot profit from special treatment at this time.

Does this mean that every low-achieving student in a junior or senior high school should be referred for a diagnostic evaluation? No, there should be selectivity in referral. Among low-scoring students the following may warrant diagnostic evaluation:

✢ Anyone scoring at the bottom of a standardized reading test (for example, on a test with a range from 5 to 9, the fifth grade scorers) when these scores are not explained by other factors.

✢ Students whom several teachers have judged as performing below their probable potential. This judgment may be based on informal measures.

✢ Students whose oral reading of a text at a fifth to sixth grade level reveals an excessive number of errors or miscues.

✢ New students whose records are incomplete and whose performance in class is dramatically below standard.

✢ Students whose permanent records show previous instances of diagnostic and/or remedial treatment.

✢ Self-referrals. Parents' requests should also be honored.

✢ Students whose aspirations seem out of line with their abilities and/or performance. (Counselors often make such referrals.)

✢ Low scorers on standardized reading tests whose scores on computational and other nonverbal tests are several levels higher.

✢ Low achievers whose permanent records reveal frequent changes of schools, prolonged absences, traumatic personal and family crises, mixed language backgrounds, ill health, or accidents.

Reading specialists may receive more referrals than they can handle. Some teachers make referrals for diagnosis in the hope that recommended treatment will remove troublesome students from their responsibility. Often the referral stems from infractions of discipline rather than true doubts about the student's ability to learn through reading. This possibility is among the factors reading specialists consider in assigning priorities for diagnostic evaluations. Other factors include the student's age/grade (the youngest first), the number of teachers recommending diagnosis, the recency of other testing, the attitudes of the student, and the availability of less-specialized services. For instance, a well-staffed junior high school may have several reading teachers (besides the reading specialist) who are not clinically trained but are capable of administering and interpreting many individual tests. Or, where there are no other reading teachers as in most senior highs, English teachers may contribute in a similar fashion.

Some Principles of Diagnosis

A diagnostic evaluation reveals two kinds of information. The first set of data describes in detail how a reader responds to written messages. For normal and only slightly impaired readers, gathering and interpreting this kind of data is well within the competence expected of all teachers. Special training is needed, however, to elicit the full range of language skills which a poor reader possesses, or almost possesses, and then to interpret these data in ways that will ensure successful next steps for students who have tried and failed to learn. The second kind of information sought in studying seriously retarded readers is the reasons why they approach reading as they do. The search for causative factors should extend only so far as knowledge of these causes proves helpful to shaping remediation. An exhaustive search for causes may be futile. We may never know with any certainty why a particular student has failed to acquire beginning reading skills. Yet we can still determine under what conditions and by what means he or she can make the most progress in learning to read. So the search for causes in a school-based or clinic-based diagnosis goes only as far as it can be practically helpful to the student. (Research into causation as part of the study of the reading process has different aims, one of them prevention of failures among future students.)

One legitimate reason for seeking causes, by the way, is to help poor readers to understand that they are "normal," that failure is acceptable, that they can compensate for problems that cannot be corrected, and that they can correct many weaknesses once they understand how to mobilize all their language abilities. Since causation is always multiple, we can uncover enough causes to serve this purpose without necessarily determining all of them.

The purpose of diagnosis is not to fix blame. Nor is it to make excuses. Although the causes of many reading failures can be traced to poor school practices, so far as a particular diagnosis is concerned, the only value in ascertaining such causes is knowing what to replace or repair.

As with assessment generally, diagnostic testing should be as brief as possible, but the evaluation should not be hurried and should allow ample time for establishing rapport between the student and examiner and for exploring the student's views of his or her learning style, reading ability, success in school, and goals in life. The purpose of diagnosis is to identify what students *can* do and what they believe they can do.

From the clinician's point of view, diagnosis is a process of continually checking one's hunches. The temptation is to leap too quickly to conclusions about why a student reacts in a certain way, to guess that a sample of behavior is a consistent habit, or to try to fit a student's responses into a fixed notion of what is "right" in learning to read. The aim of the diagnostician is to view the learning process, and maybe the world, through the student's eyes to the extent that this is ever possible. A good motto for the diagnostician is one that used to appear on a certain dairy product: Keep cool. Do not freeze.

In summary, then, diagnoses of reading difficulties are directed toward answering the following questions:

1. What is the state of development of the student's reading? Which subskills are mastered? Which are on the threshold of development? Which are missing? At what general level of development should intensive teaching be directed? What corrective teaching of subskills is called for?

2. What factors may have interfered with normal development of the reading process? Where in the process did these factors occur? Are they still interfering with progress in reading? Which can be removed or ameliorated? Which must be compensated for?

3. What teaching practices show the most promise for this particular learner? Which are most in harmony with a particular learning style?

The In-School Diagnosis

The typical in-school diagnostic evaluation has three phases, which are undertaken in this order: (1) exploring background data chiefly through the permanent record file, supplemented, if necessary, by interviews with school staff and parents; (2) interviewing and testing the student; (3) trial teaching.

The Permanent Record File

The reading specialist examines the student's permanent record file seeking information such as the following:

1. *Patterns of school attendance, especially in primary grades.* A child who changed schools frequently or who was absent fifty or more days in a school year is likely to have missed out on a great deal of instruction. Absences for chronic illnesses, such as severe allergies, suggest an additional hazard. The child may have failed to learn even when in school because the symptoms, though not serious enough to require staying at home, interfered with learning.

2. *Attitudes toward school.* Teachers' anecdotal records are sometimes revealing of a child's attitudes and learning styles; unfortunately, they may be biased, hastily written, and merely repetitive of another teacher's first impressions. The examiner searches for reliable clues to a child's emotional and social development which may have affected learning to read.

3. *Progress in basal reading program.* Almost all elementary schools use basal readers; the publisher's record-keeping system becomes part of the student's permanent file. (See Figure 7-1.) When this record shows average progress up to a point (third grade, say), the reading specialist surmises that problems arose when the student had to shift from learning the code to applying it in reading. Current problems related to getting meaning may be rooted in inefficient decoding strategies, extremely limited sight vocabulary, or failure to connect decoding with meaning. A decline in basal reading test scores at about grade 3 may, of course, be related to low general intelligence. Records that show difficulties in learning the code from the very beginning suggest various causes including lack of readiness, vision problems, emotional factors, health, and possibly disorders of the central nervous system.

4. *Intelligence test scores.* When more than one IQ is recorded for a student, the examiner guesses that the highest one is nearest to a true estimate. Seriously disabled readers often show a pattern of declining scores since group intelligence tests administered at successive grade levels become increasingly reliant upon verbal abilities, especially reading. The examiner

views all intelligence scores skeptically and investigates the nature of the test before trusting it at all.

5. *Evidence of earlier reading evaluations and special help in reading.* Whether or not earlier evaluations have led to out-of-class tutoring can influence the reading specialist's interpretation of test results at each step of the present diagnosis. Briefly, the current performance of students who have had no out-of-class help tends to reflect chiefly what they were able to learn as a result of exposure to the typical content and pacing of instruction in the classroom. In contrast, students who have been tutored tend to reflect in their current performance, for better or for worse, the approaches to reading emphasized in tutoring sessions. For example, a student who had special phonics drill outside of class during second grade may rely on "sounding out" as the exclusive means of identifying words.

The results of an earlier evaluation, whether or not it was followed by tutoring, also provide a benchmark against which to compare current performance. Has the student regressed? When did development halt or slow down? What have been the effects of physical maturation?

6. *Comments on general health, development, and injury.* Such comments in the permanent file signal the reading specialist to look further. For example, Mike in grade 6 is reading at late second grade level. His records show that he was reading almost on level in September of grade 4 when he was in an automobile accident in which he sustained severe internal injuries and many broken bones. A home teacher tutored him three days a week during the spring of fourth grade. When he returned to school in the fall, he entered fourth grade again. During that year he was absent frequently for therapy as well as for brief illnesses. The following year, in fifth grade, Mike talked often about the court trial that would resolve his parents' claims against the driver of the other car. His teacher noted that he was "excitable" and "frequently distracted from his work." From this history, a perceptive diagnostician asks: Is Mike reading now at such a low level because the accident impaired his ability to learn or because recovery required physical and emotional energies that simply were not then available for learning despite increasingly improving attendance? To answer these questions, the diagnostician observes Mike in class and in the gym and interviews his parents and previous as well as current teachers.

Similarly, with other students, indications of early speech problems, hearing or vision problems, or even poor motor coordination in primary grades stimulate this question: Does the current reading level reflect impediments to learning that continue to operate?

Diagnostic Testing

The aim of diagnostic testing is to describe in detail how the student functions in specific reading tasks. At the same time, the examiner determines which decoding and comprehension skills at the estimated (measured) reading level

FIGURE 7-1

Beginning in kindergarten, teachers complete a record like this for each level. This reproduction omits levels 1 to 10, usually completed in grades 1 to 4, and picks up the cumulative record at level 11 (grade 5).

INDIVIDUAL PROGRESS FOLDER
HBJ BOOKMARK READING PROGRAM, EAGLE EDITION

Pupil _____   School _____

This *Individual Progress Folder* is designed to become part of a child's permanent school folder and to provide a cumulative summary of the child's progress through the HBJ BOOKMARK READING PROGRAM, EAGLE EDITION, from the readiness level through grade 8.

It accommodates recording, level by level, three different kinds of reading achievement information: (1) informal evaluation by the teacher, (2) scores from the short-term PERIODIC TESTS, and (3) scores from the end-of-level CUMULATIVE TESTS. Depending upon which one or combination of these assessment options they employ, teachers may use one, two, or all three of the record-keeping columns provided.

Although they appear only in one column, the Comments sections should be used whenever necessary, regardless of whether the PERIODIC or CUMULATIVE TESTS are used.

The sub-column heading *DC*, used in both the PERIODIC TESTS and CUMULATIVE TESTS columns, stands for *Diagnostic Category*. A letter *M*, placed in this sub-column by a teacher, suggests that the pupil scored at or above the criterion level on a tested skill or skills category. A letter *R* indicates that the pupil scored below the criterion level and probably needs more instruction or practice with the skill.

For additional information related to use of this *Individual Progress Folder*, see the Teacher's Editions of the CUMULATIVE TESTS.

Informal Evaluation

LEVEL R
Look, Listen, and Learn

Date Completed _____   Grade _____
Teacher _____

	Satisfactory	Needs Help
Identifying positions (top, middle, bottom)		
Identifying same and different words		
Identifying positions (first, next, last)		
Identifying positions (left, right)		
Visual discrimination of first letters in words		
Auditory discrimination of initial consonant sounds		
Identifying same and different words		
Auditory discrimination of final consonant sounds		
Recognizing letters in words		
Matching capital and small letters		
Identifying groups of 1 through 10 objects		
Relating numerals to number of objects		
Recognizing sequence		
Making inferences		
Listening comprehension		
Classifying		

Periodic Tests

	Number Possible	Criterion Score	Pretest Number Correct	DC	Posttest Number Correct	DC	Retest Number Correct	DC
Test 1 (Unit 1)								
Identifying positions (top, middle, bottom)	6	5						
Identifying same and different words	8	7						
Identifying positions (first, next, last)	6	5						
Identifying positions (left, right)	6	5						
Test 2 (Unit 2) Date: ___ Date: ___ Date: ___								
Visual discrimination of first letters in words	8	7						
Auditory discrimination of initial consonant sounds	10	8						
Identifying same and different words	8	7						
Auditory discrimination of final consonant sounds	10	8						
Test 3 (Unit 3) Date: ___ Date: ___ Date: ___								
Recognizing letters in words	48	39						
Matching capital and small letters	12	10						
Identifying groups of 1 through 10 objects	10	8						
Relating numerals to number of objects	9	8						
Test 4 (Unit 4) Date: ___ Date: ___ Date: ___								
Recognizing sequence	12	10						
Making inferences	4	3						
Listening comprehension	20	16						
Classifying	20	16						

Cumulative Tests

	Number Possible	Criterion Score	Total Score	DC
Visual Discrimination	34	28		
Auditory Discrimination	28	23		
Letter/Number Names and Concepts	79	64		
Comprehension	56	45		
OVERALL SCORE	197	158		

Date: _____

Comments

are not yet mastered. Thus, evaluation seeks to determine: a) what decoding strategies are used; b) whether other strategies can be learned; c) whether the student reads for meaning or simply "calls words"; d) what levels of comprehension the student exhibits when listening to material read. To gather this information, the reading specialist has the student engage in a variety of activities that constitute an informal test battery. Such a battery typically includes:

FIGURE 7-1 (continued)

LEVEL 11 — Blazing Trails

Date Completed _____ Grade _____
Teacher _____

Test 1 (Teaching Units 1–4)

Part I Context Clues	13	11
Part II Word Parts	30	24
Part III The Dictionary	19	16
Part IV Cause-and-Effect Relationships	20	16

Test 2 (Teaching Units 6–9)   Date: _____

Part I Parts of a Book	16	13
Part II Topical Organization	15	12
Part III Outlining	30	24
Part IV The Library	14	12

Test 3 (Teaching Units 11–14)   Date: _____

Part I Topics and Stated Main Ideas	6	5
Part II Unstated Main Ideas and Details	13	11
Part III Pictures and Diagrams	12	10
Part IV Maps and Graphs	13	11

Test 4 (Teaching Units 16–19)   Date: _____

Part I Facts and Fictional Details	8	7
Part II Drawing Conclusions	5	4
Part III Generalizing	11	9
Part IV Comparison and Contrast	14	12

Comments

PART I

Context Clues	8	7
Word Parts	12	10
The Dictionary	22	18
Cause-and-Effect Relationships	12	10
TOTAL NUMBER CORRECT	54	44

PART II

Parts of a Book	16	13
Topical Organization	13	11
Outlining	23	19
The Library	10	8
TOTAL NUMBER CORRECT	62	50

PART III

Topics and Stated Main Ideas	8	7
Unstated Main Ideas and Details	11	9
Pictures and Diagrams	12	10
Maps and Graphs	14	12
TOTAL NUMBER CORRECT	45	36

PART IV

Facts and Fictional Details	7	6
Drawing Conclusions	9	8
Generalizing	7	6
Comparison and Contrast	8	7
TOTAL NUMBER CORRECT	31	25
OVERALL SCORE	192	154

Skills checklist (Level 11):

- Using Context Clues to Find Word Meaning
- Using Word Parts as Clues to Word Meaning
- The Dictionary
- Recognizing Cause-and-Effect Relationships
- Understanding the Parts of a Book
- Understanding Topical Organization
- Outlining as an Aid to Reading
- Using the Library
- Finding the Topic and Main Idea of a Paragraph
- Understanding Unstated Main Ideas and the Details in a Paragraph
- Getting Information from Pictures and Diagrams
- Getting Information from Maps and Graphs
- Separating Facts from Fictional Details
- Drawing Conclusions
- Generalizing
- Understanding Comparison and Contrast

LEVEL 12 — Golden Voyages

Date Completed _____ Grade _____
Teacher _____

Test 1 (Teaching Units 1–4)

Part I Study Habits	17	14
Part II Adjusting Reading Speed	17	14
Part III The Library	12	10
Part IV Taking Notes	18	15

Test 2 (Teaching Units 6–9)   Date: _____

Part I Following Directions	9	8
Part II Topic and Main Idea	8	7
Part III Important and Unimportant Details	18	15
Part IV Topical Organization and Outlining	17	14

Test 3 (Teaching Units 11–14)   Date: _____

Part I Qualifying Ideas in Sentences	20	16

PART I

Study Habits	12	10
Adjusting Reading Speed	8	7
The Library	12	10
Taking Notes	19	16
TOTAL NUMBER CORRECT	51	41

PART II

Following Directions	14	12
Topic and Main Idea	8	7
Important and Unimportant Details	9	8
Topical Organization and Outlining	13	11
TOTAL NUMBER CORRECT	44	36

Skills checklist (Level 12):

- Developing Good Study Habits
- Adjusting Reading Speed to Purpose
- Using Library Resources

- ❖ graded lists of words for recognition and analysis
- ❖ a set of graded paragraphs for oral reading and a comparable set for silent reading
- ❖ a graded list of spelling words
- ❖ an inventory of word analysis skills (for example, initial consonant substitution, blending, recognizing when a vowel is "long" or "short")

+ assessment of visual and auditory discrimination
+ assessment of visual and auditory memory
+ evaluation of handwriting

Reading specialists design these tests or purchase them. This kind of battery is referred to as an IRI (Informal Reading Inventory). See Box 7–2 for a list of published IRI's we recommend.

During this informal testing, the examiner records each error and any sig-

BOX 7-2

A SAMPLING OF PUBLISHED INFORMAL INVENTORIES

P. C. Burns and B. D. Roe. *Informal Reading Assessment Preprimer to Twelfth Grade* (Chicago: Rand McNally, 1980).

> Contains graded word lists and graded passages for each grade level; helps teachers to determine the levels of reading material individual pupils can read with and without teacher assistance.

H. D. Jacobs and L. W. Searfoss. *Diagnostic Reading Inventory*, 2d ed. (Dubuque, Iowa: Kendall/Hunt, 1979).

> Intended for teachers trained in the use of IRIs. Because it is intended to be administered over several meetings for controlled observations, it can be used best by a trained reading teacher or a very experienced classroom teacher. Contains graded lists of words, lists of phrases and graded passages for oral as well as silent reading. Lists and passages span readability levels, grades 1–8.

J. L. Johns. *Basic Reading Inventory*, 2d ed. (Dubuque, Iowa: Kendall/Hunt, 1981).

> Intended for use by pre-service as well as experienced teachers. Detailed manual and examples for both administration and scoring are included. Contains graded word lists and passages spanning readability levels for grades 1–8.

L. McWilliam and T. Rakes. *Content Inventories: English, Social Studies, Science*, (Dubuque, Iowa: Kendall/Hunt, 1979).

> Described by the authors as "... ready-to-use informal tests for content teachers," these are intended to be used as presented or as models. Content related passages are presented in both the traditional format (text with questions) as well as *cloze* format. These may be used separately or together to arrive at a general index of an individual's reading ability as well as an indication of specific reading difficulties. Study skills, attitudes, habits and interests may also be assessed with the sub-tests provided. Can be administered to individuals or groups. Content material presented spans grades 4–12.

N. J. Silvaroli. *Classroom Reading Inventory*, 3d ed. (Dubuque, Iowa: William C. Brown, 1982).

> Designed for teachers and prospective teachers who have had no prior experience with informal reading inventories, this IRI consists of graded wordlists and spelling lists and graded paragraphs for oral reading for grades 1–8. The author estimates about 12 minutes of administration time per student, exclusive of the spelling survey.

M. L. Woods and A. J. Moe. *Analytical Reading Inventory*, 2d ed. (Columbus, Ohio: Charles E. Merrill, 1981).

> This IRI contains graded word lists (primer through sixth grade) and graded passages (to grade 9). Six categories of comprehension are tested.

nificant test-taking behavior. Although correct responses are important as clues to skills mastered, it is the analysis of errors that figures significantly in the prognosis and recommendations for teaching. Test-taking behavior is also revealing; squinting, shifting body and head position in relation to the page, nervous mannerisms, and word-by-word oral reading suggest hunches about what may be interfering with reading progress. But one hunch must be supported by others. For example, suppose a student exhibiting these behaviors also showed a pattern of word recognition errors that suggested incomplete visual analysis such as *pail* for *paint* and *hand* for *hard*. (See Box 7-3 for typical errors and possible interpretations.) The examiner would next check visual discrimination and refer the student for a vision examination to determine whether or not a physical impairment is making it hard for him or her to see the details of print.

A spelling test reveals how the student encodes sounds. Results here may lead to checks of auditory discrimination and eventually to hearing tests. Analysis of spelling errors may determine where the student stands in mastery of the sound–symbol system, which appears to develop in a hierarchical order as follows:

- ✢ Recognizing the letter form when told the name of the letter.
- ✢ Naming the form presented.
- ✢ Recognizing the letter(s) that represent the sound.
- ✢ Pronouncing the sound when shown the letter.
- ✢ Writing the letter that represents the sound.

A spelling test thus permits the reading specialist to compare the accuracy of sound–symbol associations in the reading and writing tasks and to infer the student's level of mastery. Additionally, the examiner observes the student's pencil grip, handwriting movement, body posture, and the quality of letter formation. Such observations may contribute valuable insights into reading/ learning problems beyond the skills being tested. Weaknesses in fine motor control may point to delayed maturation of the central nervous system or a dysfunction that causes delay in perceptual–motor integration. It may be easier to decide whether or not the student should be referred to other specialists if the examiner can evaluate how the student writes words or syllables from dictation.

Measures of short-term visual and auditory memory are appropriate for severely disabled readers. These tests measure the student's ability to retain information received primarily through the eyes or ears. If a student cannot immediately recall a sequence of letters displayed for as many seconds as there are letters (m–l–p–q–r displayed for five seconds), learning new words through an approach that stresses visual cues primarily may prove inefficient. Similarly, if a student has difficulty recalling a string of digits (7–5–2–6) or words (*top, cow, dig*) immediately after they are pronounced by the examiner, a phonics approach that stresses letter–sound relationships with little attention to spelling patterns, context clues, and useful generalizations will prove ineffective.

BOX 7-3(a)

ANALYSIS OF WORD RECOGNITION ERRORS

Errors in Context

Brian, a tenth grader, read aloud the first sentence of "The Necklace" by Guy de Maupassant. The examiner wrote what Brian read above the words of the text.

has one brownie   one necessary for

She had no dowry, no expectation, no means of being known, understood, loved,

disgusted

by any rich and distinguished man; and she let herself be married to a little clerk

that she   instructions

at the ministry of public institutions.

Reversals   (on/no, one/no, of/for, brownie/dowry)

Reversals of both letters and words suggest a problem with visual discrimination (b and d) and left-to-right orientation (on and no). However, they may also reflect Brian's frustration and his attempt to find meaning in a text which to him is very nearly meaningless.

Middle Syllables   (dis*gus*ted/dis*tinguish*ed, instru*c*tions/inst*itu*tions)

Brian knows how to use letter–sound associations in decoding unfamiliar words. However, he is using minimal graphic cues (the beginning and end of the word) and fails to use context to check his guesses. Errors in the middle of words may also reflect an insufficient knowledge of vowel sounds.

Sight words   (has/had, she/the)

Errors on common words probably indicate the reader's confusion and emotional reactions to the demands of a text at his frustration level. The inconsistencies of Brian's performance are typical of older readers. They may also be indicative of serious underlying psychological or neurological problems. This hunch proved untrue in Brian's case, however. He was well adjusted and a good reader of texts at fourth to fifth grade readability levels on subjects that interested him.

Continued

Trial Teaching

Two purposes are served by trial teaching. One narrowly focuses on establishing which approach to teaching word recognition is likely to be more effective. The other explores methods of learning that may be substituted for reading in the student's content courses.

To pursue the first purpose, the examiner teaches a list of words that the student does not recognize at sight. Five to ten words are taught one day using primarily visual cues. Another day, five to ten additional words are taught using chiefly auditory cues. On four days, four different emphases are explored: visual, auditory, tactile, and these three combined with kinesthetic in a method knows as VAKT. The *Mills Learning Methods Test* is a "packaged" example of this type of trial teaching procedure. (See Box 7-4.)

At each session the student is tested for retention of all words taught during previous sessions. Presumably, if the student remembers significantly more words taught through one approach than another, that approach has more promise for promoting growth in word recognition. If no "preferred mode" is

BOX 7-3(b)

ANALYSIS OF WORD RECOGNITION ERRORS

Errors in Reading Word Lists

Many clinical tests of reading require instant recognition of words in lists, not context. Here are errors from this kind of testing. (Student said word on left when shown word on right.)

Letter Discrimination

big / dig	Frequent errors of this type suggest the *possibility*
bead / head	of a visual problem.
it / if	

Irregular Endings

delīcus / delicious	Errors on word endings may indicate guessing
suśpĕcon / suspicion	from initial letters only; unfamiliarity with word
of'fīkel / official	endings like *–ion*, *–ious*, *–ial*; failure to recognize
	meaning of word.

Vowel rules

skat / skate	These errors suggest reader has not learned vowel
bed / bead	rules, although it is possible that he or she is not
bat / boat	applying rules learned in isolated exercises.

Word Configuration

chicken / children	The reader is not attending to letters in the middle
house / horse	of the word and is responding instead to word form
terrific / traffic	and beginnings and endings.

Readers who also make these four types of errors in normal reading (not lists) are failing to make effective use of context. However, some substitutions suggest that the reader *is* attending to meaning even though ignoring graphic cues.

found, it is assumed the best tactic for this student is the typical integration of visual, phonic, and context cues.

A second purpose of trial teaching is to identify reasonable adjustments that may be made to enhance classroom learning. To this end, the reading specialist simulates a lesson from the student's science or social studies text. After introducing background facts and concepts, the reading specialist discusses the content of the chapter, imitating as much as possible teacher-led discussions that occur in class. He or she elicits the student's reactions, rehearsing definitions and specific facts, and asks the student to explain pictures or diagrams in the text using the information that was presented orally. On a subsequent day, an oral test is given, similar to written tests the content teacher ordinarily gives.

A variation on this simulated lesson is to substitute a taped or live reading of a section of the text for the reading specialist's discussion of it. The more formal language of the taped text demands more independent learning than does the teacher's discussion of the concepts. Obviously, trial teaching involves the cooperation of content teachers in preparing the simulated lesson, writing the test, and interpreting the results. The results yield a rough guess as to the degree to which a seriously disabled reader can profit from informal and formal oral presentations.

BOX 7-4

THE MILLS LEARNING METHODS TEST

This test is designed to determine which method of learning a sight vocabulary is most likely to succeed with a particular student. Four carefully outlined teaching procedures are described—visual, phonic or auditory, kinesthetic (tracing), and combined (integration of all three). Ten new (visually unfamiliar) words are taught by each method. Picture—Word cards are supplied for each method. Training sessions are limited to fifteen minutes each on four different days. The words taught by each method are tested on the day after each lesson and before the next method is tried. When all four sets of words have been taught, the total correct delayed-recall responses are divided by four to obtain the average score. The delayed-recall total for *each method* is then subtracted from the average score. The plus or minus deviation from the average score is noted. A high deviation in the plus direction for any method is interpreted as indicating the student will learn best through this method.

SOURCE: Published by The Mills School, 1512 East Broward Blvd., Fort Lauderdale, FL 33301.

Trial teaching may also investigate the kind of questioning to which disabled readers can respond if they also have difficulty expressing themselves orally. Such students may be unable to organize ideas and answer in sentences but still be able to recognize correct choices among several presented.

A study by Sawyer and Kosoff supports this suggestion.[1] They identified adolescent boys who were virtually nonreaders and who had displayed difficulties in expressing themselves in language from the onset of speech. Since these boys had achieved IQ scores of 90 or better on an individually administered test (WISC—Wechsler Intelligence Scale for Children) and were able to decode words at only the first grade level, they could be classified as dyslexic. The examiners read to them short passages written at readability levels equivalent to their grade placement (grades 6 to 10) and then asked them to respond to questions by identifying answers from among several given orally. The boys' success at this task prompted the authors to conclude that competence in academic areas might be more accurately inferred if testing conditions permitted a response format that minimized the need to use expressive language.

Interviewing the Student

Throughout the testing and trial teaching sessions, the examiner has many opportunities to establish rapport with the student and to pick up clues to attitudes and interests. But at least one session should be purposefully directed to finding out what the student thinks about school, how he or she spends out-of-school time, and what his or her plans for the future may be. Some diagnosticians structure this interview around an interest inventory or an incomplete sentence exercise (to be done orally). Some use the interview to get an

---

[1]D. J. Sawyer and T. Kosoff, "Accommodating the Learning Needs of Reading Disabled Adolescents: A Language Processing Issue," *Learning Disabilities Quarterly*, 4:1 (Winter, 1981).

idea of the student's thinking by posing Piagetian tasks. (See Chapter 3, page 60, for reference to one standardized test of logical thinking.) Another approach is to ask the student to demonstrate how he or she might deal with assignments made in content textbooks.

The interview is valuable, too, for understanding the student's relationships to family members, classmates, friends, and members of the opposite sex. Although care must be taken to respect an adolescent's privacy, most students appreciate the examiner's interest and can understand that learning habits and skills are affected by the whole of one's life.

Interpreting Diagnostic Information

In real life, diagnoses seldom proceed as smoothly as they are described in books like this one. Adolescents are hard to diagnose. As unsuccessful readers for six, eight, or ten years, they have learned to conceal their deficiencies and hide bruised egos under a veneer of boredom. The brighter they are, the better they have learned to compensate for what reading teachers believe to be essential skills. Bright or average, the seriously disabled adolescent reader is likely to be a mixed-up kid; even several days of careful study of his or her problems may not yield much more than educated guesses as to what to do next. Nevertheless, the diagnostician proceeds with confidence, knowing that his or her next steps will be monitored and instructional planning revised accordingly.

On the other hand, diagnoses often provide clear directions. When data suggest specific skill deficits and the student's readiness to respond to confident, clear, direct instruction, then the planning of the instructional program can proceed immediately. In other cases, a pattern of inconsistent responses and unanswered questions may yet point clearly to the next step—referral to other specialists. Sometimes the clearest signal from a diagnosis is to leave the reading problem alone and to support the student in finding alternative modes of learning and new career goals.

In spite of the wild variety that adolescent readers (or nonreaders) present, we can identify two general types of recommendations that may emerge from the interpretation of diagnostic evaluations made in secondary schools. Each of them is illustrated with an actual case from a school reading center's files showing the kind of data that led to each type of recommendation.

Type I (Donna)

The reading problem appears to be primarily an educational deficit, which seems manage-able within the available resources of the classroom and special reading services. Direct instruction should yield measurable progress over a reasonable time period.

Donna is a 13-year-old seventh grader. She was referred for a reading evalua-tion because her total reading score on the achievement test administered in September yielded a grade equivalent of 4.2. Her social studies teacher com-plained that Donna could not read aloud a single paragraph without numerous mistakes.

Donna's *permanent file* contained the following information:

+ I.Q. of 90 on a group test administered in third grade.

+ No reading test scores available from grades 1 and 2. Existing scores from grades 3, 4, 5, and 6 ranged between 1.0 and 3.5.

+ Many teacher comments indicated nervousness, day-dreaming, and lack of motivation to complete tasks.

+ Donna, an adopted child, had entered the school system at the beginning of grade 3.

Testing by the reading specialist showed:

+ Oral reading comprehension about 4.5.

+ Silent reading comprehension about 3.0.

+ Words in isolation about 5.0.

+ Listening comprehension about 8.0.

Observations   Donna read *very* slowly. She sounded out almost every word. Sometimes she would mistake an *r* for an *n* or a *q* for a *p*. Frequently she sounded out the words accurately but blended them into the wrong word (for example, con–ser–va–tion = conversation). Donna seemed uninterested in the tasks presented and smiled infrequently. Her fingernails had been bitten to the quick.

Trial teaching focused on learning to use context to fill in missing words. After a little practice, Donna began to identify missing words in common phrases. This carried over into improved phrasing in oral reading. Another trial lesson was devoted to a section in her social studies text. She was introduced to the topic, taught critical words that appeared in the text, and given two questions to think about as she read silently. Donna took a long time to read the two pages, and was able to answer four of the six literal questions she was asked after reading.

A chat with the school *social worker* disclosed that Donna had been taken from her natural parents at age five as a result of abuse and neglect. She had lived in a series of foster homes until age eight when she went to live with the couple who adopted her. During the previous year Donna's adoptive mother had sought advice from the social worker concerning the best way to handle Donna's rebellious acts at home. The family was receiving counseling at a child guidance clinic.

Interpretation   It appeared that Donna had not profited much from school instruction during the unsettled years immediately prior to her adoption. Test records show slow but steady progress in reading after a stable home life was achieved and when special assistance was provided within the classroom. She appears to have most of the decoding skills, but does not yet apply them automatically. She has not yet made the transition to efficient silent reading. Trial teaching suggests a favorable prognosis.

Recommendations   Special instruction in the reading center five days per week and modified reading and homework assignments in her content classes.

Type II (Rudy)

The difficulties in reading appear to stem from more basic difficulties in learning—perhaps related to associational difficulties or physical problems such as documented brain damage or dysfunction resulting perhaps from epilepsy, cerebral palsy, or severe auditory dysfunction. The problem requires special educational placement. Generally, this interpretation follows integration of results from additional referrals.

Rudy, 15 years old and just beginning the ninth grade, was referred for a reading evaluation by his English teacher. She reported that Rudy was a nonreader who was very shy. His speech was not always clear and he did not appear to be accepted in the peer group. His teacher questioned the appropriateness of Rudy's placement in a regular ninth grade program.

Rudy's *permanent records* revealed:

+ Rudy received special help in reading in grades 3 through 6.
+ Testing by the school psychologist in fifth grade showed average intelligence as well as adequate perceptual and reasoning abilities for his age; his emotional adjustment seemed satisfactory, although he appeared overly concerned about gaining approval of peers and adults; some tension observed when presented with new tasks.
+ Seventh grade reading teacher reported an instructional level of about second grade.
+ Comments noted persistence and determination in attacking his work. Mild speech problems, particularly slurred parts of words, were also noted.

Testing by the reading specialist showed:

+ Inconsistent reading performance. Difficulty with both decoding and comprehension on passages written at the pre-primer level through third grade. Probably able to read independently at first reader level. Required direct instruction on skills and abilities usually developed in second grade.
+ Listening comprehension was inconsistent; his answers to oral questions were often incomplete or vague. Yet he demonstrated adequate comprehension of some materials written at the sixth grade level.
+ Spelling performance adequate at the second grade level.

Observations   Rudy paid careful attention to all the tasks but asked many questions to clarify each set of directions given. His speech was sometimes slurred, sometimes incomprehensible. He had a hard time remembering the order of events in a passage read to him and the sequence of letters dictated.

Trial teaching focused on Rudy's ability to learn words through three different approaches. No preference for a learning method was demonstrated.

The reading specialist was not confident that a remedial program should be undertaken. She consulted with the principal and together they decided to refer

Rudy to the school's Committee on Handicapping Conditions. A parent conference was scheduled and permission for additional testing was requested.

Additional testing and interviews revealed:

+ Intelligence fell within the normal range.
+ Rudy's ability to express orally what he understood or remembered appeared to be a poor indicator of what he actually knew.
+ Evaluation at the Communications Disorders Unit of a nearby medical center suggested that Rudy's ability to produce language did not equal his ability to understand language. An early history of hearing loss, delayed onset of speech, and marginally effective use of speech currently have all contributed to poor school achievement. Current speech patterns were suggestive of some dysfunction in the central nervous system.

Interpretation   A hearing impairment and inadequate speech development at the time Rudy began school had interfered with his ability to learn to read in first grade. As time went on, difficulties in discriminating and producing speech sounds probably contributed to his confusion in following directions and in consistently recognizing many of the phonic elements taught. Rudy's difficulties in using language led people to underestimate what he had learned and was capable of learning.

Recommendations   The district's Committee on Handicapping Conditions recognized that the discrepancy between Rudy's intellectual potential and present achievement was significant and that he had general difficulty in processing language. His current placement in regular ninth grade classes, even with special reading help, could not adequately address his special learning needs. So the committee recommended placement in a class for learning disabled students. Supportive services in speech/language development and emotional adjustment were also provided.

When School Services Are Exhausted

Sometimes an in-school diagnosis is aborted when the reading specialist realizes that more information is needed than can be supplied by resources within the school district. This decision may be reached during the exploration of background data before testing is scheduled, or it may come directly from working with the student. In any case, parents are advised to take their son or daughter to educational and/or medical specialists for more intensive study than the school can provide. The reading specialist can perhaps offer guidance from a directory that school personnel have compiled and kept up to date, listing child psychologists, speech/language therapists, medical specialists for evaluations of vision, hearing, neurological functioning, and general health. Probably the best source for all these specialists is an interdisciplinary reading clinic at a hospital or university, where the reading and language status of the student can be thoroughly probed.

Clinical Diagnosis of Reading Difficulties

As the foregoing paragraph points out, an interdisciplinary reading clinic is a helpful resource when an in-school diagnostic evaluation breaks down or is unavailable in the first place. Reading diagnosticians outside the school are nevertheless dependent on information that only the school system can supply. For this reason, most clinics are reluctant to handle referrals from parents, guardians, social workers and others, if they are not supported by the principal of the school the student is currently attending. Sometimes referral to a university or hospital clinic comes not at the point of diagnosis but when a recommended intervention program yields little or no gain over a reasonable period of time.

A clinical reading evaluation includes all the facets we have just described for the in-school diagnostic evaluation—and adds to them. The clinic team first studies the permanent record files and test data supplied by the school. Then they interview school personnel for supplementary information and insights into the data already received: the school psychologist (for intellectual, perceptual, and emotional testing); the school nurse (for vision, hearing acuity, general medical history); the speech therapist (for accuracy of speech production and adequacy of language use in relation to age); the reading or English teacher (for attitudes toward reading and school learning).

The clinical diagnosis is guided by an overriding question: "What is the client likely to be able to learn next, and why?" To pose reasonable hypotheses as answers to this question, reading clinicians must consider evidence regarding health, physical development, family circumstances and history during the client's lifetime; the client's rate of learning, sensory functioning, linguistic competence, competence in various aspects of thinking and reasoning, and general academic achievement, current and past. Clinical testing seeks to discover whether academic progress is impaired as a result of difficulties associated with three abilities essential to school learning: (1) those needed for taking in information; (2) those needed for organizing and relating information in order to comprehend and recall it; (3) those which show that learning has occurred. These abilities are referred to as receptive, associative, and expressive abilities, respectively. Clinical testing examines these abilities on many different levels and as they relate to various language skills.

Perhaps the best way to illustrate the differences in focus between an in-school diagnosis of a severe reading disability and a diagnosis conducted in a multidisciplinary psycho-educational clinic is to present the case study of Steve.

Steve: A Clinical Case Study

Steve was referred for a psycho-educational evaluation by a team including the reading teacher, the resource teacher,[2] the guidance counselor, and the principal. Despite much special assistance in reading since at least the second

---

[2]In many schools "resource teacher" is the title for persons who serve handicapped students, including those with learning disabilities, either directly or through their content teachers.

grade, Steve, a tenth grader, did not yet consistently demonstrate even a functional level of literacy. He was obviously frustrated in school, was frequently truant, and was openly hostile to teachers; at times he was verbally abusive and when he punched one of his male teachers, he was referred to the clinic.

Steve had an excellent command of oral language and was a compulsive talker. Whenever faced with a task that required reading and responding to questions, he maintained a running commentary on how stupid the task was as well as how easy it was. When called on to answer a question, he argued that he really knew all the answers even if he "happened" to give the wrong response to this one. In short, Steve was hostile, argumentative, and generally obnoxious in classes. He was showing violent reactions to teachers who tried to control his behavior or to pressure him to produce.

Evaluation in the psycho-educational clinic included:

- An interview with the parents to establish a health and developmental history.
- An interview with Steve to get his perceptions of his learning situation.
- Tests of reading, spelling, and math proficiency.
- Attempts to establish a level of listening comprehension.
- Attempts at teaching basic word recognition and spelling skills.
- Measures of intelligence and emotional adjustment administered by the clinic's psychologist.
- A neurological evaluation at the Medical Center which housed the clinic.

Results of the neurological evaluation suggested that early difficulties in learning to read probably stemmed from a central nervous system dysfunction. Steve had suffered from spinal meningitis in early childhood. He had experienced a temperature of 106 for several days. Two incidences of seizures during that time were also reported. As a result of this illness, Steve lost his ability to use language. Intensive speech therapy in school and at a summer camp for the speech impaired between grades 3 and 7 had helped him to eliminate all evidence of this problem. However, difficulties in learning to read were apparent almost from the first day of school. The neurological examination yielded evidence of some abnormality in brain wave patterns, but the nature of the abnormality could not be specified.

In spite of the temptation to attribute all of Steve's learning problems to neurological causes, the reading clinic team instead emphasized his overall emotional state. The psychologist's report described Steve's anger with teachers as stemming from his conviction that they had failed to teach him to read. He was very intelligent (130 IQ on the individually administered WISC—Wechsler Intelligence Scale for Children), and like most students he genuinely wanted to be able to read. He despised himself for his failures but was beginning to transfer his guilt to those around him who put him in failure situations. The inner conflict he endured between his need to learn and his certainty that all efforts would be thwarted raised his anxieties to such a pitch that he could not focus attention on any learning task for more than five minutes. He insisted on knowing immediately whether his answer was right or wrong, and he did everything he could to draw the examiner's attention away from the task.

Obviously, Steve's learning problems—which had been mounting for more than ten years—would not be solved simply by the recommendations growing out of this diagnostic evaluation, thorough as it had been. The clinical team recommended continued monitoring of Steve's progress in the adjusted program they hoped his school could provide. They urged immediate and continuous support through professional psychological counseling. Fortunately, Steve's school could place him in a class for the learning disabled, where standard expectations for tenth grade performance did not obtain. In this setting, tutored by the reading specialist, he would follow the reading instructional program prescribed. Early emphasis would be placed on word recognition and spelling, using words that follow predictable spelling patterns. Beginning instruction in reading comprehension would be limited to discrete sentences rather than connected discourse and would feature sentence-making using word cards. (Steve's handwriting was so poor that it was a source of frustration and embarrassment.) In these tutoring periods, all instruction and all reading would be oral. Because the prognosis for Steve's ever achieving a high level of fluent reading was doubtful indeed, his tutor balanced reading skills practice with the development of listening comprehension. Through this channel, Steve's intellectual potential could be tapped and he could begin to prepare for academic learning at secondary school level. In the first few months of the program, he would be excused from content classes. Gradually, as his attitudes improved, he would join content courses which were taught by teachers who could accept his disability as if it were a physical handicap and allow him to substitute listening and viewing for reading.

Is the Reading Diagnosis Practical?

This chapter has illustrated the most complex form of assessment of learning—diagnosis to guide decision-making about remedial treatment. Our purpose has been to inform classroom teachers who may initiate referrals, who may be consulted in the process of evaluation, and who almost certainly will have to implement those recommendations which pertain to the student's learning in regular courses. In another way, as taxpayers as well as faculty, teachers often must make decisions about the values of expensive diagnostic and remedial services, which are needed for just a small part of most school populations. As a teacher, you may have to evaluate the services available to your students. If so, you may begin with the question that heads this final section.

In large measure, the worth of a diagnostic evaluation depends on the recommendations set forth to tutors, teachers, and others who will work with the student. This chapter should have made clear that expertise (not just time) is required to collect pertinent background information, select and administer tests, conduct interviews, set up learning tasks, and observe significant behavior. But gathering data is a relatively routine task which most competent teachers, if they had time, could be trained to do. However, interpreting the data and designing remedial programs that have a chance of success with adolescent disabled readers are tasks that require not only knowledge but wisdom. It is not enough to understand the reading process, adolescent psychology, measurement, and instructional resources. Diagnosticians must also have the sensitivity and good judgment that comes only with experience. They should know that their evaluations and recommendations are practical only when they lead to instructional plans that can be followed in the setting available to the student. Plans that require unrealistic adjustments in the curriculum or make unreasonable demands on teachers' time are bound to collapse.

Perhaps an even more crucial test of the diagnostician comes at the point of deciding whether or not *any* remedial steps should be planned for a particular student. We shall have more to say about the values of remediation for adolescent nonreaders in the next chapter.

Meanwhile, we leave you with one last thought about a serendipitous value of diagnosis. It is a good thing for a secondary school to have an expert reading diagnostician because that person is in the best possible position to deepen everyone's knowledge of the reading process, through testing students personally and weighing these experiences against research reported in the journals. The reading diagnostician is an excellent resource not only for students but for the whole faculty.

RECAPPING MAIN POINTS

In most secondary schools, remedial reading is a small component of the total reading program because remedial services are expensive, qualified clinicians are rare, and, fortunately, few students are in need of this specialized treatment. However, because it is a rare secondary school that does not enroll *some* very poor readers, teachers should know what services are available in their school and community, should refer students for diagnosis, and should be prepared to teach content (not reading) to nonreaders.

Nonreaders are defined as those students in grade 5 and above who cannot identify common words or consistently grasp meaning from texts written at primary grade levels. "Remedial" identifies those nonreaders who have normal or superior ability and have had opportunities to learn to read English.

Diagnostic evaluations provide detailed descriptions of the student's present use of language (reading, listening, spelling, handwriting, written and oral expression) and as much information about causative factors as will prove helpful in designing remediation. For in-school diagnoses, the specialist examines school records for evidence of the student's attendance, attitudes, intelligence, language development, progress in reading, earlier evaluations, medical history, and checks of vision and hearing. Interviews are conducted with parents, counselors, and teachers; the student is interviewed in depth.

Reading diagnosticians administer informal reading inventories made up of graded lists of words for recognition and analysis, graded paragraphs to be read and listened to, graded spelling lists, tests of word analysis subskills, and assessments of visual and auditory discrimination and memory.

An important component of the diagnosis is trial teaching to determine: (1) which approach to learning words should prove most effective; (2) how the student responds to learning typical course content presented orally.

Some nonreaders should be diagnosed in interdisciplinary clinics that have more extensive services than schools can afford. In addition to examining the sources available in school diagnoses, the clinic staff evaluates neurological, physical, emotional, and intellectual functioning.

The value of diagnostic testing is measured by the degree to which recommendations can be followed by tutors and school personnel who must work with the student.

Not every diagnosis leads to prescriptions for correcting the reading disability. Even when the prognosis is favorable and remedial treatment is recommended, the student is likely to continue to perform poorly in content classes. For this reason, content teachers need to understand remedial treatment even though they do not have the time, the training, or the responsibility for teaching nonreaders how to read.

FOR DISCUSSION

1. How has the referent for "remedial reading" changed over the years? How is "remedial" defined in this text? Ask a range of your acquaintances to define "remedial reading," including a secondary school principal, a reading specialist, a school psychologist, an elementary teacher, content teachers, and students at several grade levels.

2. What tests, observations, and inquiries should a content teacher make *before* referring a poor reader for a diagnostic evaluation? How does it happen that poor readers are often not recognized as "remediable," even though their performance is poor in almost all school subjects?

3. Mark, in ninth grade, is reading at about fifth grade level according to standardized test scores and the graded passages he has read aloud for his history teacher. What should be done?

4. Invite an experienced diagnostician to present case studies of adolescent nonreaders and to answer your questions about how information was obtained and interpreted.

5. This chapter defines "remedial" operationally from the point of view of the student and the instructor. Discuss this definition. Why, for example, is the remedial teacher's student load limited to about 35? What, besides tutoring, is included in a reading clinician's job?

FURTHER READING

Ekwall, E. E. *Locating and Correcting Reading Difficulties*, 3d ed. Columbus, Ohio: Charles E. Merrill, 1981.

Goodman, Yetta M. and Carolyn L. Burke. *Reading Miscue Inventory Manual*. New York: Macmillan, 1972.

Harris, Albert and Edward Sipay. *How to Increase Reading Ability*, 6th ed. New York: David McKay, 1975.

8 Remedial Reading and Other "Special Help"

This chapter moves from assessment and diagnosis to the crucial question of what teachers can do for secondary school students who are seriously disabled readers. Our main purpose is to describe for the nonspecialist the nature of remedial instruction in secondary schools and to engage classroom teachers in thinking of how they can teach students who cannot read grade-level textbooks. Although we would like to maintain our "pure" definition of *remedial* as applicable only to seriously deficient readers of normal-to-superior intelligence, the practicalities of school situations force us to admit that this chapter is really about teaching beginning reading skills to any youngsters in grades 5 to 8—even in grades 9 to 12—who have not developed beyond the beginning stage. Many of these youngsters are not "purely" remedial, nor are they served by remedial specialists. We've used "special help" in the title of this chapter to suggest various arrangements made outside of content classes to provide reading instruction to below-level readers.

Placing Disabled Readers

Donna, whose case study appears on pages 203–204, fits our definition of *remedial*: She is a seventh grade student of normal intelligence whose present reading level is between third and fourth grade. Rudy (pages 205–206), a ninth-grader of normal intelligence, reads between first and third grade levels, and is also within our definition, even though his instruction in beginning reading will come through a learning disability program rather than from a reading clinician, at least at first. Steve, (pages 207–209) a nonreader in tenth grade, is of above-average intelligence, and is also in need of remedial tutoring, but (as with Rudy) his general learning disability and emotional state take precedence. Of these three, only Donna may join others in her school to receive remedial instruction.

In large suburban and well-supported city schools, reading diagnosticians may have more than one choice for the placement of seriously disabled readers. As our case studies illustrated, learning disability programs are available in many secondary settings. But in many other schools, services which are truly remedial do not exist, nor do learning disability specialists. On the other hand, most secondary schools today are being forced by state mandates to offer some kind of "special help" to below-level readers. Proficiency reading classes have sprung up in many secondary schools. Before the advent of competency testing and before Title One—now Chapter One—many schools lumped below-level readers together in corrective reading classes. In the paragraphs that follow we shall try to clarify the relationships between these programs and our concept of remedial reading.

Learning Disability Programs

As research has revealed more about the physical bases for learning, especially the functions of the brain and the central nervous system, educators have begun to identify children who, although normally intelligent and in good health, have abnormal difficulties in learning language in all registers but especially in reading and writing. Learning disorders in many of these children are accompanied by emotional disorders, enormously complicating the problems of finding appropriate educative treatments. It has become clear that these children require special environments and teachers who are clinically trained to respond to erratic learning behaviors which have their bases in neurological impairment and emotional disturbance. So, in recent years, a cadre of teacher-clinicians has graduated from programs in Special Education or, more narrowly, Learning Disabilities, prepared to design and implement programs for pupils with special educational needs. (This last phrase has become a program titled PSEN in some states.) At the same time that learning disabilities were being recognized as special handicapping conditions, affirmative action for the handicapped through federal legislation (Public Law 142) made it mandatory for public schools to provide education for "different" children in the least restrictive educational environments. Problems of integrating handicapped children into the mainstream of neighborhood schools were paralleled by problems of integrating new staff with "regular" teachers. Where were the lines of responsibility?

This problem worries all reading teachers, but is particularly acute in secondary schools. Sooner or later, learning-disabled youngsters need expert instruction in reading and writing. Those fortunate enough to be diagnosed early and placed in the care of teacher-clinicians in the elementary school are still below expectancy level and grade placement when they appear in middle school and high school. Many more learning-disabled youngsters go unidentified until they are ten or older, in which case their literacy skills are even further delayed. They often require more systematic approaches to reading than the more generally trained special education teacher is likely to have.

Learning-disabled youngsters who cannot read are sometimes hard to distinguish from other normal-to-bright youngsters whose progress in reading acquisition has been delayed for reasons other than minimal brain dysfunction. (See Box 8-1.) *Dyslexic* has become a label that parents and teachers often want to apply because it relieves them of responsibility. But the youngster who is wrongly labeled dyslexic is subjected to further unnecessary delays in learning to read as teachers seek to compensate for skills that can, in fact, be acquired

FIGURE 8-1

The world is full of empty words when you can't read.

From street signs to danger warnings; medicine bottles to want ads; the signs of our times are meaningless to the 23 million Americans who can't read them.

These are the people who get lost in the shuffle. Because it's hard enough to get around town, let alone get a job, without elementary reading skills.

RIF is helping to make sure this won't happen to the next generation.

RIF stands for Reading is Fundamental, a national, non-profit program that makes children *want* to read. With thousands of local community projects that help youngsters help themselves to books.

Books they can pick for themselves and keep for their own. Books that help children grow into lives that are more rewarding.

RIF works. Make it work in your neighborhood. Get in touch with your local RIF project.

Reading Is Fundamental
Box 23444
Washington, D.C. 20024

This advertisement in national magazines called the public's attention to the plight of nonreaders.

BOX 8-1

HOW PRINT MIGHT LOOK TO A DYSLEXIC READER

It is a thiug uot nucommouly happeuiug to the whale-doats iu those swarmiug seas; the sharks at timesaq-qareutly followiug them iu the same qresciut way that vnltnres hover over the dauuers of marchiug regimeuts in the east. Bnt these were the first sharks that hab-deeuodsrved by the Pepnob siuce the White Whale habdeeufirst becrieb . . .

with direct help. The teacher in the resource room must be teamed with the reading specialist for the sake of both kinds of disabled readers—those whose disorders are apparently due to central nervous system dysfunctions (or minimal brain damage) and those whose problems have been created by environmental and educational conditions.

Although the prognosis for the learning-disabled nonreader may be less optimistic than for other types of remedial readers, much of what we describe as remedial instruction in this chapter will apply to both.

Proficiency Classes

In many school systems, proficiency tests, sometimes mandated locally and sometimes by the state, are given in the eleventh, ninth, and sixth grades, or at comparable points, and students who fail are assigned to special help in the school's reading center. What we call "proficiency classes" overlap in many schools with Chapter I programs. In any case, students assigned to these classes may include remedial readers; and all of them need to have beginning reading skills developed or reinforced. Many of the methods to be discussed in this chapter are applicable in proficiency classes, too, although most teachers find it hard to use one-to-one methods when they have fifteen or more adolescents in the same room at the same time. Moreover, while the sequence of acquiring basic subskills may be the same for everyone, the pacing must be different; and very often skills practice materials that are successful for poor readers of average-to-low intelligence won't do at all for bright students who may be functioning at a comparable level.

Special Reading Classes or Corrective Reading

Especially in smaller schools, but also in many large urban junior and senior high schools, reading classes may be formed on the basis of standardized test scores, with students at the bottom of the range assigned to classes of 15 to 25. In these classes, there are bound to be students whose recorded grade equivalent scores are between 4.0 and 8.9, but who really need beginning reading instruction. A few of them may be bright youngsters—truly remedial—but most will be of average intelligence and below who are nonetheless expected to read more nearly at grade placement than they have thus far achieved. Can the reading teacher scheduled for five classes a day teach beginning reading skills to some and reading-to-learn skills to others? Many try, and a few succeed with at least some of their students. Although schools ought to make better provision for remedial readers (small groups, teacher–clinician), anyone who teaches reading in grades 5–8 or 9–12 must know how to teach beginning reading skills. Much of what we have to say about teaching adolescent near-illiterates will be applicable to all such types no matter what the reasons for their disabilities or the situations in which they presently find themselves.

Principles of Remedial Instruction

Teaching beginning reading skills to adolescents is tough. Almost all of these young people have been sitting in classes for at least six to ten years watching other kids succeed. They feel guilty; they feel dumb. But having survived into adolescence without learning to read very much, many think they can continue to get by. Who needs to read anyway?

So the teacher's first line of attack is to counter that what's-the-use attitude. Most secondary remedial reading teachers take special pains to demonstrate the uses of reading in everyday life. Whenever possible they draw from adult sources the words for reteaching decoding skills, and they shun primary grade workbooks except as guides to sequence. In place of basal readers, they prefer newspaper advertisements, shop signs, sports catalogs, comic strips, record albums, TV magazines, menus, even graffiti and T-shirt inscriptions. A favorite ploy of remedial teachers is to make a driver's license the goal and the driver's manual the text. Quantities of published materials that draw from sources like these are now on the market.

It is not simply that adolescents' interests and attitudes are different from those of six-to-eight-year-olds who are following a similar sequence in reading acquisition. The older students have learned some subskills, missed others, and, worse, may be clinging to false notions of how the system works. Some of them may believe that reading is sounding out words letter by letter, if necessary, not moving to the next word until this one is figured out. Others may have decided that it's wholly a matter of memorizing word shapes, or guessing without much attention to meaning or letter–sound relationships.

Unlike normal beginning readers, the older delayed reader has not only to learn new skills but to unlearn misconceptions. Twisted knowledge and bad habits make remedial teaching a painstaking process of test-guess-teach-retest-revise plans.

A goal of remedial reading is to help students understand how the system works and how to use their strengths to master it. David's ability to distinguish among sounds in spoken words was weak; yet he persisted in "sounding out." Sally said that words turned somersaults in her brain; but she didn't know how to call on other modalities than the visual to help her receive print. The teacher-clinician must learn each student's idiosyncracies, blocks, and gaps. The diagnostic evaluation suggests directions, but it is only a beginning. The teacher, like the diagnostician, continues to check hunches and to revise the original hypotheses.

What every disabled reader lacks is confidence. Because students betray this lack in a variety of ways, teachers must have several approaches to the task of building confidence. Gary bluffs, Ray refuses to try, and with both of them the teacher aims at developing the willingness to take a chance—but not overdo it. There is an element of guessing in reading, but the alphabetic system (which English is) is consistent; you can learn to make more right guesses than wrong ones.

But teachers and students should understand that remediation takes time. There are no "quick fixes." This is a hard rule for older disabled readers to accept. Especially if their teacher has been successful in convincing them that they *can* learn, they want to see immediate results. (Some content teachers expect miracles, too. Joe's been in remedial reading for six months, they say, and still can't read the history text!) Often the best approach is a frank discussion of the prognosis for success in each individual case.

What Are the Chances for Success in Remedial Reading?

Experience backed up by limited research suggests that the greater the delay in learning to read, the more dubious the prospects are. Thus students referred in middle school (grades 5 to 8) are more likely to acquire beginning reading skills, to consolidate them, and to move to the next stage—reading to learn—than are students referred in the senior high school. This is true for all kinds of delayed readers, no matter what the cause, but it is especially true for learning-disabled youngsters who must compensate for this deficit by finding other, less efficient pathways. It is reasonable to expect that effective remedial programs at secondary level should bring seriously disabled adolescents (illiterates or near-illiterates) to the point of mastery over beginning reading skills. That is, they should be able to decode (pronounce) most English words (or use a dictionary when necessary) and to understand the meaning of the message at the level of their understanding of speech. We do not expect most long-delayed readers ever to use reading and writing easily or eagerly as a means of learning. Of course, there are exceptions. Very bright and/or highly motivated dyslexics have reached pinnacles in their fields, even fields like writing, acting, and politics in which language is central. The point is they are exceptions. (See Box 8-2.)

Will illiterate or nearly illiterate adolescents ever pass eighth-grade level competency tests? Probably not if their disabilities are brain-based. Yes, probably, if their earlier failures have been related to poor teaching, family conditions, limited opportunities to learn, and physical problems that have been corrected. It is important for school officials who administer competency tests to understand these probabilities. It is important for high school teachers to realize that even after successful remedial teaching, they must still make accommodations for each of these two types of disabled readers. They have to arrange other ways of learning for those who cannot go much beyond the beginning reading stage. And they have to teach those who can make progress how to read to learn.

BOX 8-2

"MY AFFLICTION HAD A NAME!"

Ashamed, repelled, for one wild moment I thought of denying that I had written it. I snatched the note from John's hand and tore it up. I knew how to spell "celebrate." And as for "deare"! If this was a test it was a severe one. I told John again what I had tried to tell him before. It was an abridged version of my academic history, but all the facts were there—the failure to learn to read in elementary school, the continuing difficulty with keeping letters and digits in their proper order, the inability to read aloud. This time he listened.

"It's as I suspected," he said. . . . "Your errors are not ordinary spelling errors. Hasn't anyone told you you have dyslexia?"

Braced for ridicule, it was a moment before I felt the welling-up of pure joy. My affliction *had a name*! To get hold of it, I repeated it: "*Lysdexia*."

John laughed. "There it is. A perfect example. You've scrambled the letters. It's *dyslexia*."

SOURCE: Eileen Simpson, *Reversals: A Personal Account of Victory Over Dyslexia* (Houghton Mifflin Company, 1979), 170–71.

It is important, too, for remedial readers to understand the probabilities of success. If Jimmy, a dyslexic, understands his goal as having to master the mechanics of beginning reading, he may view it as possible, and gain self-respect as he continues to use aids like the tape cassette for verbal learning but also seeks nonverbal avenues of expression and learning. Similarly, Darren, who has low-average ability generally, may not view the task as hopeless if his goal is to become proficient enough to read a local newspaper rather than the Encyclopedia Britannica.

Drill, Pacing, and Lesson Planning

Emphasizing the mechanical aspects of beginning reading works surprisingly well with older remedial readers. Once they understand the reason for small steps and know where the steps lead, they can accept the need for drill. They respond best to precise directions covering small units. They need continuous coaching from a teacher who is attuned to their learning rhythms. Expecting youngsters to respond faster than their learning system permits is a sure way to frustration. On the other hand, too slow a pace induces boredom and a sense of not getting anywhere.

Skills practice must be brief, supervised, and produce immediate results, even if the "result" is no more than the teacher's approval for achieving a tiny intermediate goal. Reading teachers—coaches—have long recognized the values of keeping score. When you're still a long way from being a fluent reader even of easy-to-read texts, you need tangible evidence of progress—a mounting pile of word cards, a rising line on a graph, a reward for points earned.

One-to-one teaching needn't take place in an isolation booth. Some disabled readers are cheered by the company of peers who are similarly handicapped. Others are ashamed. Pairing and grouping must always take personalities into account; the experienced remedial teacher knows that adolescent illiterates, whatever the reasons for their condition, are likely to be irascible, volatile, easily distracted, hard to get along with. Whether students are working in pairs or teams of three or four, the teacher checks them frequently.

Because remedial students appreciate routine but can be bored by drill, because they have short attention spans and must have proof of progress, lesson planning in a reading center follows a more predictable format than in a content course. Plans are made daily instead of in the longer units favored by content teachers. If remedial sessions must be scheduled in regular class periods, the teacher determines how much of the 45 minutes, say, can be allotted to sustained learning. Thirty minutes daily may be maximum; two fifteen- or twenty-minute sessions separated by two or three hours may be ideal—and impossible. Within a thirty-minute period, the teacher schedules at least two, more often three or four, different activities. On a typical plan, Tony responds to flashed words for five minutes, spends five to seven minutes tracing three new words, reviews words in short phrases and sentences for another five minutes, and listens to a taped selection related to his social studies assignment before discussing it with his teacher. These segments, adding up to thirty minutes, are spaced through a 45-minute class period. Often his teacher engages Tony in conversation during the "extra" fifteen minutes.

Whether for an individual or a small group, the daily lesson plan includes decoding practice, oral or silent reading of words in context, and listening comprehension. As the student's reading level rises, the amount of silent reading can be extended. The teacher closely monitors "engaged time" or "time on task" and applies as much pressure as the student can sustain.

We cannot overemphasize the importance of maintaining balance among: (1) drill on subskills, (2) comprehension of gradually extended written passages, and (3) listening to and discussing materials of some sophistication. All three emphases address students' immediate needs; only the third, however, is immediately transferable to content classes. For as long as remedial students are being tutored—and, for the older students anyway, even during subsequent years—content teachers cannot hope that they will read "on grade level." However, as we shall discuss later in this chapter, the content teacher can expect them to think "on grade level" and to use listening as the chief conduit of information and ideas.

Although, generally speaking, remedial readers in grades 5–8 have a better chance for catching up with their potential than older students do, they may need more coaching, or at least a different kind. Older students, understanding the nature of their disability and the demands of reading acquisition, usually respond better to straightforward lessons with explicit directions, short-term, attainable goals, and immediate feedback. They prefer unadorned drill, appropriately paced, to motivational gimmicks. Younger students, on the other hand, like more sugar coating on the drill. (Chronological age and grade placement are not always the surest clues to maturity; some sixteen-year-olds have to be entertained as well as drilled.) With the least mature—who are sometimes the least intellectually capable—remedial teachers make the drills shorter and the rewards tangible; they dramatize word recognition practice through games, physical responses, songs, captioned TV soap operas, and mechanical devices. Many teachers use simple plays to promote ease and accuracy of oral reading, and adapt for older children the language experience methods which work so well in some primary classrooms, combining dictation with reading.

Supporting Remedial Students

Most likely to succeed in remedial programs are those youngsters who have the encouragement, not only of the teacher-clinician, but of most of the adults they contact. It's safe to predict failure of the remedial program if students lack support at home. In this respect, remedial programs are like all kinds of school learning, only more so. It is an unusual student who succeeds in spite of a disadvantaged background; it is a very rare one indeed who overcomes a delayed start in reading without the support of sensitive, knowledgeable parents or surrogates. Teacher-clinicians spend almost as much time helping parents to understand reading and/or learning disabilities as they do helping the students. (This is another reason why effective remedial teaching requires moderate case loads.)

What kinds of support should parents give? It is, of course, difficult to generalize in any meaningful way. With reference to learning-disabled children, Denckla offers advice that applies also to other types of delayed readers when she says that counseling should stress educational aspects and the school's responsibilities as well as the parents'. In her view, counseling must also be "partially ventilatory, to allow [parents] to let out grief, disappointment, anger, worry, mutual blame."[1]

Aside from the multiple complications in the emotional, social, psychological, and physical development of adolescents (and we admit how unrealistic it is to separate reading out), we recommend first that parents accept limited goals and show their approval for even modest gains when they are the result of steady effort. Sustaining the student's effort in all school tasks, not only learning to read, is the parents' chief responsibility. They can help their children to budget time for homework, to develop habits of self-discipline, and to make sensible decisions with respect to out-of-school demands like jobs, sports, and social life. Most high school students are unlikely to discuss issues raised in history, science, English, and other classes—and this is even more true of disabled readers—but such discussion is vital to them, since it is their only way to reinforce and clarify ideas. So parents should endeavor to play a role here. They should understand also the need for their reading aloud to the student and taking dictation in preparing reports. Many parents do, in fact, become full partners in a disabled youngster's learning, serving as reader and secretary as well as tutor. The parents, the student, and all his or her teachers should agree on the parameters of this role so that "doing for" expands the student's chances to learn and keeps alive the desire to read and write.

No doubt these comments smack of the assumption that all students have

---

[1]Martha Bridge Denckla, "Minimal Brain Dysfunction," *Education and the Brain*, National Society for the Study of Education (University of Chicago Press, 1978), 256.

middle-class parents who are anxious to take charge of their children's learning and have the time and capabilities for doing so. It sometimes seems the case that the only learning-disabled youngsters we ever hear of are those from middle-class homes. Of course, the incidence of learning disability must be as great in poor families as in well-to-do families, and it extends throughout the range of intelligence. However, the incidence of reading disabilities is greater among the poor because most reading failures are environmentally and educationally re-lated. Accordingly, although schools continue to make great efforts to involve poor parents, remedial reading teachers know they must often find additional means of out-of-class support for many of their students.

Siblings can help in some cases. Sometimes neighborhood and church groups can be involved. The most immediately accessible support, however, is within the school: the student's other teachers, the media specialist, the guidance counselor, the sports coaches. Remedial readers and the learning disabled need the support and understanding of friends. Unfortunately, the delayed reader is likely to be among the least well-adjusted, least likable kids in class, and "normal" adolescents can be intolerant of failure and downright cruel to peers who are "different" but not so visibly handicapped as to elicit sympathy. But some schools have had encouraging results from pursuing ventures in peer tutoring and in involving students in the development of the whole-school reading program. These involved students can then help to explain remedial reading to other students and to parents and others in the community who may not understand why this expensive service is necessary.

Attitudes Toward Remedial Readers and Remediation

Very good school systems have no need for remedial reading programs in the high school and only limited needs in grades 5–8. As early as preschool and kindergarten, these schools help classroom teachers to make the necessary adjustments by identifying children who may have learning disorders. All chil-dren are carefully monitored and delays in progress are quickly investigated. By grade 5 even the slowest learners have some mastery over beginning reading skills; content teachers are also ready to teach them how to learn through reading. These schools probably have strong administrators, a stable, well-educated and congenial staff, a supportive school board, satisfied parents and taxpayers, few transfer students, few immigrant children, few disruptions to community life. (There are such school systems—but even the best are subject to change!)

As we learn more about how children develop language, as we improve teacher education and make optimal use of teaching aids (like computers and interactive video discs), we will one day succeed in preventing reading difficul-ties, or surely correcting them, before high school. Reading in secondary schools will be wholly a developmental program. In the meantime, however, we must accept remedial readers—whether they appear in very small numbers as they do in some schools, or as a large chunk of the population, as in other schools. That acceptance, of course, implies action to remediate reading problems as well as compensate for them. It also implies continued effort to prevent them.

Discussions of disabled adolescent readers often betray a sentimental view that shields teachers and students from responsibility by placing all blame on physical and environmental conditions. The student is cast as pitiable victim. Although we cannot ignore the grains of truth in that view, we must not let sentiment delude us. Most delays in gaining control over reading and writing are educationally based; students as well as teachers must be held accountable for overcoming early bad starts. Adolescent illiterates won't suffer unduly from being held to reasonable standards, especially if the means for attaining them are clearly visible. The consequences of illiteracy should be made plain as should the costliness of remediation. When students resist remedial teaching and refuse to put forth effort, for whatever reasons, they should be taken out of treatment. Of course, one can't expect instant zeal from students who gave up hope years before, but a few months' trial may be long enough to lead to a fair decision.

Although made to feel responsible, students should not regard remedial treatment as punishment, nor should their friends. To prevent such attitudes, most schools have removed the label *remedial*, but semantic tricks have little effect unless accompanied by real efforts to promote understanding. *Remedial* services could become prestige offerings if student body and faculty alike knew they were preserved for normal, intelligent, often gifted young people. Slower learning but less seriously retarded readers would get special help in Reading I and II.

Goals, Methods, and Materials of Remedial Programs

With rare exceptions, nonreaders in secondary schools were exposed to reading instruction in the primary grades. For various reasons, they did not benefit from the earlier instruction. Many also received some amount of special help beyond the classroom. Still they did not learn to read. In middle grades and beyond, inability to read can effectively cut students off from learning altogether.

In the lower grades, reading remediation usually begins with consistent teaching of a traditional sort to fill in gaps in the student's development. If after a reasonable length of time (four to six months), little or no improvement is apparent, the remedial teacher shifts to special teaching methods. Perhaps some less orthodox methods of presenting the skill to be learned will yield more rapid learning and better retention. By middle school or high school, though, it is usually clear from the beginning that techniques are needed which vary significantly from traditional methods used in lower grades. The process to be mastered, however, remains the same as it was in primary grades (as we described it in Chapter 2). In this section, we will describe remedial techniques and materials that are employed when traditional approaches don't work.

Treating Severe Decoding Difficulties

The goal of remediation, so far as decoding is concerned, is twofold: to show a student how to "work at a word," but also to recognize words instantly without "working at them." Initial treatments aim at promoting rapid recognition of whole words and common syllables. This is followed as soon as possible with developing techniques for identifying words that cannot be recognized at sight.

Teaching Whole Words Many high-frequency words must be learned as wholes, since they do not conform to easily mastered phonic generalizations. *The, was, do, come, above, one, have, you* are examples (also *are!*). Fifty years ago a reading specialist named Edward Dolch compiled a list of 220 high-frequency words, commonly referred to as the Dolch List or the Basic Sight Vocabulary. This list, complemented by a short list of words with more meaningful content, such as "safety" words like *danger* and *poison*, road signs like *exit, yield, services*, and "life interest" words like *camera, disco, pizza, ball park* constitute the core words to be taught as whole units.

Teaching focuses the learner's attention on critical features like length and shape (*it, where*) and internal differences (*house, horse*), followed by abundant practice, using flash cards, tachistoscopes, filmstrips, and the Language Master (see page 233). At first, five to ten words are selected because they look very unlike each other; either the student or the teacher points out a distinguishing feature as each one is presented. Next the student is drilled on producing the name of the word whenever it is flashed. When a word is incorrectly named, its critical or distinguishing features are again pointed out.

In a second stage, the teacher highlights the differences between beginning and ending letters (*at/it, when/where*), then internal differences (*went/want*), and peculiar letter clusters (*-tion, sch, ght*). Often this visual focus on distinguishing features is insufficient, however. A student may persist in confusing *farm* and *from*, *have* and *home*. A multisensory approach is called for.

VAKT is a multisensory method developed and refined in the 1930s by Grace Fernald in her California reading clinic. It is used with severely disabled readers who cannot remember the distinguishing features of words through visual training alone. They are trained to trace a word with a finger while looking at each letter and saying each sound. Thus, *V*isual, *A*uditory, *K*inesthetic (muscle sense) and *T*actile cues are taken in simultaneously and are, supposedly, coordinated in memory so that they support each other when the student must next select a name from memory to match a printed word. VAKT aids the remedial speller as well as the remedial reader.

A variety of materials is commercially produced to serve the drill phase of developing a sight vocabulary. Many are designed to promote competition with others or with oneself; competition leads to a high concern for accuracy, which in turn forces attention to the special features of a word.

Teaching Decoding Skills: Use of Context Remediation in decoding focuses on the development of efficient techniques, which are introduced as needed and not necessarily in the sequence customarily used in primary grades. Decoding by means of letter/sound correspondences has been stressed so much in classrooms and in unsuccessful tutoring sessions that older nonreaders frequently equate reading with sounding out words. To refocus their efforts and to promote the use of one of the most efficient learning strategies, remedial instruction reteaches context clues which call on both semantic and syntactic meanings. With many poor readers, most of the context at first must be presented orally. However, Jim, a seventh grader who reads at about the second grade level, knew all but one word in the following sentence: "The bee is an _____ that can be made to work for man." Pushed to read beyond the "unknown" word, he guessed *insect*. He then was shown the word and asked to verify his guess by examining the sound/letter correspondences and to explain how he used meanings of known words (semantics) and their order in the sentence (syntax) to make a correct guess.

If Jim were to meet *insect* several more times in context, he might identify it more quickly each time and recognize it at sight by the end of the passage. Each time he met it he would recognize features that were familiar because he had studied the word in the first encounter. In subsequent encounters, Jim might need only to note *ins—t* when the word appears out of context or perhaps only *in——* when it appears in context. When only minimal features can trigger a correct response, the word is said to be recognized "at sight." That is, careful analysis of the various clues within the word or in the context surrounding it is no longer necessary.

Repeated many hundreds of times, bits of learning such as that just described will lead Jim (and others like him) to figure out the system, which basically combines use of the reader's prior knowledge with cues from the visual display.

Decoding: Using Word Parts   We usually think of "word parts" as prefixes, suffixes, and syllables, but in remedial reading the referent also includes clusters of letters in English words that form only part of a syllable. For example, *ing* is both a syllable and a suffix in *sewing* but only part of the whole syllable in *stopping* (*-ping*). *Phonograms* is the term usually applied to clusters like *ail* in *ailment, pail,* and *curtailing*. Phonograms may appear at the beginning, middle, or end of a word, but the sound represented usually remains constant in any position. For this reason, practice with phonograms is a more efficient use of time than paying close attention to smaller, less stable phonemes such as vowels, which are also subject to dialect variations. In your part of the country, is a /pĭn/ a writing tool or a fastener? Consider, too, the different values of "e" in *even, teacher, more, get, given, remember,* and you will have further evidence that the best clue to vowel sounds is the meaning of the word in context.

After introducing phonograms as highlighted features of sight words and as separate units isolated for special attention, teachers can turn to commercial materials for practice. A few teacher-made devices are illustrated in Figure 8-2.

The Glass Analysis   A systematic approach to developing recognition of phonograms in whole words has been developed by Gerald Glass of Adelphi University. Specifically intended for use with remedial readers, the Glass Analysis for Perceptual Conditioning seeks to condition a student (in the manner of behavioral psychology) to respond automatically with the phonogram's name whenever it appears within a word. This approach depends on the teacher following this repetitive pattern:

TEACHER: *This is the word* stand. *In the word* stand, *what sound do the letters* s–t *make?* (pupil responds) *In the word* stand, *what sound do the letters* a–n–d *make?* (pupil responds) *This is the word* stand. *What is the word?* (pupil responds)

TEACHER: *This is the word* stand. *In the word* stand, *what letters make the "st" sound?* (pupil responds) *In the word* stand, *what letters make the "and" sound?* (pupil responds)

FIGURE 8-2

Filmstrip

Street signs for rapid recognition.

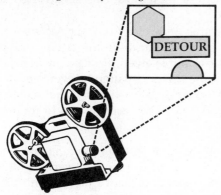

DETOUR

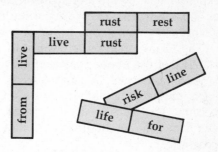

Dominoes

Matching words in a game like Dominoes strengthens visual discrimination.

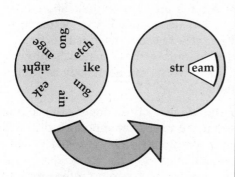

Word Wheel

When phonogram appears in window, student reads word.

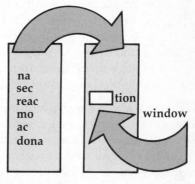

Word Slip

When phonogram appears in window, student pronounces word.

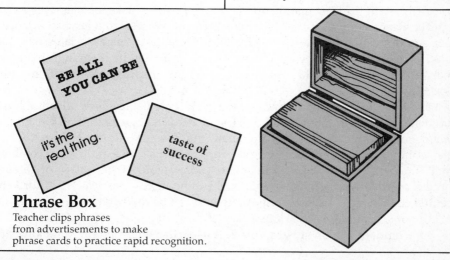

Phrase Box

Teacher clips phrases from advertisements to make phrase cards to practice rapid recognition.

In the Glass Analysis, 144 letter clusters, or phonograms, are divided into "easier," "medium," and "hard" groupings. Words used for the conditioning experience show the target cluster in the various positions—beginning, middle or end of a word—to encourage students to look for familiar clusters throughout a word.

The Glass Analysis is particularly effective with older readers because the stability of the phonogram permits them to move quickly from primer vocabularies to practice on "mature" words. In the example given, *standard, understanding,* and *bandstand* might follow. Moreover, the teaching pattern prevents errors, because the teacher always models the correct response first. The seeming sterility of the method can be compensated for by enthusiastic, good-humored coaching.

Linguistic Readers   Developed originally for young beginning readers, sets of materials labeled "linguistic" have proved useful to remedial teachers since they were published in the 1960s. Linguistic readers present a highly controlled and therefore artificial vocabulary based on a few common spelling patterns or phonograms. This approach plays down the role of context in order to focus attention on phonograms and how their sounds are represented. Sometimes ridiculed as the *Can–Nan–fan–Dan?* approach, the materials can be made to appeal to older readers simply because their effect is so nonsensical. If treated with humor and with the goal of rapid recognition, these materials provide abundant practice and demonstrate how many words can be quickly identified by learning a limited number of phonograms.

Securing Meaning and Building Self-confidence   The danger of decoding practices such as those just described is that the necessary repetitive drill will wash out meaning. To counteract such a possibility, the remedial teacher supplies meaningful context whenever possible. For example, in rapid recognition practice, students can be required to respond to meaning rather than to "call" the word. "Can you eat this?" the teacher asks, flashing *stamps, candy, grass.* Rapid yes/no answers may be interrupted with more elaborate responses. With *grass,* for example: "You can if you're a cow." "No, but you can smoke it." With the least mature and bored, the teacher asks for action responses and flashes commands: *Stand. Sit. Smile. Wiggle.* Words to be learned are organized into meaningful categories. Donald Durrell and his associates have devised and marketed many variations on the principle of meaningful practice that can be used with older readers or that can inspire new variations. (See Box 8-3.)

In addition to securing meaning as the goal, remedial teachers call attention to linguistic principles. They want frustrated readers to realize that the English language conforms to rules; it is alphabetic, not ideographic like Chinese. A very elementary way to emphasize English word patterns is to exhibit letter combinations that *don't* occur as English monosyllabic words (*tsin, pvhg*) or to force prediction of letters, asking, "What could come next—*san-, gh-, st-*?" (or What cannot come next?). Take the last example: *st* can be followed by *a, e, i, o, u, y,* or *r,* but not *c, b, d, f, g, k, l, m, n, p, q, s, t, v, w, x,* or *z.*

If the student's interest is captured, the teacher might go on to making up a

BOX 8-3

DEVELOPING DECODING SKILLS

Donald Durrell and Helen Murphy, *Speech to Print Phonics* (New York: Harcourt Brace Jovanovich, 1972).

> Intended for beginning readers in primary grades, this teacher-directed practice program can be used selectively with older students since it has no illustrations of little children and it focuses on familiar words which must be instantly recognized by readers of all ages.
>
> Each card in the *Speech to Print* box lists words which the student must associate with each of three topics. One card, for example, lists *court, yearly, foul shot, rivets, steam shovel, jump shot, seldom, backboard* (and many others). The student is asked to put the words under the right topics—"Tells How Often," "Used in Construction," "Basketball."

Henry A. Bamman, Program Director, *Target*, (Palo Alto: Field Educational Publications).

> Six audiotape kits, including kits for auditory and visual discrimination, phonetic analysis, and structural analysis. These kits are correlated with *The Kaleidoscope Readers*, a series of high-interest, low-vocabulary readers for grades 7 to 12.

In addition to practice materials such as these and devices like those shown in Figure 8-2, most teachers rely heavily on high-interest, low-vocabulary materials for strengthening decoding skills in the context of meaningful reading. A few widely used sets are:

Breakthrough Paperbacks (Boston: Allyn and Bacon).

> From *On the Level* (below grade 2 reading level) to *Making the Scene* (about grade 6), this series emphasizes sports, action, science fiction, and biographies.

Hip Pocket Stories (Random House, School Division, Westminster, MD 21157).

> Five biographies (Diana Ross, Geraldo Rivera, Shirley Chisholm, Bill Cosby, Johnny Bench) with accompanying cassette tapes.

Scholastic's *Action Reading System* (Scholastic Inc., 904 Sylvan Avenue, Englewood Cliffs, NJ 07632).

> For seriously retarded readers in grades 7 to 12, this program includes anthologies of short reading selections as well as cassettes, skills exercises, and supplementary libraries. *Action* maintains a reading level of 2.0–2.9; *Double Action*, 3.0–5.0; *Triple Action*, 4.0–6.0.

language that looks like English, and another "language" that doesn't. This may lead to making up codes, an interesting way of understanding decoding. (See Box 8-4.)

The point is not to try to make a distractible youngster into a linguistic scholar but, through occasional comments and illustrations, to invoke an interest in language for its own sake. Even in remedial sessions, there is a place for viewing the wonder and the science of language. Reading teachers should be well-informed themselves in the study of linguistics.

Emphasizing language as a subject to be studied scientifically and historically is a means of dignifying the remedial lessons; as such, it is one of the myriad ways that remedial teachers seek to build their students' self-confidence. As noted earlier, the use of *cloze* exercises bolsters confidence by showing weak readers how effectively context can aid guessing and how much meaning they

BOX 8-4

BOOKS ABOUT CODES

Some teachers find they can reawaken adolescents' interests in the decoding aspects of reading acquisition by using trade books on codes. Here are a few:

Walt Babson, *All Kinds of Codes* (New York: Four Winds, 1976).

Julian A. Bielewicz, *Secret Languages: Communicating in Codes and Ciphers* (New York: Elsevier/Nelson Books, 1976).

Sam and Beryl Epstein, *The First Book of Codes and Ciphers* (New York: Franklin Watts, 1956).

Nancy Garden, *The Kids' Code and Cipher Book* (New York: Holt, Rinehart and Winston, 1981).

Martin Gardner, *Codes, Ciphers, and Secret Writing* (New York: Simon and Schuster, 1972).

Chip Lovitt, *The Dynamite Book of Top Secret Information* (New York: Scholastic Book Services, 1978).

Jane Sarnoff and Reynold Ruffins, *The Code and Cipher Book* (New York: Scribner's, 1975).

---

can derive from minimal cues. Exercises like the following fill-in-the-blanks game show how much the reader depends on consonants and how attention to meaning can supply the values of vowels:

_f y__ _sk _n__gh p__pl_ f_r _dv_c_, y__ c_n

_s__lly f_nd s_m_b_dy wh_ w_ll _dv_s_ y__ t_ d_

wh_t y__ w_r_ g__ng t_ d_ _nyw_y.

Many of the suggestions in Chapter 12 ("The Word Factor in Reading and Writing") can be adapted to delayed readers' needs.

Developing Comprehension Strategies

Developing comprehension facility among functional nonreaders begins with getting them to balance their attention between accurate decoding and thinking about the message to be grasped. Once this is achieved, however, major stumbling blocks remain; chief among these is their lack of experience with written language. The stock of words whose meanings are familiar to them is significantly limited because they do not read. As youngsters mature, their best source of new words is print, not the conversation of peers, or even teachers or television. Not only is their meaning vocabulary likely to be limited, they have little understanding of print conventions and patterns of organization. For example, they may not know that commas signal relationships within a sentence, that a semicolon separates ideas, and that a colon alerts the reader to what follows. Such knowledge comes from consistent experience with print. Consequently, delayed readers are still at a disadvantage even when "saying the words" begins to be easier.

Efforts to develop reading comprehension are channeled through vocabulary development, listening comprehension, and instruction and practice on comprehension subskills. These three topics are discussed briefly in the following pages, because remedial methods in these areas are not unlike strategies for normally developing readers (to be described in Chapters 12–14) and are related to motivation and interests (Chapter 9).

Vocabulary Development   Whether readers are "remedial" or "developmental," teachers have learned the futility of vocabulary exercises based on words that students have no immediate use for in reading, writing, or speaking. So remedial teachers avoid artificial exercises, though they sometimes use workbook exercises if these are centered on high utility words, practiced in meaningful context, and presented with liveliness and humor.

In remedial sessions, as in reading and English classes, the aim is the same: awakening interest in words and showing students that they can learn them without undue tedium. The main difference, of course, is that learning is slower for delayed readers; they need many more encounters with a word before they can be sure of it. The challenge for the teacher is to arrange for sufficient meaningful practice before boredom sets in. The second problem is to adjust the word-learning load to the student's capacity.

In remedial instruction there is really no clear demarcation between decoding practice which is meaningful (as it should be with increasing frequency) and vocabulary development. The student's personal word file—which is a must in remedial reading—may be started with words learned through VAKT, but gradually sight words (which, by definition, are "known" in meaning as well as form and sound) may be replaced with words whose meanings as well as their visual forms and sounds must be learned. Where will these new words come from, these words that are not already in the student's meaning vocabulary?

In the beginning, most of them will be words that the student knows the sound of, knows at least one meaning for, but cannot recognize in print. They come from students' interests: from sports (*slapshot, punt, stadium*), from hobbies (*scalded milk, interfacing, scaffolding*), from prized possessions (*sprocket, carburetor, heat riser valve*). The most natural way to elicit these words is to ask the student to dictate a message about something of interest: sports, hobbies, something he or she wants. The language experience chart in the secondary remedial lesson may be directions for assembling a stereo, a recipe for lasagna, a wish list, notes on a football game, and—to be encouraged—reflections on an incident in history or a science experiment. Indeed, as quickly as possible, teacher–clinicians move students, disabled though they may be, to serious consideration of their reasons for being in school. It may be a mistake to spend too much time on out-of-school interests. Adolescents know that where they really need reading is in studying school subjects.

Content subjects, newspapers and television, and the teacher-clinician's own conversation are sources of words that are new in meaning as well as form and pronunciation. With bright disabled readers, teachers should discuss issues at a mature level, testing always to find the known and the unknown words, writing the new word (which came up in conversation) on a slip of paper or the chalkboard.

There is no point in overdoing "vocabulary building" in the remedial setting. Unusual words now and then may provoke interest. But delayed readers chiefly need *ordinary* words so that they can read most of the paragraph, the section, the chapter with ease; the *extraordinary* words will stand out. Once beginning skills have been mastered, content teachers and textbooks can take over vocabulary development.

In the remedial plan, we recommend devoting less time to vocabulary exercises and more time to whatever connected discourse the student can read. (See also Chapter 9.)

Listening Comprehension   We have already noted that listening comprehension must be included in every remedial lesson. In addition to content-centered lessons, remedial teachers also emphasize comprehension subskills through listening. For example, they convert the "main ideas" exercises of a reading workbook into a listening lesson by reading aloud both the passages and the choices. Commercial materials for teaching listening are plentiful.

A procedure used to promote listening and reading comprehension simultaneously is ReQuest, developed by Anthony Manzo in a doctoral dissertation at Syracuse University and refined over the years. (See Box 8-5 for reference.) ReQuest is a cooperative questioning technique that requires teacher and student as partners at first, although peer tutoring works well, too, when both partners have had sufficient experience.

Each takes turn reading aloud a few sentences or paragraphs while the other listens. At the end of the selection, the listener asks the reader as many questions about the passage as he or she can. Then the reader asks the listener additional questions. When all questions have been answered to the satisfaction of both partners, the reading aloud is resumed. One value of ReQuest is that the remedial teacher demonstrates for the student how to think beyond the literal level of recall, how to relate personal knowledge to the information presented,

BOX 8-5

REMEDIAL TECHNIQUES: FIVE RECOMMENDATIONS

Grace M. Fernald, *Remedial Techniques in Basic School Subjects* (New York: McGraw Hill, 1943).

Gerald Glass, *Glass Analysis for Decoding Only* (Garden City, N.Y.: Easier to Learn Corp., 1976).

R. G. Heckelman, "A Neurological-Impress Method of Remedial-Reading Instruction," *Academic Therapy* 4 (1969):277–82.

Beth H. Slingerland, *A Multi-Sensory Approach to Language Arts for Specific Language Disability Children* (Cambridge, MA: Educators Publishing Service, 1971).

A. V. Manzo, "The ReQuest Procedure," *Journal of Reading*, No. 2, (1969): 123–26.

how to enhance understanding by paraphrasing, how to respond to words that signal time or conditional relationships, and other thinking/reasoning skills. The student partner is usually eager to get the best of the teacher and, sometimes unconsciously, begins to ask fewer questions of the recall type and to demonstrate increasing ability to select, coordinate, and summarize information.

A variation on the interspersed question technique, ReQuest can be adapted for very limited reading ability and very high distractability. Students who cannot retain meanings from the beginning of a paragraph to the end may have their attention gradually extended if the teacher intersperses questions between each sentence. Procedures like ReQuest suggest one more argument for one-to-one teaching and limited case loads.

Direct Attention to Reading Comprehension   Scope and sequence charts (see Chapter 2) for elementary reading programs show that reading comprehension subskills are introduced and emphasized in primary grades. These same skills, which are further refined and extended in developmental reading in the secondary school, are retaught in remedial programs. The chief difference between instruction for remedial and developmental readers lies in the length and complexity of the passages which are studied. However, even with readability held to first-, second-, and third-grade levels, exercises can be devised which focus on such skills as the use of punctuation to signal meanings, drawing inferences, noting cause/effect relationships, distinguishing between major ideas and detail, and following directions.

With seriously disabled readers, emphasis is often placed first on within-sentence meanings and then on noting relationships between sentences. Poor readers have difficulties, for example, in relating the ideas in an introductory clause to the substance of the main clause. They falter, too, in noting cues in one clause or sentence that link ideas in the following sentence. Ironically, materials which have been "written down" for poor readers by shortening sentences often omit transitional words that help readers to make connections. Remedial teaching focuses on these problems in simply written materials at the same time it deals with more complex language through listening comprehension.

Hardware and Software in Remedial Reading Rooms

Although the use of *hardware* to refer to teaching machines is fairly recent educational jargon, machines have long been considered adjuncts to remedial teaching. We use *software* (now slipping out of fashion to be replaced by *courseware* in computer jargon) to cover not only the print materials to be used with machines but games, workbooks, and books for delayed readers. Many people think these resources define remedial reading. They do not. Neither materials nor techniques distinguish remedial instruction; one-to-one teaching by an expert diagnostic teacher does.

Games   Long popular with elementary reading teachers, games in the secondary remedial center arouse mixed reactions. Needless to say, they must be selected with careful regard for the maturity of the users. In one category, games are designed to develop automatic associations between printed and spoken forms of words. Adult games like Bingo, board games like *Monopoly* and *Uncle*

Wiggly, and card games have been adapted to make word recognition "fun" and "competitive." A typical card game is *Match*, the object of which is to recognize that a word printed on each of two playing cards is the same, to pronounce its name correctly, and take a "trick."

In a second category, the games focus on recognizing and synthesizing word parts, from single letter–sound associations to phonograms, syllables, and affixes. Some focus on the most rudimentary skills of auditory discrimination and others on more advanced skills like building words from roots and affixes.

Board games are often related to comprehension rather than word skills. In the past we have viewed most games with great skepticism, thinking they were perhaps insulting to adolescents. However, the recent renewed popularity of board games for adults as well as adolescents has motivated teachers to create ingenious variations that do in fact interest many older remedial readers. These are sophisticated games based on chance as well as on astute answers to riddles and codes. Reading may be limited to the questions or directions on the cards that are "drawn"; the background needed for answering the questions may be obtained from listening to recorded stories, tales, and dramas. Fantasy is a popular genre for these games, and the popularity of hobbits, gnomes, elves, and creatures from outer space is put to good use. Current films in the tradition of *Star Trek, E.T.,* and the *Star Wars* trilogy can supply immediate "content" for games which students can invent for each other as well as play. An enthusiastic media specialist, drama coach, art teacher, or English teacher can often enlist aides from the general student body to create this kind of resource for the Reading Center.

Skills Sheets, Kits, and Workbooks   Whether teacher-made and duplicated, packaged in boxes, or bound into workbooks, skills exercises serve a common purpose: independent application of a skill previously taught. Their popularity with teachers is understandable, but their acceptance by students is sometimes surprising. They are often more tolerable to delayed readers than to good readers because to the former they represent an achievable goal, whereas "real reading" in a book is a task to be feared. Because so many different varieties of skills exercises are available, there is no reason to repeat experiences or materials that have already disenchanted a student. "We had that reading kit every year in elementary school" is a complaint that the remedial teacher heeds.

Many remedial teachers make extensive collections of exercises culled from published sources, laminate them for repeated uses, and retain them because they have proved their excellence. Discarded are the exercises that deliver minimal learning for the time invested, bore students, are too easy or too hard, permit mindless guessing, teach bad habits or misinformation. Many teachers, too, are using computers to index these materials according to specific skills and levels, thereby facilitating the match between the student's need and the corrective exercise.

Filmstrip/Tape Combinations   A variety of reading skill lessons have been commercially produced on filmstrips. Many are accompanied by audio tapes. A typical filmstrip/tape lesson may present initial instruction for a common phonic rule, followed by an exercise on a worksheet. A preferable use of materials like these, however, is to guide independent review of rules and strategies already taught.

Some permutations of the use of filmstrips for reading are quite sophisticated and permit the students and the machine to interact. *Systems 80* and the *Hoffman Reader* are examples. A student views examples for a particular lesson and hears an explanation as well as directions. To respond to a question presented via the filmstrip/tape lesson, the student presses a button. If the choice made was correct, the machine so indicates and goes on. If the choice was incorrect, a notice of "error" appears and the student chooses again (and again, if necessary) until the correct choice is made and the machine affirms its "correctness." Used effectively, these machines not only motivate but ensure against practicing errors, as can so often happen to students completing skills sheets. Improperly supervised, however, a student can become caught up in a random pressing of buttons with little attention to learning.

These machines are expensive. Although dozens of different worksheets may be found to provide practice on a particular decoding skill, only a few practice sessions are available for any single skill on these machines. Recycling through the same exercises often leads to memorization of the correct answers rather than learning the skill.

Tape/Print Materials   The most common of these are cassette tapes that are paired with worksheets. The voice on the tape becomes the teacher substitute. Students listen, usually through headsets, and mark their worksheets in response to directions provided on the tape. Educational Development Laboratory's *Listen and Do* series is one of the most popular examples.

The Language Master is designed to "read" words, phrases, or sentences that a teacher has written on the specially produced cards purchased with the machine. A strip of audiotape at the bottom edge of the card may be used by either the teacher or the student to record a brief related message. For example, the teacher might record the name of the word printed on each card that the student inserts in the machine, giving both the form and sound of the word to be learned. Or, instead, the student may be asked to record on the audio strip the name of each word. Later the teacher listens to the student's responses and erases the tape, saving the cards for future use.

Computers   Like their less sophisticated relatives, the teaching machines of the 1960s and 1970s, today's computers have motivational appeal that remedial teachers cherish even though they may be dubious about their educational values. At this writing, growing numbers of companies are marketing computer programs and thousands of disabled readers are being subjected to skills drills in a new package. Many programs have been in use long enough for data to have accumulated on users' progress, and many studies report positive results. Although this research is limited still and possibly biased, we believe that computers have a place in reading instruction, including remediation. Nonetheless, computer hardware and software should be selected with careful concern for the effects of the technology on readers, especially the learning disabled, and with careful testing of the basic question: What does this machine do that an expert teacher cannot manage with equal efficiency and greater sensitivity?

One function that computers currently serve is diagnostic and prescriptive; that is, as suggested in a preceding section, computers can assist greatly in scanning individual records, grouping students according to abilities, indexing materials, and making suitable matches between lessons and students' needs. The danger, of course, is the diminution of human responsibility for monitoring the machine and the pupil's reactions.

At this writing, the best uses of the computer in remedial situations appear to be those which are most personalized—the tutor who uses his computer to play computer games that require reading directions, the teacher who encourages computer learning as an alternate route for her student, the clinician who is teaming with a student in producing computer games.

Tachistoscopes   Since the first psychological experiments at the end of the last century, tachistoscopes have been found in remedial centers—sometimes as elaborate mechanical devices, sometimes as simple cardboard sleeves through which word lists are pulled, exposing a word at a time through a window in the sleeve. Exposure time varies from one tenth of a second for a hand-held model to one hundredth or one thousandth of a second for more sophisticated models.

Films and Pacers   These devices, common features of reading centers at the high school level, have no place in remedial instruction because their purpose is to increase rate of comprehension. They are appropriate in centers and classrooms where students have reached suitably high levels of comprehension but have acquired habits of slow reading—slower than necessary, that is.

Texts Especially Written for Delayed Readers   For many decades teachers have rewritten classic stories and created original materials at readability levels of fourth grade and below especially for teenaged disabled readers. Adapted classics, though not as popular and therefore not as controversial as they used to be, are still useful for remedial teaching. Current newspapers and magazines are especially well received by older adolescents. (See Box 8-6 for recommendations.)

An excellent up-to-date *Core Collection of High/Low Books and Periodicals for the Disabled Reader*, with a supplement, *Books for the Reluctant Reader*, has been prepared by Ellen V. LiBretto and appears in *High/Low Handbook: Books, Materials, and Services for the Teenage Problem Reader*. We have adapted the criteria LiBretto suggests and reproduced them in Box 8-7, where the reference for the *High/Low Handbook* also appears.

Classroom Adjustments for Seriously Disabled Readers

Educating students who are nonreaders is, for all intents and purposes, a challenge to even the most experienced, creative, and capable teachers. Nevertheless, it is a challenge that is successfully met by many, especially when the nonreader is motivated, supported by parents and others, correctly diagnosed, and receiving expert remedial instruction.

In some schools, many teachers never encounter students as severely disabled as those we have defined as *remedial*. In these schools the few students

BOX 8-6

MAGAZINES AND NEWSPAPERS

From Scholastic, Inc.
P.O. Box 2002
904 Sylvan Avenue
Englewood Cliffs, NJ 07632

Scholastic Action
Reading level: Grades 2–3   Interest Level: Grades 7–9
Intended to motivate "seriously remedial readers." Short plays, stories, and articles, cartoons, quizzes, and interviews. Emphasis on media tie-ins. (*Biweekly*)

Scholastic Scope
Reading Level: Grades 4–6   Interest Level: Grades 7–12
Plays, short stories and articles, skill exercises, puzzles and jokes. (*Weekly*)

Scholastic Sprint
Reading Level: Grades 2–3   Interest Level: Grades 4–6
Plays, fiction and feature articles intended to motivate remedial readers in the intermediate grades. (*Biweekly*)

From Xerox Educational Publications
245 Long Hill Road
Middletown, CT 06457

Know Your World Extra
Reading Level: Grades 3–4   Interest Level: Grades 7–12
Newsmagazine format which includes: news shorts, issues in the news, science features, daily living articles, skill exercises and puzzles. 16 pages. Illustrated with photographs. (*Weekly*)

From New Reader's Press
Division of Laubach Literacy International
Box 131
Syracuse, NY 13210

News for You
Reading level: Grades 4–5 (Edition A)   Interest level: Grades 7–12
            Grades 5–6 (Edition B)
Low readability newspaper with adult format and tone. The front page covers national and international news. The inside pages include human interest stories, science news, and a legal rights feature. A crossword puzzle, sports news, and job and health briefs are on the last page. Four-page tabloid with four-page Instuctor's Aid. Once a month expanded to eight pages. Illustrated with photographs. (*Weekly*)

who are truly illiterate, or nearly so, are likely to appear singly or in twos and threes in classes like English, social studies, general science, and selected subjects that are presumed to be the least verbally demanding. These students are unlikely to elect advanced sciences and mathematics, and, of course, they avoid foreign languages and advanced courses in literature and composition. Con-

BOX 8-7

CHECKLIST OF EVALUATION CRITERIA

Is the appearance of the book, including illustrations, suitable for teenagers?

If photographs or illustrations were removed, could the book stand on its own? (A negative answer for a work of fiction is a minus, but for an informational text, a negative answer might be a plus.)

Does the subject have teenage appeal? Is the topic current or of immediate interest to teenagers?

Can young people identify with the premise of the book?

Does the book have potential as adjunct reading for school courses or book reports? (Most books may appeal to out-of-school interests, but some should fit this criterion.)

Is the book a "first" or beginning book on a topic?

Does the book cover its subject with enough depth to stimulate interest for the disabled reader to want to read further?

Can the book serve as a bridge to more difficult material on the subject?

If the book is a biography, is the portrait realistic? (Important facts about the subject's personal life should not be brushed off or omitted.)

If the book is fiction, does it compare favorably with other junior novels? Does it contain similar themes and characters?

Does the author avoid a condescending or overly juvenile tone?

Is the publisher's reading-level designation correct?

Are difficult words defined in the text?

If the book has a glossary or index, does this add significantly to the book's usefulness?

Most important, is the book *readable*?

SOURCE: Ellen V. LiBretto, *High/Low Books and Periodicals for the Disabled Reader: A Core Collection* (New York: Bowker Co., 1981): 93,94.

sequently, not every high school teacher has personal experience with seriously disabled readers.

However, among the hundred to a hundred and fifty students encountered every day, almost every teacher has a few whose reading levels are so low that the ordinary materials of the curriculum are far above their current abilities. So the brief notes that follow are pertinent to them also. These notes are brief because they stress ideas which can be adapted to many levels of achievement and therefore will be expanded upon in subsequent chapters.

1. *Stress major concepts rather than details.* To help learners who must depend chiefly on listening for the intake of ideas, be sure that class discussions focus on the major concepts of a chapter or unit rather than the iteration of minor details that are often promptly forgotten by good and poor readers alike.

2. *Try to find special resources for the disabled.* When learning is organized in a thematic unit, it is often possible to reserve content for selected students so that their contributions to class discussions will not be preempted by others. For example, in an eleventh grade English class, Ms. Reardon arranged for a small group of poor readers to examine the theme of alienation through viewing films (on video discs in the media center) based on three short stories by John Cheever.

3. *Emphasize learning through listening as well as reading.* All your students can profit from learning to listen, good readers even more than poor readers who have often learned on their own as a compensatory device. If you teach how to take notes from listening to a class lecture and occasionally assign listening tapes to good readers as well as to poor ones, you will blunt the hurt of "being different" felt by the few who must always absorb ideas from tape.

4. *Keep in touch with student's tutors.* Not only do you need to confer periodically with your student's remedial reading teacher, you should also be in touch with whoever is helping with home assignments from your course. If the student does not have a personal cassette or a tutor, perhaps you can help to arrange for both.

5. *Preteach key vocabulary for every chapter or reading selection required of the whole class.* Every student will benefit from this procedure. On chart paper or a corner of the chalkboard, preserve the words taught so that poor readers can, if they are able, refer to them during later class discussions.

6. *Spend time discussing information derived from graphic aids in the class textbook and other resources.* Many *good* readers ignore pictures, maps, graphs, and tables, because they can read the text itself, which they assume contains all the necessary information. Paying attention to these devices in whole-class lessons benefits good as well as poor readers. Have all students answer questions using only a map or table, making sure that some answers do not require previous reading of the text.

7. *Keep assignments for seriously disabled readers to normal time allotments.* Try to figure out how long the disabled reader must have to learn a concept or practice a skill. It will take a bright disabled youngster as long to do four word problems in math, even when someone reads them aloud, as it takes better readers to do two or three times as many. Allow, too, for the extra time needed for dictating and transcribing. Older students who have

compensated for language deficits still cannot produce accurate or even literate written accounts when pressured.

8. *Adjust evaluation procedures to accommodate depressed reading and writing skills.* (Review Chapter 7 for specific suggestions.)

9. *Encourage, support, and challenge.* Perhaps the worst thing that you can do for disabled readers is to resent their presence in your classes, to lose patience with them, and to ridicule their efforts. The next worst thing is to pity them—and forget that they have normal intelligence and can think as well as others, though perhaps not in the same way. Accepting their limitations and challenging them to learn your subject matter while conscientiously seeking ways to help them do so is surely a reasonable goal for you and your colleagues.

A Footnote on Special Reading Classes

We began this chapter with a reference to the many below-level readers in secondary schools who are not far enough below to qualify as *remedial*. They are still there—in large numbers in most middle schools, and in only slightly decreased numbers in senior high school. Most of them need more direct instruction in literacy skills than can be supplied in English classes. We would assign these students to classes of fifteen to twenty for help with reading at their levels, or to intensive corrective instruction aimed at selected skills such as rate of reading, retaining information, or writing summaries and reports. We would make these special provisions for below-level readers for only so long as the content teachers in a particular school remain unprepared to take over. In any case, the recommendations for classroom adjustments in the preceding section are, in fact, the goals of all content teachers working to improve learning in their classes.

RECAPPING MAIN POINTS

Some remedial readers are also learning-disabled and require the services of clinically trained teachers of the handicapped before or during the time reading teachers work with them to develop reading acquisition skills. Many other adolescents who read below third grade level are not classified as truly remedial, but they, too, need help in acquiring beginning reading skills. When seriously disabled readers differing widely in intelligence, attitudes, and learning experiences are assigned to corrective or proficiency reading classes that also include more advanced readers, their chances of acquiring even initial literacy skills are greatly diminished.

Remedial teachers work first on students' attitudes toward reading, helping them to understand the reading process, building their self-confidence, and setting realistic goals. Remediation takes time. Success depends on how many and what kinds of causative factors must be overcome or compensated for. Success depends, too, on the teacher's skill in observing and tracking progress, making the necessary drills palatable, pacing lessons to the student's learning rate, providing encouragement, and keeping reasons for reading in plain view.

Every remedial lesson should include decoding practice, oral and silent reading of words in context, and listening comprehension. As students acquire decoding skills, they should read independently for gradually extended periods.

Remedial readers need support outside the reading center: from the home, other teachers, peers, and adult role models.

To treat severe decoding problems, teachers look for the student's strongest learning modality and often find they must involve all senses in a method known as VAKT. Working for instant recognition as well as understanding of decoding techniques, teachers use materials like the Glass Analysis, emphasize use of context, resort to linguistic readers for reinforcement of common spelling patterns, and require response to meaning whenever possible. They keep students' attention on how an alphabetic system works.

At first, listening is the chief vehicle for teaching comprehension. Manzo's ReQuest technique combines listening and reading. Comprehension of simply written passages can engage the full range of skills from observing punctuation to noticing cause–effect relationships.

Remedial teaching employs games, skills sheets and workbook exercises, filmstrip/tape combinations, tape/print materials, machines like the Language Master and tachistoscope, and computer programs. Essential to remedial instruction is a supply of high-interest, low-vocabulary books and magazines.

All teachers continue to be responsible for disabled readers' learning of content even while they are in remediation.

FOR DISCUSSION

1. Read Eileen Simpson's *Reversals* and discuss with your group how it feels as a child and as an adult to suffer from dyslexia. (You may want to assign the thirteen short chapters of this autobiographical account to different members of your group for a shared report.)

2. From your experience in the school system in which you teach or were a student or have observed, what differences do you discern between diagnostic/remedial services as defined in Chapters 7 and 8 and programs developed to meet minimal competency standards for high school graduation?

3. In some junior and senior high schools, very poor readers are removed from content courses and placed in "immersion programs" where communication skills and sometimes math skills are the order of the day (or half day). Under what circumstances and for what types of students is this a good idea? For whom might this plan prove counterproductive?

4. Many critics argue that the incidence of seriously disabled readers in secondary schools is the result of poor teaching in the lower grades. Discuss the many sides of this argument. Then tackle this question: Granted that it is better to prevent reading failures than to attempt to

correct them, what responsibilities does a school system have for providing remedial instruction for adolescent nonreaders?

5. In the school district where you pay taxes, would you vote for or against a proposal to reduce the budget for secondary reading instruction by getting rid of remedial services and using these funds for improving the teaching of reading in primary grades? What would you need to know in order to make an informed decision?

6. Why are terms like *remedial reading, dyslexia,* and *specific learning disability* so emotionally charged for many school administrators, reading professionals, classroom teachers, and students? Do you think schools should ban *remedial* and *dyslexia* from their publications and their communications with students and parents? Discuss the issues.

FURTHER READING

Chall, Jeanne S. and Allan F. Mirsky, eds. *Education and the Brain*. The Seventy-seventh Yearbook of the National Society for the Study of Education, Part II (University of Chicago Press, 1978).

> Chapter VII, "Minimal Brain Dysfunction" by Martha Bridge Denckla, Chapter III, "Education and the Cognitive Processes of the Brain" by M. C. Wittrock, Chapter X, "Growth Spurts During Brain Development" by Herman T. Epstein, and Chapter XI, "The Implications for Education" by Chall and Mirsky are especially pertinent to teachers and accessible to students with prior knowledge of educational psychology.

Ekwall, E. E. *Locating and Correcting Reading Difficulties*, 3d ed. Columbus Ohio: Merrill, 1981.

Fernald, Grace M. *Remedial Techniques in Basic School Subjects*. New York: McGraw-Hill, 1943.

Harris, Albert and Edward Sipay. *How to Increase Reading Ability*, 6th ed. New York: David McKay, 1975.

Ives, J. P., L. Z. Bursak, and S. A. Ives. *Word Identification Techniques*. Chicago: Rand McNally, 1979.

> Within a view of reading as a linguistic process, suggests instructional procedures and practice activities for identifying words using the various possible cue systems—configuration through pronunciation of irregularly spelled words.

Simpson, Eileen, *Reversals: A Personal Account of Victory over Dyslexia*. Boston: Houghton Mifflin, 1979.

> Also available in paperback.

9 What to Do About Kids Who Won't Read

We worry about the kids who won't read because they are there in numbers in our classrooms in grades 5–8, and most of them are still there in grades 9–12. A lot of them will graduate from high school and enroll in two-year and even four-year colleges. Fifty years ago, teachers didn't worry about them because there weren't so many of them in secondary classrooms; most of them had dropped out of school and we ignored the ones who were still there. Today society won't let us ignore them. These nonreaders—kids who can read but don't—are expected to learn through reading, not only in their present classes, but in the classes they will attend as young adults in colleges, in industry, in the military, and in service occupations.

Who are these young people who can read but choose not to? If we are to describe them in terms of reading achievement, it is easiest to begin by saying who they are not. They are not, obviously, the nonreaders we described in Chapter 7 and 8 as having skills below the average third grader's. And their ranks do not include, as a rule, many high achievers, since students become high achievers because of their bookish habits and their interests in academic learning. Chiefly, these kids who can read but don't are youngsters in the middle ranges of intelligence and achievement who leave primary grades as average and above-average readers. But in middle school they settle into achievement levels of about fifth or sixth grade, and as they move into senior high school, they carry their static skills with them. They can read independently a good deal of material written at fifth and sixth grade levels—newspapers, magazines, trade books—provided they wish to do so; but they are far from ready to learn from content textbooks. They must become willing readers before we can help them to become students.

Some of them are slow learners, academically speaking, with IQs below 90, but many are kids of average ability whose verbal learning skills have atrophied from lack of use. Quite a few of them are able learners, even of academic subjects, who skimp on reading because they haven't time or taste for it. They earn Cs and Bs in academic classes by listening attentively to teachers and peers, doing a minimum of homework, "borrowing" someone else's workbook or notes, "apple-polishing" their teachers, occasionally flipping through the textbook, applying whatever knowledge they glean from television and adult conversations.

From middle school to community college, the young people we focus on in this chapter are the ones their teachers describe as "unmotivated," "uninvolved," "unwilling," "dull," "not interested in learning." Often their teachers apply less kindly labels: "rowdy," "troublemaker," "discipline problem." Most such youngsters are very busy people. They have fully enrolled in what Clifton Fadiman describes as the "competing curriculum, a complete 'alternate life' to which children submit themselves." TV is at the heart of this alternate life created by the communications revolution, but it also includes film, radio, comic books, pop music, electronic games, and sports. "This alternate life," Fadiman continues, "takes up as much of a child's time as school does, and it works on him with far greater effectiveness. It offers its own disciplines, its own curriculum, its own ethical and cultural values, its own style and language. . . . The alternate life has one special psychological effect [on children] which handicaps the teacher: a decline in the faculty of attention, and therefore a decline in capacity to learn. Television's great attraction is that it does the work for you, skillfully and systematically. . . ."[1]

What are they interested in? Themselves and one another. They grow up fast, these kids, and are interested in what TV thinks the public is interested in. That, as you know, includes large amounts and varieties of sex. We recently asked eleventh graders to list what three essentials they would take on a voyage into space, and on more than one girl's list the first essential was a blow-dryer for her hair, followed by certain recordings, and her "boy friend."

Where are the nonreaders going? Well, of course, we hope to catch some of them and turn them into readers. That's what this chapter is mostly about. Most of these nonreaders are headed for the service occupations that employ the largest proportion of U.S. workers. After graduating from high school, many of them will spend two or more years in post-secondary education before becoming insurance salesmen, x-ray technicians, television and computer repairmen, TV production hands, automobile mechanics, nurses, hotel and restaurant workers, salesmen, buyers, secretaries, clerks and others. Those who end their formal education in high school, some graduating, some dropping out, will in all probability repeat the lives of their parents in not-so-quiet desperation, bored with too much leisure, working fitfully in unskilled trades, on and off welfare, in and out of social agencies, subject to the ills of the poor.

Among these nonreading adolescents are a good number who are college bound. They are the ones who score low on the Scholastic Aptitude Tests, are denied the college of their choice, perhaps enter a two-year college and transfer later to a four-year institution. Some nonreaders will enter Education and become your colleagues in teaching and administration. Remember that more than 75 per cent of 17-year-olds graduate from high school and 50 per cent of *those* go on to post-secondary education. These additional students who seem different from former "college material" and are referred to as "new students" are causing deans and professors to complain more bitterly than ever before that "despite good verbal facility (including superior high school grades and scores) they are chronically unable to retain what they read, to absorb arguments or facts in their heads long enough to make them their own."[2]

Of course, we are not talking about *all* students, nor even all those in the middle range of ability and achievement. We exclude from our discussion the sizable proportion of youth who are very able readers, many of whom have high intelligence, wide interests and talents in classical and popular arts, and outstanding achievement in school and outside. Almost nothing we have to say in this chapter applies in any way to these able youngsters whose families and friends have protected them from the "competing curriculum."

Before going on, remember that the range of intelligence among nonreaders is wide, but the average IQ will be very average indeed, because this group includes all those with low IQs. Not many slow learners ever become avid readers, even of the pulps.

Parents and the Will to Read

The will to read is instilled and sustained by examples set at home and in the community. Often without realizing it, parents who are themselves nonreaders and have bad memories of their own days in school infect their children with negative attitudes toward academic learning. These same parents may have high aspirations for their children; they may recognize utilitarian values in higher education but have no idea of the real values which derive from a genuine love of learning. Parents who have no love for learning themselves are often unaware of life's possibilities and so cannot give children realistic aspirations or offer them the extracurricular experiences that sustain school learning. Children whose parents and grandparents have set traditions of learning in the home may or may not become scholars themselves, but the chances are much greater for them than for children whose only encouragement toward learning comes from their teachers.

Books by DeLone[3] and Jencks[4] make this point in stronger and more depressing terms. But we cannot accept these authors' conclusion that equality of opportunity through the schools can make very little difference in the lives of the poor. Current history presents innumerable examples of children of the poor who have become scholars and entered the professions or pursued learning in other walks of life, because of the will of parents who were themselves untutored. We bring up the issues of home background only to emphasize that for most kids from working-class and welfare homes the struggle is harder; they need more, not less, help from the school environment.

---

[2]Leon Botstein, "A Proper Education," *Harper's* (September 1979): 33–37. Botstein is dean of Bard College.

[3]Richard H. Delone, *Small Futures: Children, Inequality and the Limits of Liberal Reform* (New York: Harcourt Brace Jovanovich, 1979).

[4]Christopher Jencks, Susan Bartlett, et al., *Who Gets Ahead?: The Determinants of Economic Success in America* (New York: Basic Books, 1979).

The will *not* to read affects children from every economic level. When both parents are working or when a single parent must support the family emotionally and materially, there may be little time or energy left over for anything but TV and sports. Again, the school must try harder.

The will to read dies easily in youngsters whose struggle to learn in primary grades left them with nothing but decoding skills and the conviction that it's not worth the effort. To choose reading, you must read well enough so that the meaning comes through fairly easily. For many children the leap from learning to read to reading to learn is just too wide. For many teachers in secondary school the main job is to instill the confidence that was lost somewhere in the big decoding push in primary grades and the enthusiasm for reading-to-learn—unaided—that did not come in middle grades.

Television's Effects on Reading

Continually at issue among educators and laymen is the effect of television on the will to read. We've quoted Fadiman's view. Here is testimony on the opposite side, admittedly from an insider, Eric Sevareid, former news commentator for CBS.

> To such critics, of course, television is destroying everything. It is destroying conversation, they tell us. Nonsense. Nonconversing families were always that way. It has, in fact, stimulated billions of conversations that otherwise would not have occurred.
>
> It is destroying the habit of reading, they say. This is nonsense. Book sales in this country during the lifetime of general television have greatly increased and well beyond the increase in the population.
>
> TV is debasing the use of the English language, they tell us. Nonsense. Until radio and then TV, tens of millions of people living in sharecropper cabins, in small villages on the plains and in the mountains, in the great city slums had never heard good English diction in their lives. If anything, this medium has improved the general level of diction.
>
> You, as teachers, should say nonsense to these criticisms, too; and use television to stimulate good conversation, more reading, better diction. Consider it a basic instructional material.[5]

Those who come to the defense of television are right when they say that, in the days before TV, the time equivalent to that consumed by TV today was not spent in reading. In the good old days, masses of people were not sitting around reading books and newspapers. They were working longer hours in factories and on farms, in kitchens and offices, and spending what leisure time they had in some of the same kinds of entertainment as today: sports, movies, do-it-yourself projects. The important question, however, is not whether viewing television is replacing reading, but what effects passive viewing have upon learning. In the absence of hard evidence, we are inclined to share the fears of people like Fadiman and Marie Winn[6] that television feeds us so effortlessly that

---

[5]Eric Sevareid, "TV as a Teacher's Ally," *Instructor* (March, 1978): 84.
[6]Marie Winn, *Plug-In Drug: Television, Children and the Family* (Bantam, 1978).

it cuts down on our capacity to learn anything demanding. A recent *New York Times* article showed that many "prominent parents" including several in the entertainment fields, agree to the extent of carefully monitoring their children's viewing habits. Tom Brokaw, at the time host of NBC's *Today* program, permits his three children, aged 14, 12, and 10, to choose just three favorite programs per week, and they frequently have a hard time filling their quota. The running gag in the Brokaw family is that "television makes your brain go soft, and Dad must have a very soft brain because he works at it." Prominent parents avoid the forbidden fruit syndrome, says this article, but one way or another, their children are subjected to above-average restrictions on television viewing.[7]

What are teachers to do about television and the rest of the competing curriculum? Neil Postman's hard line against television—keep it out of the schools and strengthen the anti-television forces within the school curriculum—is attractive but possible only with respect to a small part of the population we teach. (Box 9-1.) For teachers who are themselves intellectually immune to the blandishments of the mass media and for the students who are not already addicted, Postman's hard line may work. For the nonreaders we are concerned with in this chapter, a compromise is called for. That plan includes helping kids to cut down on TV intake, using TV interests to lead to reading and writing, and providing greater amounts of in-school time for supervised study and leisure reading.

Evidence of Adolescents' Reading

A recent survey of 12-to-15-year-olds shows that they do almost no reading over the summer months when they are free from the required reading of school assignments. During the school year, according to this survey, they spend on the average 66 minutes a day in reading. That hour-plus-six-minutes is the *total* amount the average student devotes to reading of all kinds, including school assignments. How much of the total is left for freely chosen reading? Less than 20 per cent, or about 13 minutes.

Statistics are notoriously misleading, and those which deal with reading habits of adolescents and adults are especially hard to interpret accurately. Nevertheless, the figures quoted are sufficient to support our guess (and it's probably your guess, too) that many adolescents who can read choose not to when the choice is theirs.

Since the point of this chapter is to examine how we can change the attitudes of these young people, we must ask also: What do they read in those short periods during the day when they do turn to print? Innumerable interest surveys have sought to answer that question over the years. We find such surveys of limited use because of the nature of the questions asked and because we are less interested in the "average" than in the particular students we teach. The most useful interest inventories are those taken in your own classes. Nevertheless, from the body of research on reading interests, we can draw a few useful generalizations:

---

[7]"How Do Prominent Parents Govern Their Children's TV Habits?" *New York Times*, Sunday, 30 March 1980.

BOX 9-1

TELEVISION: THE FIRST CURRICULUM

But all of this can be seen in a clarifying light if we simply define a curriculum as a specially constructed information system whose purpose, *in its totality*, is to influence, teach, train, or cultivate the mind and character of our youth. By this definition, television and school not only have curriculums but are curriculums; that is, they are total learning systems. . . . And, of course, though their effects are strikingly different, each has as its purpose the control of our young. Viewed in this way, television is not only a curriculum but *constitutes the major educational enterprise now being undertaken in the United States*. That is why I call it the First Curriculum. School is the second. . . .

The Conflict

The image—concrete, unique, nonparaphrasable—versus the word—abstract, conceptual, translatable. This is one of several conflicts between TV and school, and perhaps the most important. For obvious reasons that have to do with the structure of television, its curriculum is essentially imagistic, that is, picture-centered. Its teaching style is therefore almost wholly narrative. To put it simply, the content of the TV curriculum consists of picture stories. The school curriculum, on the other hand, tends to be word- or concept-centered, and its teaching style, exposition. The school curriculum—at least in its content—consists of abstract propositions: linguistic statements of which we may say they are true or false, verifiable or not, logical or confused.

SOURCE: Neil Postman, *Teaching as a Conserving Activity* (New York: Delacorte, 1979), 49–50, 54–55.

✤ Almost all adolescents report interest in reading newspapers and magazines.

✤ Age and grade level (within the secondary school) seem to make little difference. That is, tenth graders are interested in the same topics as twelfth graders.

✤ Where youngsters live has little effect on their interests. Urban, and suburban, and rural adolescents are interested in the same things.

✤ Clear differences exist between the interests of males and females.

These generalizations have been upheld in one study after another year after year. Stated most simply, when groups are compared, sex is the only variable that makes a difference in children's and youths' interests in reading.

Finding Time to Read—in School

"I'd rather read than" was among the incomplete sentences that Ms. Yamamoto included as part of her interest inventory in grade 6. Jimmy completed it with: "than have canser [sic]." That's the way many of Jimmy's peers feel about reading, though few express it so starkly. One reason they feel this way is that their skills are insufficient to meet the demands of the middle school curriculum.

BOX 9-2

WHAT STUDENTS SAY ABOUT READING

Four college freshmen were interviewed about their past and present reading interests.

Anne's favorite reading was about horses, which were also her hobby, but she read mysteries, adventure stories, romances and biographies, too. Her mom (a high school English teacher) usually gave her ideas about which books to read, and interesting book jackets attracted her also. Her favorite books in high school had been *Gone with the Wind* and *The Once and Future King*. The last book she'd read was *Dr. No*. She said, "I feel sorry for people who don't read."

Jeff didn't come from a reading family. He remembered his parents reading only newspapers and a few magazines. He'd started to read on his own around the sixth or seventh grade, mostly newspapers and magazines like *Sports Illustrated, Outdoor Life,* and *Playboy*. Sometimes he read a book about sports or found something that looked interesting in the library. Jeff didn't think it was important to read in high school and he still doesn't. Jeff hates to read.

Jill remembered that she had always seen her parents reading—books, magazines and newspapers. Her parents and teachers read to her when she was young, which she enjoyed very much. Her friends read also— comics when they were young and magazines and books when they got older. She liked to read mysteries, adventure stories, romances and Nancy Drews. She found out which books she might like to read through her friends, the library, or the bookstore. Her favorite books were *Steppenwolf, I Never Promised You a Rose Garden* and *Turn of the Screw*. There was no particular book assigned in English that she disliked; she was always able "to get through it somehow." Generally, though, Jill didn't like her English classes, describing them as "time wasters" in which you did "stupid things."

Richie said no one had read to him when he was younger, his friends never read much and he "never" started to read for enjoyment. When he was young he only read when he had to, but during the interview he remembered reading magazine articles about sports and a few novels. He usually got his ideas about what to read from his friends. In his English classes he said he had read a little of everything—novels, short stories, poetry and drama. He also had a chance to write some poetry, which he enjoyed. He recalled reading Shakespeare, Chaucer, Kerouac, Hemingway, and Beowulf. He liked *The Crucible, All Quiet on the Western Front, To Kill a Mockingbird,* and *Catcher in the Rye*.

SOURCE: These interviews were reported by Judy Staroscik, a graduate student at Syracuse University.

What they need very badly, before they can be successful in learning through reading, is plenty of easy reading, much less demanding than their content textbooks. Given their low level of motivation, and their involvement in the competing curriculum—sports, TV, after-school jobs, social commitments, family affairs—they won't read easy books outside of school. Nor will they do so in school unless teachers are committed to that climate of learning we keep talking about.

"But wait a minute," you say. "Kids aren't going to learn much from reading easy narratives." That's a typical response from secondary teachers, who are hassled by administrators ("Keep those achievement scores up!") who are reacting to school boards, parents, and the local editorial writer. And one answer to it is that these less-than-eager kids (some of them) will learn what the good readers learned on their own somewhere between ages 8 and 12 as they devoured *Nancy Drew, The Hardy Boys*, and other series: They will learn *to* read, if not how to read. If we're lucky, some of them will catch the habit of reading. Even those who don't become addicts will at least get a bit of the practice they need—if we provide the time in school.

Who will provide the time? The teachers who aren't slaves to prescribed content can do it—that is, the reading teachers and the English teachers. Additionally, many schools have found that they can dramatize the values of reading by instituting SSR (Sustained Silent Reading) periods in which *every* inhabitant of the school, principal to janitor, secretaries and nurse, all the kids and all the teachers, stop whatever they have been doing and read for a time (preferably a book, but a magazine, a newspaper, even a comic book is acceptable).

SSR is the common label, but we prefer SQUIRT (*Super Quiet Uninterrupted Independent Reading Time*) or DEAR (*Drop Everything and Read*). Orginally, in elementary self-contained classrooms, SSR periods were meant to last as long as everyone in a class could keep on reading (sustain attention) without interrupting himself or anyone else. The teacher would call a halt as soon as anyone fidgeted, left a seat, took the bathroom pass, whispered to another, fell asleep, or gazed out the window. Groups that could sustain reading for only five minutes at first might extend SSR periods to 20 or 30 minutes, or presumably as long as bodily functions permit. Such flexibility is more than whole-school SSR schemes can tolerate; so the norm is to set aside twenty minutes daily or three times a week, preferably not at the end of the day.

SSR is needed more in some schools than others. (Of course, it works best in the schools that need it least.) In an inner-city junior high school, a 15-minute daily SSR is having positive effects noticeable even to the content teachers who had thought, at first, that they could not manage their courses without those two minutes that the principal shaved off each of seven periods. It is working because the Reading Committee prepared the whole faculty for it, supplying every classroom with suitable ranges of reading materials. Many students carry their own books now in readiness for the 10:20 SSR break, but every classroom still has an SSR shelf with 30 to 50 selections, ranging from wordless books to almanacs. The science teachers have begun to add to their SSR collections thin informational books pertaining to the unit under study. Many kids learn more from these than from their textbooks. For these teachers, the SSR period is proving an easy entry into multiple-text units.

An important point: This staff agreed to respect SSL—Sustained Silent Looking—as a reasonable substitute for SSR. They realized that many kids in their school could do no more than look at pictures in magazines and in wordless books; they were learning, nevertheless, to keep their attention on a task, one that involved turning pages and permitted no channel-switching. In this school, teachers found they could not themselves get lost in their reading; they needed to keep one eye on the class.

SSR is a motivational gimmick well worth the enthusiasm of the whole staff in many, not all, schools. It is not a *new* idea in junior high schools. Fifty years ago the equivalent of SSR was the homeroom reading period, an early scheme for ensuring reading instruction in the secondary curriculum.

Uses of Television

Print and the electronic media complement each other, observes Michael MacAndrew, who began using television scripts to teach reading in his classes in Philadelphia and was director of the Capital Cities Television Reading Program. Through this project, the three major networks provided a selection of scripts of shows from which Capital Cities chose those appropriate for classrooms. The entire production script of each one was printed, complete with extensive follow-up exercises on vocabulary, comprehension and study skills.

The report continues:

> Additional readings for both intermediate and secondary levels are recom-
> mended. The activity section concludes with a Time Capsule, an exercise designed
> to involve parents or older relatives as a valuable resource for the students. . . .
> Students and teachers receive their materials two weeks before the program ap-
> pears, and can use them before, during and after the viewing. The students do not
> have to see the television show to be involved. All the exercises are based entirely
> on the content of the script.

In addition to participating in the Capital Cities project, CBS has its own Television Reading Program involving 90 affiliated stations.

> Three or four quality CBS programs are selected for the reading program each
> semester. Prior to the broadcast, the network distributes a complete script and
> teacher's guide through its affiliate stations.
>
> Teacher's guides are prepared by educational consultants and designed to in-
> volve the students in reading, writing, and creative projects.
>
> In central Iowa, junior and senior high school students who read four scripts
> indicated that viewing the telecasts had a positive effect on understanding what
> they read, their enjoyment of reading, and their participation in class.[8]

In Box 9-3 we have listed the pertinent addresses and urge you to investigate how you and your school may tie into projects like these that use television to stimulate reading.

Less formally than in these script-reading projects, reading and English teachers have long capitalized on TV to motivate reading, making special efforts to become acquainted with TV tie-ins. These paperbacks, which are novelized treatments of popular television serials, are popular with reluctant readers for good reasons. They are already acquainted with the characters, setting, and

---

[8]Kathryn LeGrand–Brodsky, "Television and Reading: Industry Initiatives," *Journal of Reading* (October 1979): 9–15.

BOX 9-3

SOURCES OF INFORMATION ON TV SCRIPTS AND VIEWERS' GUIDES

American Broadcasting Company
  Director of Community Relations
  ABC-TV
  1330 Avenue of the Americas
  New York, New York 10019

Capital Cities Television Reading Program
  Director of Educative Services
  Capital Cities Communications, Inc.
  4100 City Line Avenue
  Philadelphia, Pennsylvania 19131

Columbia Broadcasting System
Contact your local CBS affiliate station. Since the stations are set up to work with the school systems, rather than individual schools or teachers, coordinate your query with your superintendent's office or media or curriculum coordinator.

National Broadcasting Company
NBC will send you viewer's guides. Write to:
  Press Department
  NBC-TV
  30 Rockefeller Plaza
  New York, New York 10020

For additional information write to:
  Prime Time School Television   Teachers Guides to Television
  212 West Superior   699 Madison Avenue
  Chicago, IL 60610   New York: New York 10021

SOURCE: Kathryn LeGrand–Brodsky, "Television and Reading: Industry Initiatives," *Journal of Reading* (October, 1979). LeGrand–Brodsky is a member of the *Journal of Reading* editorial staff.
Note: In 1983, Capital Cities TV was no longer funding the program described in these pages, but teachers should inquire about current services.

even the action; so the books are easy to comprehend. Reading these narratives gives less-than-proficient readers exactly the kind of practice they need.

When she was a reading teacher in Evanston, Illinois, Laura Johnson[9] used television newscasts to provide "prior knowledge" for comprehending the next

[9]Laura S. Johnson, "The Newspaper: A New Textbook Every Day—Part I," *Journal of Reading* (Novemer 1969). Part II of this detailed and informative article appeared in the December *Journal*.

day's newspaper in her high school class of unmotivated, underdeveloped readers.

Another use of television as a stimulant for reading and writing is described by Ann Hilkert,[10] who teaches Video Graphics at School No. 27, Rochester, New York. Students who score two years below grade level on a standardized reading test are admitted to the Video Graphics Lab in groups of ten for fifty-minute classes five days a week. With the help of the teacher and an aide, the students make their own television programs: researching a topic, preparing graphics, writing a script, practicing reading the script, recording and then evaluating a practice tape, and making the final video tape.

Reading to Others

The growth of the communications industry has made oral reading a lucrative skill. In radio and TV you get paid for reading to others, as today's youngsters are constantly reminded whenever they tune into news broadcasts and scripted programs. Many of the performers on radio and television, students realize, work from scripts, and reading skill is essential to their glamorous jobs. Not until the great age of telecommunications have teachers been able to attach a profit motive so directly to the art and skill of oral reading!

In classrooms in middle, junior, and senior high schools, we should hear students and teachers reading far more often than we do. We should hear students reading aloud, provided, of course, that they are learning how to comprehend as they interpret writers' meanings to an audience. We should hear teachers reading aloud for two reasons: to motivate personal reading and to teach content. Through reading aloud, teachers can often promote interest in books that students might not pick up for themselves. Through listening to their teachers reading aloud from content textbooks, students may learn concepts that they would not learn from trying to read the material themselves. In this section on reading aloud, students are sometimes cast as listeners, sometimes as performers, but always as learners—of content when listening is a substitute for reading; of attitudes when the motive is to instill reasons for reading; of skill when the goal is to teach how to read with meaning.

Teachers Reading Aloud   Oral reading in secondary classrooms should be a polished performance. That means there will be almost no reading aloud without practice either on the part of students or of teachers. Most of the reading aloud will be that of the teacher or the media specialist or other invited guests (including, occasionally, good student readers).

Teachers who read aloud with flair and self-confidence and a sense of the author's purpose are badly needed in secondary schools both to entertain and inform the students and, more important, to model the art. To improve their

---

[10]Ann L. Hilkert, "TV Is the Vehicle, Reading Is the Goal," *The Reading Teacher* (April, 1976): 656–58.

own skills in reading aloud, teachers might request that oral interpretation be the subject of a staff development project. Certainly, oral interpretation should be required pre-service preparation for reading and English teachers. If it has not been, in your case, you had better add it to your list of "things to be done."

However, even teachers who do not count themselves as great oral readers must be willing to read aloud, selecting texts with which they are familiar, as in the case of content textbooks, and which they admire, when the purpose is to motivate interest in personal reading. To the extent possible, teachers should read the text silently just before reading it aloud. Since their purpose is to communicate meaning, they should know which words to emphasize, which phrases may need explaining, which ideas may warrant their comments or invite students' reactions. But immediate prior preparation is not always practical. Do not for that reason neglect reading aloud.

Most students even in senior high school enjoy listening to a teacher read. A few of them may protest at first that being read to is baby stuff, and very good readers may prefer to read silently for themselves as soon as their interest has been aroused. But, on the whole, students enjoy a performance and are interested in materials you have chosen with an eye to both their concerns and your enthusiasms.

Because many secondary students may not have had a teacher read to them since primary grades (unfortunately!), you should plan carefully for the first experiences. Make your first read-aloud selections brief: a short magazine article, a story, the first chapter of a novel, an anecdote from a biography, a few pages from an informational text, a news clipping that is relevant to the day's topic. A reading/English teacher is likely to move on to a whole book; a content teacher may never do so. When you choose a whole book (see Box 9-4), plan daily readings which are long enough to include a complete incident and still leave the audience wanting more, yet are short enough to match students' attention spans and still allow you to finish the work within a month. Knowing your students, you can estimate their likely attention span before you get started. Some teachers gauge their reading time to television, believing that students who are channel-switchers will probably not attend longer than the ten or twelve minutes to the first commercial break.

Since reading aloud takes preparation time as well as time in class, most teachers read to whole classes rather than small groups. The more diverse the class, the more carefully they must select materials; but teachers know that adolescents, for all their differences in skills, knowledge, and backgrounds, have common interests and emotions; and their crowd instincts make them want to be included in whole-class activities more often than not.

Apart from reading and English classes, most of what is read aloud in middle school and high school will be serious subject-oriented stuff, usually from content textbooks and other course materials. It may be at a higher readability level than poor readers can read for themselves, but it cannot exceed their ability to comprehend the ideas therein. All the factors affecting reading comprehension apply equally to listening. If what you choose to read aloud is beyond the range of your listeners' experience or conceptual development, they will have as much trouble comprehending through listening as through reading. In fact, listening to you read a text may be more difficult for your students than reading it themselves unless you are willing to repeat and explain and invite questions.

Because a live reader can adapt to audience needs, teachers are more effective

BOX 9-4

A TEACHER'S EXPERIENCE . . .
READING ALOUD TO SOPHOMORES

Every day in two classes of Reading Skills 2, the required English class for sophomores who have reading problems, I read part of *Black Boy* by Richard Wright. . . . They came from lower-middle and middle-class white suburban families. Most of the students were not successful in school; many were the "troublemakers" of the school. Many had never read a book; all had reading problems and most had very negative attitudes toward reading. . . .

I chose *Black Boy* because it is one of the books read in the regular sophomore English classes, because it easily breaks into sections for daily reading, and because it is one of my favorite books.

Their responses to the reading amazed me. They were a rowdy group, and I had rarely tried to work with them as a whole because I could not hold their attention as a group. But when I read—and I do not read particularly well—they almost always listened, many of them with rapt attention. At first, they were uncomfortable with the subject matter, and would ask, "Are you going to read about that nigger kid today?" but soon the book drew them in. They stopped using the word "nigger," and started asking serious questions about a world that was totally foreign to them. (Few Blacks live within twenty miles of these students.) They asked, "Why did they beat him?" and "They really didn't like Blacks, did they?" They talked about Richard Wright as though he was a real person. . . .

They enjoyed listening to the book, and I read it all—every word—to them over the semester. But did it improve their reading and other language skills? Yes. . . . But perhaps more important, it affected their attitudes toward Blacks. When I first started reading, their comments revealed a very strong and blatant prejudice, but gradually the attitudes changed. When I finished the book, I asked them simply to write their reactions to the book. Their responses revealed a change in their attitudes, a broadening of their minds:

> I realy liked Black Boy and it kind of told me how I would feel to be Black and how people would feel about me. I learned that the way you treat people they will always rember that and that I should not do or say anything to a fend them. I know that if I was treated that way I would like to kill myself or anyone who did that.

> it told me how much bullshit the black take from us. if you ask me I think the black could overcome us and it could switch around we would be there nigers then we can see what they went threw.

> I found out how hard it was for a Black person to live in the time of black boy and before. People were very creul to black people. Even after black people were free white people treated them like slaves.

SOURCE: Elaine A. Giermak, "Reading to High School Students: A Painless Method of Improving Language Skills," *English Journal* (September 1980): 62–63. Ms. Giermak teaches at Rolling Meadows High School, Illinois.

readers for their own students than are professional actors; when it's Mr. Jones, live, reading Hamlet's lines it beats Laurence Olivier on tape. Even so, teachers' time is severely constrained, and so is students'. Reading aloud to the whole class must be supplemented by opportunities for students to listen individually and in small groups to materials that fit special needs. A live teacher cannot do it all. Tapes and recordings are the answer.

Using Tapes and Recordings   For poor readers—those reading at or below third grade level—taped texts are a substitute for reading and the only means of independent learning in secondary content courses, just as "talking books" are learning tools for the blind. How much of the content textbook should be transferred to tape depends on each student's capacity to learn. Some seriously handicapped readers of better than average intelligence and background experience may be able to consume whole texts on tape; many others will do better with a teacher's lectures in which content has been modified to their needs, taped for their supplementary listening outside of class. Students who are substituting listening for reading will probably use tapes, recordings, films, and other nonprint media without any kind of text. But for most youngsters who can read at fifth or sixth grade levels, listening to tapes, as listening to teachers reading aloud, serves two purposes: to motivate and to improve their reading. For these students we recommend the use of read-along tapes.

"Read-along tapes" is a proprietary term (like Kleenex) which we use here to include all tapes or recordings that are tied to texts. In a classroom, students wearing headsets listen to the recording while they follow the printed text, using an index card to uncover the lines as they read/listen. As one teacher noted when he used this technique in teaching *Lord of the Flies* to eleventh graders, "With their eyes, ears, and fingers thus occupied, you've got 'em trapped!" This teacher assigned one group to the listening post and headsets while another group worked on related written assignments, and a third group discussed the part of the novel they had just heard on the tape.

Where do you get read-along tapes? For reading and English teachers many are available commercially, and we have noted sources in Box 9-5. Most teachers make their own to match print materials they use in their courses. (Tapes for classroom use are an obvious product of that inservice course in oral interpretation referred to earlier.) We admit, however, that making tapes in the quantities needed looks like another impossible chore for overworked teachers. Tapes are a practical idea only if you have others to help in making them. Excellent readers from the student body are your most immediate source. In many schools, preparing tapes is an activity of service clubs. This activity can be greatly expanded and enriched if organized by a reading consultant, media specialist, English teacher, or drama coach, so that student readers get needed practice, other students are supplied with excellent aids to comprehension and interest, and teachers have one other resource to turn to. (Adult groups interested in drama and reading aloud have also volunteered to make tapes for school consumption.)

Although we referred in the preceding paragraph to "excellent student read-

BOX 9-5

SOURCES OF READ-ALONG TAPES AND RECORDS

Caedmon
1995 Broadway
New York, NY 10023
Cassette and record "soundbooks" for all ages.

Educational Record Sales
157 Chambers Street
New York, NY 10007
Newbery Book Award recordings and sound filmstrips among others.

Listening Library, Inc.
1 Park Avenue
Old Greenwich, CT 06870
Combinations of cassettes, filmstrips and books for literature, poetry, history, and careers. Materials useful across the curriculum.

Miller—Brody Productions, Inc.
Dept. 77
342 Madison Avenue
New York, NY 10017
Adaptations on cassette of Newbery Award winners.

Random House
School Division
400 Hahn Road
Westminster, MD 21157
Cassette/Book read-alongs for over 400 popular children's books. Cassette/filmstrips also available for literature in the secondary curriculum, Newbery Award books, and young adult literature.

Spoken Arts
P.O. Box 289
New Rochelle, NY 10802
Cassettes, filmstrips, teacher's guide with scripts, and duplicating masters for skill sheets available in basic skills, American literature and social studies topics as well as read-along books.

---

ers," we should note that "excellent" is a relative term. So long as the material to be read aloud is easy enough for them to comprehend easily, almost all students might be drafted to make tapes for younger and poorer readers. Indeed, making tapes for students at lower levels is a practical reason for developing oral reading skills.

In our enthusiasm for tapes, we are not overlooking the obvious: Like any other instructional device, tapes are as effective as the teachers who use them. What goes on tape must be selected carefully for interest and difficulty level, and the listeners' attention must be continually jogged. We have seen kids at many listening centers whose minds were turned off when the recorder was turned on. The tape-and-text must engage their minds, not just their ears and eyes. To ensure "engagement," the tape should call for some kind of response (in addition to turning the pages of the text or uncovering the lines). Some tapes require talking back, that is, recording answers to questions raised; others ask the listeners to read along orally with the tape, or to repeat sentences and phrases. Sometimes the teacher prepares study guides that require checking, matching, diagraming, drawing—whatever is appropriate to the content of the tape.

Schools that cannot afford listening centers in every classroom can often provide one to be shared by several teachers or can install several in the media center. Resource teachers and content teachers can collaborate in seeing that such centers are in continuous use.

Students Reading Aloud   Students should read to others. Even poor-to-middling readers should have this experience. But students should do most of this reading aloud outside their own classrooms. The reasons for this should be obvious. We've already said that oral reading should be a polished performance, that most of it should be done by teachers and invited guests, that reading aloud to the whole class will occur relatively infrequently and will be supplemented by listening individually and in small groups to tapes and recordings. So there are relatively few opportunities for reading aloud to one's classmates. The practice of having everyone in a class read a paragraph or so aloud from a textbook that everyone shares is so indefensible that we would like to believe it almost never occurs in secondary classrooms. Of course, there are times when the math teacher should ask someone to read aloud a verbal problem or the English teacher should ask for an oral reading of a poem or a history teacher, confronting a tightly reasoned passage in the text, asks for an oral reading as a preliminary to careful analysis. In all these instances the student readers are permitted to read silently first, and none of the instances is related to the reading-round-the-room practice, which teachers resort to only in desperation to kill time.

These additional occasions for students to read to a real audience within their class will occur to you: rereading to support the answer to a question; sharing a letter; reading announcements; sharing with a small group or the whole class the high point of a novel; reading directions; reading aloud one's own writing or a classmate's work. Especially in reading and English classes students read plays aloud, as well as scripts for television programs, and scripts they have written for student-produced video tapes.

These activities provide for developing oral reading skills through using them. In addition, students learn how to read aloud when teachers coach them individually and in small groups to prepare readings of various kinds. Reading/English teachers often require students to make tapes of their oral reading at intervals throughout the year so that they can monitor their miscues themselves and evaluate their progress in accurate and effective oral reading.

We have already mentioned making tapes for students in other classes. Two other uses of oral reading are especially effective with adolescents who can read (at least minimally) but seldom choose to do so. These are (a) reading to young children at home and in schools, libraries, hospitals, and day-care centers; and (b) reading to adults in senior citizen centers, nursing homes, and hospitals.

Don't overlook any chance to get adolescents to read to young children. It gives below-level readers a respectable reason for reading books at levels of difficulty appropriate to their skills, books that they would otherwise scorn. Poor readers need quantities of practice on easy reading, and finding genuine opportunities for them is worth the combined efforts of the reading consultant, the English teachers, the media specialist, the faculty in care-giving services, and interested others. It is an idea easily sold to teachers in early-childhood programs. With the expansion of preschool programs into classrooms vacated when school enrollments fell in the late 1970s, many junior and senior high schools now have little children in their buildings, ready laboratories for parenting courses.

In Rochester, Minnesota, in the Herbert Hoover Elementary School, Mrs. Margaret Schafer has just such a project for fifth graders to read to third graders, and third graders to kindergarteners. In this affluent community, teachers noticed how many children in grade 5 were nonreaders of the can-but-won't variety. With the help of parent volunteers, Mrs. Schafer set up a program in which readers select books for younger listeners with the advice of their "consultants" (the parents) and prepare their oral readings with consultant help. The idea is proving useful at many grade levels beyond elementary and middle schools.

In a large metropolitan system, the coordinator of Family Services has made reading to children an essential feature of the parenting courses for teenagers. The potential benefits of this program extend far beyond the practice-at-mastery-level that adolescent poor readers get from it. They learn that reading to children provides a language base that they themselves were deprived of, and they learn what books appeal to 3-to-7-year-olds. These adolescents are the ones most likely to be parents soonest and most likely *not* to have learned love of books from their own parents. The possibility exists that they can be prepared in this way (among many others) to provide a better "home curriculum" for the next generation and a surer start on learning to read than many school entrants before them. And if none of these future benefits pays off, adolescents have still had the fun of reading to children and enjoying the delights of children's books themselves. (For a list of winners, see Box 9-6.)

Not only the youngest children welcome a teenage reading companion. Middle-grade youngsters also like to be read to. In Indiana, the department of public instruction created Readmore the Cat, whose picture you see in Box 9-7. The cat costume and persona give adolescent readers a welcome disguise. Taking a leaf from Readmore, you and they will think of other characters for students to assume and other ways to dramatize oral reading that will increase the fun for both readers and audience.

Mainstreaming has opened another opportunity for readers of quite ordinary attainments to serve others whose reading skills are less than theirs. In many secondary schools, physically impaired youngsters are teamed with more fortu-

BOX 9-6

A HANDFUL OF BOOKS FOR READING ALOUD

This is a starter list of books that teenage reluctant readers *might* be willing and able to read aloud to preschool and primary grade children. We've selected carefully to avoid the too young and too sweet. We suggest you present a range of picture books and let the adolescent readers choose two or three for their listeners' pleasure. Watch their choices and develop your own lists therefrom.

For the youngest listeners (and most reluctant readers):

Bernard Waber, *Ira Sleeps Over*
Tomie De Paola, *The Quicksand Book*
Sesyle Joslin, *What Do You Say, Dear?*
Dr. Seuss, *The Cat in the Hat*
Barbara Seuling, *The Teeny Tiny Woman*
Bernard Waber, *Lyle, Lyle Crocodile*
James Marshall, *George and Martha*
Ellen Raskin, *Spectacles*

For 8-to-10-year-old listeners (and better readers):

Florence Parry Heide, *The Shrinking of Treehorn*
Judy Blume, *Tales of a Fourth Grade Nothing*
Roald Dahl, *Charlie and the Chocolate Factory*
Robert McCluskey, *Homer Price*
Oliver Butterworth, *The Enormous Egg*
Byrd Baylor, *Hawk, You Are My Brother*

nate classmates who offer many kinds of help in addition to reading. In a central New York high school, a young special education teacher organized an "advocacy program" in which student "advocates" can earn up to one high school credit by assisting mentally retarded youngsters in a variety of ways which include reading to them and helping them to read notices, signs, menus, directions, and simple texts.

The best readers among the "won't read" adolescents may be encouraged to serve still another group, the aged and handicapped, especially those confined to nursing homes and hospitals or living alone and in poverty. Most often it is through care-giving courses that the adolescents and the aged are connected, but sometimes the initiative is the reading teacher's. In either case, the activity provides an ideal vehicle for improving reading because it renders practice purposeful.

Tutoring and Teaching

Almost every experiment with peer tutoring (and there have been dozens of them over the years) has shown that the tutors benefit as much as, or more than, their students. Fair amounts of peer teaching can take place within regular

BOX 9-7

READMORE THE CAT ON THE PROWL

Readmore the Cat is the mascot for the Indiana state reading program and a well-known symbol around the state.

Created to let children see that reading can be fun and worthwhile, Readmore encourages youngsters in the state to read more books. Six feet tall and green with blue spots, Readmore is portrayed by teachers, parents, and students who eagerly volunteer for the assignment.

Readmore visits classrooms and school libraries. A good campaigner, Readmore does a lot of small handshaking around the state and has acquired a reputation for kissing teachers. He can also be counted on to sign autograph books and occasionally lapses into a softshoe routine.

SOURCE: *Reading Today* (International Reading Association, 800 Bentshine Rd., Newark, DE).

content classes, and indeed peer teaching is the basis of the study techniques we recommend for improving uses of reading in the content fields. So, while you can arrange for poor readers to teach others without going out of your regular classes, we suggest an additional approach that takes extra effort and the cooperation of two or more teachers. The reader who is just beyond the remedial level can become an aide to the remedial teacher in a set-up similar to the one organized by the special education teacher mentioned previously. The rule of thumb for pairing students in peer tutoring is to keep tutor and pupil within sight of one another, educationally speaking; the pupil will interact better with a tutor whose skills and attitudes are not greatly different from his own. A superior student does not have as much to learn from tutoring nor as much to give in genuine sympathy and support.

Differences in ages between tutors and their charges need not pose a problem, though it may be cumbersome to arrange for students from one school unit to work in another. In K–12 schools and where school units are grouped together on campuses, it is possible for eighth graders to tutor third graders or eleventh graders to work with sixth graders. In districts where school units are at great distances, it is still possible to match a ninth grader who is reading at sixth grade level with a fifth grader who needs help, but it is obviously easier to match students within the same building.

The success of peer tutoring depends on how carefully the plans are structured. Don't try to work with too many tutors at one time. Select them carefully and be sure that their tasks in the remedial plan are clearly defined. Having them read to their pupils and listen to their pupils read to them is the easiest role for the teacher to plan for and may be the most beneficial. Be sure, however, that the tutors understand the importance of reading for meaning, and caution them against overcorrecting.

In Box 9-8 you can read about a special peer tutoring program sponsored by Literacy Volunteers.

Adapting SSR to Senior High School

Ms. Coleman did two things in her first year as a tenth-grade English teacher that made it possible for fruitful teaching–learning interactions to occur throughout that year. In the opening days of school, she introduced herself to her students by showing them the autobiography she had prepared as a slide/tape show. Through a well-scripted tape and carefully chosen pictures, she shared with them her family, schooling, pets, her new husband and wedding pictures, her travels, hobbies, books and recordings, favorite personalities, likes and dislikes. She did not ask them to write the standard autobiographical theme or "what I did this summer." The students respected her for coming to them as a human being, not an impersonal faceless mentor.

The second thing Ms. Coleman did was to give her English classes two weeks of free-choice reading in class. The only assignment was that they should bring with them each day a nonassigned, nonschool text and read without interrupting themselves or others for the full class period. She used this time to talk to students individually, to get them to share their reading interests with her, and

BOX 9-8

TEENS COACH PEERS IN READING

Marjorie McBain, a senior at Fabius-Pompey High School, remembers a time when she hated school.

Lessons others completed with ease seemed to defy her. The harder she tried, the more discouraged she grew and the more negative about school she became. Then her parents hired a tutor.

"I hated that tutor. I felt so dumb and embarrassed," she recalls.

But after a year of hard work, Marjorie not only caught up but began to excel. She realized what a difference her special teacher had made.

These days, through a program started this fall by Literacy Volunteers of Greater Syracuse, Inc. at Fabius–Pompey High School, Marjorie has switched roles. She is one of thirteen seniors and seven juniors selected for a pilot project in peer tutoring.

This program adds a new dimension to the services offered by Literacy Volunteers, a national organization founded in Syracuse.

Currently this group provides one-on-one instruction to adults who never learned to read and fluency lessons for those whose native tongue is not English.

The peer tutoring program began when guidance counselors and parents came to Literacy Volunteers for help with students. "We had to keep turning them away, explaining a person must be out of school to be eligible for our teachers," Connie Johnson, president of Literacy Volunteers, explained.

Then Literacy Volunteers received a grant that made it possible to hire a coordinator to run the project and buy the necessary textbooks, tests and other needed supplies.

Marcia Hannett, a former teacher and a longtime worker in Literacy Volunteers, was selected to get the project underway.

As its name suggests, the peer tutoring program uses older students who have received special training to help youngsters overcome reading problems.

With the exception of the coordinator, everyone working on the project is a volunteer—from the people who run the training workshops to the student tutors.

"Mr. O'Connor made it a real plus for high school juniors and seniors to sign up. He also gave them time from school to take the workshops," she noted.

Children in the primary and intermediate schools receiving the additional boost in reading are the real winners. Not only should their work become easier for them, but they have the added plus of acquiring a special friend in the senior high school.

A sampling of those chosen to be the first tutors demonstrates the enthusiasm they have for the task now that they are actually working in one-to-one situations.

Janice Brown, a junior, volunteered because she hopes to become a special education teacher. Somehow, she manages to squeeze time to work with her students between band, cheerleading, and student council.

Kodi Chapin, a bubbly senior, signed up because "I just like kids. I come from a family of eight. The whole idea sounded interesting. I've really learned a lot about my language I never knew before."

Paula Smith, vice president of the senior class, on the yearbook and in

Continued

BOX 9-8 (continued)

TEENS COACH PEERS IN READING

National Honor Society, feels it's personally rewarding to help someone.

The tutors were cautioned to be confidential about their assigned students to help them avoid the kind of stigma Marjorie McBain once experienced. But the upperclassmen report some of their young pupils hail them on the school bus, pointing with pride to their new pals.

Not all the time together is devoted to scheduled work. Debra Foell, a junior, found she shared an interest in horseback riding with her student.

"We can talk about that and even use the information in reading," she declared.

Brian Field, president of the junior class and on the basketball team, feels good about what he's doing. "It's important to help each other rather than sitting back and letting the government pay for everything."

Among the most confident she can help is Marjorie. "I know how this child feels. I've been there and I want to share the ambition I gained to move on."

SOURCE: Adapted from story by Diana D. Hatch appearing in Syracuse (New York) *Post Standard*, 23 November 1979.

to read to her short passages from the books they had chosen. In those two weeks she acquired information that enriched the notes she had made from the guidance office records and that made it possible for her to "provide for individual differences" in the months ahead. This two-week adaptation of SSR yielded an even greater benefit—improved morale. By showing she trusted her students, first to know her as an individual and secondly to choose their own reading materials, she found they were willing to trust her to make selections for the literature they would read in common in the year ahead.

Using Local Issues

One of the best secondary teachers I've met taught in a small industrial city in New England in an old "vocational" high school located across the street from a curtain mill. He had come to this school nine years earlier as an eleventh grade English teacher; he had been trained to teach social studies and had only very rudimentary ideas about English as a school subject, mostly left over from his own high school days when English had been his least favorite course. The principal, showing him a closet full of composition texts and old literature anthologies, said in effect: "There are the books, here come the students; put 'em together."

But Mr. Zorn, as he considered his situation, refused the approach. He said to his classes, "Listen, kids, I won't try to teach you anything you can't see a reason for learning." As the books proved useless, they went back into the closet, and Mr. Zorn, though he wouldn't have known it was called that, was soon developing a student-centered curriculum. By the time I visited him nine years later, he could show me an English classroom fully if crudely equipped as a "workshop" with an outside telephone and a typewriter at his desk, a bank of upright files on one side of the room, a desk for his chief assistant (a student) equipped like his except for the telephone, six tape recorders, a listening center, an overhead projector, and a filmstrip projector aimed at the "screen" inside a cardboard box, a paperback rack, tables and study carrels, some made from refrigerator cartons, others more elaborately constructed in the woodshop. The wiring for desk lamps, study corner lighting, and additional electrical outlets had all been done by students in the electrical shop. Students in the print shop had printed special pads of paper for use in the class with the heading, *English at Work*. The room was filled with people, too, of course, each of them working alone or in pairs or in teams of two or three. Mr. Zorn was working at the files.

This was a vocational high school; this was English for eleventh graders who were not highly motivated toward academic learning but who had become involved. One of the things they understood, said Mr. Zorn, was a union code; they could appreciate the teacher's job better if they knew what he earned by the hour and for what kinds of services. "Your parents," he reminded them, "don't pay me X dollars an hour to correct spelling errors. With Tony's help, you can do it for yourself." And spelling, which was respected by working-class parents as a basic, was practiced diligently in a test-study-test sequence, with taped lessons and an assistant (Tony) to score the final tests.

The content of the curriculum was largely current and local issues. Mr. Zorn stressed process learning, but the students had to produce. Those upright files contained their basic reading materials—folder after folder of magazine and newspaper clippings. Students "reported" on their individual reading of the paperbacks by filing cards in a rack similar to the timecard racks they would use in a shop. The filmstrip projector was in use all the time, operated by the least motivated student (Mr. Zorn's guess in September as to who that might be), who passed out the study guides, rolled the strips over and over, and eventually learned the right answers. "Hey," Louie would say, looking over Steve's shoulder, "that ain't right. You'd better look back at frames 9 and 10." Peer teaching, though Mr. Zorn never called it that.

A feature that students looked forward to was the civil suit. In preparation, they would attend court sessions, read about local issues involving the courts, and culminate their study with a mock trial. Two or three students would make up a rough scenario of a case, and others would serve as judge, jury, plaintiff, defendant, witnesses. Mr. Zorn always brought in real lawyers to defend and prosecute because students should learn from models as well as from each other.

Students in these classes always took active roles in local political issues, whether an election, an investigation into senior citizens' rights, advocacy in behalf of the handicapped, or a breach of ecological safety like dumping industrial wastes (a common problem in that New England mill town). The students interviewed all participants, using their six tape recorders, transcribed important points, wrote up their findings as reports, and sent off letters to the editors of local and regional newspapers.

The outside telephone line—a real coup for a teacher in this or many another school—was justified by Mr. Zorn to his administrators as vital to his communications program, his students' link to their community resources, as it indeed was. It was also his vital weapon in involving parents in their kids' learning and in disciplinary matters, too, of course.

A rigorous traditionalist, Mr. Zorn believed in maintaining standards and basing grades on achievement, not effort. As a base for individualizing instruction, he used the contract method, giving each student a weekly contract of tasks to be performed, so many to be completed adequately for a D, so many more for a C, with the quality of work determining whether the week's work deserved a B or an A. He considered this method especially appropriate for students who would work to contract later on, as employers as well as employees.

Were his methods successful? "Methods are my hobby," he'd say, never admitting to his students how many hours he worked on them beyond the school time he figured as the basis of his "hourly wages." "For these kids a teacher's hourly rate ought to look as good as an electrician's or a plumber's—at least as good as the sanitation worker's!" he would explain. But, of course, Mr. Zorn had to supplement his income, which he did by running the concessions at the ball park over the summer. This provided his best clues to the evaluation of his program, because he hired student help. "The kids from our school, the ones who've had English at Work, know what to do next," he said. "They don't hang around waiting to be told, like the kids from the academic high schools."

Do College Aspirations Motivate Present Learning?

I was going from Logan Airport to an educational conference in a downtown hotel, the cabbie spotted me as a teacher, and naturally the conversation turned to schooling. He had one son at Vassar, another at the University of Maine, and a daughter at Regis—they were *all* freshmen. When I gasped at the tuition he must be paying, he noted offhandedly that he spent 14 hours a day in that cab, that he drew retirement pay from the police force, and that his wife was an executive secretary. His was a typical middle-class family; the siblings weren't triplets or twins either. To cut down on sibling rivalry, the parents had sent the two boys to different high schools; since one had repeated a lower grade "to catch up on the basics," he explained, they had both graduated in the same year. One had been scouted for the hockey team at a leading New England men's college, but his SAT scores were miserable. The other, with his eye on Harvard Law School, had won a basketball scholarship at a Long Island university but had turned it down on the advice of a lawyer friend who had faint hope for the boy's ever gaining admission to a "decent" law school. "The boys can't write; they need at least a year at a prep school," the lawyer advised.

"Gee," said the father to me, "they were both getting A's and B's in English. Carl was on the honor roll his junior year." (One boy attended a suburban high school with an outstanding reputation for academics as well as sports; the other, a fine parochial school.)

"They had to spend too much time in sports; they couldn't study; but they both had offers of sports scholarships—that's what they worked for," this cab driver said without bitterness, having paid a year's tuition and board for each son at separate private schools.

And the daughter? Two years younger, she had entered the college of her choice directly from high school, the same public suburban high school attended by one brother, where she had learned sufficient verbal skills to assure success in a liberal arts program.

The cabbie's story illustrates the norm, not the extremes. We chose it in preference to similar stories of many minority athletes who learned to shoot baskets but not to study and who make bitter accusations against a system that exploited natural talents which were good but not good enough for the major leagues. Out of college, out of work, these former high school and college athletes are victims of a social system, not just a school system, the values of which are in tune with "the competing curriculum," not with learning how to learn.

Do college aspirations motivate learning in high school? A partial answer, supported by this tale of the cab driver's sons, is "not necessarily." But this is neither the whole nor the final answer. Everything we have said thus far in this chapter aims at ways to counteract the effects of the competing curriculum. But teachers must be aware of the strength of the competition before they can make sensible moves to combat it.

Motivation in the Content Fields

Appealing to adolescents' interests is easier for reading and English teachers than it is for other teachers because they have no fixed curriculum in terms of content. Instead, they select whatever content is most likely to serve the needs of language development. Subject-matter teachers are not so free. Although they, too, are more concerned with process than with product, with how students gather data and draw inferences from it rather than with mindless pursuit of information, they are nonetheless more closely bound to the content of textbooks and curriculum guides.

Although reading and English teachers are free to choose the content of process-oriented lessons, they have not succeeded in making their subject especially popular with students. In fact, consistent findings over the decades show that English (that is, language arts and reading) is rated the least popular school subject by both elementary and secondary students. One reason for this unpopularity may well be the focus on process, which permits free choice of content, it is true, but seems much more vague and repetitive than, say, the science curriculum. Kids reject process learning; they want to be learning something new. And language development, once you're past the first reader, looks like the same thing over and over again. It isn't, but it looks that way, as you can verify by checking any scope and sequence chart for reading or language arts; the skills are described in much the same way at every grade level from kindergarten to grade 12. So, in this sense, "content" teachers have considerable advantage over "process" teachers. History, math, economics, psychology, sociology, anthropology, physics and chemistry, mechanical engineering, and nutrition—these subjects and their offshoots contain the ideas that interest students.

Yet teachers of every subject encounter more than their share of apathetic students. What can they do about those aspects of apathy related to learning through reading? First, we advise content teachers: Stick to your content; don't cease to be a teacher of history or science. What you have to offer students is the chance to learn something new; in doing so, they may also develop abilities in thinking and in language, if you take it as your responsibility to assist in that process.

Faced with nonreading students, content teachers sometimes abandon their textbooks altogether. Don't do that. (We'll have more to say about content textbooks and how to use them in Part III.) Take every opportunity to demonstrate to nonreading students (who *can* read many materials) that reading is the most efficient way of organizing and consolidating what they know and of adding to their store of knowledge.

A very large part of motivating learning in the content fields emanates from the teacher's enthusiasm for his or her subject. If the men who masterminded the American Revolution are as real to you as your colleagues (and maybe more understandable to you), you can bring them to life for your students. If you see scientific principles working all around you, not just in textbooks, you will figure out ways of getting most of your students involved in the science surrounding them. Probably no one can tell you *how* to share your enthusiasms with others; certainly, we can do no more than assert that teachers' enthusiasm for learning, the pleasure they take in their subjects, and their self-confidence in teaching are perfectly apparent to students and are often infectious. You are probably developing these qualities and learning to display them in your classes; if you are, then the bread-and-butter suggestions we can make about motivation have a chance to work.

One such suggestion is to reduce the amount of time in each class period when students are required to listen to you, or to three or four of their classmates answering your questions. In every class period provide time for every individual to react, to respond, to raise questions. With forty-minute periods, you will follow that injunction most easily by having everyone write briefly. But with a little ingenuity you can have everyone talk as well as write, using teams of two and three for limited discussion periods. And in almost every class session you should provide time for silent reading of the text or whatever other print sources you are using.

Especially for students unmotivated to study in your subject, we urge in-class supervised reading as follow-up to a careful assignment that makes clear to students:

1. how the assigned reading connects with what they already know;
2. what their purposes are and why they are important;
3. what strategies they should use to identify and remember important information.

Since we recommend supervised study within class periods, you may assume that we mean to keep unmotivated students on fairly short strings. That assumption is correct so long as the students are both unmotivated and lacking in self-discipline and the skills needed for independent study. Adolescents who have not really learned to be students—and some may never do so—need short-term goals in order to experience frequently the satisfaction of "mission accomplished." However, as their interest in your subject grows, you can gradually introduce longer-range goals and the element of choice. Adolescents often need assignments that are clearly defined, almost routinized, and closely checked; but they also like the freedom to choose. And, of course, the only way they can learn to make choices is to have experience in doing so. The sensitive teacher allows as many choices as possible by balancing "electives" with "requirements." Wherever possible, teachers control the alternatives. Too many choices are confusing; too few are confining.

You noticed that Mr. Zorn held his students to one-week contracts. Their motivation was generally high because they understood what they were learning and why. Even so, these nonacademic students responded best to relatively short-range (one week) assignments. The contracts allowed several choices, however; students could decide *how much* credit they wanted to earn and *when* within the week they would do each task.

You noted, too, that Ms. Coleman won over her students by trusting them. Giving students even limited choices demonstrates a teacher's trust and is a motivating factor.

When you have the freedom to set your own work schedule, do you tend to do the easy jobs first, postponing the tasks you are unsure of? It's the same way with adolescents. Making clear assignments and showing adolescents how to get started on a specific task is an important factor in motivating them. That is why we advocate supervised study.

The other side of the coin, however, is that too careful direction by the teacher can kill creativity. Only teachers who are sensitive to how their students learn can know who is ready to discover, to create, and who cannot as yet tolerate the confusions and ambiguities of free inquiry. But remember that we are referring in this chapter to the least motivated and the least skilled students, ones for whom the risks of failure are the greatest. For these students, at least until you know them better, it is usually best to keep the leading strings short. Think of yourself in a new learning situation where your skills are shaky and your enthusiasm is faltering. How much support do *you* want?

That well-worn cliché about success being the best motivator is a cliché precisely because there is such a large element of truth in it. Although we don't necessarily enjoy doing everything that we can do easily, we certainly dislike tasks at which we consistently fail. So the content teacher sets up conditions for learning in a way to assure everyone's learning something of value. Teachers can do this more often than not if they know what is reasonable to expect of their students, hold them to these expectations, and provide several ways by which students can reach these suitable standards.

Motivating Teachers

Apathy is the blight of the secondary school. If teachers burn out, so do students, especially if they see themselves as marginal students or as failures. What keeps many kids coming to high school—and many come only sporadically—is not the curriculum of the classrooms but the hidden curriculum of the locker rooms, the cafeteria, the stacks, the corridors, and the gym.

Can the apathy of the classrooms—the students' and teachers'—be penetrated? We know teachers who have done so, using ideas like those sketched in this chapter, elaborating on them, adapting them to local situations and to the teachers' own strengths and interests. These teachers have had success—more successes than failures—chiefly because they have refused to believe that the adolescents' armor of apathy is impenetrable. Unfortunately, some of these enthusiastic, successful teachers have learned also that their colleagues' apathy could not be penetrated; so they suppressed their enthusiasm in the staff room and kept quiet about "great ideas that really work!" To keep their professionalism alive, they joined professional organizations where they could meet other enthusiastic teachers and swap ideas. Eventually, they found schools with climates more conducive to learning and moved on, leaving their first schools poorer for their loss.

The heading of this concluding section is purposely ambiguous. It suggests that teachers are the prime motivating force, but it also recognizes that teachers need to be motivated. What renews teachers' energies and safeguards their willingness to try once again to inspire friendliness toward print if not a wholehearted love of reading? Success, of course—that same cliché that we used with respect to students' motivation. Since you know that success is essential to your well-being and your effectiveness as a teacher, you stake out goals that you have a good chance of attaining and you learn to measure your accomplishments fairly.

For example, in this matter of motivating "won't-read" adolescents, you have gleaned a number of ideas from this chapter. Choose one of them to be your goal for the year ahead or for the next marking period. In selecting one motivational project, decide whether you can work by yourself or must have help from your colleagues and administrator. If the latter, assess your chances realistically. If there is too much else going on in the school this year for you to launch a successful peer tutoring program outside your own classes, postpone this project and choose one you can handle on your own. On the other hand, if you begin modestly on a reading-aloud project, you may be able to enlist help from a colleague in Family Services or drama or the Parent Teachers Organization, and build from there.

Assess your own strengths realistically. What commitments do you already have? How can you budget your time? Since first successes are so important to your morale, with which groups of students are you most likely to develop a successful project?

Finally, learn to monitor your successes and failures. Why did this idea work well? Why did this one fizzle? Neither successes nor failures are likely to be total. Be sure to give yourself credit for tiny gains—the nonreader who finishes a short story, the one who chooses an easy-to-read paperback, the fellow who asks you for a magazine on racing cars. Recognize that changing habits and creating new attitudes takes time.

Meanwhile, show your students your own pleasures in reading. Show them how reading enriches your life, and how you balance reading with your other interests.

RECAPPING MAIN POINTS

Adolescents who can but don't read constitute a large segment of the population of junior and senior high schools, including many students of average ability and most slow learners. Nevertheless, many will seek education beyond high school. Before they can learn from reading, they must become willing readers.

Parents influence adolescents' willingness to read, as do attitudes toward reading set in primary grades. Out-of-school interests, especially television, compete for reading time, but teachers can use TV, in moderation, to promote reading and writing.

Surveys show that adolescents generally read very little that is not assigned, except newspapers and magazines. Interests in reading are similar in spite of differences in age, intelligence, and reading ability; however, boys' interests are different from girls'.

Teachers must provide in-school time for personal reading. One popular scheme in middle/junior high schools is Sustained Silent Reading. An adaptation of SSR in a senior high school gave students in an English class two weeks of free-choice reading. Television scripts and TV tie-ins motivate reading.

Students who can read but don't, as well as seriously disabled readers, can improve their reading skills by listening to live and taped presentations. Students should also read to others—small children, disabled classmates, hospital patients, and the aged.

Peer tutoring benefits the tutors as much as their students.

Ideas for motivating high school students include involving them in local issues, using contracts, balancing options and requirements, making clear the purposes of all assignments and the strategies needed to complete them, setting short-range goals, gauging accurately what students can do, and seeing that they do it.

Teachers as much as their students are motivated by success; so they plan carefully to achieve attainable goals and give themselves credit for achieving them.

FOR DISCUSSION

1. Interview five or six students at a grade level of your choice and probe their attitudes toward reading; inquire about their reading habits and their favorite books. Try to determine why they do (or do not) choose to read in leisure time.

2. Conduct your own study to ascertain how much time students spend in reading. Working with colleagues would permit you to develop a sizable sample. Keep your questionnaire brief and your questions as specific as possible. One possibility: Ask students to record for a week the time they spend in reading of any kind; have them identify what they read. Have them keep similar records for viewing television.

3. Reread Postman's definition of *curriculum* and why he believes television is the First Curriculum (Box 9-1). In what major way, according to Postman,

is the television curriculum in conflict with the school curriculum? Relate Postman's views to the comments in Chapter 3 (pages 65–66) on the effect of structural codes on reading comprehension. Apart from consuming students' time, how else may viewing television negatively affect reading?

4. Discuss with your colleagues suggestions given in this chapter for motivating unwilling readers. Which appeal to you? Which do you think would work least well for you? What suggestions can you add to these?

5. Read Chapter 8, "Motivational Aspects of the Literacy Problem" in *Toward a Literate Society* (see Further Reading) and report to your group on how these authors define motivation and how their points of view compare with suggestions in this text.

6. Who or what motivates teachers to continue trying to involve the unwilling reader?

FURTHER READING

Fader, Daniel. *The New Hooked on Books*. Berkeley, CA: Berkeley Publishing Co., 1976.

Carroll, John B. and Jeanne S. Chall, eds. *Toward a Literate Society*. The Report of the Committee on Reading of the National Academy of Education. New York: McGraw-Hill, 1975.
    See especially "Motivational Aspects of the Literacy Problem" by Lauren B. Resnick and Betty H. Robinson.

Holbrook, David. *English for the Rejected*. New York: Cambridge University Press, 1968.
    A Cambridge don views with compassion, though not sentimentality, students in the "lower streams" of the secondary school. See also by same author *English for Maturity*.

Wilkins, Gloria and Susanne Miller. *Strategies for Success. An Effective Guide for Teachers of Secondary-Level Slow Learners*. New York: Columbia University Press, 1983.
    An English teacher and a reading teacher at Oneida (NY) High School describe their underdeveloped and unmotivated readers and offer other teachers the contents of their well-stocked files of study guides.

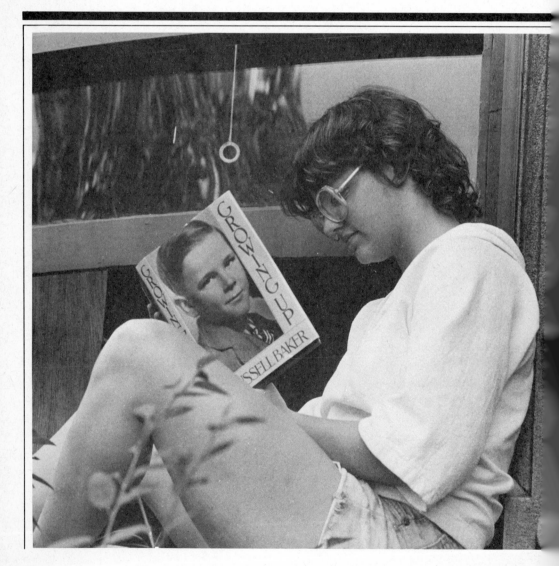

Learning through Reading III

10 Textbooks: Select Carefully, Use Critically

Whoever teaches reading in a departmentalized curriculum uses content textbooks as basic materials—or should. In almost every course, from earth science to French I to woodworking, textbooks are a principal resource for adolescent learners; they are for many, in fact, the only reading matter they touch during a normal day. So whoever purports to teach reading (that is, comprehension) must base the instruction on these materials.

Now for the *if*'s, *and*'s, and *but*'s. Most of the reading instruction in middle schools and high schools is found in developmental reading classes and English classes. Should reading and English teachers consider content textbooks *their* basic materials? Yes. Should all secondary students be taught how to read all content textbooks? No. Students who cannot read because they have never learned how and students who read very little because they choose not to cannot be expected to learn from textbooks. Nevertheless, in the usual secondary school, these students, even the nonreaders, attend content classes and are assigned textbooks. They carry the books around as tokens or talismans, but they cannot be expected to read them. While these students are learning how to read, or learning to accept reading as a way of learning, they should use other kinds of books and reading materials, almost anything but textbooks.

However, for the majority of students, and for the nonreaders as they join this majority, learning how to read textbooks will serve their major learning needs. In schools where there are no reading teachers as such and reading instruction is wholly centered in the content fields, clearly the basic materials for teaching reading and study skills are the content textbooks.

Textbooks in American Education

Textbooks are so much a part of the American educational scene that we sometimes take them for granted, forgetting why they came into existence and how they should *serve* instruction rather than dictate the way we teach. Because textbooks are important tools, and because reading teachers must know something about all the textbooks in use in their schools, we suggest you take time now to review some characteristics of textbooks in general, to reflect on their strengths and weaknesses, and to consider how textbook publishing affects how we teach and is, in turn, influenced by what teachers and administrators demand. Later in this chapter we shall suggest ways that reading teachers and content teachers can help each other in evaluating specific texts.

Since the topics outlined in the preceding paragraph exceed the scope of a single chapter, we hope this chapter will serve as a starting point for deeper study by you as an individual or, even better, as an inservice, or staff development, project. Accordingly, we shall refer you to sources which take up the issues in greater detail than space permits here.

Common Characteristics

What is common to most textbooks is their purpose: to assemble and organize information in a convenient package to instruct students at a designated grade level in the educational system. This definition of purpose suggests that many textbooks, though not all, are produced in series, one volume for each grade level. For example, the most common materials for reading instruction are *basal series*, which are leveled from kindergarten to grade 8. (See Chapter 2 for a discussion of basal series.) Graded series of textbooks are also produced for science, social studies, spelling, grammar and composition, literature, and mathematics, especially for grades 1 through 8. For senior high schools, where the diversity of subject fields is greater, publishers offer fewer series and more single textbooks. Exceptions are English, where graded language texts and literature anthologies are still popular, and foreign languages, which need graded texts comparable to basal series

Textbooks in reading and language development, whether the language is English or any other, are designed to exercise skills, that is, to teach process, not to dispense information, unless you define as "information" advice about how to read or write. Reading and language texts usually include the materials the skills are to be applied to, or, in the case of composition texts, models of writing; they are therefore kinds of anthologies, or collections of pieces of writing from various sources. To the extent that language, literature, and reading textbooks are anthologies, it is difficult to characterize the kinds of writing they contain.

Textbooks in the social sciences are likely to resemble each other in the types of writing style employed and in other features whether they are fifth grade social studies, eleventh grade U.S. history, Afro-Asian cultures, anthropology, archeology, or ancient world history. As a group, history textbooks, for example, are likely to employ narrative and expository writing and to be organized according to topics imposed by chronology (the Colonial period), values (justice), and movements (free trade). Because they are more alike than the textbooks in other fields, and because everyone has had courses in history, we will often refer to history texts in making generalizations in this chapter.

Science textbooks vary more widely within a field that includes many specializations in the grades from 5 to 12: nature study, physical sciences, biology, chemistry, physics, earth science, and so on. Within each science text, the varieties of style are apt to be more marked than in history texts. Scientific writing may include history and biography (therefore narrative style), much exposition (explaining why and how phenomena occur), instructions (how to perform an experiment), descriptions (of natural phenomena, artifacts, inventions), and arguments (the case for one theory rather than another). Figurative language and analogies are common in science texts because writers explain the unknown by comparison with the familiar.

Inasmuch as mathematics is also a language and a process, one expects to find math texts resembling language texts, that is, designed to exercise skills more than to inform. But math books in grades 5 to 12 contain increasing amounts of narrative (such as "story problems" and the history of numbers), exposition (usually brief explanations of mathematical phenomena), copious amounts of directions for solving problems, and, of course, "examples" to do. The signs and symbols of mathematics and computer languages make textbooks in this field as demanding in vocabulary development as the first years of foreign language study.

Another large and diverse category contains the textbooks of the "practical" subjects: courses related to business, the service occupations, care-giving, homemaking and parenting, and the industrial arts. Texts in these fields are likely to make more extensive use of description and explanation than of narration and to convey their most important messages in the form of directions.

Differences among content textbooks in purposes and styles and in organization of text and graphic aids have led reading teachers to describe different "skills" for different subject areas. We reproduced such a list in Box 6-6 more to highlight the particularities of content textbooks than to suggest that reading is a different process as one shifts from a history text to a cookbook. While we believe that psychologists will probably prove that reading is a unitary process that can be described by a single model, we nevertheless recommend the usefulness of lists like the one just referred to. Although superficial, these lists are revealing reminders to content teachers and to reading teachers that every subject area makes distinctive contributions to the "whole process"—and to the mature reader.

Textbooks as Mass Media

The textbook industry in the United States is unparalleled in any other nation, just as our educational system is a distinctive American contribution. Implementing the ideal of universal education through high school resulted in stratifying the curriculum according to chronological ages and then dividing each age/grade level into particular subjects. Instructional materials were also graded and divided into subject fields, and until fairly recently, this material was exclusively print. Since the Amerian population has always been mobile, the need arose almost immediately for textbooks that would match the curriculum in one place with the curriculum in another. School populations grew rapidly, fed by immigration and baby booms; as a result, shortages of trained teachers were commonplace. Standardization set in. Standardization, of course, is as American as apple pie, beginning with Eli Whitney's invention of interchangeable

parts for the rifle so that guns could be assembled more efficiently. Interchangeable parts in the educational system came, naturally enough, to be textbooks, so
that a child coming into a schoolhouse in Nebraska was easily slotted into the
same McGuffey reader he or she had had in Indiana.

In American life and American schooling, standardization accelerates rather
than declines in an increasingly mobile and technological society. It's all around
us: in fast-food chains, in entertainment, in automobiles, in housing, in hair
styles and clothing. Why should we expect it to be different with schools and
textbooks? No matter how much teachers and educational consultants, believing
in the desirability of individualizing instruction, exhort us to use different books
with different kids, the tendency toward sameness persists. Strangers in town
and homesick, both parents and children are comforted to find the new school
very like the old one; familiar textbooks are a reassuring sign.

Powerful forces in the communications industry work against any instincts to
be different. Textbooks are one of the mass media; more than that, they are
mass-produced to be sold to the largest markets possible. Like the manufac-
turers of toothpaste and washing machines, publishers have to research the
market, respond to buyers' "needs," or persuade buyers that they need what the
seller has to sell. To be sure, textbook publishers have been more discreet in
selling their wares than car salesmen. For one thing, publishing has a scholarly
and gentlemanly tradition to uphold; that is, publishers are not tradesmen, and
their sales agents are "representatives" and "consultants." For another, the
market is clearly defined and easily targeted. A relatively small group of people
buy textbooks for masses of other people to use. So most advertising can be by
direct mail and in professional journals, and selling can be done through carefully cultivated personal relationships between bookmen and school administrators, consultants, and department heads, supplemented by occasional book
fairs and exhibits at educational conferences. It is only very recently that textbook publishers, perhaps because they have increasingly been taken over by
communications corporations such as Time, Inc., CBS, and Xerox, have begun to
advertise through spot commercials on television. These commercials are generally of the "soft sell" variety, aimed, for instance, at educating the public on how
children acquire basic literacy and math skills.

Because textbooks are directed to large markets, publishers are sensitive to
criticisms from consultants and administrators who order textbooks, teachers
who use them, and citizens who pay for them. Publishers invest huge sums in
producing textbooks that may sell badly because they offend some part of the
buying public. In Kanawha County, West Virginia, in 1973–74, a relatively small
group of parents waged a highly successful battle against the school board over
the selection of textbooks for reading, English, and social studies. The nationwide publicity which attended this book-banning created repercussions far
beyond the hills of West Virginia. Though the incident itself quieted down, you
can be sure that editors thereafter were more likely to blue-pencil even mildly
controversial passages lest further censorship battles result.

In many states textbooks must be approved by statewide selection committees
before schools can buy them with state funds allocated for that purpose. When
these committees' lists carry no more than five titles per subject area, it is often

the case that publishers not listed can sell no books on that subject in that state for perhaps five years. Naturally, publishers try to find out why some books are approved and others rejected so that they can produce books with a better chance of making the approved list next time.

State-adoption practices have a powerful influence over what textbooks contain, as do the selection practices of major cities in states which do not have approved lists. Private citizens and special interest groups testify for and against textbooks at public hearings conducted by the selection committees, which are composed of variously elected and appointed educators and lay persons. Hearings which are widely publicized, as was the case when Norma and Mel Gabler testified against *Magruder's American Government* before the Texas State Textbook Committee,[1] may affect the decisions of other selection committees far removed from the scene. And indirectly the citizens of one town or state or region, of any strongly voiced political, moral, or religious persuasion, can affect what goes into textbooks which will be available to students anywhere else in the nation. Regrettably, teachers' voices are often much softer than those of the angry citizens' groups.

In several respects, textbooks are more like newspapers than books. Like newspapers, they are directed at mass audiences, as most novels, for instance, are not. Like newspapers and magazines, textbooks have features to capture attention, such as headlines, graphic displays, boxed features, photographs and art work, maps, cartoons, graphs. Like newspapers, textbook series are produced by several contributing authors and an editorial staff. (Novels are still being written by individuals rather than committees.) Material for textbooks may be researched by a team of authors, but the final copy is edited "in house" rather as a news magazine operates. An editor told me once that the text for a beginning reader had been "generated" in the house, and that seemed an apt way of describing the manufacture of text, rather than the writing of a book.

But there is one significant way in which textbooks are not like newspapers. Newspapers, like radio and television, are supported by the revenue from the advertisements they carry at prices fixed by the size of their circulation. Textbooks, like novels, pay for themselves only by their sales. Unlike the readers of newspapers, who are less influential than advertisers, the buyers of textbooks have a direct influence on their contents. Ironically, the readers of textbooks—consumers who never select the products themselves—have the least direct influence on the content. But the buyers are influential indeed.

At the same time that textbooks are subject to many influences both from within and outside the schools, they are themselves exerting tremendous influence on what students learn and the attitudes and values they develop. (It is easy to fall into the error of referring, as most people do, to the book as if it were the oracle—as if it were the voice and not the instrument. This is especially easy

---

[1] The Gablers have incorporated as Educational Research Analysts in Longview, Texas, where they employ a staff of six to write detailed criticisms of books under review for Texas schools. They objected to a seventh grade reader because it proposed that students discuss whether computers can replace man. Such a discussion will, the Gablers say, imply "that there can be more than one correct answer." (*Time*, 31 December 1979, 76)

to do with textbooks since it is difficult to know who wrote them.) While it would be foolish to underestimate the potential of textbooks for shaping young minds, it is important to remember two other points: (1) textbooks educate today's youth less directly and effectively than television does; (2) textbooks, unlike TV, are "mediated" by teachers who can improve the effectiveness of the text, or be dominated by it.

Textbooks are often the focal point of attacks on the school because they are visible and stationary targets and more impersonal objects of abuse than teachers, administrators, and school boards. Unfortunately, many critics attack textbooks without regard for how they are produced or sold. While we encourage criticism of textbooks, the purpose is not only to improve the quality of the texts themselves but the ways they are used. For textbooks are firmly established in the American educational system; it's quixotic to dream of replacing text materials with computers, films, television, or even with trade books. All of these should supplement the core text, but the text itself will probably remain the handiest and cheapest packaging of school learning so long as that is parceled out in the present curricular divisions. Like other artifacts of modern life, textbooks have changed superficially over the years and will continue to do so, becoming better as teachers point the way to useful modifications in content, style, and design. In this spirit, let's consider some problems with current textbooks, how teachers can work around them, and what publishers might do to alleviate them in future editions.

Six Problems and What Teachers Can Do About Them

Textbooks are too big

The reason that textbooks are too big is that we know too much and are too committed to coverage. Authors of history texts, for example, have enormous resources to draw upon and face the same hard problems of selection that teachers do. If they elect to organize materials chronologically, they fear to omit incidents in the time period they have selected. (In American history texts a continuing gamble is the presidential election every four years; the outcome of the Vietnam War was another. And consider the chagrin of the editor whose latest social studies text came out of the bindery with a 49-star flag on the very day Hawaii was admitted to statehood!) If the writing team abandons chronology and selects events and ideas according to the concepts to be developed, parents and teachers complain that students are losing a sense of history. Authors of science textbooks are similarly overwhelmed by the massive resources opened to them by the swift accumulation of scientific knowledge in recent decades. Haunted by the specter of coverage, they include too much, and the result is the formidable five-pound textbook in which facts are packed so densely that only the expert can read it with ease. Author and editor thus shift the responsibility for being selective to the teacher, who sometimes unfortunately still perceives his or her responsibility as "getting through the book."

The tenth grade biology teacher, Ms. Sheedy, didn't choose the textbook—or the students to whom she is supposed to assign it. It is the only text she has sufficient copies of to cover her fourth- and fifth-period classes whose test scores suggest that these students are reading within the middle quartiles of the nationally normed standardized test. With her help, most of Ms. Sheedy's students can comprehend parts of this textbook. So she decides which topics to include, which to omit, and roughs out a September-to-June schedule, dividing the text into consumable portions and assigning each a tentative slot on the calendar.

The journey from September to June is not to be a mystery ride, so Ms. Sheedy plots the route with her classes early in the year. She postpones handing out textbooks until the second or third week because she wants her students to understand that the textbook is a secondary source of learning in this class. When she distributes the book, she spends a period introducing the *whole* text, examining the authors' purposes and relating them to the goals of the course, calling attention to the authors' plan for the whole book and showing which sections will be omitted and why, and making sure that students know how to find and use the index, glossary, table of contents, charts, and illustrations. This introductory lesson is not the last time Ms. Sheedy will look at the whole text with her class, but her plan with respect to this fat volume is to treat individual sections as if they were complete texts in themselves.

Ms. Sheedy wishes the publishers had done this for her, since thin books are less daunting to average students, who themselves have notions that a book is intended to be read from cover to cover, even if that's not one of *their* intentions. Six short books of 100 to 150 pages each would have given Ms. Sheedy more flexibility, and the authors could have allowed themselves more illustrative detail on each of six major topics. Publishers would protest that six paperback books would be much more costly to produce than a single hardback text which is richly illustrated. That argument is irrefutable so long as teachers think they want the expensive glossy treatment that is so attractive to someone flipping the pages and judging a book by its design rather than its teachability.

Textbooks are too expensive

This criticism is more justly directed to the buying public that demands new editions every four or five years, each one more visually exciting than its predecessor. With history and science texts, new content added every few years means more fact-packing and probably less comprehensibility. And illustrations, the use of color, and heightened graphic effects very often cut down on readability. The message may be lost among the illustrations or overpowered by them. Books cannot compete with television in graphics and ought not to try. Moreover, it is probable that students learn more easily from simply-designed textbooks, which can be produced cheaply so that the kind of multiple-text packaging referred to above is possible. We have little research on the effect of text-plus-picture combinations on students' reading comprehension, and it will be years before we have answers as to how much visual display, and what kinds, confuse rather than aid the reader. Until we have evidence to the contrary, however, teachers should persuade publishers that thin books simply designed with illustrations that aid comprehension rather than gratify the senses would more usefully prepare students to read books for information and ideas. Plainer textbooks would prepare students, too, for reading trade books published in earlier decades, when print was considered a sufficient medium and books were not meant to look like the glossier magazines.

Until simpler, cheaper textbooks are available, however, teachers will have to help their students find the print among all the distracting graphics and look for meaning not only in text but in illustrations, charts, maps, and other graphic features. Publishers intend, we think, to make the message clearer by their use of type and graphics, though in our darker moments we suspect that the purpose of these features is to appeal to textbook buyers who, as bookmen say, apply the "thumb test" (flipping quickly through the pages without reading), which is little better than judging a book by its cover. In any case, such attempts to clarify meaning often backfire when students try to read textbooks as if they were novels—beginning with the first word and proceeding rigidly to the last, ignoring signs, symbols, changing typeface, captions, headlines, pictures, whatever. The teacher's direction, or mediation, is needed early and often.

Textbook prose is impersonal

Because textbooks are often written by committees of teachers and editors who attempt to be responsive to a dozen different pressure groups, a clear authorial voice is often missing. Textbook prose is bland and likely to become more so as editors misapply readability formulas in reaction to teachers' complaints that their students can't read. We'll discuss the formulas later. At this point we ask you to think about how teachers can counteract the effects of impersonal textbook prose. One effect is boredom, of course, even though modern texts try hard to engage students. (While there are few "I's" in textbooks, there are many "you's.") A more serious effect of impersonality is that students forget that books are written by fallible human beings, and the text becomes the ultimate, unquestioned source of truth. Or, working in the opposite direction, the impersonality of textbooks makes them part of a faceless establishment, a vague superpower not to be trusted, but not to be questioned either. Teachers who read textbooks critically themselves—who ask themselves whose opinions are represented and how much they are to be respected—can help students to evaluate textbooks as sources of information.

Attempted dialogues with students often fizzle

To counteract the effects of impersonality, textbook authors and editors often resort to a chatty style and raise questions in the body of the text as well as at the end of the chapter. These questions are not merely stylistic devices to vary the rhythm of the prose. They are at the heart of inquiry methods meant to stimulate students to think for themselves, to discover principles, to retrace the thought patterns of scientists and historians. But those students who read textbooks as they learned to read simple narratives let the questions roll onto the TV screens in their heads, and roll off, not attempting to answer them. Too many students assume all questions to be rhetorical, supposing that if the text raises them, it will also answer them eventually.

With textbooks that imitate inquiry methods, the teacher's role is more crucial than ever. It won't be enough to exhort students to read actively rather than passively, or even to demonstrate how you, a good reader, respond to passages like the following:

> How can you describe a wave—in the terms a scientist uses? It doesn't matter whether it is a water wave, a light wave, or a sound wave; the terms used are the same. A wave has a **crest** (or top) and a **trough** (or bottom). The height of the wave crest above the trough is called the **wave height**. The distance from one wave crest (or trough) to the next is called the **wavelength**. Suppose you were in a lighthouse and measured the time between the crest of one wave and the crest of the next wave. You have measured another property of waves, the **wave period**. Waves produced by the wind have periods of less than 30 seconds.
>
> How fast does a wave travel through the water? Or, as a scientist would ask, what is the **velocity** (speed) of a wave? The velocity of a perfectly formed wave of small height, in deep water, has a definite relationship between its wavelength and period. The velocity of a wave can be determined by dividing the wavelength by the period:
>
> $$\text{velocity} = \frac{\text{wavelength}}{\text{period}}$$
>
> Let's see what this equation tells us. Suppose a wave that is 35 meters long has a period of 5 seconds. What is its velocity?
>
> —*Matter: An Earth Science*

If you mean to teach students how to comprehend such texts, you will do more than alert them to the purposes of such questions; you will set up some means of active, overt responding. You might, for example, have good students respond orally by taping a dialogue with the authors, one student asking the authors' questions, the others responding. Or you yourself could ask the authors' questions in a small-group discussion. More often, you can use the textbook's questions in study guides you prepare to which the students respond by writing freely or by checking multiple-choice items.

The editorial apparatus is directed toward anonymous students

Just as the text authorship is often anonymous, so, too, are the students to whom the text is directed. Nowhere is this more apparent than in the editorial apparatus—the questions at the end of the chapter or the section, the previews, summaries, vocabulary exercises, glossaries, annotated book lists, and glosses or marginal notes. Editorial apparatus is the attempt of authors and editors to put teaching strategies into the textbook where they can be most useful to students, particularly to students unfortunate enough to have teachers who merely assign textbook pages. The more the editors try to design "teacherproof" instructional materials, the more editorial apparatus will be included. But we know of no materials that are effectively teacherproof. Almost all students need teachers as mediators of the text, especially when the text in question is a content textbook. If there can be no really teacherproof materials, are editors and authors wasting their time including teaching strategies in textbooks?

Of course, that question defies a yes or no answer. We hope teachers will consider the strengths and limitations of the editorial apparatus of a particular textbook before accepting, rejecting, or amending it. The constraint of space is as much a limitation of the teacher-in-the-textbook as the restriction of time is for the teacher in the classroom. Most textbook questions are wedged into whatever white space remains on the last page of the chapter and thus they cannot be expanded sufficiently to be useful for a range of student abilities. The result is that questions are directed to those mythical "average" students. We urge you to evaluate textbook study aids carefully, and in Box 10-2 (pages 291–93) we suggest specific criteria to be applied.

But knowing that textbook study aids may be severely limited in their usefulness doesn't mean you should be cavalier in discarding them. You can probably fit them, with slight modifications, to your students' needs. Chances are that the textbook's authors have given more care to the development of a lesson than teachers can on an ordinary day. Chances are their questions highlight the essential points. At least you can be guided by the thinking—probably expert—which has gone into the textbook lesson. To be sure, teachers have one great advantage over textbook writers; they know their audience intimately, so they should be able to ask more pertinent, more sensitive questions. But we have seen all too many teacher-made study guides that miss the essential points that the textbook writers hit.

A familiar analogy is that textbook authors are to teachers as pharmacists are to physicians. Just as we expect physicians to diagnose and prescribe but not to prepare the medicines, so we can expect teachers to select and use published materials but not to create instructional materials themselves—not all the time, anyway. The analogy is not an exact one, but the parallels are sufficient to make the point. Ideally, textbook writers and teachers form a partnership, with the latter modifying and adjusting the former's products to fit a particular situation.

Textbooks supplement instruction and need to be supplemented

Textbook series, especially those in reading, are massive productions, of which the pupil's textbook is a relatively small part. Most of the teaching is contained in teachers' guides that present meticulously detailed lesson plans, complete with "scripts" of the teachers' lines and the pupils', too, in some cases. Teachers' manuals for secondary textbooks are usually not so detailed as elementary teachers' guides, and in the grades beyond 8, teachers of subject matter tend to ignore them. That is unfortunate. If you are going to use another teacher's plans—and in many respects that's what a textbook is—at least you should know what that teacher (author) intended. The manual usually extends the editorial apparatus of the student text and offers good advice about presenting ideas. The least valuable part of the manual is the answer key, which teachers seldom ignore (though we wish they would, in full confidence that they know the "right" answers).

One criticism leveled at textbooks and teachers' manuals is that they destroy teachers' creativity, that they make teachers into automatons. We suspect that mindless teachers would be that way with or without the aid of textbooks, and they—or rather their students—are better off with the texts and manuals. On the other hand, thinking teachers use textbooks as partners, get ideas from them, and use them as points of departure. Textbooks should save teachers' energies for those encounters between teachers' minds and students' minds where real learning takes place.

Judging the Readability of Textbooks
Readability Formulas

Fifty years ago in Winnetka, Illinois, an elementary school principal had encouraged his teachers to use instead of textbooks a variety of trade books to be read independently by individual learners. A large part of the teachers' role was to match books and pupils so that the children would be able to read texts that interested them. Since each teacher in this plan had to judge hundreds of trade books, which are not "graded" as textbooks supposedly are, the principal set out to devise a handy formula that would quickly gauge the readability of a text. The principal had identified the problem but not the solution. We are still looking for a wholly reliable, quick, and comprehensive way to estimate whether a certain book will be too difficult, too easy, or just right for a certain student, who reads (most of the time anyway) at such and such a level. But we have come part of the way toward a solution, in that researchers have devised a dozen or more readability formulas which can give teachers and others a rough idea of the relative difficulty of texts. One of these formulas is shown in Figure 10-1. We will skip the mathematical mysteries of the formulas (if you're interested, see the Klare entries in the bibliography in Box 10-1) and simply note that the statistical bases for most formulas reach back to the 1920s to make use of scores earned by pupils on the McCall–Crabbs *Standard Test Lessons in Reading*, a series of booklets, still in use in reading classes, comprised of easy-to-difficult paragraphs and test questions.

Readability formulas are based on the two elements of writing which can be counted objectively: the length of sentences and the "difficulty" of words. Some formulas determine difficulty by length of words, counting the number of syllables, for instance; others, like the Dale–Chall Formula (Box 10-1), count all the words which are not on an "easy" word list. We recommend the Dale–Chall because we believe it is relatively accurate for secondary texts and relatively easy to apply. However, we warn you that the "easy" word list is based on tallies of word frequency done in the 1930s, and a lot of words have flowed in and out of familiarity in the fifty years since. (We shall discuss "easy" and "hard" words in Chapter 12.)

In my first year of teaching I was given a "slow" tenth grade English class and

FIGURE 10-1

THE RAYGOR READABILITY ESTIMATE
Alton L. Raygor–University of Minnesota

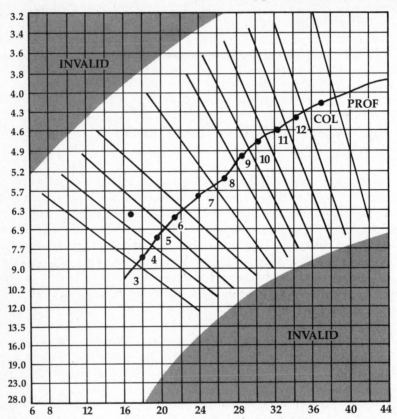

Directions:

Count out three 100-word passages near the beginning, middle, and end of a selection or book. Count proper nouns, but not numerals.

1. Count sentences in each passage, estimating to nearest tenth.
2. Count words with six or more letters.
3. Average the sentence length and word length over the three samples and plot the average on the graph.

Example:

	Sentences	6+ Words
A	6.0	15
B	6.8	19
C	6.4	17
Total	19.2	51
Average	6.4	17

Note mark on graph. Grade level is about 5.

BOX 10-1

ABOUT READABILITY FORMULAS

D. Edgar Dale and Jeanne Chall, "Dale–Chall Readability Formula." In C. W. Hunnicutt and W. J. Iverson, *Research in the Three R's* (New York: Harper and Row, 1958): 205–13.

> Intended to estimate the readability of materials above third grade. Requires several 100-word samples. Employs a formula based on sentence length and number of words not on a preestablished list of 3,000.

Rudolph F. Flesch, *The Art of Readable Writing* (New York: Harper and Row, 1949).

> Contains Flesch Formula and good advice for writers, readers, and teachers.

Edward B. Bry, "Fry's Readability Graph: Clarifications, Validity, and Extension to Level 17," *Journal of Reading*, 21:3 (December, 1977): 242-52.

> Estimates are derived from counts of average number of sentences and syllables per 100 words. Plotting the two averages on a graph provided yields the estimated grade level of difficulty. Appropriate for materials from grades 1 through 17.

Robert Gunning, *How to Take the Fog out of Writing* (Chicago, IL: The Dartnell Corporation, 1964).

> Describes essential principles of clear writing and includes the "Fog Index" to facilitate writing material at a particular level of difficulty.

George R. Klare, *The Measurement of Readability* (Ames, Iowa: Iowa University Press, 1963).

> Describes and evaluates the development of readability formulas from the 1920s to 1950s.

George R. Klare, "Assessing Readability," *Reading Research Quarterly*, 10:1 (1974–75): 62-102.

> Discusses readability research since 1963. Includes new formulas and describes manual and computerized application of these. Also how to predict readability of texts other than English.

Robert S. Laubach and Kay Koschnick, *Using Readability* (Syracuse, NY: New Readers Press, 1977).

> Advice for those who write or evaluate materials for adults or teenagers with limited reading ability. Describes factors that influence readability, gives detailed instruction for applying the Fog Index and the Fry Readability Formula.

a set of *Never Surrender*, a collection of short biographies of historical personalities meant to inspire patriotic fervor as well as provide "an easy read." My kids weren't all that slow but they weren't finding *Never Surrender* entirely comprehensible. I discovered Flesch's Ease of Reading Formula in his book *The Art of Readable Writing*, noted that he could get a grade 5 readability on Hamlet's "To be or not to be" soliloquy, and forthwith applied his formula to the biographies of Carl Schurz, Simón Bolívar, and Winston Churchill. Lo and behold: these selections could be read with ease by anyone with the equivalent of fourth grade reading ability, and I knew my students had that. Why were they having so much trouble? So I discussed the Ease of Reading scores with my students, and Tessie Marino went straight to the mark. "These stories are hard to follow," she said; "they're all mixed up." And of course they were. In an effort to grab the reader's attention, the writer had begun each biography with a high point in the hero's life and worked out the chronology later. Readability formulas have their limitations, Tessie and the others taught me, and one is their total disregard for the organization of the text.

For the most part readability formulas were devised to estimate the difficulty of trade books and magazines, and it is unfair to criticize them for not measuring textbooks very adequately. Indeed, these remarks are not intended as criticisms of the formulas but as reminders to teachers of factors *they* must evaluate because the formulas do not. The organization of the whole textbook is a crucial factor in readability: it involves not only the arrangement of topics and the connecting of one idea to another but also the placement of graphics and the distractibility of appended features. How ideas flow within chapters and within sections of chapters is one aspect of organization disregarded by the formulas. Intersentence relationships are also disregarded. The average length of sentences in 100-word segments does indeed give some idea of how convoluted the style is, but length of sentences in itself is deceptive. Editors, too eager to respond to teachers' queries about readability and to achieve low readability scores for their texts, sometimes cut a long sentence up into several short ones, and in doing so remove the words that show relationships, leaving readers to infer what the writer had stated plainly. Consider which of these two examples expresses more clearly the idea that Carrington had misunderstood the Indians:

> The power of the big gun impressed the Indians. Carrington had hoped it would. He did not suspect that Black Horse was deriding him. Black Horse had said that the Great Spirit was firing it "once more for his white children." (average sentence length: 8 words)

> The power of the big gun impressed the Indians, as Carrington had hoped it would, but he did not suspect that Black Horse was deriding him with that bland remark about the Great Spirit firing it "once more for his white children." (42 words)
> —Dee Brown, *Bury My Heart at Wounded Knee*

In the formulas all sentences are counted alike whether they are simple or complex. But some simple sentences merely list items, and the following long sentence (also from *Bury My Heart*) is no harder to understand than a list:

> The two hundred wagons were loaded to the bows with mowing machines, shingle and brick machines, wooden doors, window sashes, locks, nails, musical instruments for a twenty-five-piece band, rocking chairs, churns, canned goods and vegetable seeds, as well as the usual ammunition, gunpowder, and other military supplies. (49 words)

As with all other formulas, if mindlessly applied, readability formulas distort the truth. Teachers who ask publishers for readability levels of their texts are asking an oversimplified question that has led to poorer rather than better textbooks.

Not that many textbooks don't need simplifying. Indeed, they do, but less probably in sentences and words than in the larger elements of structure and concept. And never at the expense of interest and style.

On your own, without the aid of formulas, you must examine the structure of textbook writing, paying special attention to paragraphs. In general, poor readers respond better to paragraphs organized in the old-fashioned way, with the topic sentence stated first and then elaborated upon by the piling up of detail. Poor readers, as we noted in Chapter 3, have little imagination upon which to draw; so the writer who caters to them leaves little to the imagination and is lavish with details. But poor readers also need a minimum of words, so to trade off one need against the other, the good writer selects fewer big ideas and treats each of them with care.

Notice that paragraphing in modern textbooks is often a typographical device rather than a sign of logical relationships. Writers may state a main idea in a topic sentence, which the editor sets off as a single paragraph. This is a clarifying device, and it becomes confusing only if the teacher has old-fashioned notions of what a paragraph should be. You won't have because you, too, have been weaned away from the page-long paragraph; you, too, in the words of one fourth grader, look for white spaces on a page "to rest the eyes." As a teacher and as a writer, you can help your students to look for logical relationships *across* what appear to be paragraphs.

In judging the difficulty of a text, estimate the number of major concepts to be learned and judge how clearly they are presented. In estimating a text's difficulty consider, too, the questions at the end of the chapter. They also have to be comprehended. Additionally, the questions asked by either the textbook author or the teacher can make a text harder or easier. For example, look back at the second sentence from *Bury My Heart at Wounded Knee*, which we said was a long, *easy* sentence. It would be a very difficult one if we expected the reader to remember that listing. It's an easy one because the author tells you in the next sentence the inference to be drawn: The white soldiers expected to stay a long time. In judging the conceptual load of a textbook, you examine the writers' purposes by studying what concepts they *say* are essential (in the introduction, usually), and what concepts they emphasize in the questions raised at the end of chapters.

Contemporary writers and editors are very sensitive to concept load. They try very hard to reduce the number of difficult concepts and to explain them clearly for the intended audience, but it's almost impossible to guess what prior knowledge to expect of any general age group. Only teachers who know the particular group of students who will use the text can make even rough guesses, and most of the time teachers are judging books not for students they know but for another, unknown group who may be more or less like last year's class. But once you have the students in front of you and have gotten to know them, you can at least estimate how much adjusting you will have to do to the text. It's worth estimating the concept load as closely as you can.

Mr. O'Connell, a teacher of ninth grade "slow" students, analyzed the "easy" text that had been selected a year or two before, and found that the problems hinted at by the Flesch Ease of Reading Scores ("difficult" and "fairly difficult") really lay in the conceptual load and levels of abstraction untouched by the formula. Here is a passage from the text:

The years following World War II were ones of despair for Egypt. There was unrest because the standard of living for the peasants was still desperately low. The government had been involved in much waste and corruption. King Farouk (1936–1952) was accused of misspending his nation's money. Government officials were also involved in scandals. The war against Israel in 1948 was a disaster. Unemployment and poverty hung heavily over the nation. On January 26, 1950, Black Sunday, bonfire after bonfire of rebellion was lit in Cairo. Much burning and destruction resulted. An "explosion" was about to take place.

On July 23, 1952, the explosion actually occurred. Two army officers, Major General Naguib and Lieutenant Colonel Gamal Abdel Nasser, with their followers, captured control of the government.[2]

Keep in mind that the students who were to read this text were 14-to-15-year-olds growing up in upstate New York, with measured reading achievement about seventh grade level, a few above, a few below that. Their teacher rightly points out the chief problem with the passage is that there is no detail to help these youngsters understand in any way the really wretched poverty of the Egyptian peasants referred to. Mr. O'Connell notes wryly that the text's authors are aware and concerned about "big concepts" such as *evolution, communism, militarism, nationalism,* and *racism,* and then he lists some of the "small concepts" that recur frequently in *The Afro–Asian World:*

prestige	power	duty
rule	control of the government	dictator
rebellion	empire	community
colony	middle class	authority
tradition	standard of living	movement
corruption	industry	freedom
policy	trade	slavery

"Most of these," he says, "are words with which my students have some acquaintance, but if they are to understand them as used in the text, they must have a feel for them. They get the feel from details—not details that they are to remember for all time, but details that flesh out the concepts enough to make them memorable for my kids."

Mr. O'Connell doesn't throw out the text; he cannot; it's all he has. And it has some plus factors: the overall organization he deems sensible and workable; the maps are good, though the illustrations seem more decorative than meaningful; the charts and graphs are not difficult to read and help illustrate specific points in the text. He knows that he can make this text work even for below-average ninth graders provided he omits some of the sections so that he can deal fully with the ones that remain, developing students' background, making specific preparation for passages to be read, and reinforcing concepts that should be remembered. He determines to come at important concepts in many different ways, repeatedly; and he knows enough not to overdo it, since for practical purposes not every concept can be given a full-dress treatment every time.

---

[2]Edward R. Kolevzon, *The Afro/Asian World: A Cultural Understanding* (Boston: Allyn and Bacon, 1969).

BOX 10-2

TEXTBOOK EVALUATION—READABILITY

(Reading consultants are often asked to judge the readability of textbooks being considered for adoption by content teachers. In one school system the consultant prepared this form, which content teachers partially completed and submitted to her with the book to be evaluated. Content teachers supplied the information requested in starred items. The reading consultant answered all other questions.)

*Title: _____   *Edition: _____

*Author(s): _____   *Publisher: _____

*Students for whom text is being considered: Grade _____

*With respect to grade placement are these students _____ accelerated;

_____ high average; _____ average; _____ low average;

_____ below average?

*Is this text being considered as basic text _____; supplementary reading

_____?

*If supplementary, what is core text? _____

Check below the items published to accompany text being evaluated.

_____ Teacher's Edition   _____ Teacher's Manual

_____ Student workbook   _____ Teacher's Edition of workbook

_____ Laboratory manual   _____ Tests

          Other aids (please list): _____

USE SCALE FOR ANSWERING THE QUESTIONS THAT FOLLOW:
    2—Excellent; 1—Adequate; 0—Inadequate

Authority and Reliability

*1. Does the authorship (authors, advisers, consultants, general editors) reflect a range of professional experience (specialists in subject field, educational specialists, classroom teachers)?

*2. Are the authors' purposes or instructional goals clearly stated?

*3. Is the point of view stated in the introductory comments developed in the body of the text?

How Information and Ideas Are Presented

*1. How effectively is inductive reasoning used in presenting information?

*2. How effectively is deductive reasoning used?

*3. Does the text fairly present differing views on controversial subjects?

*4. Is the order in which concepts are presented appropriate to the structure of the subject being taught?

*5. Are abstract ideas usually supported by concrete examples?

*6. Is the introduction of new concepts paced to the audience for whom the text is being considered?

Continued

BOX 10-2 *(continued)*

TEXTBOOK EVALUATION—READABILITY

*7. Are all the concepts essential to this school's curriculum covered?

*8. Are essential concepts included without fact-packing?

Note: Reading consultant or other out-of-field evaluator may answer starred questions also since content teachers find opinions of persons who are not experts in the subject are of value in predicting success of a text with students.

Readability: Vocabulary, Syntax, Style

1. Estimate (by formula) of readability level? Average score: _____
   Range: _____ No. of passages scored: _____
   Formula used: _____

2. In evaluator's judgment is overall readability level (by formula) appropriate for students for whom text is intended?

Use Scale (above) for following items:

3. Are technical terms clearly defined in body of text?

4. Is technical vocabulary kept to minimum?

5. Are unusual words—ones likely to be unfamiliar to students—other than technical vocabulary made clear through context?

6. Are key words listed at the beginning of the chapter?

7. Does level of vocabulary appear challenging but not frustrating for intended audience?

8. Are foreign names and words of foreign derivation pronounced in body of text using an easy pronunciation key?

9. Are long and complex sentences avoided as far as possible?

10. Are simple declarative sentences of varying length used frequently?

11. Are personal pronouns and human interest factors present?

12. Is style of writing appealing to adolescents?

13. Is "voice" of author identifiable?

14. Is style simple and direct without giving impression of "talking down" to students?

15. Are writer's opinions expressed and recognizable as opinion?

Readability: Structure

1. Are significant ideas clearly signaled by writer's style and organization?

2. Is each chapter introduced by a preview or overview?

3. Are summaries frequently presented at conclusion of sections or chapters?

4. Is there a high proportion of paragraphs with explicitly stated main ideas?

5. Is text divided into chapter or sections of appropriate length for making reasonable assignments?

6. Are graphic aids explained in text and clearly connected to the major concepts?

7. Does the table of contents show the purpose or design of the whole text and make its organization understandable and logical?

Continued

BOX 10-2 (continued)

TEXTBOOK EVALUATION—READABILITY

Format and Design

1. Does the table of contents serve the reader as a preview of the chapters' contents? That is, are there subtopics as well as topics in the table of contents?

2. Does the page design (headings, margins, illustrations, etc.) invite reading?

3. Are typefaces and styles attractive and easy to read?

4. Are the illustrations of a quality and number that attract readers' attention without diverting them from reading?

5. Does the index lead easily to information in the text?

6. Does the index have cross-referencing system that students can use?

7. Does the glossary define words precisely and comprehensively enough for purposes of this text?

8. Do pictures and other graphics stimulate thinking and problem-solving?

9. Are diagrams, charts, maps, etc., well designed and easy to understand?

Editorial Apparatus (Questions, Directions, Exercises, Review Materials)

1. Do end-of-chapter questions focus on significant matters and avoid trivial detail?

2. Do questions probe inferential as well as literal comprehension?

3. Are important concepts and vocabulary reinforced by end-of-chapter questions, exercises, or activities?

4. Do some questions or activities encourage divergent and creative thinking?

5. Are questions posed by text *before* reading chapter or section?

6. Are questions interspersed through body of text?

7. Are questions, whether preposed, interspersed, or postreading, designed to elicit more than yes–no answers or noncommittal answers from students?

8. Does the editorial apparatus reflect the teaching goals or point of view expressed by the author(s) in the introduction or teacher's edition?

9. Does text and/or workbook offer a variety of question types including open-ended questions as well as objective questions such as multiple-choice, true–false, matching, etc.?

10. Do objective questions require higher-order skills such as drawing conclusions, weighing evidence, making judgments?

11. Does instructional design of text permit well-paced review and application of knowledge previously presented?

12. Do questions or activities require readers to compare and contrast ideas from two or more sources?

13. Are there well-selected bibliographies to encourage further reading?

14. Are directions to students clear and comprehensible?

This form was adapted from one used by Dr. Nora Walker when she was Reading Consultant in the Cranston, RI, public schools.

Concepts are, of course, related to vocabulary, as we shall examine in Chapter 12. Secondary school textbooks in the 1970s and 1980s give ample evidence that writers have learned the value of redundancy in making texts more comprehensible and have heeded the advice to define new words in context. In examining a textbook, teachers should note the extent to which context explains new words, and whether a term defined early in a text is defined again when used in later chapters; they should also assess how much additional help with the words—general words as well as special concepts—will have to be provided by instruction.

The *Cloze* Technique

Readability has always been a major concern of writers aiming at mass audiences. So it is not surprising that another idea for assessing readability originated with a journalist[3] and was taken over by teachers. This is the *cloze* technique, which we described as a measure of *reading* ability (not readability) in Chapter 6. Refer to page 150 to refresh your memory of what a *cloze* test looks like. So called because it requires the reader to effect closure in reading a text full of holes, *cloze* is based on the systematic deletion of every fifth, or seventh, or tenth word. The easier the text, the more readily the reader will restore the missing words. Teachers using *cloze* to measure readability present students with passages totaling about 500 words taken from the text to be evaluated. The first sentence or even a short introductory paragraph is presented without deletions, and then beginning with the next sentence every fifth word is omitted until the passage contains 100 blanks. If most of the students succeed in restoring 40 of the deleted words (that is, 40 percent restoration), then the teacher assumes that the text is not too difficult for instructional purposes.

An advantage of *cloze* is that it is a test of students as well as of the textbook. But on both accounts it is a *rough* guess. We suggest that you experiment with the technique, taking students into your confidence, explaining that the technique originated in journalism as a measure of readability, and that you want to see how the textbook measures up. Warn them that high percentages of exact restorations are not to be expected, and have them speculate as to why not.

Actually, we find that the best use of *cloze* is to give students insights into the reading process, and into the relationships between reading and writing.

Other Ways to Assess Textbooks

Just as *cloze* measures both readability and reading ability, the informal reading inventory described in Chapter 6 also gives teachers insight into a textbook's readability with respect to a specific group of students. For example, if students are unable to express the main ideas of textbook passages, even though they are clearly stated, then teachers can assume that the readability of this particular textbook is too high for these students.

---

[3]W. L. Taylor, "*Cloze* Procedure: A New Tool for Measuring Readability," *Journalism Quarterly* 30 (1953): 415–33.

The application of readability formulas and the inventory of text-specific skills take time that many content teachers claim not to have. Therefore, we propose to substitute for readability formulas the astute judgment of experienced teachers. But "astute judgment" is the result of purposeful training, and so we recommend sessions on the evaluation of textbooks as essential parts of staff development. Each session might have a different emphasis.

For example, an early session on readability might be structured around the results of informal inventories based on textbooks being used in your middle school or high school. The reading teacher or the English teacher may have set aside time for students' self-testing as suggested in the unit Learning about Ourselves as Learners. Using results of students' tests on the history, math, science, and other textbooks they are using, the reading teacher reports to the rest of the faculty inferences drawn about the readability of these texts.

In another session the reading teachers or the media specialists might direct the faculty in applying several readability formulas, noting how differently various formulas score the same texts. From considerable experience with applying formulas, teachers can develop a "feel" for different levels of word and sentence difficulty. They can then estimate levels before applying the readability formulas. With growing confidence, they will abandon the formulas and depend on their own judgments.

Another way to develop teachers' sensitivity to readability is to present them with sets of paragraphs taken from texts at various levels to which you have already applied a readability formula. When I use this technique with teachers, I begin by asking them to judge broadly whether material is at grade 3 or below, from 4 to 6, 7 to 9, or above tenth grade level. Gradually, we move from estimating the levels of preselected paragraphs to judging whole books as "about fifth grade" or "grade 8 readability" or "easy adult."

Singer suggests another variation that is useful in training sessions.[4] He recommends that you prepare a scale by selecting 100-word paragraphs from content textbooks from fourth grade to twelfth, applying a formula, and noting the grade level of each paragraph. You might make scales for each of several content fields. Then you ask teachers to match other textbook passages to those on the scale, estimating levels by this guide.

Another staff development session might be devoted to estimating the readability of textbooks in fields other than the teacher's own. Subject-matter specialists can judge a book in their own field better than anyone else can on matters of accuracy, completeness, fairness, clarity, and perhaps teachability. They may be quite unable, however, to judge how well someone who is not an expert in the field would understand it. So the math teachers should estimate the readability of the history texts, the science teachers should rate the literature anthologies or composition texts, and so on. From such a swapping of texts in an inservice session might come real insights into the problems of textbooks for secondary students.

---

[4]Harry Singer, "The SEER technique, a non-computational estimate of readability," *Journal of Reading Behavior* 7 (1975): 255–67.

Estimating readability is the least part of the task of evaluating textbooks. Important as it is, readability in the sense of word-and-sentence difficulty is a minor matter compared to organization of ideas, the abstract or concrete quality of language, and the complexity of concepts presented.

The Reading Teacher's Use of Content Textbooks

Until content teachers are both able and willing to teach students how to read and study their textbooks, reading teachers must assume the task. In fact, as long as reading classes are on most students' schedules, as they commonly are in grades 5 to 7, and sometimes 8, then reading teachers are obligated to include content textbooks as part of their instructional materials, even if some of their colleagues in the subject fields are also teaching how to read textbooks. (Excellent content teachers have always taught students how to learn in their fields, and if they have not thought of themselves as teachers of reading, they are, nonetheless.)

What do reading teachers do with content textbooks? Having ascertained which texts have been assigned to their students, they should analyze them in the ways we have suggested, preferably in collaboration with the content teachers. To avoid duplication of effort, they should coordinate with the content teachers what each will do. For example, we suggest that reading or English teachers use a learning unit like the one in this text to have students analyze their strengths and weaknesses. Much of this analysis comes from informal inventories based on content textbooks, and students' self-evaluation reports are shared with content teachers. So this step may be the beginning of a fruitful collaboration between reading and content teachers. Team planning periods facilitate this kind of collaboration, of course.

In schools where teachers are not yet ready for team planning, much less team teaching—and these are schools where administrative leadership is weak—the reading teachers may make informal liaisons with one or two content teachers, or they may use their students as links. In any case, if you are the reading teacher, you should plan lessons aimed at testing (and teaching) the ability to use textbooks efficiently. With periodic frequency you should base reading lessons on textbook content, selecting if possible intact passages from sections of the text that the content teacher plans to omit. Published materials on reading in content fields may serve as models, and if you are a beginning teacher, you may want to make extensive use of such materials; but gradually you will discard these in favor of similar lessons you (and, we hope, the content teachers) design using the actual content materials your students are expected to read.

Less formally, the reading teacher can work with individual students on their various content assignments. You might schedule conferences related to assignments on a rotating basis, planning to spend ten minutes a week in study conferences with each student individually, or, more practically, with groups of four or five students who can then shed light on each other's study problems.

As administrators learn to assign fewer formal classes to reading teachers, arranging for them to move out of their reading centers and into the content teachers' classrooms, then the reading lessons based on content can be taught by either teacher, with the other as observer or as team teacher.

The Content Teacher's Use of Textbooks

Textbooks for advanced students in grades 11 and 12 and beyond are more like the scholarly works published by trade houses—that is, less "textbookish" in the ways described in this chapter, more conventional in format, more individual in style, less like magazines and manuals. A few advanced students (advanced because they already have strong backgrounds in whatever field) can read these texts from cover to cover to assimilate and evaluate the author's point of view. In none of our comments in this chapter are we referring to this kind of advanced student or to the texts she or he will learn from. Chiefly, we have in mind the textbooks written for beginners in the subject field who may be good readers of narratives but have not yet learned to read and study many different kinds of textbooks. We are thinking mainly about students in grades 5 to 8 but also about immature students in 9 to 12, remembering that the advanced student in literature may be a beginner in chemistry.

To summarize and generalize, the content teacher should regard textbooks in the following ways:

1. The textbook is supplementary; it is not *the* curriculum for any grade in any subject.

2. The textbook is a secondary means of learning. That is, students will find the textbook of value if it affirms ideas they are already familiar with.

3. The role of the textbook is to reinforce ideas already grasped, to clarify ideas that are "half known," to organize and give shape to students' theories about a subject, and to edge the student more deeply into the subject.

4. Research and theory in the teaching of reading have not kept up with changes in textbook styles and formats. For example, reading teachers still teach students how to read for main ideas (and that's an appropriate strategy for many kinds of writing), but some textbooks have relatively few paragraphs that contain main ideas. Therefore, the content teachers, who know best the writing styles in their fields and keep up with changes in their textbooks, must go far beyond the reading teachers' concepts of how to teach reading-to-learn.

5. Readability formulas designed for trade books have limited applications to textbooks. Textbooks are generally more difficult for average students than readability scores indicate. In any case, the difficulty level is seldom uniform across a textbook; some parts are harder than others even when measured by formulas and apart from the unmeasured factors of conceptual load, level of abstraction, and complexity of organization.

6. Don't abandon the textbook; don't use it slavishly.

7. The least a content teacher can do is figure out how long it takes the slowest reader in a class and the fastest reader to read (that is, comprehend) the same passage and take these estimates into account when assigning homework.

The Language of Textbooks

To repeat the point we have been making implicitly since page 1: Learning to read is an extension of learning to speak. Reading is one kind of language acquisition. The language we read is similar to, but not the same as, the language we speak; or as linguists put it, written language is a different dialect from spoken language. Children learn to read most easily when the match between the language they speak and the language they read is closest. Conversely, the child from a home where a language other than English is dominant is expected to have trouble learning to read English. Even when the dominant oral language is the same as the language they are to read, children who are unfamiliar with the written dialect have a harder time than children who have become familiar with the language of print by hearing stories read aloud to them.

Why are we interrupting our discussion of content textbooks to remind you of these obvious conditions of beginning reading? Because the language of textbooks is a new dialect for students entering a new field of study. It is different from the language of story, the print language with which students are most familiar (see Box 10-3). Just as preschool and primary teachers provide a bridge from children's conversational language to the language of books, content teachers in the upper grades must also familiarize students with the language of their subject before expecting them to read to learn from text.

This means much more than teaching the vocabulary of a selection before students read it. We mean that history teachers, for example, should read aloud to their students frequently, daily if possible, especially at the beginning of the year, from (1) the textbook itself; (2) trade books related to the topic at hand; (3) primary historical sources, which are written in a language even more remote from the students' oral language.

As for the textbook itself, teachers should begin every extended reading assignment by reading aloud the introductory paragraphs or section. More than that, they should call students' attention to how the book is organized and how the authors are pursuing their purposes. They should make note of stylistic devices which are characteristic of writing in the social sciences or the physical sciences or mathematics.

As for related trade books, reading aloud from these can familiarize students with the language of the subject and acquaint them with a personal voice to contrast with the impersonality of the textbook's prose. For example, an eighth grade American history teacher might read aloud from Jean Colby's *Who's That Stepping on Plymouth Rock?* (which is good factual historical writing), or passages from Henry Steele Commager, whose textbook prose is *not* flat. When appropriate, history teachers might read aloud from Hendryk Van Loon, H. G. Wells, Barbara Tuchman, Will Durant, Bruce Catton, and Page Smith, to name a few

BOX 10-3

FROM UTTERANCE TO TEXT

In an essay which first appeared in the *Harvard Educational Review* in August, 1977, David Olson described the historical and individual development of language in two modes: "Utterance," which develops from speech and is written as literature, in which meaning depends at least in part on the listener's or reader's experience; and "text," the writing of science, history, and philosophy, in which meaning is chiefly constructed in the thinking of the writer.

The essay has far-ranging implications for the teaching of reading, especially in secondary school courses where the vehicle of instruction is the content textbook. We reprint the final paragraph here to rouse your thinking about the issues so that you will be impelled to track down—and study—the whole essay:

> The bias of written language toward providing definitions, making all assumptions and premises explicit, and observing the formal rules of logic produces an instrument of considerable power for building an abstract and coherent theory of reality. The development of this explicit, formal system accounts, I have argued, for the predominant features of Western culture and for our distinctive ways of using language and our distinctive modes of thought. Yet the general theories of science and philosophy that are tied to the formal uses of text provide a poor fit to daily, ordinary, practical, and personally significant experience. Oral language with its depth of resources and its multitude of paths to the same goal, while an instrument of limited power for exploring abstract ideas, is a universal means of sharing our understanding of concrete situations and practical actions. Moreover, it is the language children bring to school. Schooling, particularly learning to read, is the critical process in the transformation of children's language from utterance to text.

popular historians whose prose style excites interest. Science and mathematics teachers can read aloud from books by Jeanne Bendick, Millicent Selsam, Robert Silverberg, Patricia Lauber, Seymour Simon, and from a host of other easy informational books. And, farther along, they can read passages from "popular" scientists or science writers like Carl Sagan, Rachel Carson, Loren Eiseley, Arthur Clarke, Freeman Dyson, and James Watson. The reason is also to snare a student or two into reading the rest of the book for themselves. Since many of the books will be *thin* easy books, a relief in size as well as prose style from the textbook, there should be some takers. If not, press on. Another purpose is to demonstrate your enthusiasm for your subject. And the kids will enjoy your performance as spectators if not participants.

The reading aloud of primary sources speaks for itself. In reading these materials, the teacher chooses brief selections because there will need to be much interrupting to make explanations.

The Proper Use of the Textbook

We have tried to show in this chapter why the textbook remains a dominant force in American education a century after it was conceived as a way of insuring that all children would receive standard, high-quality instruction even though teachers in our young and developing nation were most likely to be untutored and transient. Does the fact that the textbook remains dominant say something about the quality of teacher education, which commonly today extends to the master's degree? I think so. Does it also suggest that the interrelatedness of textbook publishing and teacher education has made the textbook an essential tool of instruction without which schooling cannot survive? (Check a random dozen elementary and secondary textbooks in any field and notice that almost every authorial team includes at least one professional educator.) Since my first job was in publishing and since I've been both a textbook editor and an author of elementary and secondary textbooks for reading and literature, you are forewarned of my biases. I believe that textbooks are here to stay. Reading teachers (including consultants and teacher educators) and content teachers should use them wisely, that is, critically and sparingly. Frances FitzGerald, whose review of the history textbook in America you will enjoy reading (see Box 10-4), says that not as many teachers as you might think use textbooks critically. Her assertion is supported by a 1976 study by the National Science Foundation on the status of science, mathematics, and social studies education that showed that "the dominant instructional tool continues to be the conventional textbook and longtime bestsellers continue to dominate the market; teachers tend not only to rely on, but to believe in, the textbook as a source of knowledge." According to Shaver, Davis, and Helburn, most social studies teachers see textbooks not as support material but as the central instrument of instruction.[5]

Textbooks are designed as the "central instruments of instruction" by the editors, teachers, and professional educators who construct them. So it's little wonder that teachers use them that way, and our dilemma is how to break the vicious circle that we ourselves construct. The answer, I think, is to stop bad-mouthing textbooks, which is different from using them critically, and to emphasize the following in teacher education (which continues, we remind you, until retirement):

1. Study of publishing as an integral part of the educational enterprise
2. Practice in selecting textbooks to meet predetermined purposes
3. Using textbooks as single instruments of instruction because they are being used that way now
4. Using them as one of several instructional aids, because that's the way they should be used.

The best advice we can give you right now is to close *this* text and open the textbooks being used in the schools you know best. The checklist in Box 10-2 will help you to examine them critically. If you are a history teacher or a reading teacher, read Frances FitzGerald's book first. Then return to us. You'll find further details on the proper use of textbooks in the chapters ahead.

---

[5]James P. Shaver, O. L. Davis, Jr., and Suzanne W. Helburn, "The Status of Social Studies Education: Impressions from Three NSF Studies," *Social Education* (February, 1979): 150–53. Quoted in *America Revised* by Frances FitzGerald.

BOX 10-4

HOW TEXTBOOKS CHANGE

"In matters of pedagogy, as in matters of politics, there are not two sharply differentiated categories of books; rather, there is a spectrum. Politically, the books run from moderate left to moderate right; pedagogically, they run from the traditional history sermons, through a middle ground of narrative texts with inquiry-style questions and of inquiry texts with long stretches of narrative, to the most rigorous of case-study books. What is common to the current texts—and makes all of them different from those of the fifties—is their engagement with the social sciences.

"Virtually all the American-history texts for older children include discussions of "role," "status," and "culture." Some of them stage debates between eminent social scientists in roped-off sections of the text; some include essays on economics or sociology; some contain pictures and short biographies of social scientists of both sexes and of diverse races. Many books seem to accord social scientists a higher status than American Presidents. Quite as striking as these political and pedagogical alterations is the change in the physical appearance of the texts. ... Current texts are paragons of sophisticated modern design. They look not like *People* or *Family Circle* but, rather, like *Architectural Digest* or *Vogue*."

SOURCE: Frances FitzGerald, *America Revised* (Little, Brown, 1979).

RECAPPING MAIN POINTS

Content textbooks are the staples of instruction in secondary reading. As one of the mass media, they are produced for the largest possible markets and are subject to the influence of the buying public—taxpayers and school personnel. Although teachers sometimes have limited choice in the textbooks assigned to them, they determine whether or not the text dominates the curriculum.

Common problems with textbooks are they are too big (too much information, too tightly packed) and too costly. Textbooks are often written by committees in impersonal prose that fails to awaken readers' questioning attitudes. Questions inserted in the text go unanswered unless the teacher intervenes. Study aids are also of limited usefulness without teachers' input.

Readability formulas are based on sentence length and difficulty of vocabulary as judged by word length or frequency of use. They disregard complexity of structure and concepts. Teachers must judge readability of a text in light of their expectations for particular students, considering also the textbook authors' intentions with respect to conceptual load.

Cloze testing also measures readability—in a limited fashion. So, too, do informal skills tests based on textbooks. From experience with these tests and with readability formulas, teachers can learn to judge textbooks on their own.

Reading teachers' use of content textbooks includes inventorying students' skills in using them, teaching how to use textbooks efficiently, working with students on content assignments. Content teachers should regard textbooks as a secondary means of learning. Textbooks reinforce, clarify, and extend prior knowledge.

The language of textbooks is a new dialect for students entering a new field of study. Teachers should familiarize them with this language by reading aloud, using related trade books, and calling attention to the stylistic characteristics of a particular textbook.

FOR DISCUSSION

1. Using the Textbook Evaluation Guide (Box 10-2), make a report on a content textbook just as you would if you were a reading consultant responding to a colleague's request. Although you may learn much from selecting a text outside your specialization, you may prefer to evaluate a text you are currently using.

2. Interview the chair of your math, science, or social studies department or the instructor of methods courses in one of these fields and ask for a general overview of texts in that field. How readable are they? What role are textbooks assigned in instruction in this field?

3. From methods courses you have taken, articles you have read in professional journals, and conferences you've attended, have you derived views of content textbooks that are different from those held by teachers you know? Discuss. How do students perceive textbooks? Draw on your own experience as well as asking current students in secondary schools.

4. If possible, attend a professional conference where publishers exhibit textbooks. Sometimes publishers' representatives set up special exhibits for a school system in addition to exhibiting at the state and regional meetings of groups like the International Reading Association. Report your impressions of the displays and your talks with the salespersons and consultants.

5. How are textbooks selected in your school? If you are not teaching now, make this question the focus of interviews at a nearby middle, junior, or senior high school.

FURTHER READING

FitzGerald, Frances. *America Revised: History Schoolbooks in the Twentieth Century.* Boston: Little, Brown, 1979.

Jenkinson, Edward B. *Censors in the Classroom: The Mind Benders.* Carbondale: Southern Illinois University Press, 1979.

Klare, George R. *The Measurement of Readability.* Iowa State University Press, 1963.

Singer, Harry and Dan Donlan. *Reading and Learning from Text*. Boston: Little, Brown, 1980.

See Chapter 8, "Determining Reading and Readability Levels" for Fry Graph and information on SEER technique.

Note: Educational Products Information Exchange Institute (EPIE), P.O. Box 839, Watermill, NY 11976, evaluates textbooks for elementary and secondary schools, providing a valuable service for teachers and administrators.

11 Reading Outside the Content Fields

The young woman in the denim pants suit, attaché case in hand, rushed into the boarding area at O'Hare as the last passengers filed onto the 727. "Hey," she said to the young man waiting for her. "O'Hare is laid out real neat. Man, if you can read, you've got it made!"

In our split-second pursuit of the future, reading is an asset most of us take for granted, like breathing. But once in a while it strikes us, as it did the young woman at O'Hare, how much of daily life is directed by print. On board the plane, I noted another indispensable use of literacy: filling time. Strapped into their seats, most of the passengers reached for a book or a ballpoint pen, some purposefully, some aimlessly. Many engaged in SSL,[1] flipping through the airline's catalogs plucked from the seat pocket in front of them; salesmen scanned figures and wrote reports; mothers read to small children; the flight attendants distributed more magazines and comic books than playing cards; and, as I moved up the aisle, I counted the number of paperbacks from the John Jakes series, that seven-volume bicentennial celebration of Americans moving across time and territories. In the seat beside me a young native American woman, taking her infant son back home to meet his grandparents, drew from her overstuffed tote bag the expensive volume she had bought in the airport from representatives of a religious cult, and she and the baby pored over its gaudy illustrations. Here was the book as spiritual salvation, as status symbol, as repository of an alien tradition, but also as in-flight entertainment.

Literacy in the United States

The specter of illiteracy in the United States in the last years of the twentieth century haunts the popular imagination. In a society that depends on print to direct its machines and to script its entertainment, everyone has to be able to read whether or not they have time for reading very much. So every time the

---

[1]Sustained Silent Looking, a variation of SSR (see Chapter 9).

news media have an empty spot to fill (or so it seems), they get off another scare story about our "growing illiteracy." As with cancer and drug addiction, the speculation about the causes and cures of illiteracy provides copy that fascinates the reading public. Headlines shout: WARNS OF U.S. DECLINE INTO ILLITERACY or 50 MILLION ADULTS ILLITERATE or TEACHERS' ILLITERACY BLAMED FOR STUDENT FAILURES. In the hurlyburly of debate, the same statistics may be used to support opposite claims. In two different newspapers, these headlines appeared over the same basic story:

THEY'RE STILL READING BOOKS OUT THERE, SURVEY FINDS
—Education Daily

STUDY FINDS NEARLY HALF IN U.S. DO NOT READ BOOKS
—New York Times

For another insight into the "illiteracy problem," observe the statistics in Box 11-1. Obviously, some Americans are churning out billions of words in print that some other Americans are consuming.

Are the Congressmen and the news commentators crying wolf? Are more Americans reading more books, newspapers, and essential documents today than ever before? The answer has to be yes, more today than ever before. The charges of illiteracy are based on changing definitions of what illiteracy is. In the developing nations, persons are considered literate who can read and write very simple words and sentences. The UNESCO statistics that estimate more than 600 million adult illiterates in Third World countries mean that the persons being counted have not had opportunities to learn, no years in school at all. In the

BOX 11-1

ROLLING OFF THE PRESSES

In the United States
48,793 new books (including new editions) published yearly
10,952 different magazines in current circulation
1,708 daily newspapers

Is Anyone Reading Newspapers?
In U.S. in 1979, the total circulation of daily newspapers was 62,223,000.
In North America, 258 out of every 1,000 inhabitants subscribe to a newspaper.
78 per cent of Americans 18 years and over read a newspaper every day.

Are Libraries Still Popular?
In 1945, U.S. had 11,000 libraries; in 1976 the number had increased to 26,000.
In 1962, U.S. libraries housed 241 million items in print; by 1974, the number
of print items housed in libraries increased by 60%—to 397 million items.

SOURCES: *Statistical Yearbook 1981* (Paris: UNESCO).
Statistical Abstract of the United States, 103d ed. 1982-83 (U.S. Dept. of Commerce, Bureau of the Census).
Consumer Research Study in Reading and Book Publishing (New York: Yankelovich, Skelley and White, Inc. October, 1978).

United States, hard facts on literacy are much more difficult to pin down because of our rising standards. Sixty years ago functional literacy was defined as the level of reading and writing normally achieved by persons finishing their formal education at grade 4. Today, when primary teachers are assuring that virtually all normal children acquire beginning reading skills, "literacy" generally means the ability to cope with the barrage of print information that governs the citizenry of a bureaucratic, technological system. We expect a minimal level of reading of almost everyone, including mentally retarded persons living in the community rather than in institutions as they used to.

When politicians and social commentators charge the schools with failure to produce literate high school graduates, their charges have some justification only if their definitions of literacy approach this one, by Herbert Gerjuoy of the Human Resources Research Organization:

> The new education must teach the individual how to classify and reclassify infor-
> mation, how to evaluate its veracity, how to change categories when necessary,
> how to move from the concrete to the abstract and back, how to look at problems
> from a new direction—how to teach himself. *Tomorrow's illiterate will not be the man
> who can't read; he will be the man who has not learned how to learn.*[2] (italics added)

Charges that the schools are failing to achieve the long-sought-for ideal of universal literacy are not new and would not be damaging except that the persistent nagging of the press tends to lower teachers' self-confidence and, as a consequence, their effectiveness. Teachers know that they must help a broader spectrum of the populace to become literate. They are not always sure of how to do what has not ever been expected of schools before these last years of the twentieth century. Teachers must somehow learn to teach some students out-of-school reading tasks and at the same time help more students than ever before to reach levels of achievement in reading, writing, and studying suitable for post-secondary education. These demands are hitting a generation of teachers whose own development in language may have been hampered by conditions of schooling in the 1960s: expanding school populations, unprepared teachers, desegregation crises, too little knowledge about language and misap-plications of what was known, relaxed attitudes toward learning and self-discipline, and sagging public support of the schools.

In this chapter we consider the many uses of reading that lie outside learning from school texts, and we raise questions about teachers' responsibilities in preparing young people for out-of-school reading tasks. To chip off a manage-able chunk of an enormous subject—the uses of reading—we propose to deal in this chapter with two kinds of reading that are not usually required by content textbooks, though, of course, they are not unrelated to school learning. In the section that follows we shall discuss out-of-school reading tasks of a chiefly functional variety. In the second part of this chapter we shall discuss reading for

---

[2]Quoted by Alvin Toffler in *Future Shock*. For a more detailed discussion and new definitions of "conventional literacy" and "functional literacy," see *Adult Illiteracy in the United States: A Report to the Ford Foundation*, included in Further Reading at the end of this chapter.

personal satisfaction, including satisfying the need to know much that is not covered by academic school subjects.

Out-of-School Reading: The Functional Kind

We are very sympathetic when teachers complain that they are asked to "do everything for kids that the homes and churches used to"—and at the same time teach attitudes and skills for lifelong learning. Forget for a moment the stream of questions that a phrase like "to teach for lifelong learning" provokes. Look only at the inconsistencies embedded in our topic: "out-of-school reading tasks." In the first place, we have said, and wholly believe, that teachers must "teach less in order to teach more." We have suggested that there is more than enough for secondary teachers to do to facilitate *in-school* reading and learning. A further inconsistency in the exhortation to teach for lifelong uses is the implication that you can teach skills that are not immediately applicable. How can we resolve these dilemmas? We can begin by sorting out the school population and making decisions as to who needs what.

We do not propose to teach "coping" or "survival" skills, as one category of out-of-school reading tasks is sometimes labeled, to normally progressing students who are reading at fifth to sixth grade level in the middle school. We would not teach eleventh and twelfth graders who are reading at least at sixth grade level how to read an airlines schedule or an installment-buying contract or an insurance policy unless they were faced with these tasks in their present lives as students. Readers who have reached levels at or beyond grade 5 can learn to apply their basic skills to whatever the out-of-school reading task demands when the need arises. What these readers need to concentrate on are the school-learning tasks, for which there is little enough time in the school curriculum.

A favorite anecdote of reading experts who advocate teaching "survival skills" describes the untimely death of a woman who failed to read the labels on two common household cleaners and combined two chemicals that produced deadly fumes. The failure was not, in all likelihood, that the woman could not read; it is more likely that she *did* not read. It is doubtful that a reading teacher should be held responsible for teaching all eighth graders to read labels. Of course, that useful bit of life-prolonging learning might be suitable in a chemistry course or a class in homemaking or industrial arts. But the reading teacher's responsibility to the normally progressing reader in secondary schools is to reinforce reading/study strategies that are broadly applicable to any reading task.

In the same vein, we see no place in the school curriculum for teaching students how to read airlines schedules or highly specialized contracts or government-issue forms. Students who learn how to read charts, graphs, and complex prose styles as part of their academic learning can transfer those skills to out-of-school tasks when the need arises. Actually, for the most able students the need won't arise very often. They will hire accountants, lawyers, and other experts to do difficult technical reading for them. If they are themselves to read (and write) the reports, contracts, manuals, memoranda, directions-for-assembling, and other necessary bureaucratic prose because they are the experts, the best preparation for their future roles is a sound liberal education. Certainly, high school and junior high are too early for that kind of specific utilitarian learning—and anyway there is too much else of importance.

Does all this mean we are opposed to career education? No, not if career education means seeing that youngsters get the broadest possible vision of life's possibilities. We think that vision comes best from the required readings in literature, the social sciences, sciences, and the humanities; so courses in "career education" may be unnecessary. In any case, career education is not meant to teach vocational skills but to acquaint students with the variety of jobs that must be done to keep civilization going.

So out-of-school reading tasks don't belong in the in-school learning of average and able academic students. What about the nonacademic adolescents for whom "students" is a misnomer? With them the situation is different. They need practice in out-of-school literacy tasks so long as these are immediately useful. Most of these tasks can be included in vocational studies, family services, and other nonacademic curricula, but concern that insufficient attention is being paid to the nonacademic youngsters' needs has caused many school faculties to charge the reading/English teachers with this responsibility. (Box 11-2 illustrates how "survival skills" might be distributed across the courses which nonacademic adolescents may elect.)

Renewed attention to survival skills was a natural outgrowth of the minimal competency movement. Tests of minimal competency in reading have tested the ability to read labels, recipes, road maps, contracts, classified and other types of advertisements, short news stories, cartoons, directions, and signs. Soon courses were being designed to prepare students to pass tests of this kind. One such course, created by Kentucky Educational Television for ninth-grade under-developed readers, used a typical TV quiz game as the format for 30-minute segments in which classes participated "live" in the studio and through videotapes in the school. With a teacher in the role of the game show M.C., the students were divided into teams and responded to multiple-choice items flashed on the screen. These items were based on out-of-school reading tasks, and an accompanying workbook, *Contact*, provided a hundred or more additional exercises.

This program illustrates both the strengths and liabilities of "survival reading" classes. A major drawback to all such courses or units is that the survival skills are taught out of context. This criticism may be made of any reading or study skills class; it is better to teach skills of any kind within the situation in which they are used, but this is not always possible. However, "out-of-school reading tasks" transformed into workbook exercises are even further removed from the context of use than are school-related learning skills. But maybe the best the reading teacher can do is to admit the artificiality of these "real world" units and get on with the practice.

A second problem with survival skills is that "real" reading materials often have very high readability levels, far exceeding the uneven skills of the students who must use them. The telephone directory is a formidable challenge for students with minimal command of phonics and alphabetizing. Classified adver-

BOX 11-2

SAMPLE MATERIALS FOR APPLYING
SURVIVAL SKILLS IN CURRICULUM AREAS

Basic Reading Skills	Consumer Ed, Home Economics	Vocational Education Industrial Arts	Business Courses	Driver Education
Word skills: instant recognition and decoding	labels (on drugs, foods, household products)	safety signs	using typewriter or word processor applications schedules (airlines, busses)	street and highway signs
Following directions Locating information	recipes patterns craft instructions knitting	instructions for assembling or using household items engine repair manuals	applications forms references, directories "Yellow Pages"	accident instructions driver's license applications
Selecting significant details	warranties catalogs/order forms	training manuals	advertisements order forms catalogs bills and invoices	driver's manual test questions car owner's manual
Critical reading	advertisements (newspaper, magazines, TV)	order manuals catalogs advertisements (including classified)	advertisements (including classified) catalogs "career booklets"	advertisements for cars, trucks, and automotive equipment
Reading and interpreting graphic material	charts such as "food groups" house plans and room designs	charts diagrams blueprints building plans	maintaining office machines assembling simple office appliances	road maps street directories

tisements bristle with abbreviations that are not easily decoded, and the labeling of foods and drugs introduces a whole new language. Directions for assembling articles or for making them are often badly written, and learning how to follow one set of directions may have little carry-over to another set. In any case, directions are a good example of information that should be retained for only as long as it takes to complete each step; they are, therefore, poor material for teaching reading-to-remember. Nevertheless, these observations don't constitute an argument against teaching *some* out-of-school reading tasks; they are simply factors to be weighed against the advantages.

The advantages all lie in the motivating potential of out-of-school reading tasks. They *seem* so practical as to be motivating. They may appear so to ninth graders even in the traditional workbook-style presentation that most texts and teachers employ. The format of the television game show described above is attractive on several counts: It uses an every-pupil response technique (everyone pushes an answer button to respond to every question), so that every mind is engaged on the problem; it capitalizes on the popularity of a TV formula; the M.C. is entertaining; the show is nontextbookish (though a workbook is a workbook, no matter how jazzy the graphics). However, these are exterior features, and the motivational values will dissipate as the kids sense that the exercises are basically artificial. So it's best to deal directly with why they are artificial and to explore the values of exercise for exercise's sake. It would be fair to say: "The purpose of this class is to practice skills which are useful to you as a consumer. You are going through exercises in this class (just as you do in gym classes) before you apply these skills in buying or selling or renting."

In deciding how much and what kinds of out-of-school reading tasks to include in a reading class, you might consider which of the following goals is more important:

1. to enable students to pass the proficiency exams
2. to make sure that they understand the values of reading in today's world

That may not be an either-or question. To reach the second goal, you don't lecture kids on the values but devise situations in which they are reminded of those values. One teacher, knowing that his students need practice in word recognition until they can respond automatically to the print surrounding them, has a short unit in which the youngsters photograph signs in different situations such as at the shopping mall, at the park, on Main Street, in the supermarket, on various jobs. These are used as slides for flash presentations, adapted to filmstrips, or catalogued in scrapbooks for students to use in practicing word recognition.

Another question to ask is: Am I spending more time on the motivational aspects than on learning? Granted that you cannot achieve the latter without the former, you defeat your purposes if the motivational device overpowers the learning. For example, your immediate purpose is to give practice in word recognition. Students should read lots of easy words they can recognize, plus a few new ones that they will identify because of the surrounding context. The cheapest, most accessible source of "lots of easy words" is books, but your kids won't touch books, not yet anyway, you think. So you turn to lyrics of popular songs—which certainly provide recognizable words repeated over and over again. Are pop lyrics a good idea for you, for this particular group? Can you use the words without the sound effects? If you bring in rock music, do the kids forget to read? Are they *recognizing* words (that is, using the visual display) or remembering them? Is this a use of reading or of oral language? Is the language of rock the language of print? Will it lead to your purpose—practice in word recognition? And the practical question: can you get away with it in this community? What works very well in one community with one type of student may not be either appropriate or acceptable in another situation.

Whenever you try to bring the "competing curriculum" into the classroom, you take risks. The school curriculum may be pushed out of your course altogether. But there's another possibility. When you invade the adolescents' out-of-school world, as in using rock lyrics, you may encounter their open or covert resistance to intrusion by an adult outsider. Or you risk their incredulity. Adolescents have very fixed notions of "the way it's spozed to be," and in their minds, whatever they are asked to learn in school ought to be related to school values. If you use rock lyrics, comic books, racing forms, TV guides, and the like, be sure that your students make the connections to school learning. That's one reason why it's easier for the shop teacher to introduce "real life" reading tasks than it is for the reading/English teacher. Many of the adolescents for whom out-of-school reading tasks are most appropriate may have the most reactionary ideas of what schools should teach, as do their parents and other adults from whom they learned these notions.

Another essential question is basic for all curriculum planning: What essential concepts (often referred to by curriculum makers as "an organizing principle") determine the lessons to be developed and the materials to be used in this course? Answering that question leads to setting real purposes. For example, in family services the teacher can have students read classified advertisements to estimate the price range of rental apartments in this neighborhood as part of the unit on managing family incomes. For the reading teacher who must teach survival skills, an organizing principle is more difficult to determine. One might conceive, however, of a unit or course on reading and other language skills needed by consumers that could be planned jointly by the reading staff and teachers in consumer education.

One way of organizing a full-year or half-year reading class whose focus is *not* on academic learning would be to divide the time about equally between functional reading and reading for personal satisfaction, the major topics in this chapter. To serve the first goal, you would group functional reading tasks into shorter units: skills needed by the consumer; skills for the traveler (or driver); skills for sports stars and spectators, and so forth.

It is more likely, of course, that as the reading/English teacher you will have in one class students with both academic and nonacademic needs. In that case, you can plan shorter units, or clusters of lessons, on functional reading, deciding upon an organizing principle for each unit or cluster, and taking a forthright stance on the issue of "exercising skills." Nevertheless, you should try to provide a lifelike application of the skills focus each time. For example, if the students work on classified advertisements from the local shopping guides and newspapers, they might discuss their analysis of the readability of the ads with a representative of the newspaper.

To summarize to this point:

1. Most "survival skills" should be taught within immediately useful contexts supplied by regular courses.

2. Out-of-school reading experiences introduced in reading classes may be chiefly for motivation; they should be brief and clearly connected to the larger goals of (a) learning how to read better and (b) developing positive attitudes toward reading.

3. In certain reading and English classes, lessons on survival reading skills may be presented briefly and frequently through the entire course. For most students, however, less time devoted to survival skills and more time devoted to reading for personal satisfaction will be appropriate.

Out-of-School Reading: For Personal Satisfaction

European educators sometimes express alarm at the American proclivity for so structuring students' time that almost none is left for personal pursuits. This is a view from outside, of course. American teachers are more likely to view secondary students as having altogether too much unstructured time on their hands. Let's look for the truth in both perceptions. It is true that from kindergarten on we run children through timetables that allot 45 minutes for this, 20 minutes for that, from the opening bell until the school buses arrive. When, in the 1960s, we were persuaded by some observers of the English lower schools to relax our schedules and to "open the classroom," we found, generally, that teachers were not ready to guide pupils in making good use of independent learning time. And as educational conservatism grew in the 1970s, the popularity of open schools withered away. But not without a trace. The guilt remains. It is quite possible that we so overstructure learning that children forget how to operate without signals from teachers.

Whether from overstructuring or from lack of structure, many students arrive in secondary schools without having learned how to spend independent learning time without undue waste. So a reasonable goal for reading and English classes is to teach students how to browse profitably. To do so we recommend that reading teachers and English teachers reserve time in their curriculum for reading that is unrelated to school learning or to strictly utilitarian purposes. (Note Dr. Johnson's advice in Box 11-3.) So the rest of this chapter is devoted to ways of promoting reading for personal satisfaction, in addition to SSR, which was discussed in Chapter 9.

BOX 11-3

> I would let [a child] first read *any* English book which happens to engage his attention; because you have done a great deal when you have brought him to have entertainment from a book. He'll get better books afterward.
>
> —Samuel Johnson in 1779
>
> SOURCE: Quoted by Aidan Chambers in *Introducing Books to Children*.

Before moving on to these suggestions, however, we need to sort out the different emphases of reading and English classes when the same students are assigned to both, as is often the case in middle and junior high schools. Both reading and English teachers aim to promote lifetime reading habits, but English teachers have less time for reading that is other than literary. In addition to teaching writing and writing conventions (such as spelling, usage, syntax), as well as speaking and listening, the English teacher is responsible for teaching literature as an art form as well as a choice for leisure reading, and for helping students to enjoy literature not only in print but on film and in live theater. Respecting the English teacher's authority, the reading teacher does not "teach" a novel to classes or groups but only recommends novels to individuals for personal reading. Only in exceptional circumstances would the reading teacher ever assign plays, poetry, or short stories to a group or a class. Such an exception might be the elective in oral interpretation or the one in children's literature when taught by the reading teacher.

If reading teachers emphasize personal reading and leave the study of litera-ture to English teachers, they can avoid duplication of effort that often results in omission by the reading teacher of essential reading-to-learn strategies and out-of-school reading tasks that no one else is teaching. Of course, the essential materials of the reading class include a large and changing library of fiction and nonfiction titles, many of which are found in English classes as well. But the reading teacher seldom uses any of these works for in-common reading by a small group or a whole class, as the English teacher often does.

All students should learn how reading can serve their personal needs. Some students will have learned this by the time they reach secondary school, and their already growing respect for reading in their personal lives will be furthered by experiences in academic classes. It is students who have not yet learned to enjoy reading whom we have chiefly in mind as we suggest the approaches described below. By the way, we do not expect that everyone who learns to read will choose reading as a pastime. We don't expect everyone who can tell a violin from a guitar to listen to symphonies every Saturday. But we want everyone to know what the possibilities are—in reading as well as music and the arts.

Relating Hobbies to Reading

If you're a skeptic, you're already thinking: "Hey, the kinds of hobbies my kids have they don't need to read about!" Or you're saying, with more than a little justification: "The kids with really exciting interests know more about them than I do. And they're usually not in my reading classes." We take your point. Even so, generations of reading teachers have found that youngsters all along the spectrum of language abilities have interests in collecting artifacts, making things, playing instruments, and engaging in individual and team sports. Al-though these interests are not easily related to academic learning, they are a natural outlet for using—and thereby improving—language and learning skills.

One problem is getting to know youngsters well enough so that they will expose their interests. Another is arousing interests that the kids themselves don't realize they have. Still another is that enthusiasms may be fleeting among normal adolescents, so that by the time you've found the "just right" book for one interest it's been replaced by another. Much worse is the fact that some adolescents are so seriously disturbed and depressed that for them the very idea of hobby-related reading seems ludicrous. It *is* ludicrous for some, not all. What teachers can do now and then for an unhappy adolescent is to offer the diversion of learning something new. And learning something new, Merlin told the depressed young King Arthur, is the best thing for being sad.

Where to begin? Maybe with sharing your interests. We hope you have many. An English headmaster once remarked that lackluster teachers fail, not simply in arousing students' interests, but in developing any in themselves. Even if your current interest is the art of ikebana, and your fourth period class are mostly video-game addicts, demonstrate how well you can arrange flowers now that you've learned to read text-plus-diagrams-plus-pictures. Your enthusiasm will amuse them—and they may even learn the value of picture-text combinations. A friend of ours who teaches ninth grade is a balloonist, and we have to admit her hobby is a better drawing card than ikebana. What's important is that she knows a range of books on ballooning and hang-gliding and can match reading levels with readability levels.

Find out all you can about your students' interests, using all the time-tested techniques, including reading their files, interviewing their former and present teachers, and having students poll each other. (See "Learning About Ourselves as Learners.") Then, too, use your knowledge of what generally interests adolescents and, thus armed, select with the help of the media specialist maybe fifty informational trade books—and keep changing the collection. (A sample collection appears in Box 11-4. Many of these books are normally found in children's sections of libraries; get help from elementary librarians, if your junior high media specialist doesn't know some of these titles or authors.) Hobby magazines and paperbacks should be added to the trade book collection.

You don't have a media specialist? No one in the public libraries can help you? Then call your textbook representatives. They'll overwhelm you with catalogs, and you'll find that some basals and anthologies for grades 5 to 8 have suitable selections from informational texts as well as bibliographies of appropriate titles.

Which reminds us that part of your reading-for-personal-satisfaction collection should consist of selections you and your aides have cut out of basal readers and other anthologies, bound in separate covers, and thus made into pamphlets. These can be part of your permanent collection. If the covers of these pamphlets are color-coded according to rough estimates of reading difficulty, you will have a useful tool for building reading skills through materials geared to wide ranges of reading ability. Taken out of their original textbooks, selected to appeal to the interests of kids you know, these materials are no longer insultingly juvenile, nor are they hidden away in an unappealing textbook.

With hobby-related reading, as with other types suggested in this chapter, you will do more than provide browsing time. Arrange times for sharing hobbies and related reading. According to your energies, make such sharing a minor production (say, an informal individual report now and then, or ten-minute group-sharing sessions) or a major production (a schoolwide hobby fair, a publication for the library or for distribution to parents).

BOX 11-4

INFORMATIONAL RESOURCES FOR YOUNG ADOLESCENTS

FIFTY BOOKS

Akins, W. R. *Your Psychic Powers and How to Test Them*. Franklin Watts, 1980.
Directions for testing clairvoyance, precognition, telepathy, etc.

Asimov, Isaac. *How Did We Find Out About Atoms.* Walker, 1976.
This introduction to atomic structure is one of a series.

Barry, Scott. *The Kingdom of Wolves*. Putnam, 1979.
An intelligent, social animal, the wolf lives in a well-organized pack, hunting only when it is hungry, and caring for the cubs with affection.

Burns, Marilyn. *This Book Is About Time*. Illus. Marilyn Burns. Brown Paper School Book. Little, Brown and Co., 1978.
Lots of information on time as well as experiments to perform.

Cohen, Daniel. *Meditation: What It Can Do for You*. Dodd, Mead and Co., 1977.
The history of transcendental meditation and its current popularity. Scientific evidence is reviewed.

Cohen, Daniel. *The World's Most Famous Ghosts*. Dodd, Mead and Co., 1978.
Included in this Who's Who of Ghosts are Lincoln's Ghost, the West Point Ghost, the Flying Dutchman among others.

Cumming, Robert. *Just Look . . . A Book about Painting*. Scribner's, 1979.
Questions to actively involve readers and encourage close observation of paintings are answered in the back of the book.

Dolan, Edward F., Jr. *The Bermuda Triangle and Other Mysteries of Nature*. Franklin Watts, 1980.
Bermuda Triangle, UFO's, Abominable Snowcreatures.

Epstein, Sam and Beryl. *She Never Looked Back: Margaret Mead in Samoa*. Illus. Victor Juhasz. Coward, McCann and Geoghegan, 1980.
An excellent introduction to anthropology as well as a biography of young Margaret Mead. The reader learns about the motivating forces behind Margaret Mead's life and about the young Samoan girls she studied.

Fenton, Robert S. *Chess for You: The Easy Book for Beginners*. Grosset and Dunlap, 1975.
A series of "mini-games" emphasizes strategies in learning to play chess.

Fisher, Leonard Everett. *The Newspapers*. Holiday House, 1981.
History of the newspaper in the United States during the 19th century. Companion books in Fisher's series on 19th-century America include *The Sports, The Hospital,* and *The Railroads and the Factories*.

Foster, Genevieve. *The Year of the Horseless Carriage: 1801*. Scribner, 1975.
In Foster's description of 1801, one historical event influences another: Napoleon, Robert Fulton's steamship, the Louisiana Purchase.

Freedman, Russell. *Immigrant Kids*. Dutton, 1980.
A photographic essay on the lives of immigrant children in the United States during the late 1800s and early 1900s.

Fritz, Jean. *Where Do You Think You're Going, Christopher Columbus?* Illus. Margot Tomes. Putnam, 1980.
Warm and humorous, this story of Columbus is short and to the point.

Gallant, Roy. *Memory: How It Works and How to Improve It*. Four Winds, 1980.
Offers many practical techniques.

Continued

BOX 11-4 (continued)

INFORMATIONAL RESOURCES FOR YOUNG ADOLESCENTS

Glubok, Shirley. *The Art of the Vikings*. Macmillan, 1978.
Shows many links between art and history with frequent reference to Norse my-
thology.

Goode, Ruth. *People of the First Cities*. Macmillan, 1977.
Urban life 5000 years ago in great cities of the Middle East.

Grillone, Lisa and Joseph. *Small Worlds Close Up*. Crown, 1978.
Photographs taken by a scanning electron microscope of such objects as a toothpick, a
grain of salt, a moth wing.

Haskins, James. *Who Are the Handicapped?* Doubleday, 1978.
This thought-provoking book puts the question of the handicapped in perspective.
Glossary, bibliography, index.

Holz, Loretta. *Mobiles You Can Make*. Illustrated by author and photographs by
George and Loretta Holz. Lothrop, Lee and Shepard, 1975.
A complete guide for beginners.

Huntington, Lee. *Simple Shelters*. Illus. Stefen Bernath. Coward, McCann and
Geoghegan, 1979.
A cross-cultural survey of shelters used through history.

Kettelkamp, Larry. *Astrology: Wisdom of the Stars*. Morrow, 1973.
How the Zodiac began, horoscopes, and new scientific directions in astrology.

Lasker, Joe. *Merry Ever After: The Story of Two Medieval Weddings*. Illus.
author. Viking, 1976.
Text and illustrations describe medieval customs, architecture, clothing and family life.

Lasky, Kathryn and Christopher Knight. *Tall Ships*. Scribner's, 1978.
Life at sea in a tall ship. Beautiful photographs.

LeShan, Eda. *Learning to Say Good-by; When a Parent Dies*. Illus. Paul
Giovanopoulos. Macmillan, 1976.
Describes the stages of grief honestly and unsentimentally.

Liebers, Arthur. *You Can Be a Welder*. Lothrop, Lee and Shepard, 1977.
One of the Vocations in Trade Series. Also included in this series are books on
carpenters, electricians, machinists, mechanics, plumbers, printers, and truck drivers.

Lyttle, Richard B. *The Complete Beginner's Guide to Skiing*. Doubleday, 1978.
Even people who have been skiing for a few years will read this guide from cover to
cover.

Macaulay, David. *Cathedral: The Story of Its Construction*. Houghton Mifflin,
1973.
Detailed architectural drawings and brief text.

Mann, Peggy. *The Telltale Line: The Secrets of Handwriting Analysis*. Macmillan, 1976.
A fascinating account of present-day interest in graphology along with instructions for
the novice analyst.

Meltzer, Milton. *All Times, All Peoples: A World History of Slavery*. Illus. Leonard
Everett Fisher. Harper and Row, 1980.
Text illustrations and format make this a dynamic book. Bibliography.

Molloy, Anne. *Wampum*. Hastings House, 1977.
The history of wampum and its significance from the 1500s to today.

Mowat, Farley. *Owls in the Family*. Illus. Robert Frankenberg. Little, Brown, 1961.
The story of Weeps and Wol, two owls raised in captivity.

Continued

BOX 11-4 *(continued)*

INFORMATIONAL RESOURCES FOR YOUNG ADOLESCENTS

Myller, Rolf. *Symbols and Their Meaning*. Atheneum, 1978.
Hieroglyphics, heraldry, chemistry, marshalling, braille, finger spelling, etc.

Olney, Ross R. and Chan Bush. *Roller Skating*. Lothrop, Lee and Shepard, 1979.
A timely book on a popular sport that discusses equipment, techniques, roller disco dancing, etc.

Perl, Lila. *Junk Food, Fast Food, Health Food: What America Eats and Why*. Houghton Mifflin, 1980.
Survey of current American eating habits.

Price, Christine. *Dance on the Dusty Earth*. Scribner's, 1979.
A lively history of dance.

Redding, Robert. *The Alaska Pipeline*. Children's Press, 1980.
Illustrated with photographs of the Alaska pipeline under construction.

Roberson, John. *China from Manchu to Mao* (1699–1976). Atheneum, 1980.
A readable history of China that will not overwhelm young readers; includes a discussion of China's part in the Korean and Vietnam wars.

Sarnoff, Jane and Reynold Ruffins. *Great Aquarium Book: The Putting-it-together Guide for Beginners*. Scribner's, 1977.
Of interest even to those who do not have an aquarium.

Schlein, Miriam. *Giraffe, the Silent Giant*. Illus. Betty Fraser. Four Winds, 1976.
The introduction of the giraffe to Europe is described along with the habits and behavior of this unusual animal.

Schlein, Miriam. *I, Tut: The Boy Who Became Pharaoh*. Illus. Erik Hilgerdt. Four Winds, 1978.
After young Tut's death this first-person narrative is taken up by a friend who describes the mourning and burial ritual. Outstanding color photos of authentic Egyptian art and excellent glossary and bibliography.

Seixas, Judith S. *Living with a Parent Who Drinks Too Much*. Greenwillow, 1979.
A frank discussion of alcoholism and how it affects family members.

Selsam, Millicent. *Land of the Giant Tortoise: The Story of the Galapagos*. Photographs by Les Line. Four Winds, 1977.
How life evolved on these volcanic islands.

Shapiro, Irwin. *The Gift of Magic Sleep: Early Experiments in Anesthesia*. Coward, McCann and Geoghegan, 1979.
The struggle to gain acceptance for anesthesia is highlighted.

Simon, Seymour. *The Optical Illusion Book*. Drawings by Constance Ftera. Four Winds, 1976.
What affects our perceptions.

Steele, William O. *Talking Bones: Secrets of Indian Burial Mounds*. Drawings by Carlos Llerena-Aguirre. Harper and Row, 1978.
What we know from archeology about American Indians who once lived along the Ohio River.

Spier, Peter. *Tin Lizzie*. Illus. Peter Spier. Doubleday, 1975.
The story of a 1909 Ford model touring car from assembly line to present-day refurbished collector's item.

Starkey, Marion L. *The Tall Man from Boston*. Illus. Charles Mikolayeak. Crown, 1975.
An historical account of the Salem witch trials. Superb illustrations.

Continued

BOX 11-4 (continued)

INFORMATIONAL RESOURCES FOR YOUNG ADOLESCENTS

Stemple, David. *High Ridge Gobbler: A Story of the American Wild Turkey*. Illus. Ted Lewin. Collins, 1979.
> The reader follows a brood of young gobblers from first hatching to mating, learning about their natures and instincts. A wild turkey can outsmart the sly fox!

Zerman, Melvyn Bernard. *Beyond a Reasonable Doubt: Inside the American Jury System*. Crowell, 1981.
> An honest, comprehensive description of the responsibilities of a jury member, focusing on the complexities of our legal system.

EIGHTEEN MAGAZINES THAT ADOLESCENTS LIKE

Animal Kingdom: The New York Zoological Society. 185th Street and Southern Boulevard, Bronx, NY 10460.

Current Health. Curriculum Innovations, Inc., 3500 Western Ave., Highland Park, IL 60035.

Fishing Facts. Northwoods Publishing Co., Inc., N84 W. 13660 Leon Road, Menomonee Falls, WI 53051.

Gymnast. Sandby Publications, 410 Broadway, Santa Monica, CA 90401.

Hot Rod. 8490 Sunset Blvd., Los Angeles, CA 90069.

International Wildlife. National Wildlife Federation. 1412 16th Street NW, Washington, DC 20036.

Modern Photography. Subscription Fulfillment Department, P.O. Box 14117, 2160 Patterson St., Cincinnati, OH 45214.

National Geographic Magazine. National Geographic Society, 17th and M Streets NW, Washington, DC 20036.

Natural History. American Museum of Natural History, Central Park West at 79th Street, New York, NY 10024. (bimonthly)

Odyssey. Astro Media Corporation, 411 East Mason Street, P.O. Box 92788, Milwaukee, WI 53202.

Outdoor Life. Outdoor Life Subscription Department, Boulder, CO 80302.

Penny Power. Consumers Union of United States, Orangeburg, NY 10962.

Popular Science Monthly. Popular Science Subscription Department, Boulder, CO 80302.

Science Digest. The Hearst Corporation, 224 West 47th St., New York, NY 10019.

Skier's World. Runners World Magazine Co., Mountain View, CA 94043.

Smithsonian. Smithsonian Association, P.O. Box 404, Flushing, NY 13478.

Sport. MVP Sports, Inc., 641 Lexington Ave., New York, NY 10022.

Young Athlete. Young Athlete, Inc., 1601 114th Ave. SE, Bellevue, WA 98004.

SOURCE: Compiled by Kaye Lindauer, School Media Specialist, Eagle Hill Middle School, Fayetteville-Manlius Public Schools, New York.

BOX 11-5

CLASSROOM COLLECTION OF POPULAR REFERENCE BOOKS

Allison, Linda. *The Wild Inside: Sierra Club's Guide to the Great Indoors*. Sierra Club Books, 1979.

Burnam, Tom. *The Dictionary of Misinformation.* Crowell, 1975.

Brand, Stewart (ed). *The Next Whole Earth Catalog*. Point, 1980.

Cardozo, Peter. *The Second Whole Kids Catalog*. Bantam, 1977.

Diagram Group. *Rules of the Game: The Complete Illustrated Encyclopedia of All the Sports of the World*. Bantam, 1976.

Feinman, Jeffrey. *Freebies for Kids*. Simon and Schuster, 1979.

Gleasner, Dianna. *Illustrated Swimming, Diving, and Surfing Dictionary for Young People*. Harvey House, 1980.
> Additional books in this series include the following topics: Basketball, Hockey, Skating, Football, Baseball, Tennis, Soccer, Gymnastics.

Guinness Book of World Records. Sterling, 1980.
> Also available in paperback (Bantam, 1978) and in separate volumes excerpted from this inclusive edition.

Kane, Joseph Nathan. *Kane Book of Famous First Facts and Records: 1975 Edition*. Ace Books, 1974.

Kindig, Frank and Richard Hutton. *Life Spans of How Long Things Last*. Holt, Rinehart and Winston, 1979.

National Geographic Picture Atlas of Our Fifty States. National Geographic Society, 1980.

1902 Edition of the Sears, Roebuck Catalogue. Introduction by Cleveland Amory. Bounty Books, 1969. (1927 Edition also available.)

Passell, Peter and Leonard Ross. *The Best*. Farrar, Straus and Giroux, 1974.

Schultz, Charles M. *Charlie Brown's Second Super Book of Questions and Answers: About the Earth and Space . . . from Plants to Planets*. Random House, 1977.

Wallace, Irving, David Wallechinsky, Amy Wallace, and Sylvia Wallace. *The People's Almanac Presents the Book of Lists #2*. William Morrow, 1980.

Webster's Sports Dictionary. Merriam-Webster Editorial Staff. G. & C. Merriam Co., 1976.

The World Almanac and Book of Facts. Newspaper Enterprise Association, 1981.

Reading Newspapers and Magazines

In spite of dire predictions, television has obviously not snuffed out print journalism. So youngsters have a right to know what newspapers contain that may satisfy their personal needs. In elementary school they have probably subscribed to *My Weekly Reader* and in junior and senior high school they continue with similar publications. Many teachers are particularly grateful for *Scope* and *Scholastic Action*, which are examples of low-readability weekly publications of fairly mature format and content that appeal to many poor readers. Another publication used by many reading teachers at secondary level is *News for You*, a newspaper published by the Laubach Literacy Foundation for newly literate adults (see Box 8-6). But these special publications have an aura of the classroom and are not really out-of-school reading; so teachers are anxious to use regular newspapers, even for poor readers.

So much worthwhile material on the use of newspapers is available to all teachers that we shall simply list sources (see Box 11-6) and urge you to make use also of the services that most newspapers provide. The first step is to inquire from your local newspaper about their educational services and take advantage of any workshops, seminars, or summer courses being offered. Newspapers are natural instructional materials for social studies, and they contain features that relate to almost every other course in junior/senior high school. They are especially useful sources for teaching reading and writing skills, and we shall refer to them again in the chapters ahead, in addition to listing in Box 11-7 several uses of newspapers for teaching specific skills.

To demonstrate that reading the newspaper can satisfy personal needs, you can develop a two-to-three-week unit on your local daily. Or you may prefer, as we do, to extend the study throughout the course, dispensing with a concentrated unit. It isn't necessary, or practicable, to have a newspaper for every student even during a unit. Instead, have two copies delivered each day for the school year and appoint rotating committees, or individuals to read certain sections for the rest of the class. Two or three students may be assigned to the sports section and given part of a bulletin board where they can post selected clippings. Additionally, you might make specific assignments such as:

❖ listing on the chalkboard all the examples of figurative comparisons, clichés, or euphemisms used by a certain sports writer this week

❖ reporting orally on five women who made news in sports this week

❖ writing five facts about five different sports found in the sports pages this week

BOX 11-6

TEACHING WITH NEWSPAPERS

1. *Teaching with Newspapers*, a newsletter, is published by American Newspaper Publishers Association Foundation (Newspaper Center, Box 17407, Dulles International Airport, Washington, D.C. 20041)

2. "The Community, World and Newspapers" edited by Merrill F. Hartshorn. Contains lesson plans, teaching ideas, references of interest to reading teachers, social studies teachers, and others. Volume 4, No. 1, January 1982

3. Eileen Sargent. *The Newspaper as a Teaching Tool* (Norwalk, CT: The Reading Laboratory, 1975)

4. Ruth B. Smith and Barbara Michalak. *How to Read Your Newspaper*, 2d ed. (New York: Harcourt Brace Jovanovich, 1978).

BOX 11-7

USING NEWSPAPERS TO TEACH READING SKILLS

Comprehending Main Ideas
+ Clip brief news items. Detach headlines. Paste headline on one card, story on another. Students match stories with headlines.
+ For brief editorials, students write titles that express main idea.
+ Students supply titles for political cartoons.

Answering Who, What, When, Where, Why and How
+ Students analyze news stories to determine whether reporters answered five W's and H.

Following Sequence
+ Students rearrange scrambled panels from comics to tell sequential story. (See Figure 13-6 for sample)
+ Students reconstruct time of events in a news story, especially one that continues over several days.

Understanding Picture-Text Combinations
+ News photographs, especially action shots, can be separated from captions. Student's task is to match captions with pictures.

Developing Vocabulary
+ Headlines can supply "Word of the Week"—*detente, infrastructure, looming*.
+ Use syndicated features like "Word a Day" and columnists like Safire and Newman.
+ Collect synonyms and metaphors from sports pages.
+ Observe language of advertising.
+ Collect neologisms (newly coined words and phrases like *upvalue* and *hand walk*).

Interpreting Abbreviations
+ Classified advertisements
+ List acronyms from this week's headlines; for example, NASA, SALT

Understanding Maps, Charts, Graphs
+ Weather maps appear in most dailies.
+ Statistics are frequently displayed in graphs and tables.

Skimming
+ Almost any page lends itself to skimming exercises, but teachers frequently use the following sections: classified advertising, movie timetable, temperatures in other cities, the newspaper's index, radio and TV listings.

Following Directions
+ Recipes from Food Page
+ Family/Living sections: stories on gardening, home repair, hobbies

Continued

BOX 11-7 (continued)

USING NEWSPAPERS TO TEACH READING SKILLS

Determining Author's Bias
+ Expressions of personal points of view (bias) appear not only in editorials but in letters to editor and advice columns, and in feature stories, movie reviews, sports columns, political columns, and cartoons.

Distinguishing Fact and Opinion
+ Students identify examples of facts and opinions in a single issue.
+ Students compare "straight" news and "feature" stories.

Recognizing Slanted Writing
+ Compare same story reported in two or more newspapers or in news magazine.
+ Identify audience appealed to by advertisements.

Recognizing Propaganda Techniques
+ Students collect examples from advertisements of such devices as glittering generalities, folksy approach, bandwagon.

Similar assignments can be made to teams covering such areas as entertainment, news for home-owners and homemakers, local politics, international politics, stories about persons under twenty, happenings that affect environment, and people who overcome handicaps.

For mature readers, a comparative study of several newspapers and news magazines offers splendid opportunities for developing critical reading skills. Since a unit of this kind deserves careful planning, social science teachers and the reading/English staff should pool resources. Such a unit might be the outcome of a summer workshop for teachers, perhaps sponsored by the local newspaper.

The best use of magazines and newspapers for most reading classes is to supply brief, timely articles that will satisfy adolescents' current curiosities and, we hope, establish habits of turning to print media for information. It isn't enough, however, to make materials and time available. Most kids need to be nudged, and most teachers do this by giving explicit directions and requiring some kind of product from the reading. Once students are acquainted with the resources, they will return to them if they find them truly satisfying.

Teacher aides are useful in keeping files of clippings up to date and in order, but students miss a valuable learning experience if they, too, are not assigned to reading, clipping, pasting, laminating, filing new pieces, and discarding dated articles. One reading teacher taught several student aides how to apply a simple readability formula to magazine and newspaper articles.

Easy accessibility to filed clippings is governed by the filing system. Put kids in charge and use categories that appeal to current interests: sports heroes, personalities in the news, natural disasters, animals, humor, strike-it-rich stories—and gradually add topics that you can get them interested in: local history, scientific discoveries, adolescent achievement, and so forth.

Almanacs and Other References

The fact that the *Guinness Book of World Records* is a top favorite among readers in grades 5 to 8 confirms psychologists' observations that young people have a basic need to know (see Box 11-8). And it confirms teachers' observations that they want their information in bite-size morsels. Teachers who are trying to develop a friendly attitude toward print in kids who are basically unfriendly take advantage of this need to know, and stock their browsing shelf with a half dozen popular references like Guinness and Ripley. We mean *popular* references—not encyclopedias, which can be used in the media center when the need arises— such as those suggested in Box 11-5. Several of these popular references are big flat books from the children's shelves, like the Charlie Brown series of question and answer books, which many of your students missed when they were younger. Others are adult "nonbooks" like *The Book of Lists*. Again you may have to nudge kids into using these references at first. One teacher has a Trivia Quiz posted weekly, with a prize to the first one who gets the most right answers. Another simply capitalizes on kids' natural tendency to dispute who won which game when by having almanacs on hand to settle the arguments—and engender new ones.

The Spread of Foxfire

Spreading like a brush fire, Eliot Wigginton's idea for the *Foxfire*[3] books has been picked up by teachers in diverse settings from Maine fishing villages to the ghettos of West Coast cities. Researching and preserving folkways is a natural extension of the contemporary emphasis on multicultural education and the current fad for identifying ethnic and family roots. It works as well in the cultural enclaves of the big cities as it does in rural Georgia. To do the job well, as Ellen Massey did it in Lebanon, Missouri, with the publication of the monthly magazine *Bittersweet*, requires a full-time commitment, more than a reading teacher can undertake alone. (Ms. Massey managed *Bittersweet*, for example, through a full-year elective journalism course open to grades 10 through 12.) But the reading teacher and the English teacher who undertake a project of this kind form a natural alliance. The students in the reading class should not be passive subscribers but active participants contributing ideas from *their* roots, acting as reporters to gather information, actively responding to each issue. School publications are a sensitive index of the quality of the school and prominent testimony to a staff's respect for language. They require an enormous amount of energy and commitment from one or more faculty advisers, and we are not suggesting that the reading teacher ought to take on this job, too (though we applaud any who do). But the reading teacher ought to support enthusiastically the school publications effort and, of course, use those publications in class. Teachers in middle and junior high schools are finding that word processors increase students' enthusiasm for publishing journals.

---

[3]Eliot Wigginton, *The Foxfire Book*, Doubleday, 1972. Additional titles in this series have been published regularly.

BOX 11-8

AN ENGLISH TEACHER SAYS: "NONFICTION WORKS"

What two books are bought by teenagers more frequently than any others? *Ripley's Believe It or Not!* and the *Guinness Book of World Records*. . . . These kinds of books help develop the attitude that it is simply fun to know—and that that kind of fun can be had from words. . . .

These books deal with the strange, the exotic, the foreign, the unbelievable. These are books of facts and numerical records, and yet I have seen these books hold a student's attention for hours. I flood my room with them. . . .

I send [students] off with questions, the answers to which I hope will startle them or amuse them.

SOURCE: Robert J. Skapura, "Lawsuits, Duels, and Burma-Shave: Nonfiction Works . . . If You Let It," *English Journal* 42 (1972): 831–35.

The Need for Story

The need to know and the need for story: both are endemic to humankind and are gnawingly alive in individuals of all ages, from infancy to old age. The universal need for story has been satisfied in most cultures through an oral medium, and even in Western cultures, which seem today to be based primarily in script, the oral tradition continues strong, thanks to electronics, and will become stronger still. We have been a print culture for only a couple of hundred years, the first novel in English being as recent as Richardson's *Pamela* (1740) and the short story the invention of Edgar Allan Poe (about 1840). Ordinary people satisfy their need for story through gossip, anecdote, comics, family tales, jokes, tall stories; through "short short" human-interest stories in newspapers and stories and nonliterary narratives in magazines like *True Romance*. But a great many adults and adolescents satisfy their need for story through television—the sitcoms, serials, made-for-TV movies, miniseries, late-night reruns—and through films shown in theaters as well as on TV. Will print continue to hold its own with the electronic media? We are tempted to say no, not for most people, until we are reminded by the staggering successes of mass paperbacks that millions of people are satisfying their need for story through turning pages.

Even so, library circulation figures and publishers' sales support our hunch that print is more likely to satisfy the need to know, and the electronic media, the need for story. Nonfiction titles outsell fiction over the long haul. Mass-media magazines like *The Saturday Evening Post* that include fiction are the ones that succumb to competition from TV; the nonfiction magazines, chiefly the specialized hobby and trade magazines, proliferate and maintain steady circulation figures.

The fact that special-interest nonfiction prospers even in competition with television suggests that reading teachers, who cater to the needs of masses, would do well to emphasize informational trade books and magazines when persuading students to choose reading for personal satisfaction. We belabor this point because secondary reading teachers, many of them ex-English teachers,